❖

A LIBRARY OF PROTESTANT THOUGHT

❖

DEDICATION

❖

To the memory of three good priests
my fathers in the Catholic faith

SIDNEY CHILDS

CHARLES HOWARD BOULDEN

WILLIAM HOLMES DAVISON

and other disciplines can gain a more balanced view of how the Protestant mind has thought and spoken since the Reformation.

The Board is grateful to the Hazen Foundation for an initial grant enabling it to begin its work; to the Sealantic Fund, Inc., for a grant making possible Board meetings, consultations, and editorial assistance in the preparation of specific volumes; and to the Oxford University Press for undertaking the publication of the Library.

THE EDITORIAL BOARD

Preface

No doubt there is an element of incongruity in the appearance of a volume of Anglo-Catholic classics in a Library of Protestant Thought. After all, the Oxford Movement and the developed Anglo-Catholicism which has issued from it form the most strongly anti-Protestant strain in the entire history of Anglicanism. In view of the demonstrated capacity of the Anglican Communion to conceive and nurture such a way of belief and worship and life, one might even wonder whether anything Anglican could safely be identified as "Protestant" without serious reservations. In the case of Keble and Newman, Pusey and Williams, Ward and Wilberforce, the answer seems obvious the moment the question is raised; they do not sound Protestant, and they have no desire to be Protestant as that term is commonly understood.

Yet a case can be made for the appearance of Anglo-Catholic authors in the present series. To begin with, while the historical development of the Anglican Communion has made it plain that Anglicanism cannot meaningfully be described as a Protestant "confession," the English Church's experience of the Reformation has left deep and enduring marks on the formularies and the life of the Anglican churches. Consequently, it would be impossible to give a sufficient account of the theological outcome of the Reformation without letting typical Anglican voices be heard. But it would be no less impossible to paint a true picture of Anglicanism without representing the type of "High Church" thought which the Oxford Movement shaped. Furthermore, although the Oxford Movement certainly was, among other things, a "Counter-Reformation," it differed in one significant particular from the Roman Catholic Counter Reformation. The Council of Trent encountered Protestantism as an external force, but the Oxford Movement knew it as an outlook and a party firmly rooted by history within the same comprehensive Church of England to which the Tractarians themselves belonged. Indeed, some of the Movement's major figures had themselves grown up in the atmosphere of Evangelical Anglicanism, strong in its Protestant conviction, and their laborious progress to

Abbreviations

ACW	*Ancient Christian Writers*, Johannes Quasten and Joseph C. Plumpe, eds. (Westminster, Md., 1946–)
ANF	*Ante-Nicene Fathers* (Buffalo, 1885–97)
B.C.P.	English Book of Common Prayer, 1662
CSEL	*Corpus Scriptorum Ecclesiasticorum Latinorum* (Vienna, 1866–)
FC	*Fathers of the Church* (New York, 1947–)
GCS	*Die griechischen christlichen Schriftsteller der ersten drei Jahrhunderten* (Leipzig, 1897–)
LCC	*Library of Christian Classics* (Philadelphia, 1953–)
LF	*Library of Fathers of the Holy Catholic Church*, E. B. Pusey and others, eds. (Oxford, 1838–85)
NPNF [1]	*Nicene and Post-Nicene Fathers of the Christian Church*, 1st ser., Philip Schaff, ed. (Buffalo–New York, 1886–90)
NPNF [2]	*Nicene and Post-Nicene Fathers of the Christian Church*, 2d ser., Philip Schaff and Henry Wace, eds. (New York, 1890–1900)
PG	*Patrologiae Cursus Completus: Series Graeca*, J. P. Migne, ed. (Paris, 1857–1912)
PL	*Patrologiae Cursus Completus: Series Latina*, J. P. Migne, ed. (Paris, 1844–64)

Part Four: The Heart of the Matter   199

    I. Edward Bouverie Pusey · Tract Sixty-seven: Scriptural Views
       of Holy Baptism (Selection), 201
          Chapter II: On the Meaning of Baptismal Regeneration, and
          the Passages of Holy Scripture Which Speak of or Im-
          ply the Greatness of Baptism, 203

   II. John Henry Newman · Lectures on Justification (Selection), 215
          Lecture VI: On the Gift of Righteousness, 219
          Lecture VII: The Characteristics of the Gift of Righteous-
          ness, 233
          Lecture VIII: Righteousness Viewed as a Gift and as a Qual-
          ity, 247

  III. Isaac Williams · Tract Eighty-seven: On Reserve in Communi-
       cating Religious Knowledge (Parts IV–VI) (Selection), 260
          Part V: The Principle Opposed to Certain Modern Re-
          ligious Opinions, 263

  IV. Edward Bouverie Pusey · Entire Absolution of the Penitent (Se-
       lection), 271

Part Five: Discerning the Lord's Body   281

    I. Robert Isaac Wilberforce · The Doctrine of the Incarnation of
       Our Lord Jesus Christ in Its Relation to Mankind and to the
       Church (Selection), 283
          Chapter XI: Christ Is Present with Men in His Church or
          Body Mystical, 288
          Chapter XII: Of Common Worship as a Means of Union
          with the Mystical Body of Christ, 309
          Chapter XIII: Of Sacraments, as Means of Union with the
          Manhood of Christ, 335
          Appendix to Chapter XIII: Wilberforce's Doctrine of the
          Holy Eucharist, 362

   II. Edward Bouverie Pusey · The Presence of Christ in the Holy
       Eucharist (Selection), 368

  III. John Keble · On Eucharistical Adoration (Selection), 377
          Chapter I: Promptings of Natural Piety, 379

A SELECT BIBLIOGRAPHY, 385

INDEX, 393

THE OXFORD MOVEMENT

to consideration of the abuses of the church itself, especially in its finance and administration. A long overdue reorganization of dioceses in Ireland had led to Keble's call to arms in 1834 [*sic*], his sermon on "National Apostasy." Then the *Tracts for the Times* laid down the program for the next six or eight years.[2]

Yet to other interpreters, no less worthy of credence, such a view would seem superficial and misleading.

. . . We have ever to remember [an English statesman declared] that what is called the catholic revival was not in England that which the catholic counter-revolution had been on the continent of Europe, primarily a political movement. Its workings were inward, in the sphere of the mind, in thought and faith, in idealised associations of historical grandeur.[3]

The English Catholic movement [a British theologian wrote] . . . was distinguished from the Continental by its being more personal and religious in character, aiming at reform and resistance rather than counter-revolution. . . . The arena of action and change was mainly subjective, in minds that had feared the unsettling influence of the critical and progressive tendencies then active, and were alarmed for religion in the degree that they loved it. The revolution that was dreaded was internal, in the region of thought and belief.[4]

It is clear that we shall have to find our own way through a welter of conflicting opinions.

It can scarcely be denied that the men of the Oxford Movement were conservative-minded, with little feeling for political reform as such; that they shared in the widespread reaction against the dry "rationality" of eighteenth-century culture; that their poetic sensibility — which cannot be ignored, in view of the fact that Keble, Newman and Williams were all fluent, if minor, poets — was "romantic" in its tone. But it would be a great mistake to suppose that, as a group, they had any interest in the preservation of political monarchy or aristocracy; that they relied on — or indeed even knew — the great systems of idealistic metaphysics in which German thought attempted to transcend the inhibitions of the earth-bound understanding; that the "nature-mysticism" of romantic poetry was determinative for their conception of religion. On the contrary, it was the Church, not the existing social order, that they defended; it was on dogma, not on metaphysics, that they relied as the

2. J. H. Nichols, *Romanticism in American Theology* (Chicago, 1961), 78.
3. J. Morley, *The Life of William Ewart Gladstone* (New York, 1904), I, 159.
4. A. M. Fairbairn, *Catholicism, Roman and Anglican*, 5th ed. (London, 1903), 114 f.

sure witness to suprarational reality; it was in the Church and its sacraments, as "extensions" of the redemptive Incarnation of God the Word, that they found the core of vital Christianity. Their view of the contemporary ecclesiastical situation was well put by Pusey, when he wrote:

> I could have been a Tory; but 1830 ended Toryism. I could not be a mere Conservative, i.e. I could not bind myself, or risk the future of the Church on the fidelity or wisdom of persons whose principle it is to keep what they think they can, and part with the rest. I believe that we are in the course of an inevitable Revolution; that the days of Establishments are numbered, and that the Church has to look to her purity, liberty, faithfulness to Catholicism, while I fear that the Conservatives would corrupt her in order to increase the numerical strength of the Establishment.[5]

To sum up tentatively: the Oxford Movement was unquestionably an affirmation of the Church's God-given authority and inherent power, but this affirmation was part of an attempted renewal of the Church in the interests of supernatural religion. Over against the aridities of empiricist philosophy and Utilitarian ethics, the Tractarians sought a renewed awareness of transcendent mystery and a renewed sense of human life as guided by a transcendent power to a transcendent goal. If they insisted on the authority of the Church, they did so because they saw in the Church an indispensable witness to the grace and truth that came by Jesus Christ — not because they looked to it as one more bulwark of a threatened social order.

If we take the next obvious step, and ask why the Tractarians — unlike the Evangelicals, who, for the better part of a century before the Oxford Movement began, had been striving mightily in the service of a grace-centred Christianity, without developing an elaborate ecclesiology — felt it necessary to lay such emphasis on the Church, both in theory and in practice, the answer must be this: the Tractarians held a significantly different view of the gospel and its communication. Influenced both by the traditional High Church appeal to history and by the deepened historical interest characteristic of the early nineteenth century, they saw the gospel as the story of God's real intervention in human history and the Church as the tangible, historical link between the historical Incarnation and believers in each and every age.

5. Pusey to E. Churton, July 25, 1865, in H. P. Liddon, *Life of Edward Bouverie Pusey, D.D.*, 4th ed. (London, 1894–98), IV, 199.

and the "liberal" state was no mere voluntary association of Christians whose acts rested simply on the collective authority of its members or whose teaching was simply a set of private interpretations of Scripture. On the contrary, the Church was a divinely created body with a divinely authorized order and a divinely inspired faith — a body anything but helpless if only it would look to its inherent powers of authoritative teaching and action.

> What is that Church [Newman inquired] but a pledge and proof of God's never-dying love and power from age to age? . . . He set it on the foundation of His Twelve Apostles, and promised that the gates of hell should not prevail against it; and its presence among us is a proof of His power. . . . Much and rightly as we reverence old lineage, noble birth, and illustrious ancestry, yet the royal dynasty of the Apostles is far older than all the kingly families which are now on the earth. . . . The presence of every Bishop suggests a long history of conflicts and trials, sufferings and victories, hopes and fears, through many centuries. His presence at this day is the fruit of them all. He is the living monument of those who are dead. He is the promise of a bold fight and a good confession and a cheerful martyrdom now, if needful, as was done by those of old time. We see their figures on our walls, and their tombs are under our feet; and we trust, nay, we are sure, that God will be to us in our day what He was to them.[10]

In the dual reassertion of apostolic authority with which the Oxford Movement faced the "liberal" revolution there was nothing really novel from the standpoint of traditional Anglican churchmanship — and yet in the end it led to a revolution of another sort.[11] The great paradox of the Anglo-Catholic Revival lay in the fact that, in attempting to rescue and renew the Anglican Church by means of a thoroughgoing application of historic Anglican standards, it actually wrought a massive transformation. It is hard to think of a significant Tractarian thesis for which substantial precedent cannot be found in earlier Anglican theology. Yet it is impossible to deny that the Oxford Movement, for all its profound conservatism, seriously altered the accepted patterns of Anglican thought and practice.

Perhaps the best way to illustrate the nature of the Tractarian revolution is to note how the Oxford Movement, in the very process of affirming long-recognized views of apostolic authority, undermined the con-

10. J. H. Newman, *Parochial and Plain Sermons*, 4th ed. (London, 1844), III, 271–73.
11. See below, Part Three, The Anglo-Catholic Revolution.

ventional definition of the English Church's position in relation to other Christian bodies. From the Reformation onwards it had commonly been supposed that the Church of England shared a common "Protestantism" with the Lutheran and Reformed Churches, over against medieval and Counter-Reformation Rome. In reality, however, ever since the Reformation Settlement in the time of Elizabeth I an influential school of Anglican theologians had been steadily moving away from typically Protestant teaching on a number of more or less distinct issues — grace and justification, Church order and episcopacy, the eucharistic sacrifice (to name only the more conspicuous). This trend found definite (if discreet) expression in the Restoration Settlement of 1662, which led directly to the separation of Protestant Nonconformists from the Church of England, and it continued over the next century or so in the several parts of the gradually expanding Anglican Communion, notably among the English and Scottish Nonjurors and the High Churchmen of Connecticut, New York, and New Jersey. In essence, the Tractarian revolution was simply the carrying of this quiet Anglican "Counter-Reformation" to an explicit and logical conclusion, under the pressure of the conviction that "Protestantism," by drawing Anglicans away from that sure foundation of apostolic succession and apostolic tradition on which the English Church had stood firm through all the storms of the Reformation, had exposed the Church to the onslaughts of "Erastianism" and "liberalism."

Given their diagnosis of the Church of England's ills and their consequent rejection of the Protestant Reformation and of the Protestant aspects of Anglican history, it was natural enough that the Tractarians should seek ecclesiastical salvation in a "Catholicism" which affirmed all that Protestantism had denied. From this deliberate decision the positive features of the Anglo-Catholic revolution readily followed. While Newman's transitional ecclesiology of the *via media* looked to the formulation of a distinctively Anglican version of Christianity, neither Protestant nor Roman,[12] the dominant and enduring tendency of Anglo-Catholicism has been to assimilate doctrine and worship alike to the common "Catholicism" of the Roman Catholic and Eastern Orthodox churches — or even, in the case of "papalist" Anglo-Catholics, to the complete system of the post-Tridentine Roman Catholic Church. The end result has been the firm rooting within the Anglican Communion of a wide range of

12. The vision of Anglicanism as a kind of "Western orthodoxy," which has caught the fancy of many later Anglo-Catholics, does not seem to have occurred to Newman.

III

The aims and convictions just outlined are far from being the whole point of the Oxford Movement, but taken together they do much to explain its most conspicuous results in the life of the Anglican Church. At least a few words must be said about some of these results.

For one thing, the Oxford Movement recovered long-forgotten forms of spiritual discipline. It cannot be claimed that modern Anglicans are a race of ascetics, worn out by fasting; that they are notable for the intensity of their prayer life; that the majority of Anglican priests spend long hours in the confessional. But it must be said that the Lenten observance, the fast before Communion, the Friday abstinence and other forms of self-discipline have been very widely restored among Anglicans; that the daily "divine office," retreats, mental prayer, and other traditional practices are once again an important element in Anglican spirituality, lay as well as clerical; that private confession and sacramental absolution are once more a recognized part of the Anglican priest's "cure of souls." All these developments are largely the result of the Tractarian call to personal holiness.

A second Anglo-Catholic achievement, closely related to the first, has been the widespread revival of the "religious life" as a recognized path to Christian perfection. Men's and women's communities, almost all of them established amidst manifold difficulties and in the face of strong opposition, have become an important feature of modern Anglicanism. From these centres the spiritual influence of Tractarianism continues to penetrate the Church.

Thirdly, in its "ritualistic" continuation the Oxford Movement has contributed largely to a spectacular transformation of Anglican eucharistic worship. While the early Tractarians had little taste for elaborate ceremonial, they did try to promote the more frequent and more reverent celebration of the Eucharist, and in the long run their doctrine of the eucharistic sacrifice and presence inevitably led to sweeping changes in liturgical usage. One famous parish priest expressed the genuinely Tractarian spirit of the "ritualistic" pioneers very clearly, in a comment on the practice of his own parish:

> . . . The Ritual of S. Peter's [London Docks] is not a mere aesthetic embellishment, but the outward expression of a great reality. It exactly meets the wants of those who have been taught to value their Lord's Sacramental Presence; they rejoice to see His Throne

made glorious, His priests ordering themselves as His representatives, and the whole arrangement of the service typical of its
heavenly counterpart. The poor and uneducated are thus taught
by the eye and ear, as well as by the understanding; and when they
find that those who set these great truths before them in the Ritual
of the Church are at the same time commending their priestly office
in the daily sacrifice of their lives, they acknowledge the truth and
consistency of the doctrine.[18]

Predictably, "ritualism" has not been wholly free from eccentricity
and superficiality, but the sacramental piety and dignified worship of
countless Anglican congregations are a living witness to the real spiritual
power of this phase of the Anglo-Catholic Revival.

Finally, the Oxford Movement did much to prepare the Anglican
Communion for the modern "ecumenical dialogue." Insular though the
Movement was in its original concern and conception, its inner logic
has compelled its sons to open their eyes to Christendom. It may be that
the alienation of the Tractarians from Protestantism as they knew it has
kept Anglo-Catholics, as a body, from doing full justice to the churches
of the Reformation. But the serious questioning of the separate existence
of the Anglican Church, which inevitably arose out of the Tractarians'
growing sense of kinship with traditional Catholicism, has led not only
to a persistent quest for reunion with Rome and with the Orthodox East,
but also in due course to a vital concern for the reunion of all believers
in one visible fellowship. Furthermore, the Oxford Movement's effective
demonstration of the Anglican Church's freedom from "confessional"
ties and of its sole dependence on the Bible and the historic standards of
faith and order common to East and West has shed more than a little
light on the true "ecumenical" vocation of Anglicanism.

IV

In the nature of the case, *solvitur ambulando* had to be the working
principle of the Tractarian theologians. Their theology was first and
foremost a spiritual medicine for the ailing Church of England, and like
all medicines it had to be compounded and administered as the course
of the patient's illness dictated. Consequently, in the theological literature
of the Oxford Movement we find a great many explorations and expositions of particular controversial issues, but relatively little in the way of
wide-ranging systematic construction, and it is tempting to conclude that

18. C. F. Lowder, *Twenty-One Years in S. George's Mission* (London, 1877), 163 f.

PART ONE

❖

The Babylonian Captivity
of the
English Church

I

JOHN HENRY NEWMAN

The Usurpations of Reason

Editor's introduction. The Oxford Movement was a good deal more than John Henry Newman in action, but without John Henry Newman to guide it and speak for it the Oxford Movement would have been much less spectacular and much less effective. For most of the crucial period 1833–45 he was the Movement's dominant figure and clearest voice. At least twenty-eight of the ninety *Tracts for the Times* were written or edited by him. Sunday by Sunday his sermons at St. Mary's, Oxford, spelled out the Movement's essential message in one of England's most influential pulpits. His theological lectures and essays add up to the first comprehensive statement of the Tractarian position.

Newman's leading role in the Oxford Movement was something of a surprise — and an unpleasant surprise, at that — to his family and his old friends. Born in London in 1801, he grew up in the atmosphere of Evangelical Anglicanism. After an undergraduate career which ended in apparent failure, he won the prize, coveted by every young Oxford intellectual, of an Oriel fellowship. Despite his sensitive disposition and angular manner, he blossomed out wonderfully among the "noetics" of the Oriel common room and became the close friend and associate of Richard Whately, their most forceful spokesman. By 1825 he was apparently on the way to becoming a theological liberal.

Three events helped to change the direction of his thinking. In 1826 Richard Hurrell Froude, dashing young heir of the Cavaliers, became a fellow of Oriel College. In November 1827 Newman suffered a devastating nervous collapse. On January 5, 1828, his dearly loved sister, Mary, died suddenly at the age of nineteen. When Froude wrote, in September 1828, that he "would give a few odd pence" if Newman "were not a heretic," [1] the latter was already ripe for conversion to the un-compromising High Churchmanship which Froude expounded with an engaging impertinence and lived with an almost frightening intensity.

In reality, Newman's theological liberalism had never gone very deep, and in his time of distress and sorrow he readily turned to what was soon to be known as "Anglo-Catholicism," for the simple reason that it seemed to him to offer a sounder foundation than the rather thin theology of the Evangelicals could provide for the dogmatic religion which he had cherished from his boyhood. In his own words:

> From the age of fifteen, dogma has been the fundamental principle of my religion: I know no other religion; I cannot enter into the idea of any other sort of religion; religion, as a mere sentiment, is to me a dream and a mockery. As well can there be filial love without the fact of a father, as devotion without the fact of a Supreme Being. What I held in 1816, I held in 1833, and I hold in 1864. Please God, I shall hold it to the end. Even when I was under Dr. Whately's influence, I had no temptation to be less zealous for the great dogmas of the faith, and at various times I used to resist such trains of thought on his part, as seemed to me (rightly or wrongly) to obscure them. Such [he concluded, emphatically and significantly] was the fundamental principle of the Movement of 1833. [2]

Newman's sermon on "The Usurpations of Reason," preached before the university on December 11, 1831, clearly articulated the convictions which were soon to take tangible shape in the Oxford Movement. All its themes were key Tractarian themes: unwavering faith in the self-disclosure of the transcendent God; the authority of the Church as interpreter of divine revelation; the impotence of mere human reason to demonstrate the mysterious truth given in revelation; the necessity of a moral submission to the message of judgment and grace.

Even on Newman's own terms this sermon is one-sided, in so far as it minimizes the inherent dignity of human intelligence and passes over the proper role of reason in the interpretation of Christian truth. But to his mind the days are too evil and dangerous for a nice concern for balanced statement. The mounting Utilitarian criticism of the English Church is but one expression — though from the churchman's standpoint admittedly a particularly ominous expression — of the rationalistic *Zeitgeist*, and nothing less than a slashing attack on every manifestation of a narrowly

---

1. *Remains of the late Reverend Richard Hurrell Froude, M.A.* (London, 1838), I, 233.
2. J. H. Newman, *Apologia pro vita sua* (Garden City, N.Y., 1956), 163.

empirical and earth-bound view of human knowledge and human life can really speak to the times. In another sermon of the same period Newman sharply asserts the need of his age for bitter medicine:

> Here I will not shrink from uttering my firm conviction, that it would be a gain to this country, were it vastly more superstitious, more bigoted, more gloomy, more fierce in its religion, than at present it shows itself to be. Not, of course, that I think the tempers of mind herein implied desirable, which would be an evident absurdity; but I think them infinitely more desirable and more promising than a heathen obduracy, and a cold, self-sufficient, self-wise tranquillity.[3]

"The Usurpations of Reason" would seem to have been composed in a similar mood.

❖   ❖   ❖   ❖

Mt. 11:19. Wisdom is justified of her children.

1. Such is our Lord's comment upon the perverse conduct of his countrymen, who refused to be satisfied either with St. John's reserve or his own condescension. John the Baptist retired from the world, and when men came to seek him, spoke sternly to them. Christ, the greater prophet, took the more lowly place, and freely mixed with sinners. The course of God's dealings with them was varied to the utmost extent which the essential truth and unchangeableness of his moral government permitted; but in neither direction of austereness nor of grace did it persuade. Having exposed this remarkable fact in the history of mankind, the divine speaker utters the solemn words of the text, the truth which they convey being the refuge of disappointed mercy, as well as a warning addressed to all whom they might concern. "Wisdom is justified of her children": as if he said, "There is no act on God's part, no truth of religion, to which a captious reason may not find objections; and in truth the evidence and matter of revelation are not addressed to the mere unstable reason of man, nor can hope for any certain or adequate reception with it. Divine Wisdom speaks, not to the world, but to her own children, or those who have been already under her teaching, and who, knowing her voice, understand her words, and are suitable judges of them. These justify her."

2. In the text, then, a truth is expressed in the form of a proverb, which

3. J. H. Newman, *Parochial and Plain Sermons* (London, 1908–18), I, 320.

is implied all through Scripture as a basis on which its doctrine rests — viz., that there is no necessary connexion between the intellectual and moral principles of our nature; that on religious subjects we may prove anything or overthrow anything, and can arrive at truth but accidentally, if we merely investigate by what is commonly called reason, which is in such matters but the instrument at best, in the hands of the legitimate judge, spiritual discernment. When we consider how common it is in the world at large to consider the intellect as the characteristic part of our nature, the silence of Scripture in regard to it (not to mention its positive disparagement of it) is very striking. In the Old Testament scarcely any mention is made of the existence of the reason as a distinct and chief attribute of mind; the sacred language affording no definite and proper terms expressive either of the general gift or of separate faculties in which it exhibits itself. And as to the New Testament, need we but betake ourselves to the description given us of him who is the only-begotten Son and express Image of God, to learn how inferior a station in the idea of the perfection of man's nature is held by the mere reason. While there is no profaneness in attaching to Christ those moral attributes of goodness, truth, and holiness which we apply to man, there would be an obvious irreverence in measuring the powers of his mind by any standard of intellectual endowments, the very names of which sound mean and impertinent when abscribed to him. St. Luke's declaration of his growth "in *wisdom* and stature" [Lk. 2:52], with no other specified advancement, is abundantly illustrated in St. John's Gospel, in which we find the almighty Teacher rejecting with apparent disdain all intellectual display, and confining himself to the enunciation of deep truths, intelligible to the children of wisdom, but conveyed in language altogether destitute both of argumentative skill and what is commonly considered eloquence.

3. To account for this silence of Scripture concerning intellectual excellence by affirming that the Jews were not distinguished in that respect is hardly to the point, for surely a lesson is conveyed to us in the very circumstance of such a people being chosen as the medium of a moral gift. If it be further objected that to speak concerning intellectual endowments fell beyond the range of inspiration, which was limited by its professed object, this is no objection, but the very position here maintained. No one can deny to the intellect its own excellence, nor deprive it of its due honours; the question is merely this, whether it be not limited in its turn, as regards its range, so as not without intrusion to exercise itself as an independent authority in the field of morals and religion.

4. Such surely is the case; and the silence of Scripture concerning intellectual gifts need not further be insisted on, either in relation to the fact itself or the implication contained in it. Were a being unacquainted with mankind to receive information concerning human nature from the Bible, would he ever conjecture its actual state, as developed in society, in all the various productions and exhibitions of what is called talent? And, next viewing the world as it is, and the Bible in connexion with it, what would he see in the actual history of revelation but the triumph of the moral powers of man over the intellectual, of holiness over ability, far more than of mind over brute force? Great as was the power of the lion and the bear, the leopard, and that fourth nameless beast, dreadful and terrible and strong exceedingly, God had weapons of their own kind to bruise and tame them. The miracles of the Church displayed more physical power than the hosts of Pharaoh and Sennacherib.[1] Power, not mind, was opposed to power; yet to the refined pagan intellect, the rivalry of intellect was not granted. The foolish things of the world confounded the wise far more completely than the weak, the mighty. Human philosophy was beaten from its usurped province, but not by any counter-philosophy; and unlearned faith, establishing itself by its own inherent strength, ruled the reason as far as its own interests were concerned, and from that time has employed it in the Church, first as a captive, then as a servant; not as an equal, and in no wise (far from it) as a patron.

5. I propose now to make some remarks upon the place which reason holds in relation to religion, the light in which we should view it, and certain encroachments of which it is sometimes guilty; and I think that, without a distinct definition of the word, which would carry us too far from our subject, I can make it plain what I take it to mean. Sometimes, indeed, it stands for all in which man differs from the brutes, and so includes in its signification the faculty of distinguishing between right and wrong, and the directing principle in conduct. In this sense I certainly do not here use it, but in that narrower signification, which it usually bears, as representing or synonymous with the intellectual powers, and as opposed as such to the moral qualities, and to faith.

6. This opposition between faith and reason takes place in two ways, when either of the two encroaches upon the province of the other. It would be an absurdity to attempt to find out mathematical truths by the purity and acuteness of the moral sense. It is a form of this mistake which

1. [ED.] Cf. "The Miracles of Early Ecclesiastical History" (written in 1842–43), in J. H. Newman, *Two Essays on Biblical and on Ecclesiastical Miracles* (London, 1918), 95–393.

had led men to apply such Scripture communications as are intended for religious purposes to the determination of physical questions. This error is perfectly understood in these days by all thinking men.[2] This was the usurpation of the schools of theology in former ages, to issue their decrees to the subjects of the senses and the intellect. No wonder reason and faith were at variance. The other cause of disagreement takes place when reason is the aggressor, and encroaches on the province of religion, attempting to judge of those truths which are subjected to another part of our nature, the moral sense.[3] For instance, suppose an acute man, who had never conformed his life to the precepts of Scripture, attempted to decide on the degree and kind of intercourse which a Christian ought to have with the world, or on the measure of guilt involved in the use of light and profane words, or which of the Christian doctrines were generally necessary to salvation, or to judge of the wisdom or use of consecrating places of worship, or to determine what kind and extent of reverence should be paid to the Lord's Day, or what portion of our possessions set apart for religious purposes; questions, these, which are addressed to the cultivated moral perception, or what is sometimes improperly termed "feeling" — improperly, because feeling comes and goes and, having no root in our nature, speaks with no divine authority; but the moral perception, though varying in the mass of men, is fixed in each individual, and is an original element within us. Hume, in his "Essay on Miracles," has well propounded a doctrine, which at the same time he misapplies. He speaks of "those dangerous friends or disguised enemies to the *Christian Religion*, who have undertaken to defend it by the principles of human reason. Our most holy Religion," he proceeds, "is founded on *Faith*, not on reason." [4] This is said in irony; but it is true as far as every important question in revelation is concerned, and to forget this is the error which is at present under consideration.

7. That it is a common error is evident from the anxiety generally felt to detach the names of men of ability from the infidel party. Why

2. [ED.] Newman's clear rejection of a crude "fundamentalism" is worth noting.

3. [ED.] It is clear enough from the context that Newman does not mean to adopt the "moral sense" theory, associated with Shaftesbury and Hutcheson. *Cf.* J. H. Newman, *Parochial and Plain Sermons* (London, 1908–18), I, 312: "Conscience is no longer recognized as an independent arbiter of actions, its authority is explained away; partly it is superseded in the minds of men by the so-called moral sense, which is regarded merely as the love of the beautiful; partly by the rule of expediency. . . ."

4. [ED.] David Hume, *Enquiries concerning the Human Understanding and concerning the Principles of Morals*, L. A. Selby-Bigge, ed. (Oxford, 1902), 129 f.

should we be desirous to disguise the fact, if it be such, that men distinguished, some for depth and originality of mind, others for acuteness, others for prudence and good sense in practical matters, yet have been indifferent to revealed religion — why, unless we have some misconceived notion concerning the connexion between the intellect and the moral principle? Yet is it not a fact, for the proof or disproof of which we need not go to history or philosophy, when the humblest village may show us that those persons who turn out badly, as it is called — who break the laws first of society, then of their country — are commonly the very men who have received more than the ordinary share of intellectual gifts? Without turning aside to explain or account for this, thus much it seems to show us, that the powers of the intellect (in that degree, at least, in which, in matter of fact, they are found amongst us) do not necessarily lead us in the direction of our moral instincts, or confirm them; but if the agreement between the two be but matter of accident, what testimony do we gain from the mere reason to the truths of religion?

8. Why should we be surprised that one faculty of our compound nature should not be able to do that which is the work of another? It is as little strange that the mind, which has only exercised itself on matters of literature or science, and never submitted itself to the influence of divine perceptions, should be unequal to the contemplation of a moral revelation, as that it should not perform the office of the senses. There is a strong analogy between the two cases. Our reason assists the senses in various ways, directing the application of them, and arranging the evidence they supply; it makes use of the facts subjected to them, and to an unlimited extent deduces conclusions from them, foretells facts which are to be ascertained, and confirms doubtful ones; but the man who neglected experiments and trusted to his vigour of talent would be called a theorist; and the blind man who seriously professed to lecture on light and colours could scarcely hope to gain an audience. Or suppose his lecture proceeded, what might be expected from him? Starting from the terms of science which would be the foundation and materials of his system, instead of apprehended facts, his acuteness and prompt imagination might carry him freely forward into the open field of the science, he might discourse with ease and fluency, till we almost forgot his lamentable deprivation; at length on a sudden, he would lose himself in some inexpressibly great mistake, betrayed in the midst of his career by some treacherous word which he incautiously explained too fully or dwelt too much upon; and we should find that he had been using words without

corresponding ideas — on witnessing his failure, we should view it indulgently, qualifying our criticism by the remark that the exhibition was singularly good for a blind man.

9. Such would be the fate of the officious reason, busying itself without warrant in the province of sense. In its due subordinate place there, it acts but as an instrument; it does but assist and expedite, saving the senses the time and trouble of working. Give a man a hundred eyes and hands for natural science, and you materially loosen his dependence on the ministry of reason.

10. This illustration, be it observed, is no adequate parallel of the truth which led to it; for the subject of light and colours is at least within the grasp of scientific definitions, and therefore cognizable by the intellect far better than morals. Yet apply it, such as it is, to the matter in hand, not, of course, with the extravagant object of denying the use of the reason in religious inquiries, but in order to ascertain what is its real place in the conduct of them. And in explanation of it I would make two additional observations. First, we must put aside the indirect support offered to revelation by the countenance of the intellectually gifted portion of mankind; I mean, in the way of *influence*. Reputation for talent, learning, scientific knowledge, has natural and just claims on our respect, and recommends a cause to our notice. So does power; and in this way power, as well as intellectual endowments, is necessary to the maintenance of religion, in order to secure from mankind a hearing for an unpleasant subject; but power, when it has done so much, attempts no more; or if it does, it loses its position, and is involved in the fallacy of persecution. Here the parallel holds good — it is as absurd to argue men, as to torture them, into believing.

11. But in matter of fact (it will be said) reason *can* go farther; for we can reason about religion, and we frame its evidences. Here, then, secondly, I observe, we must deduct from the real use of the reason in religious inquiries, whatever is the mere setting right of its own mistakes. The blind man who reasoned himself into errors in optics might possibly reason himself out of them; yet this would be no proof that extreme acuteness was necessary or useful in the science itself. It was but necessary for a blind man; that is, supposing he was bent on attempting to do what from the first he ought not to have attempted; and, after all, with the uncertainty whether he would gain or lose in his search after scientific truth by such an attempt. Now, so numerous and so serious have been the errors of theorists on religious subjects (that is, of those who have specu-

lated without caring to act on their sense of right; or have rested their teaching on mere arguments, instead of aiming at a direct contemplation of its subject matter), that the correction of those errors has required the most vigorous and subtle exercise of the reason, and has almost engrossed its efforts. Unhappily, the blind teacher in morals can ensure himself a blind audience, to whom he may safely address his paradoxes, which are sometimes admitted even by religious men, on the ground of those happy conjectures which his acute reason now and then makes, and which they can verify. What an indescribable confusion hence arises between truth and falsehood, in systems, parties and persons! What a superhuman talent is demanded to unravel the chequered and tangled web; and what gratitude is due to the gifted individual who by his learning or philosophy in part achieves the task! — yet not gratitude in such a case to the reason as a principle of research, which is merely undoing its own mischief, and poorly and tardily redressing its intrusion into a province not its own; but to the man, the moral being, who has subjected it in his own person to the higher principles of his nature.

12. To take an instance. What an extreme exercise of intellect is shown in the theological teaching of the Church! Yet how was it necessary? chiefly, from the previous errors of heretical reasonings, on subjects addressed to the moral perception. For while faith was engaged in that exact and well-instructed devotion to Christ which no words can suitably describe, the forward reason stepped in upon the yet unenclosed ground of doctrine, and attempted to describe there, from its own resources, an image of the Invisible.[5] Henceforth the Church was obliged, in self-defence, to employ the gifts of the intellect in the cause of God, to trace out (as near as might be) the faithful shadow of those truths, which unlearned piety admits and acts upon without the medium of clear intellectual representation.

13. This obviously holds good as regards the evidences also, great part of which are rather answers to objections than direct arguments for revelation; and even the direct arguments are far more effective in the confutation of captious opponents than in the conviction of inquirers. Doubtless the degree in which we depend on argument in religious subjects

5. [ED.] Cf. J. H. Newman, *The Arians of the Fourth Century* (London, 1908), 34: ". . . Canons grounded in physics were made the basis of discussions about possibilities and impossibilities in a spiritual substance, as confidently and as fallaciously, as those which in modern times have been derived from the same false analogies against the existence of moral self-action or free-will."

varies with each individual, so that no strict line can be drawn: still, let it be inquired whether these evidences are not rather to be viewed as splendid philosophical investigations than practical arguments; at best bulwarks intended for overawing the enemy by their strength and number, rather than for actual use in war. In matter of fact, *how* many men do we suppose, in a century, out of the whole body of Christians, have been primarily brought to belief, or retained in it, by an intimate and lively perception of the force of what are technically called the evidences? [6] And why are there so few? Because to the mind already familiar with the truths of natural religion, enough of evidence is at once afforded by the mere fact of the present existence of Christianity; which, viewed in its connexion with its principles and upholders and effects, bears on the face of it the signs of a divine ordinance in the very same way in which the visible world attests to us its own divine origin — a more accurate investigation, in which superior talents are brought into play, merely bringing to light an innumerable alternation of arguments, for and against it, which forms indeed an ever-increasing series in its behalf, but still does not get beyond the first suggestion of plain sense and religiously trained reason, and in fact, perhaps, never comes to a determination. Nay, so alert is the instinctive power of an educated conscience, that by some secret faculty, and without any intelligible reasoning process, it seems to detect moral truth wherever it lies hid, and feels a conviction of its own accuracy which bystanders cannot account for; and this especially in the case of revealed religion, which is one comprehensive moral fact — according to the saying which is parallel to the text, "I know my sheep, and am known of mine" (Jn. 10:14).

14. From considerations such as the foregoing, it appears that exercises of reason are either external, or at least only ministrative, to religious inquiry and knowledge: accidental to them, not of their essence; useful in their place, but not necessary. But in order to obtain further illustrations, and a view of the importance of the doctrine which I would advocate, let us proceed to apply it to the circumstances of the present times. Here, first, in finding fault with the times, it is right to disclaim all intention of complaining of them. To murmur and rail at the state of things under which we find ourselves, and to prefer a former state, is not merely indecorous, it is absolutely unmeaning. We are ourselves neces-

---

6. [ED.] Newman is referring to the attempts (so frequent in the eighteenth century) at rational demonstration of the divine origin of Christianity. A famous example is William Paley, *A View of the Evidences of Christianity* (London, 1794).

sary parts of the existing system, out of which we have individually grown into being, into our actual position in society. Depending, therefore, on the times as a condition of existence, in wishing for other times we are, in fact, wishing we had never been born. Moreover, it is ungrateful to a state of society, from which we daily enjoy so many benefits, to rail against it. Yet there is nothing unbecoming, unmeaning, or ungrateful in pointing out its faults and wishing them away.

15. In this day, then, we see a very extensive development of an usurpation which has been preparing, with more or less of open avowal, for some centuries — the usurpation of reason in morals and religion. In the first years of its growth it professed to respect the bounds of justice and sobriety: it was little in its own eyes; but getting strength, it was lifted up; and casting down all that is called God, or worshipped, it took its seat in the temple of God, as his representative [cf. 2 Thess. 2:4]. Such, at least, is the consummation at which the oppressor is aiming — which he will reach, unless he who rids his Church of tyrants in their hour of pride, look down from the pillar of the cloud, and trouble his host [cf. Ex. 14:24].

16. Now, in speaking of an usurpation of the reason at the present day, stretching over the province of religion, and in fact over the Christian Church, no admission is made concerning the degree of cultivation which the reason has at present reached in the territory which it has unjustly entered. A tyrant need not be strong; he keeps his ground by prescription and through fear. It is not the profound thinkers who intrude with their discussions and criticisms within the sacred limits of moral truth. A really philosophical mind, if unhappily it has ruined its own religious perceptions, will be silent; it will understand that religion does not lie in its way: it may disbelieve its truths, it may account belief in them a weakness, or, on the other hand, a happy dream, a delightful error, which it cannot itself enjoy — anyhow, it will not usurp. But men who know but a little are for that very reason most under the power of the imagination, which fills up for them at pleasure those departments of knowledge to which they are strangers; and, as the ignorance of abject minds shrinks from the spectres which it frames there, the ignorance of the self-confident is petulant and presuming.

17. The usurpations of the reason may be dated from the Reformation. Then, together with the tyranny, the legitimate authority of the ecclesiastical power was more or less overthrown; and in some places its ultimate basis also, the moral sense. One school of men resisted the Church;

another went farther, and rejected the supreme authority of the law of conscience. Accordingly, revealed religion was in a great measure stripped of its proof; for the existence of the Church had been its external evidence, and its internal had been supplied by the moral sense. Reason now undertook to repair the demolition it had made, and to render the proof of Christianity independent both of the Church and of the law of nature. From that time (if we take a general view of its operations) it has been engaged first in making difficulties by the mouth of unbelievers, and then claiming power in the Church as a reward for having, by the mouth of apologists, partially removed them.

18. The following instances are in point, in citing which let no disrespect be imagined towards such really eminent men as were at various times concerned in them. Wrong reason could not be met, when miracle and inspiration were suspended, except by rightly directed reason.

19. (*i*) As to the proof of the authority of Scripture. This had hitherto rested on the testimony borne to it by the existing Church. Reason volunteered proof, not different, however, in kind, but more subtle and complicated in its form — took the evidence of past ages, instead of the present, and committed its keeping (as was necessary) to the oligarchy of learning: at the same time, it boasted of the service thus rendered to the cause of revelation, that service really consisting in the external homage thus paid to it by learning and talent, not in any great direct practical benefit, where men honestly wish to find and to do God's will, to act for the best, and to prefer what is safe and pious, to what shows well in argument.

20. (*ii*) Again, the evidences themselves have been elaborately expanded; thus satisfying, indeed, the liberal curiosity of the mind and giving scope for a devotional temper to admire the manifold wisdom of God, but doing comparatively little towards keeping men from infidelity or turning them to a religious life. The same remark applies to such works on natural theology as treat of the marks of design in the creation, which are beautiful and interesting to the believer in a God; but, when men have not already recognized God's voice within them, ineffective, and this moreover possibly from some unsoundness in the intellectual basis of the argument.[7]

21. (*iii*) A still bolder encroachment was contemplated by the reason

---

7. [ED.] Writing in 1870, Newman expressed a favourable view of a general theistic argument from *order*, as distinct from apparent instances of *design*. Cf. J. H. Newman, *An Essay in Aid of a Grammar of Assent* (Garden City, N.Y., 1955), 74 f.

when it attempted to deprive the moral law of its intrinsic authority and to rest it upon a theory of present expediency. Thus, it constituted itself the court of ultimate appeal in religious disputes, under pretence of affording a clearer and more scientifically arranged code than is to be collected from the obscure precedents and mutilated enactments of the conscience.

22. (iv) A further error, connected with the assumption just noticed, has been that of making intellectually gifted men arbiters of religious questions, in the place of the children of wisdom. As far as the argument for revelation is concerned, it is only necessary to show that Christianity has had disciples among men of the highest ability; whereas a solicitude already alluded to has been shown to establish the orthodoxy of some great names in philosophy and science, as if truly it were a great gain to religion, and not to themselves, if they *were* believers. Much more unworthy has been the practice of boasting of the admissions of infidels concerning the beauty or utility of the Christian system, as if it were a great thing for a divine gift to obtain praise for human excellence from proud or immortal men. Far different is the spirit of our own Church, which, rejoicing, as she does, to find her children walking in truth [*cf.* 2 Jn. 4; 3 Jn. 4], never forgets the dignity and preciousness of the gifts she offers; as appears, for instance, in the warnings prefacing the Communion Service, and in the Commination [8] — above all, in the Athanasian Creed, in which she but follows the example of the early Church, which first withdrew her mysteries from the many, then, when controversy exposed them, guarded them with an anathema — in each case, lest curious reason might rashly gaze and perish.

23. (v) Again — another dangerous artifice of the usurping reason has been the establishment of societies in which literature or science has been the essential bond of union, to the exclusion of religious profession. These bodies, many of them founded with no bad intention, have gradually led to an undue exaltation of the reason, and have formed an unconstitutional power, advising and controlling the legitimate authorities of the soul. In troubled times, such as the present, associations, the most inoffensive in themselves, and the most praiseworthy in their object, hardly escape this blame. Of this nature have been the literary meetings and societies of the last two centuries, not to mention recently established bodies of a less innocent character.

24. (vi) And lastly, let it be a question, whether the theories on gov-

8. [ED.] The special penitential service for Ash Wednesday, B.C.P.

ernment which exclude religion from the essential elements of the state
are not also offshoots of the same usurpations.

25. And now, what remains but to express a confidence, which cannot
deceive itself, that, whatever be the destined course of the usurpations of
the reason in the scheme of divine providence, its fall must at last come,
as that of other proud aspirants before it? "Fret not thyself," says David,
"because of evildoers, neither be thou envious against the workers of
iniquity; for they shall soon be cut down like the grass, and wither as the
green herb" [Ps. 37:1 f.]; perishing as that high-minded power, which the
prophet speaks of, who sat in the seat of God, as if wiser than Daniel, and
acquainted with all secrets, till at length he was cast out from the holy
place as profane, in God's good time (Ezek. 28:3, 16). Our plain business, in
the meantime, is to ascertain and hold fast our appointed station in the troubled scene, and then to rid ourselves of all dread of the future; to be careful,
while we freely cultivate the reason in all its noble functions, to keep it
in its subordinate place in our nature: while we employ it industriously
in the service of religion, not to imagine that, in this service, we are doing
any great thing, or directly advancing its influence over the heart; and,
while we promote the education of others in all useful knowledge, to
beware of admitting any principle of union, or standard of reward, which
may practically disparage the supreme authority of Christian fellowship.
Our great danger is, lest we should not understand our own principles,
and should weakly surrender customs and institutions which go far to
constitute the Church what she is, the pillar and ground of moral truth
[cf. 1 Tim. 3:15] — lest, from a wish to make religion acceptable to
the world in general, more free from objections than any moral system
can be made, more immediately and visibly beneficial to the temporal
interests of the community than God's comprehensive appointments
condescend to be, we betray it to its enemies; lest we rashly take the
Scriptures from the Church's custody and commit them to the world,
that is, to what is called public opinion; which men boast, indeed, will
ever be right on the whole, but which, in fact, being the opinion of men
who, as a body, have not cultivated the internal moral sense, and have
externally no immutable rules to bind them, is, in religious questions,
only by accident right, or only on very broad questions, and tomorrow
will betray interests which today it affects to uphold.

26. However, what are the essentials of our system, both in doctrine
and discipline; what we may safely give up and what we must firmly

hold; such practical points are to be determined by a more mature wisdom than can be expected in a discussion like the present, or indeed can be conveyed in any formal treatise. It is a plainer and a sufficiently important object to contribute to the agitation of the general subject, and to ask questions which others are to answer.

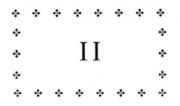

JOHN KEBLE

National Apostasy

Editor's introduction.

Long before the Oxford movement was thought of, or had any definite shape, a number of its characteristic principles and ideas had taken strong hold of the mind of a man of great ability and great seriousness, who, after a brilliant career at Oxford as student and tutor, had exchanged the university for a humble country cure.[1]

The true and primary author of it [the Oxford Movement], . . . as is usual with great motive-powers, was out of sight. Having carried off as a mere boy the highest honours of the University, he had turned from the admiration which haunted his steps, and sought for a better and holier satisfaction in pastoral work in the country. Need I say that I am speaking of John Keble?[2]

John Keble, thus definitively identified as the true begetter of the Anglo-Catholic Revival, was no self-assertive controversialist. Born at Fairford, in Gloucestershire, in 1792, he learned in his father's country parsonage to love the Anglican tradition, as soberly interpreted by the best representatives of the High Church school.

Next to a sound rule of faith [he was to write in 1827], there is nothing of so much consequence as a sober standard of feeling in matters of practical religion: and it is the peculiar happiness of the Church of England to possess, in her authorized formularies, an ample and secure provision for both.[3]

Crowning a spectacular undergraduate career by winning an Oriel fellowship in 1811, he became a college tutor in 1817, but in 1823 he retired

1. R. W. Church, *The Oxford Movement: Twelve Years, 1833–1845*, 3d ed. (London, 1892), 23.
2. J. H. Newman, *Apologia pro vita sua* (Garden City, N.Y., 1956), 137.
3. John Keble, *The Christian Year, Lyra Innocentium, and Other Poems* (London, 1914), xix.

to the Cotswolds to serve as his father's curate. Four years later he published *The Christian Year*, whose "soothing" verse — the adjective is
his own [4] — pleasantly expressed his serene piety, but by the same token
gave little indication of his potential boldness in conflict.

For all his love of retirement, however, there was a firm (not to say
stubborn) side to Keble's character. ". . . To his attainments," Dean
Church tells us, "he joined a temper of singular sweetness and modesty,
capable at the same time, when necessary, of austere strength and strict-
ness of principle." [5] Given a sufficient stimulus, that strength and strict-
ness would emerge with surprising effect. As it happened, the decisive
stimulus was twofold: a personal friendship and a political event.

Like most serious churchmen in the age of reform, Keble anxiously
contemplated the probable impact of political change on ecclesiastical
institutions, but he apparently had no clear notion of an appropriate
counterstrategy. One man in particular did a good deal to prepare him
for action. When Keble withdrew to the country in 1823, he organized
a reading party of three of his Oriel pupils: Robert Isaac Wilberforce,
Isaac Williams, and Richard Hurrell Froude.

> Keble won the love of the whole little society; but in Froude he
> had gained a disciple who was to be the mouthpiece and champion
> of his ideas, and who was to react on himself and carry him forward
> to larger enterprises and bolder resolutions than by himself he would
> have thought of. Froude took in from Keble all he had to com-
> municate — principles, convictions, moral rules and standards of
> life, hopes, fears, antipathies. And his keenly-tempered intellect,
> and his determination and high courage, gave a point and an im-
> pulse of their own to Keble's views and purposes.[6]

As a result, when the critical moment came, Keble was ready to speak
out as a leader.

He did not have to wait long for an occasion to speak. In 1828-29, by
repealing the Corporation and Test Acts and enacting the Roman Catholic
Relief Bill into law, the Parliament of the United Kingdom relieved both
Protestant Dissenters and Roman Catholics of most of their civil disabilities, thereby seriously affecting the political position of the United
Church of England and Ireland. Within four years conservative churchmen thought that their worst fears were being realized when Earl Grey's
Whig administration introduced the Church Temporalities Bill into the
reformed Parliament.

4. *Ibid.*   5. Church, *Oxford Movement*, 24.   6. *Ibid.*, 27 f.

At first glance, perhaps, it is hard to see why the measure aroused such fierce opposition. Its aim was a badly needed reorganization of the Irish Church. The government had at first hoped to divert a considerable portion of the Church's revenues to public purposes, but in the end, owing to the resistance of the House of Lords, it had to be content with a partial rationalization of the Church's internal finances. The very uneven distribution of ecclesiastical income made such action seem eminently reasonable, and in view of the fact that the native Irish population was overwhelmingly Roman Catholic in religion, there was obviously a good case for the further step of partial disendowment.

In Anglican eyes, nonetheless, the administration's proposal was extremely dubious, for one definite reason. Even in its milder form it involved a drastic reduction of the Irish hierarchy — and that without the consent of the Church. (Since both the English and the Irish convocations had been silenced for over a century, the Church had no canonical means of giving or refusing consent, but of course for many Anglicans the impotence of the historic synods was one more serious grievance.) When the episcopate, on which, according to the stricter Anglican view, the Church's very existence depended, was being arbitrarily cut down by an ecclesiastically dubious Parliament, English churchmen found it hard to take an unbiased interest in the economic and political problems of Ireland. There may well have been "something feverish, a touch of absurdity," [7] about some Anglican reactions to the Church Temporalities Bill, but we must realize that for many Anglicans a serious religious issue seemed to be at stake.

In the crisis of 1833 more than one voice spoke in tones that had scarcely been heard since the passing of the Nonjurors. The Regius Professor of Divinity at Oxford, for example, had this to say:

> I contend, that the Irish Church was not bound to comply with the provisions of this unrighteous Bill. If the clergy of the diocese of Waterford [8] had elected a Bishop according to the forms of the primitive Church, and if the Primate of Ireland had thought fit to consecrate him, he would have been as much a Bishop of the United Church of England and Ireland, as any of the Bishops appointed by the Crown. But Roman Catholics and Dissenters have decided it to be convenient that the Irish Church should henceforth have

7. E. L. Woodward, *The Age of Reform, 1815–1870* (Oxford, 1938), 493.
8. The first effect of the Church Temporalities Act was the union of the see of Waterford and Lismore, vacant through the death of Richard Bourke in 1832, with Cashel.

fewer Bishops: and thus the Church . . . is "bound and fettered and enslaved." But will she not burst her bonds? [9]

Although at least a few churchmen do seem to have contemplated open rebellion,[10] no overt action was taken — and yet in fact an ecclesiastical revolution was already in the making. On July 9, 1833, Newman returned to England from an extended Mediterranean tour.

The following Sunday [he records], July 14th, Mr. Keble preached the Assize Sermon in the University Pulpit. It was published under the title of "National Apostasy." I have ever considered and kept the day, as the start of the religious movement of 1833.[11]

❖ ❖ ❖ ❖

1 Sam. 12:23. As for me, God forbid that I should sin against the Lord in ceasing to pray for you: but I will teach you the good and the right way.

On public occasions, such as the present, the minds of Christians naturally revert to that portion of Holy Scripture which exhibits to us the will of the Sovereign of the world in more immediate relation to the civil and national conduct of mankind. We naturally turn to the Old Testament when public duties, public errors, and public dangers are in question. And what in such cases is natural and obvious, is sure to be more or less right and reasonable. Unquestionably it is a mistaken theology which would debar Christian nations and statesmen from the instruction afforded by the Jewish Scriptures, under a notion that the circumstances of that people were altogether peculiar and unique, and therefore irrelevant to every other case. True, there is hazard of misapplication, as there is whenever men teach by example. There is peculiar hazard, from the sacredness and delicacy of the subject; since dealing with things supernatural and miraculous as if they were ordinary human precedents would be not only unwise but profane. But these hazards are more than counterbalanced by the absolute certainty, peculiar to this history, that what is there commended was right, and what is there blamed, wrong. And they would be effectually obviated if men would be careful to keep in view this caution — suggested everywhere, if I mistake not, by the manner

9. Edward Burton, *Thoughts on the Separation of Church and State* (London, 1834), 62.

10. *Cf.* E. R. Fairweather, " 'National Apostasy': A Contemporary View of the Irish Church's Duty," *Canadian Journal of Theology,* VIII (1962), 50–54.

11. Newman, *Apologia,* 152.

in which the Old Testament is quoted in the New — that, as regards re-ward and punishment, God dealt formerly with the Jewish people in a manner analogous to that in which he deals now, not so much with Chris-tian nations, as with the souls of individual Christians.

Let us only make due allowances for this cardinal point of difference, and we need not surely hesitate to avail ourselves, as the time may re-quire, of those national warnings which fill the records of the elder Church: the less so, as the discrepancy lies rather in what is revealed of God's providence than in what is required in the way of human duty. Rewards and punishments may be dispensed, visibly at least, with a less even hand; but what tempers, and what conduct, God will ultimately reward and punish — this is a point which cannot be changed: for it depends not on our circumstances but on his essential, unvarying at-tributes.

I have ventured on these few general observations because the im-patience with which the world endures any remonstrance on religious grounds is apt to show itself most daringly when the Law and the Prophets are appealed to. Without any scruple or ceremony, men give us to understand that they regard the whole as obsolete: thus taking the very opposite ground to that which was preferred by the same class of persons two hundred years ago; but, it may be feared, with much the same pur-pose and result.[1] Then, the Old Testament was quoted at random for every excess of fanatical pride and cruelty: now, its authority goes for nothing, however clear and striking the analogies may be, which appear to warrant us in referring to it. The two extremes, as usual, meet, and in this very remarkable point: that they both avail themselves of the supernatural parts of the Jewish revelation to turn away attention from that which they, of course, most dread and dislike in it: its authoritative confirmation of the plain dictates of conscience in matters of civil wis-dom and duty.

That portion, in particular, of the history of the chosen people, which drew from Samuel, the truest of patriots, the wise and noble sentiment in the text, must ever be an unpleasing and perplexing page of Scripture to those who would fain persuade themselves that a nation, even a Chris-tian nation, may do well enough, as such, without God, and without his Church. For what if the Jews were bound to the Almighty by ties common to no other people? What if he had condescended to know them in a way in which he was as yet unrevealed to all families of the earth besides? What if, as their relation to him was nearer, and their ingratitude

1. [ED.] Keble is referring to the Puritan extremists of the Civil War period.

more surpassing, so they might expect more exemplary punishment? Still, after all has been said, to exaggerate their guilt, in degree, beyond what is supposed possible in any nation whatever now, what can it come to, in kind and in substance, but only this — that they rejected God, that they wished themselves rid of the moral restraint implied in his peculiar presence and covenant? They said what the prophet Ezekiel, long after, represents their worthy posterity as saying, "We will be as the heathen, the families of the countries" (Ezek. 20:32). "Once for all, we will get rid of these disagreeable, unfashionable scruples, which throw us behind, as we think, in the race of worldly honour and profit." Is this indeed a tone of thought which Christian nations cannot fall into? Or, if they should, has it ceased to be displeasing to God? In other words, has he forgotten to be angry with impiety and practical atheism? Either this must be affirmed, or men must own (what is clear at once to plain unsophisticated readers) that this first overt act, which began the downfall of the Jewish nation, stands on record, with its fatal consequences, for a perpetual warning to all nations, as well as to all individual Christians, who, having accepted God for their King, allow themselves to be weary of subjection to him, and think they should be happier if they were freer, and more like the rest of the world.

I do not enter into the question, whether visible temporal judgments are to be looked for by Christian nations transgressing as those Jews did. Surely common sense and piety unite in representing this inquiry as, practically, one of no great importance. When it is once known for certain that such and such conduct is displeasing to the King of kings, surely common sense and piety concur in setting their mark of reprobation on such conduct, whether the punishment, sure to overtake it, come tomorrow, or a year hence, or wait till we are in another world.

Waiving this question, therefore, I proceed to others, which appear to me, I own, at the present moment especially, of the very gravest practical import.

What are the symptoms by which one may judge most fairly, whether or no a nation, as such, is becoming alienated from God and Christ?

And what are the particular duties of sincere Christians whose lot is cast by divine providence in a time of such dire calamity?

The conduct of the Jews, in asking for a king, may furnish an ample illustration of the first point: the behaviour of Samuel, then and afterwards, supplies as perfect a pattern of the second, as can well be expected from human nature.

I. The case is at least possible, of a nation, having for centuries acknowledged, as an essential part of its theory of government, that, as a Christian nation, she is also a part of Christ's Church, and bound, in all her legislation and policy, by the fundamental rules of that Church [2] — the case is, I say, conceivable, of a government and people, so constituted, deliberately throwing off the restraint, which in many respects such a principle would impose on them, nay, disavowing the principle itself; and that on the plea that other states, as flourishing or more so in regard of wealth and dominion, do well enough without it. Is not this desiring, like the Jews, to have an earthly king over them, when the Lord their God is their King? Is it not saying in other words, "We will be as the heathen, the families of the countries," the aliens to the Church of our Redeemer?

To such a change, whenever it takes place, the immediate impulse will probably be given by some pretence of danger from without — such as, at the time now spoken of, was furnished to the Israelites by an incursion of the children of Ammon; or by some wrong or grievance in the executive government, such as the malversation of Samuel's sons, to whom he had deputed his judicial functions. Pretences will never be hard to find; but, in reality, the movement will always be traceable to the same decay or want of faith, the same deficiency in Christian resignation and thankfulness, which leads so many, as individuals, to disdain and forfeit the blessings of the gospel. Men not impressed with religious principle attribute their ill success in life — the hard times they have to struggle with — to anything rather than their own ill-desert: and the institutions of the country, ecclesiastical and civil, are always at hand to bear the blame of whatever seems to be going amiss. Thus, the discontent in Samuel's time, which led the Israelites to demand a change of constitution, was discerned by the unerring eye, though perhaps little suspected by themselves, to be no better than a fresh development of the same restless, godless spirit which had led them so often into idolatry.

> They have not rejected thee, but they have rejected me, that I should not reign over them. According to all the works, which they have done since the day that I brought them up out of Egypt even

---

2. [ED.] Cf. John Keble, *Sermons, Academical and Occasional*, 2d ed. (Oxford, 1848), 152: ". . . Instead of representing the Church as dependent on the State, the holy prophet intended to point out the entire submission which the State owes to the Church: that is, in other words, the entire submission which God's ministers in temporal things owe to that great enduring plan, which he has set on foot in a lost world for subduing all things to himself." (From a sermon on Is. 49:23, preached on June 26, 1835.)

unto this day, wherewith they have forsaken me, and served other gods, so do they also unto thee (1 Sam. 8:7 f.).

The charge might perhaps surprise many of them, just as, in other times and countries, the impatient patrons of innovation are surprised at finding themselves rebuked on religious grounds. Perhaps the Jews pleaded the express countenance which the words of their law, in one place (Deut. 17: 14–20), seemed, by anticipation, to lend to the measure they were urging. And so, in modern times, when liberties are to be taken, and the intrusive passions of men to be indulged, precedent and permission, or what sounds like them, may be easily found and quoted for everything. But Samuel, in God's name, silenced all this, giving them to understand that in his sight the whole was a question of motive and purpose, not of ostensible and colourable argument — in his sight, I say, to whom we, as well as they, are nationally responsible for much more than the soundness of our deductions as matter of disputation, or of law; we are responsible for the meaning and temper in which we deal with his holy Church, established among us for the salvation of our souls.

These, which have been hitherto mentioned as omens and tokens of an apostate mind in a nation, have been suggested by the portion itself of sacred history, to which I have ventured to direct your attention. There are one or two more, which the nature of the subject, and the palpable tendency of things around us, will not allow to be passed over.

One of the most alarming, as a symptom, is the growing indifference, in which men indulge themselves, to other men's religious sentiments. Under the guise of charity and toleration we are come almost to this pass, that no difference, in matters of faith, is to disqualify for our approbation and confidence, whether in public or domestic life./Can we conceal it from ourselves, that every year the practice is becoming more common, of trusting men unreservedly in the most delicate and important matters, without one serious inquiry, whether they do not hold principles which make it impossible for them to be loyal to their Creator, Redeemer, and Sanctifier? Are not offices conferred, partnerships formed, intimacies courted — nay (what is almost too painful to think of), do not parents commit their children to be educated, do they not encourage them to intermarry, in houses on which apostolical authority would rather teach them to set a mark as unfit to be entered by a faithful servant of Christ?

I do not now speak of public measures only or chiefly; many things of that kind may be thought, whether wisely or no, to become from time to time necessary, which are in reality as little desired by those who lend them a seeming concurrence as they are, in themselves, undesirable. But I speak of the spirit which leads men to exult in every step of that kind; to congratulate one another on the supposed decay of what they call an exclusive system.

Very different are the feelings with which it seems natural for a true churchman to regard such a state of things, from those which would arise in his mind on witnessing the mere triumph of any given set of adverse opinions, exaggerated or even heretical as he might deem them. He might feel as melancholy — he could hardly feel so indignant.

But this is not a becoming place, nor are these safe topics, for the indulgence of mere feeling. The point really to be considered is, whether, according to the coolest estimate, the fashionable liberality of this generation be not ascribable, in a great measure, to the same temper which led the Jews voluntarily to set about degrading themselves to a level with the idolatrous Gentiles. And, if it be true anywhere, that such enactments are forced on the legislature by public opinion, is APOSTASY too hard a word to describe the temper of that nation?

The same tendency is still more apparent, because the fair gloss of candour and forbearance is wanting in the surly or scornful impatience often exhibited, by persons who would regret passing for unbelievers, when Christian motives are suggested and checks from Christian principles attempted to be enforced on their public conduct. I say, "their public conduct," more especially; because in that, I know not how, persons are apt to be more shameless, and readier to avow the irreligion that is in them — amongst other reasons, probably, from each feeling that he is one of a multitude, and fancying, therefore, that his responsibility is divided.

For example — whatever be the cause, in this country of late years (though we are lavish in professions of piety) there has been observable a growing disinclination, on the part of those bound by VOLUNTARY OATHS, to whatever reminds them of their obligation; a growing disposition to explain it all away. We know what, some years ago, would have been thought of such uneasiness, if betrayed by persons officially sworn, in private, legal, or commercial life. If there be any subjects or occasions, now, on which men are inclined to judge of it more lightly, it concerns them deeply to be quite sure that they are not indulging or encouraging a profane dislike of God's awful presence; a general tendency, as a people, to leave him out of all their thoughts.

They will have the more reason to suspect themselves in proportion as they see and feel more of that impatience under pastoral authority which our Saviour himself has taught us to consider as a never-failing symptom of an unchristian temper. "He that heareth you, heareth me; and he that despiseth you, despiseth me" (Lk. 10:16). Those words of divine truth put beyond all sophistical exception what common sense would lead us to infer, and what daily experience teaches — that disrespect to the successors of the apostles, as such, is an unquestionable symptom of enmity to him who gave them their commission at first, and has pledged himself to be with them for ever [cf. Jn. 20:21 ff.; Mt. 28:20]. Suppose such disrespect general and national, suppose it also avowedly grounded not on any fancied tenet of religion, but on mere human reasons of popularity and expediency, either there is no meaning at all in these emphatic declarations of our Lord, or that nation, how highly soever she may think of her own religion and morality, stands convicted in his sight of a direct disavowal of his sovereignty.

To this purpose it may be worth noticing that the ill-fated chief whom God gave to the Jews, as the prophet tells us, in his anger (Hos. 13:11), and whose disobedience and misery were referred by himself to his "fearing the people, and obeying their voice" (1 Sam. 15:24), whose conduct, therefore, may be fairly taken as a sample of what public opinion was at that time supposed to require — his first step in apostasy was, perhaps, an intrusion on the sacrificial office (1 Sam. 13:8–14), certainly an impatient breach of his engagement with Samuel, as the last and greatest of his crimes was persecuting David, whom he well knew to bear God's special commission. God forbid that any Christian land should ever, by her prevailing temper and policy, revive the memory and likeness of Saul, or incur a sentence of reprobation like his. But if such a thing should be, the crimes of that nation will probably begin in infringement on apostolical rights; she will end in persecuting the true Church; and in the several stages of her melancholy career, she will continually be led on from bad to worse by vain endeavours at accommodation and compromise with evil. Sometimes toleration may be the word, as with Saul when he spared the Amalekites; sometimes state security, as when he sought the life of David; sometimes sympathy with popular feeling, as appears to have been the case when, violating solemn treaties, he attempted to exterminate the remnant of the Gibeonites in his zeal for the children of Israel and Judah (2 Sam. 21:2). Such are the sad but obvious results of separating religious resignation altogether from men's notions of civil duty.

II. But here arises the other question on which it was proposed to say a few words; and with a view to which, indeed, the whole subject must be considered if it is to lead to any practical improvement. What should be the tenor of their conduct, who find themselves cast on such times of decay and danger? How may a man best reconcile his allegiance to God and his Church with his duty to his country, that country which now, by the supposition, is fast becoming hostile to the Church, and cannot therefore long be the friend of God?

Now in proportion as anyone sees reason to fear that such is, or soon may be, the case in his own land, just so far may he see reason to be thankful, especially if he be called to any national trust, for such a complete pattern of his duty as he may find in the conduct of Samuel. That combination of sweetness with firmness, of consideration with energy, which constitutes the temper of a perfect public man, was never perhaps so beautifully exemplified. He makes no secret of the bitter grief and dismay with which the resolution of his countrymen had filled him. He was prepared to resist it at all hazards, had he not received from God himself directions to give them their own way; protesting, however, in the most distinct and solemn tone, so as to throw the whole blame of what might ensue on their wilfulness. Having so protested, and found them obstinate, he does not therefore at once forsake their service; he continues discharging all the functions they had left him, with a true and loyal, though most heavy, heart. "God forbid that I should sin against the Lord in ceasing to pray for you: but I will teach you the good and the right way."

Should it ever happen (which God avert, but we cannot shut our eyes to the danger) that the apostolical Church should be forsaken, degraded, nay trampled on and despoiled by the state and people of England, I cannot conceive a kinder wish for her, on the part of her most affectionate and dutiful children, than that she may consistently act in the spirit of this most noble sentence; nor a course of conduct more likely to be blessed by a restoration to more than her former efficiency. In speaking of the Church, I mean, of course, the laity as well as the clergy in their three orders — the whole body of Christians united, according to the will of Jesus Christ, under the successors of the apostles. It may, by God's blessing, be of some use, to show how, in the case supposed, the example of Samuel might guide her collectively, and each of her children individually, down even to minute details of duty.

The Church would, first of all, have to be constant, as before, in INTER-

CESSION. No despiteful usage, no persecution, could warrant her in ceasing to pray, as did her first fathers and patterns, for the state and all who are in authority [*cf.* 1 Tim. 2:1 f.]. That duty once well and cordially performed, all other duties, so to speak, are secured. Candour, respectfulness, guarded language — all that the apostle meant in warning men not to "speak evil of dignities" [Jude 8], may then, and then only, be practised, without compromise of truth and fortitude, when the habit is attained of praying as we ought for the very enemies of our precious and holy cause.

The constant sense of God's presence and consequent certainty of final success, which can be kept up no other way, would also prove an effectual bar against the more silent but hardly less malevolent feeling of disgust, almost amounting to misanthropy, which is apt to lay hold on sensitive minds when they see oppression and wrong triumphant on a large scale. The custom of interceding, even for the wicked, will keep the Psalmist's reasoning habitually present to their thoughts:

> Fret not thyself because of the ungodly, neither be thou envious against the evil doers: for they shall soon be cut down like the grass, and be withered even as the green herb. . . . Leave off from wrath, and let go displeasure: fret not thyself, else shalt thou be moved to do evil (Ps. 37:1-2, 8).

Thus not only by supernatural aid, which we have warrant of God's word for expecting, but even in the way of natural consequence, the first duty of the Church and of churchmen, INTERCESSION, sincerely practised, would prepare them for the second — which, following the words of Samuel as our clue, we may confidently pronounce to be REMONSTRANCE. "I will teach you the good and the right way." REMONSTRANCE, calm, distinct, and persevering, in public and in private, direct and indirect, by word, look, and demeanour, is the unequivocal duty of every Christian, according to his opportunities, when the Church landmarks are being broken down.

Among laymen, a deep responsibility would appear to rest on those particularly whose profession leads them most directly to consider the boundaries of the various rights and duties which fill the space of civilized society. The immediate machinery of change must always pass through their hands: and they have also very great power in forming and modifying public opinion. The very solemnity of this day may remind them, even more than others, of the close amity which must ever subsist between equal justice and true religion; apostolical religion, more precisely, in proportion to her superior truth and exactness.[3] It is an amity made still more sacred, if possible, in the case of the Church and law of England, by historical recollections, associations and precedents, of the most engaging and ennobling cast.

But I return to the practical admonition afforded her, in critical periods, by Samuel's example.

After the accomplishment of the change which he deprecated, his whole behaviour, to Saul especially, is a sort of expansion of the sentiment in the text. It is all earnest INTERCESSION with God, grave, respectful, affectionate REMONSTRANCE with the misguided man himself. Saul is boldly rebuked, and that publicly, for his impious liberality in sparing the Amelekites, yet so as not to dishonour him in the presence of the people. Even when it became necessary for God's prophet to show that he was in earnest, and give the most effectual of warnings, by separating himself from so unworthy a person — when "Samuel came no more to see Saul" (1 Sam. 15:35) — even then, we are told, he still "mourned for him."

On the same principle, come what may, we have ill learned the lessons of our Church if we permit our patriotism to decay, together with the protecting care of the state. "The powers that be are ordained of God" [Rom. 13:1], whether they foster the true Church or no. Submission and order are still duties. They were so in the days of pagan persecution; and the more of loyal and affectionate feeling we endeavour to mingle with our obedience, the better.

After all, the surest way to uphold or restore our endangered Church will be for each of her anxious children, in his own place and station, to resign himself more thoroughly to his God and Saviour in those duties, public and private, which are not immediately affected by the emergencies of the moment: the daily and hourly duties, I mean, of piety, purity, charity, justice. It will be a consolation understood by every thoughtful churchman, that let his occupation be, apparently, never so remote from such great interests, it is in his power, by doing all as a Christian, to credit and advance the cause he has most at heart; and what is more, to draw down God's blessing upon it. This ought to be felt, for example, as one motive more to exact punctuality in those duties, personal and official, which the return of an assize week offers to our practice; one reason

3. [ED.] It should be recalled that this sermon was preached before His Majesty's Judges of Assize.

more for veracity in witnesses, fairness in pleaders, strict impartiality, self-command, and patience in those on whom decisions depend; and for an awful sense of God's presence in all. An apostle once did not disdain to urge good conduct upon his proselytes of lowest condition, upon the ground that, so doing, they would adorn and recommend the doctrine of God our Saviour (Tit. 2:10). Surely, then, it will be no unworthy principle if any man be more circumspect in his behaviour, more watchful and fearful of himself, more earnest in his petitions for spiritual aid, from a dread of disparaging the holy name of the English Church, in her hour of peril, by his own personal fault or negligence.

As to those who, either by station or temper, feel themselves most deeply interested, they cannot be too careful in reminding themselves that one chief danger, in times of change and excitement, arises from their tendency to engross the whole mind. Public concerns, ecclesiastical or civil, will prove indeed ruinous to those who permit them to occupy all their care and thoughts, neglecting or undervaluing ordinary duties, more especially those of a devotional kind.

These cautions being duly observed, I do not see how any person can devote himself too entirely to the cause of the apostolical Church in these realms. There may be, as far as he knows, but a very few to sympathize with him. He may have to wait long, and very likely pass out of this world before he see any abatement in the triumph of disorder and irreligion. But if he be consistent, he possesses, to the utmost, the personal consolation of a good Christian: and as a true churchman, he has that encouragement which no other cause in the world can impart in the same degree — he is calmly, soberly, demonstrably, SURE, that, sooner or later, HIS WILL BE THE WINNING SIDE, and that the victory will be complete, universal, eternal.

He need not fear to look upon the efforts of antichristian powers, as did the holy apostles themselves, who welcomed the first persecution in the words of the Psalmist:

Why do the heathen rage, and the people imagine a vain thing?
The kings of the earth stand up, and the rulers take counsel together, against the Lord, and against his Anointed.
For of a truth against thy holy Child Jesus, whom thou hast anointed, both Herod and Pontius Pilate, with the Gentiles, and the people of Israel, were gathered together,
FOR TO DO WHATSOEVER THY HAND AND THY COUNSEL DETERMINED BEFORE TO BE DONE (Acts 4:25-28).

ADVERTISEMENT TO THE FIRST EDITION
(JULY 22, 1833)

Since the following pages were prepared for the press, the calamity, in anticipation of which they were written, has actually overtaken this portion of the Church of God. The legislature of England and Ireland (*the members of which are not even bound to profess belief in the atonement*), this body has virtually usurped the commission of those whom our Saviour entrusted with *at least one voice* in making ecclesiastical laws, on matters wholly or partly spiritual.[1] The same legislature has also ratified, to its full extent, this principle — that the apostolical Church in this realm is henceforth only to stand, in the eye of the state, as *one sect among many*, depending, for any pre-eminence she may still appear to retain, merely upon the accident of her having a strong party in the country.

It is a moment, surely, full of deep solicitude to all those members of the Church who still believe her authority divine, and the oaths and obligations by which they are bound to her, undissolved and indissoluble by calculations of human expediency. Their anxiety turns not so much on the consequences, to the state, of what has been done (*they* are but too evident), as on the line of conduct which they are bound themselves to pursue. How may they continue their communion with the Church *established* (hitherto the pride and comfort of their lives), without any taint of those Erastian principles on which she is now avowedly to be governed? What answer can we make henceforth to the partisans of the Bishop of Rome when they taunt us with being a mere parliamentarian church? And how, consistently with our present relations to the state, can even the doctrinal purity and integrity of the MOST SACRED ORDER be preserved?

The attention of all who love the Church is most earnestly solicited to these questions. They are such, it will be observed, as cannot be answered by appealing to precedents in English history, because, at most, such could only show that the difficulty might have been raised before. It is believed that there are hundreds, nay thousands, of Christians, and that

---

1. In the suppression of certain Irish sees, *contrary to the suffrage of the Bishops of England and Ireland*. [ED.] This did not happen without some episcopal connivance; *cf.* W. A. Phillips, ed., *History of the Church of Ireland, from the Earliest Times to the Present Day*, III (London, 1933), 302 ff.

soon there will be tens of thousands, unaffectedly anxious to be rightly
guided with regard to these and similar points. And they are mooted
thus publicly, for the chance of eliciting, from competent judges, a correct and early opinion.

If, under such trying and delicate circumstances, one could venture to
be positive about anything, it would seem safe to say that in such measure
as it may be thought incumbent on the Church, or on churchmen, to
submit to any profane intrusion, it must at least be their sacred duty to
declare, promulgate, and record their full conviction that it *is* intrusion;
that they yield to it as they might to any other tyranny, but do from
their hearts deprecate and abjure it. This seems the least that can be
done: unless we would have our children's children say, "There was
once here a glorious Church, but it was betrayed into the hands of liber-
tines for the real or affected love of a little temporary peace and good
order."

PART TWO

❖

Declaration
of
Independence

❖ ❖ ❖ ❖ ❖ ❖ ❖ ❖
❖   ❖
❖   I   ❖
❖   ❖
❖ ❖ ❖ ❖ ❖ ❖ ❖ ❖

JOHN HENRY NEWMAN

Tract One:
Thoughts on the Ministerial Commission

Editor's introduction. On July 28, 1830, as the July Revolution was gathering speed in France, Newman wrote to Hurrell Froude:

> The French are an awful people. How the world is set upon calling evil good, good evil! This Revolution seems to me the triumph of irreligion. What an absurdity it is in men saying, "The times will not admit of an establishment," as if the "times" were anything else than the people. It is the people who will not admit of it. Yet coxcombs wag their heads and think they have got at the root of the matter when they assure one that the times, the spirit of the times, makes it chimerical to attempt continuing the Catholic Church in France. The effect of this miserable French affair will be great in England.[1]

By the beginning of 1832 (he tells us later) both his fears for the Church of England and his idea of what must be done in her defence had taken definite shape.

> . . . I felt affection for my own Church, but not tenderness; I felt dismay at her prospects, anger and scorn at her do-nothing perplexity. I thought that if Liberalism once got a footing within her, it was sure of the victory in the event. I saw that Reformation principles were powerless to rescue her. As to leaving her, the thought never crossed my imagination; still, I ever kept before me that there was something greater than the Established Church, and that that was the Church Catholic and Apostolic, set up from the beginning, of which she was but the local presence and organ. She was

---

1. Anne Mozley, ed., *Letters and Correspondence of John Henry Newman during His Life in the English Church* (New York, 1911), I, 204 f.

nothing, unless she was this. She must be dealt with strongly, or she would be lost. There was need of a second Reformation.[2]

Before long he heard the call to do his part in getting the "second Reformation" under way. In December 1832 he set out for the Mediterranean with Hurrell Froude and his father, Archdeacon Froude. In the spring, leaving his friends in Rome, he made a solitary journey to Sicily, where he fell dangerously ill.

> I got to Castro-Giovanni [he records], and was laid up there for nearly three weeks. Towards the end of May I set off for Palermo, taking three days for the journey. Before starting from my inn in the morning of May 26th or 27th, I sat down on my bed, and began to sob bitterly. My servant, who had acted as my nurse, asked what ailed me. I could only answer, "I have a work to do in England." [3]

When he finally reached England in early July, Newman found various projects of "Church defence" in the air: the presentation of clerical and lay addresses to the Archbishop of Canterbury, in support of the Establishment; the formation of an association; the issuing of manifestoes by a committee. He was not greatly impressed by these proposals. In his view the one thing needful was a direct and personal affirmation of definite religious conviction. On September 9, 1833, he opened his own campaign with the publication of the first three *Tracts for the Times*.

The first and most famous of these early *Tracts* has sometimes been construed as a mere assertion of Anglican superiority and clerical privilege. Its most obvious feature was certainly its peremptory reaffirmation of the High Church doctrine of apostolic succession. But Newman was not much interested in scoring a point for Anglicanism or in defending the clergy as a privileged caste. He reaffirmed the old doctrine because he was convinced that apostolic succession was the sure foundation of the Church's spiritual independence. It was precisely because they saw what he and his friends were making of it that many of his contemporaries turned so fiercely against both Newman and the traditional teaching.[4]

❖ ❖ ❖ ❖

2. J. H. Newman, *Apologia pro vita sua* (Garden City, N.Y., 1956), 149.
3. *Ibid.*, 152.
4. *Cf.* the retrospective comment of a Tractarian veteran, Bishop John Medley of Fredericton, in *A Sermon Preached before the Provincial Synod of Canada* (Montreal, 1877), 5: ". . . The notion of any powers wholly spiritual, and independent of the state, appeared so novel and so foreign to men's minds, that men lashed themselves into fury at the thought."

To my brethren in the sacred ministry, the presbyters and deacons of the Church of Christ in England, ordained thereunto by the Holy Ghost and the imposition of hands.

Fellow-labourers, I am but one of yourselves — a presbyter; and therefore I conceal my name, lest I should take too much on myself by speaking in my own person. Yet speak I must; for the times are very evil, yet no one speaks against them.

Is not this so? Do not we "look one upon another" [cf. Jn. 13:22], yet perform nothing? Do we not all confess the peril into which the Church is come, yet sit still each in his own retirement, as if mountains and seas cut off brother from brother? Therefore suffer me, while I try to draw you forth from those pleasant retreats, which it has been our blessedness hitherto to enjoy, to contemplate the condition and prospects of our Holy Mother in a practical way; so that one and all may unlearn that idle habit, which has grown upon us, of owning the state of things to be bad, yet doing nothing to remedy it.

Consider a moment. Is it fair, is it dutiful, to suffer our bishops to stand the brunt of the battle without doing our part to support them? Upon them comes "the care of all the churches" [2 Cor. 11:28]. This cannot be helped; indeed it is their glory. Not one of us would wish in the least to deprive them of the duties, the toils, the responsibilities of their high office. And, black event as it would be for the country, yet (as far as they are concerned) we could not wish them a more blessed termination of their course than the spoiling of their goods and martyrdom.

To them then we willingly and affectionately relinquish their high privileges and honours; we encroach not upon the rights of the successors of the apostles; we touch not their sword and crozier. Yet surely we may be their shield-bearers in the battle without offence; and by our voice and deeds be to them what Luke and Timothy were to St. Paul [cf. 2 Tim. 4:9–11].

Now then, let me come at once to the subject which leads me to address you. Should the government and the country so far forget their God as to cast off the Church, to deprive it of its temporal honours and substance, on what will you rest the claim of respect and attention which you make upon your flocks? Hitherto you have been upheld by your birth, your education, your wealth, your connexions; should these secular advantages cease, on what must Christ's ministers depend? Is not this a serious practical question? We know how miserable is the state of religious bodies not supported by the state. Look at the Dissenters on all sides of you, and you will see at once that their ministers, depending simply upon the people, become the *creatures* of the people. Are you content that this should be your case? Alas! can a greater evil befall Christians, than for their teachers to be guided by them, instead of guiding? How can we "hold fast the form of sound words" [2 Tim. 1:13], and "keep that which is committed to our trust" [1 Tim. 6:20], if our influence is to depend simply on our popularity? Is it not our very office to *oppose* the world? Can we then allow ourselves to *court* it? to preach smooth things and prophesy deceits [*cf.* Is. 30:10]? to make the way of life easy to the rich and indolent, and to bribe the humbler classes by excitements and strong intoxicating doctrine? Surely it must not be so — and the question recurs, *on what* are we to rest our authority when the state deserts us?

Christ has not left his Church without claim of its own upon the attention of men. Surely not. Hard Master he cannot be, to bid us oppose the world, yet give us no credentials for so doing. There are some who rest their divine mission on their own unsupported assertion; others, who rest it upon their popularity; others, on their success; and others, who rest it upon their temporal distinctions. This last case has, perhaps, been too much our own;[1] I fear we have neglected the real ground on which our authority is built — OUR APOSTOLICAL DESCENT.

We have been born, not of blood, nor of the will of the flesh, nor of the will of man, but of God [Jn. 1:13]. The Lord Jesus Christ gave his Spirit to his apostles [*cf.* Jn. 20:22]; they in turn laid their hands on those who should succeed them; and these again on others; and so the sacred gift has been handed down to our present bishops, who have appointed us as their assistants, and in some sense representatives.

1. [ED.] *Cf.* William Paley, "A Distinction of Orders in the Church Defended upon Principles of Public Utility" (sermon preached at an episcopal consecration in 1782), in his *Works* (London, 1825), VII, 97: "It is equally impossible to invest every clergyman with the decorations of affluence and rank, and to maintain the credit and reputation of an order which is altogether destitute of these distinctions. . . . At present, every member of our ecclesiastical establishment communicates with the dignity which is conferred upon a few — every clergyman shares in the respect which is paid to his superiors — the ministry is honoured in the persons of prelates. Nor is this economy peculiar to our order. The professions of arms and of the law derive their lustre and esteem, not merely from their utility (which is a reason only to the few), but from the exalted place in the scale of civil life which hath been wisely assigned to those who fill stations of power and eminence in these great departments. And if this disposition of honours be approved in other kinds of public employment, why should not the credit and liberality of ours be upheld by the same expedient?"

Now every one of us believes this. I know that some will at first deny they do; still, they do believe it. Only, it is not sufficiently, practically impressed on their minds. They *do* believe it; for it is the doctrine of the Ordination Service, which they have recognized as truth in the most solemn season of their lives. In order, then, not to prove, but to remind and impress, I entreat your attention to the words used when you were made ministers of Christ's Church.

The office of deacon was thus committed to you:

Take thou authority to execute the Office of a Deacon in the Church of God committed unto thee; In the Name, etc.

And the priesthood thus:

Receive the Holy Ghost for the Office and Work of a Priest in the Church of God, now committed unto thee by the Imposition of our hands. Whose sins thou dost forgive, they are forgiven; and whose sins thou dost retain, they are retained. And be thou a faithful Dispenser of the Word of God, and of his holy Sacraments; In the Name, etc.

These, I say, were words spoken to us, and received by us, when we were brought nearer to God than at any other time of our lives. I know the grace of ordination is contained in the laying on of hands, not in any form of words — yet in our own case (as has ever been usual in the Church) words of blessing have accompanied the act. Thus we have confessed before God our belief that the bishop who ordained us gave us the Holy Ghost, gave us the power to bind and to loose, to administer the sacraments, and to preach. Now *how* is he able to give these great gifts? *Whence* is his right? Are these words idle (which would be taking God's name in vain), or do they express merely a wish (which surely is very far below their meaning), or do they not rather indicate that the speaker is conveying a gift? Surely they can mean nothing short of this. But whence, I ask, his right to do so? Has he any right, except as having received the power from those who consecrated him to be a bishop? He could not give what he had never received. It is plain then that he but *transmits;* and that the Christian ministry is a *succession.* And if we trace back the power of ordination from hand to hand, of course we shall come to the apostles at last. We know we do, as a plain historical fact; and therefore all we who have been ordained clergy, in the very form of our ordination acknowledged the doctrine of the APOSTOLICAL SUCCESSION.

And for the same reason we must necessarily consider none to be *really* ordained who have not *thus* been ordained. For if ordination is a divine ordinance, it must be necessary; and if it is not a divine ordinance, how dare we use it? Therefore all who use it, all of *us*, must consider it necessary. As well might we pretend the sacraments are not necessary to salvation, while we make use of the offices in the liturgy; for when God appoints means of grace, they are *the* means.

I do not see how anyone can escape from this plain view of the subject, except (as I have already hinted) by declaring that the words do not mean all that they say. But only reflect what a most unseemly time for random words is that in which ministers are set apart for their office. Do we not adopt a liturgy *in order to* hinder inconsiderate idle language, and shall we, in the most sacred of all services, write down, subscribe, and use again and again forms of speech which have not been weighed and cannot be taken strictly? [2]

Therefore, my dear brethren, act up to your professions. Let it not be said that you have neglected a gift; for if you have the Spirit of the apostles on you, surely this *is* a great gift. "Stir up the gift of God which is in you" [2 Tim. 1:6]. Make much of it. Show your value of it. Keep it before your minds as an honourable badge, far higher than that secular respectability, or cultivation, or polish, or learning, or rank, which gives you a hearing with the many. Tell *them* of your gift. The times will soon drive you to do this, if you mean to be still anything. But wait not for the times. Do not be compelled, by the world's forsaking you, to recur as if unwillingly to the high source of your authority. Speak out now, before you are forced, both as glorying in your privilege and to insure your rightful honour from your people. A notion has gone abroad that they can take away your power. They think they have given and can take it away. They think it lies in the Church property, and they know that they have politically the power to confiscate that property. They have been deluded into a notion that present palpable usefulness, producible results, acceptableness to your flocks, that these and suchlike are the tests of your divine commission. Enlighten them in this matter.

2. [ED.] The general line of argument in the preceding paragraphs is strongly reminiscent of Richard Hooker, *The Laws of Ecclesiastical Polity*, Bk. V, chap. 77 (*Works* [Oxford, 1845], II, 455–68). Some of the most important Anglican sources of Newman's view of "apostolical succession" are quoted in E. R. Fairweather, *Episcopacy Re-Asserted* (London, 1955), 25–27, 30–32. For a fuller presentation of the evidence, *cf.* A. J. Mason, *The Church of England and Episcopacy* (Cambridge, 1914).

Exalt our holy fathers the bishops as the representatives of the apostles and the angels of the churches; and magnify your office as being ordained by them to take part in their ministry.

But, if you will not adopt my view of the subject, which I offer to you, not doubtingly, yet (I hope) respectfully, at all events, CHOOSE YOUR SIDE. To remain neuter much longer will be itself to take a part. *Choose* your side; since side you shortly must, with one or other party, even though you do nothing. Fear to be of those whose line is decided for them by chance circumstances, and who may perchance find themselves with the enemies of Christ, while they think but to remove themselves from worldly politics. Such abstinence is impossible in troublous times. HE THAT IS NOT WITH ME IS AGAINST ME, AND HE THAT GATHERETH NOT WITH ME SCATTERETH ABROAD [Mt. 12:30].

II

JOHN KEBLE

Primitive Tradition Recognized in Holy Scripture

Editor's introduction.

Towards the end of 1834 a question appeared in Oxford interesting to numbers besides Mr. Newman and his friends, which was to lead to momentous consequences. The old, crude ideas of change in the Church had come to appear, even to their advocates, for the present impracticable, and there was no more talk for a long time of schemes which had been in favour two years before. The ground was changed, and a point was now brought forward on the Liberal side, for which a good deal might be plausibly said. This was the requirement of subscription to the Thirty-Nine Articles from young men at matriculation; and a strong pamphlet advocating its abolition, with the express purpose of admitting Dissenters, was published by Dr. Hampden, the Bampton Lecturer of two years before.[1]

For the future of the Oxford Movement the consequences of the developments thus outlined were indeed momentous. The Irish Church, against which the critics of the Anglican Establishment had aimed their first hard blow, was somewhat remote from the field of influence of the Tractarian group. The University of Oxford, on the other hand, was their home ground, where their responsibilities were most definite and their influence strongest. Consequently, when Oxford became at least momentarily the main centre of ecclesiastical controversy, they inevitably found themselves playing a conspicuous role in public affairs. In the process they grew in unity and stature as a party, but at the same time made enemies whose hostility was to tell strongly against them in the critical years 1841–45.

1. R. W. Church, *The Oxford Movement: Twelve Years, 1833–1845*, 3d ed. (1892), 152 f.

The little drama at Oxford really comprised two episodes, linked by the appearance in both of the enigmatic figure of Renn Dickson Hampden. The first episode, in which Hampden appeared as a champion of the admission of non-Anglicans to the university, was significant chiefly because it set the stage for the second and more spectacular act — the agitation connected with his appointment as Regius Professor of Divinity. On the one hand, it fixed a strong prejudice against him in the minds of Oxford conservatives. On the other hand, it brought to light certain serious ambiguities in his theological position, which had hitherto lain concealed in the turgid prose of his Bampton Lectures of 1832.[2] By the time the Prime Minister, Viscount Melbourne, singled him out for promotion in 1836, he was probably Oxford's most unpopular theologian.

To some observers it has seemed obvious that the Tractarians were nothing but peculiarly virulent examples of Oxford conservatism outraged by Hampden's generous attitude towards Dissent. Thomas Arnold, for instance, saw them as fanatical defenders of ecclesiastical custom and priestly privilege, whose like had scarcely been seen (except for some earlier High Churchmen) since the Jewish or Judaizing opponents of St. Paul and of Christ himself.[3] Much of their later unpopularity was unquestionably due to such unfavourable impressions, created by their part in the "Hampden persecution."[4]

It is true that Newman and his circle consistently opposed any dilution of the Anglicanism of Oxford. (Their reason was the firm conviction that a church, a definite creed, and a recognized pastoral relationship must play a decisive role in all genuine education.) The primary motive of their polemic against Hampden lay, however, in a wider and deeper theological issue. In a word, Hampden's great offence lay in his apparent undermining of the historic dogmas of Catholic Christianity by a rationalistic method of Biblical interpretation.[5]

2. R. D. Hampden, *The Scholastic Philosophy Considered in its Relation to Christian Theology*, 3d ed. (Hereford, 1848).

3. Cf. Thomas Arnold, "The Oxford Malignants and Dr. Hampden," *Edinburgh Review*, LXIII (April–July, 1836), 225–39.

4. E. Jane Whately, *Life and Correspondence of Richard Whately, D.D., late Archbishop of Dublin* (London, 1866), I, 390.

5. Cf. Anne Mozley, *Letters and Correspondence of John Henry Newman during His Life in the English Church* (New York, 1911), II, 69. (Newman to Hampden, November 28, 1834): "While I respect the tone of piety in which the pamphlet [on dissent] is written, I feel an aversion to the principles it professes, as (in my opinion) legitimately tending to formal Socinianism." Cf. also H. A. Woodgate, *A Letter to Viscount Melbourne*, 2d ed. (London, 1836), 18: "Dr. Hampden's whole view of the

Hampden's conscious intentions do not, in fact, seem to have gone so far. His published sermons were strictly orthodox, to the point of including not only a Biblical vindication of the dogma of the Trinity but even a defense of the Athanasian Creed.[6] Nevertheless, his declared principles were pregnant with radical consequences. He could write, for example, in an analysis of the causes of schism:

> The real causes of separation are to be found in that confusion of theological and moral truth with Religion, which is evidenced in the profession of different sects. Opinions on religious matters are regarded as identical with the objects of faith; and the zeal which belongs to dissentients in the latter, is transferred to the guiltless differences of fallible judgments. Whilst we agree in the canon of Scripture — in the very words, for the most part, from which we learn what are the objects of faith — we suffer disunion to spread among us, through the various interpretations suggested by our own reasonings on the admitted facts of Scripture. We introduce theories of the Divine being and attributes — theories of human nature and of the universe — principles drawn from the various branches of human philosophy — into the body itself of revealed wisdom. And we then proceed to contend for these unrevealed representations of the wisdom of God, as if it were that very wisdom as it stands forth confessed in his own living oracles. "The wisdom that is from above" is at once "pure" and "gentle" [Jas. 3:17]. Surely it has no resemblance to that dogmatical and sententious wisdom which theological controversy has created.[7]

Even if Hampden merely meant to correct exaggerated views of the authority of the Thirty-nine Articles, his actual line of argument at once subverted the authority and questioned the content of traditional Christian dogma itself.

To make matters worse — from the standpoint of the Oxford Move-

---

origin and nature of the doctrines of the Christian Church, and of the relation in which they stand to the Holy Scriptures, is radically wrong, and opposed to the opinion and practice of the Church in every age."

6. Cf. R. D. Hampden, *Parochial Sermons on the Revelation of God in Jesus Christ* (London, 1828). In 1847 Hampden became Bishop of Hereford; the one notable act of his long episcopate was a denunciation of the "infidelity" of *Essays and Reviews*. (This volume of essays by seven authors, including Benjamin Jowett, Mark Pattison, and Frederick Temple, appeared in 1860. Theological conservatives, led by Bishop Samuel Wilberforce, attacked it bitterly, and in 1864 it was condemned by the convocation of Canterbury.) Cf. Arnold Haultain, ed., *A Selection from Goldwin Smith's Correspondence* (Toronto, n.d.), 269: ". . . His Liberalism was not robust, and when he had been made a bishop became extremely weak."

7. R. D. Hampden, *Observations on Religious Dissent*, 2d ed. (London, 1834), 7 f.

ment — it was impossible to regard Hampden simply as an eccentric individual. Wittingly or unwittingly, he spoke for a world-wide tendency to define the essence of Christianity in a way which effectively excluded dogma as traditionally conceived.[8] It was this wider context of his teaching that made his appointment as Regius Professor quite intolerable to the Tractarians. In their eyes, his promotion marked a new phase in the rationalistic attack on the Church's faith, just as truly as the Irish Church legislation had begun the overt liberal onslaught on the Church's order.

The Tractarians did not call themselves "Apostolicals" for nothing. In 1833 they had met the political challenge with a reassertion of "apostolical succession." In 1836 they responded to the theological threat with a reaffirmation of "apostolical tradition." One of the best examples of this apologetic is Keble's sermon on "Primitive Tradition," preached in Winchester Cathedral on September 27, 1836.[9]

❖   ❖   ❖   ❖

2 Tim. 1:14. That good thing which was committed unto thee keep by the Holy Ghost which dwelleth in us.

Whatever men may severally anticipate concerning the final issue of the many anxious discussions which at present occupy the Catholic Church in England, all, I suppose, must feel that for the time they occasion a great perplexity and doubtfulness of mind. We are beset on every side (the clergy more especially) with conflicting difficulties, and temptations to unworthy compromise. That man must be either very confident in the accuracy of his own views, or very highly favoured in respect of clearness of judgment, or very successful in keeping himself out of the way of all controversy, who has not repeatedly found himself at a loss, within the last seven years, on such points as the following: What are the limits of the civil power in ecclesiastical matters, and how far we may venture in the way of submission without sacrifice of church

8. Cf. *Tract Seventy-three: On the Introduction of Rationalistic Principles into Revealed Religion* (Oxford, 1835); "Apostolical Tradition," *British Critic*, XX (July–October, 1836), 166–99 (both by Newman). In addition to Hampden, Whately, and the ex-Roman Catholic Blanco White, the Tractarian list of antidogmatic writers included a Scotsman (Thomas Erskine), an American (Jacob Abbott) and a German (Schleiermacher).

9. The sermon is printed here in full, but most of Keble's lengthy notes are replaced by brief editorial notes, and the "Postscript" to the published sermon (Keble, *Sermons, Academical and Occasional*, 2d ed. [Oxford, 1848], 341–421) is omitted.

principle; how the freedom of the Anglican Church may be vindicated against the exorbitant claims of Rome, and yet no disparagement ensue of the authority inherent in the Catholic Apostolical Church; again, how the method of voluntary combination, so generally resorted to in our days for important ecclesiastical objects, may be reconciled with entire deference to episcopal prerogative; how Christ's ministers may "study to be quiet" [1 Thess. 4:11], and yet do their duty as watchmen, and not let their people slumber in the midst of danger; and how they may best unite unwearied meekness in judging, and active Christian love, with strict reserve and timely censure towards everyone that walketh disorderly [cf. 2 Thess. 3:6, 11]. The time was, not long since, when many of these points appeared to most of us as mere historical curiosities. We felt, perhaps, that they were, abstractedly, of grave importance, but we thanked God that our lot was cast in times which required not of us, as pastors and stewards in Christ's service, any distinct consideration and settled views concerning them. Now things are different; the course of God's providence has permitted the enemies or prompted the defenders of the Church to lay bare her very foundations; and it has become imperative on us all, in discharge of our ordination vows, to make up our minds as well as we can, and endeavour to see our own way, on points which we should gladly, if we might, have taken on trust.

It cannot be safe to shrink from this duty, and say, as many seem inclined to do, that we could bear persecution itself better than the perplexity of considering such things, or the responsibility of deciding for ourselves, and agitating others, concerning them. We have put our hand to the plough, and we must not — we dare not — look back [cf. Lk. 9:62]. It is too late for sworn and ordained priests and ministers in the Church of God to dream of drawing back from responsibility. The nature of the case contradicts the very thought. For what responsibility can be more fearful than *his*, who indolently and unthinkingly gives his assent to changes, which, for aught he knows, may prove not only ruinous in the event, but in theory and principle also opposed to the truths and ordinances wherewith Christ has put him in trust? Dismissing, therefore, as a snare of our great enemy, the false comfort which many of us, perhaps, are too much inclined to take to ourselves, from a notion that by not interfering we keep ourselves irresponsible, let us see whether the unprejudiced study of those parts of Scripture which are obviously best suited to our case may not supply us with a better and more genuine comfort, by furnishing some one clear and unquestionable rule, which may go a good way in guiding us rightly, independent of all results:

showing us where our chief responsibility lies, and to which, among interests and duties apparently conflicting, we are bound always to give the preference.

It is natural, in such an inquiry, to turn immediately to the two Epistles to Timothy, especially the last. For undoubtedly it must have been to that holy bishop a time of very great perplexity, when his guide and father in the faith was on the eve of departing from him: the heretics also, as appears from many passages, already beginning to infest the Asiatic churches, according to St. Paul's own prophecy [*cf.* 1 Cor. 11:19]. It appears from the opening of the second Epistle, that when all doubt was taken away as to St. Paul's approaching martyrdom, his affectionate disciple was in danger of being overwhelmed by his sorrow for so great a loss, joined to his sense of the heavy burden which would be laid on himself, now left comparatively alone. To these two feelings in the breast of Timothy, the apostle in his farewell letter addresses himself: remembering, as he says (2 Tim. 1:4), the tears which Timothy had shed, perhaps when they had last parted from each other, and longing the more for the satisfaction of seeing him again. In the meantime, there are two words which he seems studiously to repeat over and over, that he may leave them sounding, as it were, in his disciple's ears, for remembrancers of the two duties most pressing at the moment: ΚΑΚΟΠΑΘΗΣΟΝ, and ΠΑΡΑΚΑΤΑΘΗΚΗ: "endure hardness," and "keep that committed to thy charge."

First, with reference to the dejection of mind by which Timothy was then suffering: "endure hardness," says the apostle (2 Tim. 2:3), "as a good soldier of Jesus Christ"; "endure affliction, make full proof of thy ministry" (2 Tim. 4:5); "be thou partaker of the affliction of the gospel, according to the power of God" (2 Tim. 1:8). The drift of all which warnings is the same as where he reminds the Thessalonians (1 Thess. 3:4), "When we were with you, we told you that we should suffer tribulation; even as it came to pass, and ye know." Affliction, hardness, trial, tribulation, is the very atmosphere of the gospel ministry: we never had cause to expect anything else. "Do not, therefore" — so the apostle implies — "do not shrink thus overtenderly from the thought of losing me, which, you now see, comes into your ordained portion of trouble." "Be not ashamed of the testimony of our Lord, nor of me his prisoner" [2 Tim. 1:8]; do not carry your affectionate regret so far as almost to cause an appearance of defective faith. Do not take it to heart so very bitterly, as if you in some sort regretted your Christian engagement, finding so much to be borne beyond your expectation; as if you were sorry that you had put so much confidence in me. But, instead of vain regret, take comfort in doing your duty; resort to that fountain of supernatural grace which was opened for you when you were consecrated to be an apostle. "Remember that thou stir up the gift of God which is in thee by the imposition of my hands. For the Spirit which we both of us then received was not a spirit of fear" [2 Tim. 1:6 f.], of unworthy sadness and cowardice; excessive, unreasonable dejection can be no fruit of it.

Such were the tender expostulations and chidings of St. Paul, well beseeming the kindest and most thoughtful of parents recalling his own son in the faith [cf. 1 Tim. 1:2] to a manly firmness. Then, in the temper of a noble and true soldier, he propounds his own example, teaches his younger comrade the way of consolation which he found most effectual for himself. "Because I am ordained a herald and apostle and teacher, I suffer these things: but I am not ashamed, for I know in whom I have believed, and am persuaded that he is able to keep that which I have committed unto him against that day" [2 Tim. 1:11 f.]. And elsewhere (2 Tim. 2:9), "I suffer evil, as a malefactor, even unto bonds, but the word of God is not bound." What can be more animating, what more affecting, than to witness a person like St. Paul, full of conscious energy, power, and usefulness, thus devoutly reconciling himself to that which, humanly speaking, would have seemed the most untimely interruption of his labours? It is clear, I think, that even St. Paul found this a severe struggle; but he cheers himself, as in his former imprisonment, when he wrote to the Philippians, that the taunts of his enemies on his confinement had turned out rather to the furtherance of the gospel, causing his bonds in Christ to be spoken of in the palace of the Caesars, and in all places: so that even those who in speaking of his sufferings meant nothing but envy and strife, did in a manner "preach Christ" (Phil. 1:15–18) — make his gospel known, and draw popular attention to his name. Such I take to be the true meaning of that often alleged text; far from conveying the encouragement, which some think they find in it, to irregular and schismatical efforts, but fraught with abundant consolation for those, who being anxious for the Church in evil times, feel themselves precluded from active exertions on her behalf.[1] They can always say to themselves, "The word of God is not bound: he can make even envy

1. [ED.] In support of his exegesis Keble cites Tertullian, *Against Marcion*, V, 20 (*ANF*, III, 472; *PL*, 2, 554); Cyprian, *Epistle* 73, 14 (*ANF*, V, 382 f.; *CSEL*, III, 788); John Chrysostom, *Homilies on Philippians*, II, 3 (*NPNF*[1], XIII, 190; *PG*, LXII, 193).

and strife involuntary heralds of his cause." Their fidelity in acting while they could is rewarded with the assurance of a strong faith, that when *their* work is over, God's eternal and glorious work is still in progress, although they cannot see how.

But we dare not take this comfort to ourselves — we dare not, in those instances where we find the Church bound and fettered, mitigate our regret by exulting remembrance of the expansive inherent force of divine truth — except we be really, in some tolerable measure, doing our best for her, so far as we are at liberty. The sense of our own responsibility, and of our faithfulness to it, must lie at the root of all true and solid consolation.

To this, therefore, as the one thing needful, both for the cause and for himself, the apostle most emphatically bespeaks his disciple's attention. He loses no opportunity of reminding him of the $\pi a \rho a \kappa a \tau a \theta \acute{\eta} \kappa \eta$, the charge, trust, deposit, which had been left jointly in both their hands, and in the hands of all commissioned as they were. Observe how naturally, with what dexterity of affection, he passes from the mention of his own trust to that of the same trust as committed to Timothy: "I am not ashamed, for I know in whom I have believed, and am persuaded that he is able to keep my deposit, $\tau \grave{\eta} \nu \ \pi a \rho a \kappa a \tau a \theta \acute{\eta} \kappa \eta \nu \ \mu o \nu$, against that day. Hold fast the form," or, "abide by the pattern or standard, of wholesome words which thou hast heard from me, by faith and love which is in Christ Jesus. That good thing committed unto thee" (literally, the good and noble deposit) "keep, by the Holy Ghost which dwelleth in us" [2 Tim. 1:12–14].

Surely these are words in which we ourselves are concerned, as deeply as he was, to whom they were first written. We are so far in Timothy's case that we are full of sorrow and perplexity at the condition in which we find the Church and Body of Christ Jesus; we would fain lay hold of Timothy's and St. Paul's consolation; let us first see to it that we neglect not the warning given. To the companion of apostles that warning was plain and simple. The duty imposed on him, paramount to all others, was simply to keep safe and entire a certain trust committed to his charge; to that one vital object all considerations of present expediency, temporal comfort, visible, apparent edification, were to give way. What that treasure was, Timothy could not be ignorant; nor yet could he be doubtful as to the celestial aid by which, if not wanting to himself, he would surely be enabled to preserve it. But in both respects some consideration is requisite before we of this day can fully apply the case to ourselves. It is not obvious at first sight what this trust or treasure was, nor (of course) whether we are partakers of it; and even supposing those points settled, there might still remain a doubt whether we have the same help for the faithful discharge of our trust, the Holy Ghost dwelling in us. The consideration of these points in their order may not unfitly employ us on the present occasion.

1. And, first, as to the exact notion which we are to attach to the word παρακαταθήκη, "trust or deposit," in this place: I observe that the very use of so general a word with the article implies that it had been by that time received among Christians as a term (if one may so speak) of their own, a part of the vocabulary of the holy Catholic Church. A diligent eye may detect, in St. Paul's Epistles, many traces of the like use of language: current sayings, or senses of words, or formulae, which the apostle only just alludes to, as well known to all his readers. For instance, the expression, "This is a faithful saying," which occurs repeatedly in these latter Epistles, indicates, in all probability, so many Christian proverbs, familiar in the mouths of that generation of believers. Thus in the First Epistle to Timothy we have, "This is a faithful saying, and worthy of all men to be received, that 'Christ Jesus came into the world to save sinners' " (1 Tim. 1:15); "This is a faithful saying, 'If a man desire the office of a bishop, he desireth a good work' " (1 Tim. 3:1); "This is a faithful saying, 'That therefore we both labour, and suffer reproof, because we trust in the living God, who is the Saviour of all men, especially of them that believe' " (1 Tim. 4:9 f.). In the Second Epistle, "It is a faithful saying, 'If we be dead with him, we shall also live with him; if we suffer, we shall also reign with him; if we deny him, he also will deny us' " (2 Tim. 2:11 f.). And to Titus, after a brief summary of the gospel way of salvation, which by the exact rhythm and order of its members might almost appear to be part of a primitive hymn [Tit. 3:4–7], St. Paul adds the same clause, "Faithful is the saying." From all which I argue that there was a certain set of "sayings" current among the Christians of that time, to which any allusion or appeal, however brief, would be presently understood. Nor will it be hard to find examples of single words which had evidently acquired by that time a Christian sense; so that, even when used absolutely, they could only be taken by Christians in a particular relation: such words, I mean, as τὸ μυστήριον [Eph. 3:3], for "the scheme of supernatural truth revealed in the gospel, and more especially in the doctrine of our Lord's incarnation"; ὁ ἐχθρὸς [Lk. 10:19], for "the evil spirit"; ἡ ὁδὸς [Acts 24:14], for "the profession of Chris-

tianity." These, and other examples which might be mentioned, make it surely not incredible, that ἡ παρακαταθήκη, "*the* deposit, trust, or charge," conveyed to Christian ears in those days a peculiar and definite, I had almost said, a technical, meaning.

Now both this word and its kindred term, ἡ ἐντολὴ, "the commandment," are mentioned in connection with errors to be avoided in *doctrine*. Thus, Timothy is warned to "keep the deposit, avoiding profane and vain babblings, and oppositions of science falsely so called" (1 Tim. 6:20). Again, on mention made of the "good confession," made by the same Timothy "before many witnesses," at the time of his first calling to eternal life — which "good confession" can only mean the Apostles' Creed, or some corresponding formula, recited at baptism — St. Paul proceeds thus: "I exhort thee before God and the Lord Jesus Christ, who before Pontius Pilate witnessed a good confession, that thou keep *the commandment* without spot, unrebukeable, until the appearing of our Lord Jesus Christ" [1 Tim. 6:13 f.]. Does not this appear as if "the confession" in the former verse had suggested the caution about "the commandment" or "commission" in the latter? — and if so, what more probable than that "the commission" means the same treasure of doctrine which we know to have been embodied in the confession or creed?

This interpretation of the noun παρακαταθήκη,[2] "deposit," is confirmed by the repeated use of the kindred verb, παρατίτεσθαι, "to entrust, or commit," in reference to Christian doctrine. For example, "This *commandment* I *commit* unto thee, son Timothy, that thou mightest charge some that they *preach no other doctrine* (1 Tim. 1:18, 3). Elsewhere (a passage which seems to be sufficient alone to warrant the proposed interpretation) Timothy is instructed concerning the things which he had heard from St. Paul, "before many witnesses," that is, as it should seem, at a kind of public charge at his ordination — these he is directed to commit or entrust "to faithful men, who shall be able to teach others also" (2 Tim. 2:2). Ability to *teach* is the thing required; it is plain, therefore, that the test related principally to *doctrine*.

Further, it will be observed that the phrase of the apostle is absolute: *the* trust, not *your* trust; the great trust of all, in which whosoever participates has reason to consider himself especially responsible to the great Judge of heaven and earth. And it is implied that the charge of St. Paul and that of Timothy were one and the same. "Keep the good deposit,"

2. [ED.] Keble consistently reads παρακαταθήκην, with the *textus receptus*, rather than παραθήκην, in 2 Tim. 1:14.

says the apostle, "by the Holy Ghost which dwelleth *in us*" (2 Tim. 1:14). Now what St. Paul's trust was, the trust uppermost in his heart, he himself teaches, exclaiming, "I have fought a good fight, I have finished my course, *I have kept the faith*" (2 Tim. 4:7). He does not say, "I have kept the flock, I have kept those left in my charge"; but, "I have kept the *faith,* the *truth* of Christ, the *doctrine* of the gospel. I have watched it, and preserved it entire." Great as was the holy apostle's anxiety for the souls which God had put under his care, his anxiety for the system of Christ, the kingdom of heaven, did at that moment apparently engross him more entirely. And it is clearly probable that what he felt himself to be the main care, the chief trust of all, that he would recommend to his disciple in such words as those of the text, "That good thing which is committed unto thee, keep"; especially considering that those words immediately follow a caution which can only relate to doctrinal formulae: "Hold fast," as a model for thyself, "the form of sound words," the course of healthful, orthodox interpretations and doctrines, "which thou hast heard of me" (2 Tim. 1:13). That "form of sound words," is it not obviously the same with "the good deposit" in the next verse?

Thus the context leads to the same exposition which, as we have seen, the parallel passages suggest — an exposition ratified also by the general consent of Christian antiquity. The good deposit is commonly understood by the Fathers to mean the *truths* committed by St. Paul to Timothy. Thus, in the paraphrase ascribed to St. Jerome: "Watch over the deposit *of the faith,* entrusted to thy keeping by us. What thou hast not heard of me, though it were spoken by an angel, receive it not willingly." [3] And a venerable Father of the third century, Hippolytus, having quoted the expressions, "O Timothy, keep that which is committed to thy charge," and, "The things which thou hast heard of me before many witnesses, the same commit to faithful men," remarks that "the blessed apostle used religious care in delivering these *truths,* which were easily accessible to all." [4] And Vincent of Lérins: " 'Keep,' says the apostle, 'that which is committed to thy charge; *the Catholic faith,* as a talent, preserve thou inviolate and unalloyed.' " [5]

3. [ED.] Pseudo-Jerome (John the Deacon?), *Comm. in Epist. I ad Tim.,* on 1 Tim. 6:20 (*PL,* XXX, 888).

4. [ED.] Hippolytus, *On Christ and Antichrist,* 1 (*ANF,* V, 204; *GCS,* I/2, 4, where the text as quoted by Keble appears in the margin). The word "truths" is supplied by Keble.

5. [ED.] Vincent of Lérins, *Commonitorium,* 22 (*NPNF* [2], XI, 147; *PL,* L, 667).

Upon the whole we may assume with some confidence that the good thing left in Timothy's charge, thus absolutely to be kept at all events, was the treasure of apostolical doctrines and Church rules: [6] the rules and doctrines which made up the charter of Christ's kingdom.

2. The next question to be settled is, whether the precept in the text apply literally to us: that is, in other words, whether we have yet in our possession the identical deposit which St. Paul left with Timothy. For, *if* we have, mere natural piety would teach us to reverence and guard it as he was required to do.

Some will reply to this question at once: We have the holy Scriptures, and we know for certain that they contain all that is important in Timothy's trust. These would resolve the custody of the good deposit into the simple duty of preserving the Scriptures incorrupt, and maintaining them in their due estimation among Christians. Undoubtedly this would be in some respects the least troublesome if it could be proved the most correct and dutiful way. But can it be so proved?

We are naturally, if not reasonably, jealous of the word "tradition," associated as it is in our minds with the undue claims and pernicious errors of Rome. Yet must it not be owned, on fair consideration, that Timothy's deposit did comprise matter, independent of, and distinct from, the truths which are directly scriptural — that it contained, besides the substance of Christian doctrine, a certain form, arrangement, selection, methodizing the whole, and distinguishing fundamentals; and also a certain system of Church practice, both in government, discipline, and worship; of which, whatever portion we can prove to be still remaining, ought to be religiously guarded by us, even for the same reason that we reverence and retain that which is more properly scriptural, both being portions of the same divine treasure?

To these conclusions we are led by the consideration, first, that the truths and rules committed to Timothy's charge were at the time almost or wholly unwritten. This is clear from the very date of the Epistles which mention that charge: the latest of which must have been composed many years before St. John's Gospel, and in the first of them the deposit in question is spoken of, not as an incomplete thing on its progress towards perfection, but as something so wholly sufficient, so unexcep-

6. The insertion of "Church rules" here has been objected to, as not being warranted by the preceding citations. But the sacraments, at least, were from the beginning Church rules; and were not they part of the trust committed to Timothy, in common with all "stewards of the mysteries of God" [1 Cor. 4:1]?

tionably accurate, as to require nothing but fidelity in its transmitters (1 Tim. 1:3; 6:14, 20). The holy writings themselves intimate that the persons to whom they were addressed were in possession of a body of truth and duty totally distinct from themselves and independent of them. Timothy, for instance, a few verses after the text, is enjoined to take measures for the transmission, not of holy Scripture, but of the things which he had heard of St. Paul among many witnesses (2 Tim. 2:2). The Thessalonians had been exhorted to hold the traditions which they had received, whether by word or apostolical letter (2 Thess. 2:15). They could not be exhorted to hold the Christian Scriptures, since at that time in all probability no Christian Scriptures yet existed, except perhaps St. Matthew's Gospel. Much later we find St. Peter declaring to the whole body of Oriental Christians that in neither of his Epistles did he profess to reveal to them any new truth or duty, but to "stir up their minds by way of remembrance of the commandment of the apostles of the Lord and Saviour" (2 Pet. 3:1 f.). St. John refers believers, for a standard of doctrine, to the word which they had heard from the beginning (1 Jn. 2:24), and intimates that it was sufficient for their Christian communion if that word abode in them. If the word, the commandment, the tradition, which the latest of these holy writers severally commend in these and similar passages, meant only or chiefly the Scriptures before written, would there not appear a more significant mention of those Scriptures — something nearer the tone of our own divines when they are delivering precepts on the rule of faith? As it is, the phraseology of the Epistles exactly concurs with what we should be led to expect: that the Church would be already in possession of the substance of saving truth, in a sufficiently systematic form, by the sole teaching of the apostles. As long as that teaching itself, or the accurate recollection of it, remained in the world, it must have constituted a standard or measure of Christian knowledge, though it had never seemed good to the Almighty to confer on us the additional boon of the books of the New Testament.

It can hardly be necessary to remind this audience [7] that these scattered notices are abundantly confirmed by the direct and formal testimony of the ecclesiastical writers of the age immediately following the apostles. As often as Tertullian and Irenaeus have false teachers to reprove, or unevangelical corruptions to expose, do they not refer to the tradition of the whole Church, as to something independent of the written word,

7. [ED.] Keble was preaching to the clergy assembled for the "Visitation" of the Chancellor of the Diocese of Winchester.

and sufficient at that time to refute heresy, even alone? Do they not employ Church tradition as parallel to Scripture, not as derived from it, and consequently as fixing the interpretation of disputed texts, not simply by the judgment of the Church, but by authority of that Holy Spirit which inspired the oral teaching itself, of which such tradition is the record? Their practice is throughout in accordance with the following sentence of Irenaeus:

> We ought not to be still seeking among others for the truth, which it is easy to receive from the Church; since therein, as in a rich depository, the apostles did most abundantly lodge all things appertaining to the truth: so that whoever will, may receive from her the waters of life. For the Church is the entrance to life; all the rest are but thieves and robbers. . . . And what if the apostles themselves had left us no Scriptures? Ought we not to follow the course of tradition, such as they delivered it to those whom they entrusted with the churches? Which rule is followed by many nations of the barbarians, those I mean who believe in Christ, without paper or ink, having salvation written in their hearts by the Spirit, and diligently keeping the old tradition.

Then, having recited the substance of the Apostles' Creed as a specimen of that tradition, he adds:

> This faith those who without letters have believed, in respect of our language are indeed barbarians, but in respect of their views, habits, and conversation, have attained by faith a very high measure of illumination, and please God, walking in all justice, chastity, and wisdom. And if anyone should relate to them in their own language the new inventions of the heretics, they would presently shut their ears and escape as far as possible, not enduring so much as to hear the profane discourse.[8]

This noble passage I the rather quote, because it shows that the case which was just now put, of persons left without the Scriptures to depend on tradition alone, is not a mere dream of imagination, but at that time actually existed in some parts of the Christian world. There were instances, it seems, known to Irenaeus, of true believers who did not as yet know anything of the New Testament, yet were able to stop the mouths of heretics by merely avouching the ancient apostolical tradition. As was the condition, duty, and privileges, of those faithful and simple men, such would have been those of the whole Christian world had the inspired Scriptures either remained unwritten or perished with

8. [ED.] Irenaeus, *Against the Heresies*, III, 4 (*ANF*, I, 416 f.; *PG*, VII, 855 f.).

so many other monuments of antiquity. Faith in those divine truths with which the Church was originally entrusted would still have been required at the hands of Christian men; but the task of ascertaining those truths would have been far harder and more delicate. Now that it has pleased our gracious God to bestow on us, over and above, the use of his written word, can we be justified in slighting the original gift, on pretence of being able to do without it? Surely, in whatever respect any tradition is really apostolical, to think lightly of it must be the same *kind* of sin, as if those unlearned and remote Christians, of whom Irenaeus speaks, had thought lightly of the New Testament when it came to be propounded to them. We see at once in what manner sincere reverence for God's truth would lead them to treat the portions of his *written* word as they were brought successively under their notice. If we will be impartial, we cannot hide it from ourselves, that his *unwritten* word, if it can be anyhow authenticated, must necessarily demand the same reverence from us; and for exactly the same reason: *because it is his word.*

But further: the fact is clearly demonstrable from Scripture, that as long as the canon of the New Testament was incomplete, the unwritten system served as a test even for the apostles' own writings. Nothing was to be read as canonical except it agreed with the faith delivered once for all to the first generation of the saints. The directions of St. Paul on this subject are perfectly clear, and without reserve. "Though we or an angel from heaven preach any other gospel unto you than that which we have preached unto you, let him be anathema" [Gal. 1:8]. And St. John, in his Epistles, strikes continually on the same chord. His language sounds like an emphatical protest against any suspicion of novelty or originality in his teaching. "Brethren, I write no new commandment unto you, but the old commandment which ye had from the beginning. The old commandment is the word which ye heard from the beginning" (I Jn. 2:7). He writes to them as to persons knowing the truth; knowing all things; not needing that any man teach them (1 Jn. 2:20 f., 27). He forbids their acquiescing without trial in any pretensions to spiritual gifts: he would have the spirits tried, whether they be of God, whatever their claim to be confirmed even by miracle; and the test or touchstone which he recommends is agreement with the orthodox doctrine of the incarnation. "Every spirit that confesseth that Jesus Christ is come in the flesh, is of God; and every spirit that confesseth not that Jesus Christ is come in the flesh, is not of God" (1 Jn. 4:1-3). And his Second Epistle speaks just the same language: "Whosoever transgresseth, and abideth not in the doctrine of Christ, hath not God; he that abideth in the doctrine of Christ, he hath both the Father and the Son" (2 Jn. 9).

I do not see how we can be wrong in inferring, from these and similar passages, that the faith once for all delivered to the saints [Jude 3], in other words, apostolical tradition, was divinely appointed in the Church as the touchstone of canonical Scripture itself. No writing, however plausible the appearance of its having come from the apostles, was to be accepted as theirs if it taught any other doctrine than what they at first delivered; rather both it and its writers were to be anathema.

This use of apostolical tradition may well correct the presumptuous irreverence of disparaging the Fathers under a plea of magnifying Scripture. Here is a tradition so highly honoured by the Almighty Founder and Guide of the Church, as to be made the standard and rule of his own divine Scriptures. The very writings of the apostles were to be first tried by it, before they could be incorporated into the canon. Thus the Scriptures themselves, as it were, do homage to the tradition of the apostles; the despisers, therefore, of that tradition take part, inadvertently or profanely, with the despisers of the Scripture itself.[9]

On the other hand, it is no less evident that Scripture, being once ascertained, became in its turn a test for everything claiming to be of apostolical tradition. But on this part of the subject there is the less occasion to dwell, it being, I suppose, allowed on all hands. Only it may be well to notice a distinction not always sufficiently kept in view by modern writers on the rule of faith; viz., that whereas Scripture was from the beginning appealed to, of course, as a test of *positive* truth, it could only then be appealed to *negatively,* that is, its silence could then only be quoted as excluding any point from the list of truths necessary to salvation, when itself had attained a certain degree of completeness. And this perhaps may be one reason why the doctrine of the sufficiency of Scripture is nowhere expressly affirmed in Scripture itself.[10] The character which our Article justly assigns to the Bible, of "so containing all things necessary to salvation, that whatsoever is not read therein, nor may be proved thereby, is not to be required of any man that it should be believed as an article of faith, or be thought requisite or necessary to

9. It is assumed in this paragraph that where Scripture is silent or ambiguous, consent of the Fathers is a probable index of apostolical tradition.

10. This is not said without recollection of such texts as Jn. 5:39; 2 Tim. 3:15-17. But it is plain that both these passages speak of the *Scriptures of the Old Testament* only; and therefore, if understood exclusively, prove too much. . . .

salvation" [11] — this character the Bible could not, from the very force of the terms, acquire, until a sufficient portion of its contents had appeared, to include in one place or another every one of such fundamentals. Nor are we sure of this condition having been fulfilled until the appearance of St. John's Gospel and First Epistle, the latest, probably, of those canonical Scriptures, "of whose authority was never any doubt in the Church." [12] This consideration may serve to account for the comparative rareness of quotations from the New Testament in the writings of the first century; in the Epistle of St. Clement, for instance, who, while he produces in almost every paragraph some testimony from the Jewish Scriptures, has only three or four references to the New Testament: where such might be expected, he rather uses to remind men of "the depths of divine knowledge, which they had looked into"; [13] of "the immortal knowledge, whereof they had tasted"; [14] and of the apostolical examples which they had seen. Whereas the writers of the following age, Irenaeus, Tertullian, and the rest, add to the argument from tradition, on which in itself they lay as much stress as St. Clement, authorities and arguments from the New Testament, much in the manner of controversialists of our own time.

From all this I gather that in the interval between Clement and Ignatius on the one hand, Irenaeus and Tertullian on the other, the canon of the New Testament had first become fixed and notorious, and then the fact had been observed, which is stated in our Article: that every fundamental point of doctrine is contained in the unquestioned books of that canon, taken along with the Hebrew Scriptures. And this observation, being once made, would of course immediately suggest that golden rule, not of the Anglican only, but of the Catholic Church: that nothing is to be insisted on as a point of faith necessary to salvation, but what is contained in, or may be proved by, canonical Scripture. At any rate it is unquestionable that by the time of Irenaeus, that is, towards the end of the second century, the fact had been universally recognized, and the maxim thoroughly grounded and incorporated into the system of the Catholic Church. [15]

Reserving thus the claim of Scripture to be sole and paramount as a rule of faith, we may now, I think, venture to assume, from the nature

---

11. [ED.] Thirty-nine Articles, VI.   12. [ED.] *Ibid.*

13. Clement of Rome, *First Epistle to the Corinthians,* 40 [*LCC,* I, 62; *PG,* I, 288].

14. Clement of Rome, *First Epistle to the Corinthians,* 36 [*LCC,* I, 60; *PG,* I, 281].

15. [ED.] In a supporting note Keble quotes Irenaeus, *Against the Heresies,* II, 27; II, 30 (*ANF,* I, 398, 404; *PG,* VII, 802, 818).

of the case, the incidental testimony of Scripture, and the direct assertions of the Fathers, that it was an unwritten system which the holy writers spoke of when they so earnestly recommended the deposit, the commandment, the word heard from the beginning, to the reverential care both of pastors and of all Christian people.

Will it be said, "This is no concern of ours; it may be true in fact, but it yields no practical result; the traditionary system, whatever it was, having long ago passed away, except so far as it has been preserved in inspired writings"? This may be stated, and often is so, but can hardly be proved.

For in the first place, as long as it is only doubtful whether any statement or precept is part of the apostolic system or no, so long a mind imbued with true devotion will treat that statement or precept with reverence, will not rudely reject or scorn it, lest he refuse to entertain an angel unawares. So long, the mere fact of its not being contained in Scripture cannot be felt as a justification for casting it aside, any more than we should venture to disparage it on account of its not being revealed in any particular *book* of Scripture which we might happen to value above the rest. Although not in Scripture, it may yet be a part of *their* rule, concerning whom the Son of God has declared, "He that heareth you, heareth me: and he that despiseth you, despiseth me" [Lk. 10:16].

But in truth it may be proved to the satisfaction of any reasonable mind that not a few fragments yet remain, very precious and sacred fragments, of the unwritten teaching of the first age of the Church. The paramount authority, for example, of the successors of the apostles in Church government; the threefold order established from the beginning; the virtue of the blessed Eucharist as a commemorative sacrifice; infant baptism; and above all, the Catholic doctrine of the most Holy Trinity, as contained in the Nicene Creed. All these, however surely confirmed from Scripture, are yet ascertainable parts of the primitive, unwritten system, of which we yet enjoy the benefit. If anyone ask how we ascertain them, we answer, by application of the well-known rule, *Quod semper, quod ubique, quod ab omnibus* [16] — Antiquity, Universality, Catholicity — tests similar to those which jurists are used to apply to the common or unwritten laws of any realm. If a maxim or

16. [ED.] The "Vincentian Canon" — properly *quod ubique, quod semper, quod ab omnibus* — is derived from Vincent of Lérins, *Commonitorium*, 2 (*NPNF* [2], XI, 132; *PL*, L, 640).

custom can be traced back to a time whereof the memory of man runneth not to the contrary; if it pervade all the different courts, established in different provinces for the administration of justice; and, thirdly, if it be generally acknowledged in such sort, that contrary decisions have been disallowed and held invalid: then, whatever the exceptions to it may be, it is presumed to be part and parcel of our common law. On principles exactly analogous, the Church practice and rules above mentioned, and several others, ought, we contend, apart from all Scripture evidence, to be received as traditionary or common laws ecclesiastical. They who contend that the very notion of such tradition is a mere dream and extravagance; who plead against it the uncertainty of history, the loss or probable corruption of records, the exceptions, deviations, interruptions which have occurred through the temporary prevalence of tyranny, heresy, or schism; must, if they would be consistent, deny the validity of the most important portion of the laws of this and of most other old countries.

It is not, therefore, antecedently impossible that a system of tradition, subsidiary to the Scriptures, might yet exist in the commonwealth or city of God. The rest is matter of investigation in each case, whether any given rule, interpretation, or custom, be traditionary in the required sense. But it will not be going too far into particulars, and may help to the understanding and application of the whole argument, if I point out three distinct fields of Christian knowledge, in neither of which can we advance satisfactorily or safely without constant appeal to tradition, such as has been described.

The first is, the *system and arrangement of fundamental articles*, so far as they have come down to us systematic and arranged. We, that is all of the Anglican Church who have had any regular training in theology, are so early taught to trace the creed in the Scriptures, and to refer at once certain portions of both Testaments to certain high mysteries of the Catholic faith, that it commonly appears to ourselves as though we had learned those mysteries directly from the Scriptures. But there are few, surely, who on careful recollection would not be compelled to acknowledge that the creed, or some corresponding catechetical instruction, had prepossessed them with these truths before ever they thought of proving them from Holy Writ. I need hardly remind you of the un-questioned historical fact, that the very Nicene Creed itself, to which perhaps of all *formulae* we are most indebted for our sound belief in the proper divinity of the Son of God — even this creed had its origin, not from Scripture, but from tradition. The three hundred bishops who joined in its promulgation did not profess to have collected it out of the Bible, but simply to express the faith which each of them had found in the church which he represented, received by tradition from the apostles.[17] Nor is this any disparagement to Scripture, nor need it excite any alarm for the great fundamental verity itself, which the creed was meant to assert; any more than it would disparage the works of God, or shake the foundation of our faith in natural religion, were one to affirm that the power and Godhead of the Creator, although unquestionably provable from the things which are made, would yet have remained unknown to the mass of mankind but for primitive tradition, or subsequent revelation of it.

The second great subject, on which most of us are unconsciously indebted to the ancient Catholic tradition, is the *interpretation of Scripture*, especially those parts of [it] which less obviously relate to the mysteries of the gospel. Catholic tradition bears upon Scripture interpretation, not only indirectly, by supplying, as just now stated, certain great landmarks of apostolical doctrine, conformably to which the written statements are all to be interpreted; but also, in numerous cases, directly; setting the Church's seal, as it were, upon one among many possible expositions of particular passages. For example: how else could we know with tolerable certainty that Melchizedek's feast is a type of the blessed Eucharist;[18] or that the book of Canticles is an allegory, representing the mystical union betwixt Christ and his Church;[19] or that "Wisdom," in the book of Proverbs, is a name of the second person in the most Holy Trinity?[20] All which interpretations, the moment they are heard, approve themselves to an unprejudiced mind, and must in all

17. [ED.] *Cf.* Athanasius, *Letter concerning the Decrees of the Council of Nicaea*, 3 (*NPNF*², IV, 152; *PG*, XXV, 420).

18. [ED.] On this point Keble cites Cyprian, *Epistle* 63, 4 (*ANF*, V, 359; *CSEL*, III, 703); Augustine, *The City of God*, XVI, 22; XVII, 20 (*NPNF*¹, II, 323, 358; *CSEL*, XL/2, 164, 260); Jerome, *Epistle* 46, 2 (*NPNF*², VI, 61; *CSEL*, LIV, 331); John Chrysostom, *Homiliae in Genesim*, XXXV, 5 (*PG*, LIII, 328); and the Roman Canon of the Mass.

19. In this I believe all the Fathers who quote that divine book (and most of them do so often) are agreed. [ED.] On the typological exegesis of this and other parts of the Old Testament, *cf.* J. Keble, *Tract Eighty-nine: On the Mysticism attributed to the Early Fathers of the Church* (Oxford, 1840).

20. The disputes on the text, Prov. 8:22, at the Nicene Council, are sufficient to prove agreement on this point. It is well known that the Arians alleged it, as it stands in the LXX, . . . as a proof of the Son's inferiority. The Catholics never disputed the application of the text to our Lord, but denied the deduction from it.

likelihood have come spontaneously into many readers' thoughts. But it may be questioned whether we could ever have arrived at more than a plausible conjecture regarding them, but for the constant agreement of the early Church, taking notice everywhere, in these and the like instances, of the manner in which the Old Testament was divinely accommodated to the wonders of Christ's religion.

The third great field of apostolical tradition lies among *practical* matters, the *discipline, formularies,* and *rites* of the Church of Christ: in regard of which, reason tells us that the Church apostolical must here have had *some* method and system; yet it is evident to the very eye that the New Testament exhibits no such system in form, but only fragments and other indications of one in full operation at the time, and well known to those for whom the apostles were writing. These fragments being found to coincide with similar but more copious indications in later Church records; consideration also being had of the religious reverence wherewith in those ages everything primitive was regarded, and of the charitable jealousy of the churches, watching each other for the purpose of remonstrating against unwarrantable deviations; we need not fear to accept in its fulness, on all such matters, the well-known rule of St. Augustine, which I give in the words of Hooker: "Whatsoever positive order the whole Church everywhere doth observe, the same it must needs have received from the very apostles themselves; unless, perhaps, some general council were the authors of it." [21] In this kind no one at all versed in Church history can be at a loss for examples of the benefit which the present Church derives from the chain of primitive tradition. Without its aid, humanly speaking, I do not see how we could now retain either real inward communion with our Lord through his apostles, or the very outward face of God's Church and kingdom among us. Not to dwell on disputable cases: how, but by the tradition and practice of the early Church, can we demonstrate the observance of Sunday as the holiest day, or the permanent separation of the clergy from the people as a distinct order; or where, except in the primitive liturgies, a main branch of that tradition, can we find assurance that in the Holy Eucharist we consecrate as the apostles did, and, consequently, that the cup of blessing which we bless is the communion of the Blood of Christ, and the bread which we break the communion of the Body of Christ [1 Cor. 10:16]?

21. Richard Hooker, *The Laws of Ecclesiastical Polity,* Bk. VII, chap. 5 [*Works* (Oxford, 1845), III, 157]. Cf. Augustine, *Epistle* 54 [*NPNF* [1], I, 300; *CSEL,* XXXIV, 159].

Whether, then, we look to discipline, to interpretation, or to doctrine, every way we see reason to be thankful for many fragments of apostolical practice and teaching, most needful to guide us in the right use of Holy Scripture.

So it is, however, that either from impatience of authority, or dislike of trouble, or excessive dread of Romish error, tradition has become to most of us an unpalatable word, and we love not to allow that in any sense we rest our faith and practice upon it. And, as commonly happens when the mind is first made up and reasons are to be found afterwards, objections the most contradictory are brought to justify this our determined disregard of antiquity. Sometimes it is urged that the matters involved are so many, so intricate and various, and demand such minute research, that it is out of the question bringing them within the reach of the great body of the clergy, however learned; sometimes, on the contrary, it is maintained, that the points agreed on in the whole ancient Church are obviously so few, there have been such constant discussions and waverings of opinion, that after all there is no such thing as primitive Catholic tradition; what is called such being merely the register of the dictates of that which has proved, on the whole, the strongest and most fashionable party in the Church.[22] The one statement makes the field so wide that it is impossible not to lose one's way in it; the other so contracted that occupying it is no advantage. It is obvious that both objections cannot stand together; and as might be expected, the truth lies between the two. On the one hand, we are not to imagine that every usage which has prevailed in any part of the Church, every opinion which has been upheld even among orthodox Fathers, claims to have been part of the system of the apostles. On the other hand, we cannot surely deny such claim to those rules in which *all* primitive councils are uniform, those rites and formularies which are found in *all* primitive liturgies, and those interpretations and principles of interpretation in which *all* orthodox Fathers agree; more especially when they produce them as undoubted and authoritative. Now the genuine canons of the primitive councils, and the genuine fragments of the primitive liturgies, are reducible into a small space; even although we go so low down in both as the division of

22. [ED.] By way of illustration, Keble quotes Chillingworth's famous statement beginning: "The Bible, I say, the Bible only, is the religion of Protestants" (William Chillingworth, *Works* [Oxford, 1838], II, 410 f.). He adds Clarendon's observation that Chillingworth was for a long time "sceptical, to say the least of it, on the highest points of faith." Cf. *The Life of Edward, Earl of Clarendon* (Oxford, 1857), I, 56.

the Eastern and Western churches, including the six first councils general,[23] and excluding image-worship and similar corruptions by authority.[24] As far, therefore, as the councils and liturgies are concerned, tracing the remnant of apostolical tradition need not prove such a very overwhelming task. To establish consent among the Fathers is, doubtless, a far more laborious process; easiest, however, where it is most desirable, namely, in the great points of faith and worship, as recurring continually, and implied in all other discussions. What remains is chiefly interpretation of Scripture; a precious, inexhaustible mine of primitive knowledge to such as have the zeal to explore it, but not essential to the fixing of the main outlines. Leaving out, for the present, all such incidental discussions, and confining our view to that which touches the foundation, we shall find that the matters are neither few nor unimportant, which are settled by traditionary evidence within reach of common students. Were they much fewer than they are, and less important, still, as unquestionable relics of the apostles, a devout and thoughtful mind would prize them for their authors' sake, and for the sake of the lost treasure, whereof they are portions. To forget and disparage them would be a hard and unnatural thing, like coldly refusing due reverence to the dead. As it is, by the gracious providence of Almighty God, the points of Catholic consent known by tradition constitute the knots and ties of the whole system; being such as these: the canon of Scripture, the full doctrines of the Trinity and incarnation, the oblation and consecration of the Eucharist, the apostolical succession — truths and orders soon enumerated, but such as to extend in vital efficacy through every part of the great scheme of the Church. What, then, if the Church in our time, for the sins of Christians, should have lost more or less of "that good thing," the perfect apostolical body of government, doctrine, and sacramental grace, committed to St. Paul first, and by him to Timothy? It is not the less our duty, and by God's grace we will regard it as our high privilege, to keep unwearied watch over what remains, and to preserve it, "by the Holy Ghost which dwelleth in us."

3. These concluding words, while they supply an additional reason for extreme jealousy of our precious apostolical relics, open to us the appointed way of guarding what remains, and if one might be so happy,

23. [ED.] Nicaea I (A.D. 325), Constantinople I (381), Ephesus (431), Chalcedon (451), Constantinople II (553), Constantinople III (680–81).

24. [ED.] Clearly Keble, following the older Anglican tradition, does not recognize Nicaea II (787) as an ecumenical council.

of recovering more: a way not our own, but strictly and properly super-natural. And thus we are conducted to the final point of our enquiry: whether we, the existing ministers of the Church, have the same grace dwelling in us by which Timothy was exhorted to maintain his trust.

Now certainly the obvious meaning of the text is that the treasure of sound doctrine was to be guarded by the grace of the apostolical suc-cession. For St. Paul speaks of the Holy Ghost dwelling *in us*, that is, in himself and Timothy; and how it had passed from him to Timothy had been expressed a few verses before: "I will that thou stir up the grace of God which is in thee by the imposition of my hands." The Church of England, you will remember, supplies full warrant for this inter-pretation by directing the same phrase to be solemnly repeated at the consecration of every bishop: "Remember that thou stir up the grace of God *which is given thee by the imposition of our hands*"; and also where, in ordaining a bishop or presbyter, the solemn words are spoken, "Receive the Holy Ghost." Our Church, therefore, does not teach us to consider the Holy Ghost dwelling in St. Paul and Timothy as properly miraculous, a gift of extraordinary grace; but as their portion of that Spirit which was to be poured out on all apostles, and successors of the apostles, for ever. It was not what is commonly called miraculous, yet it was altogether supernatural. For no natural or acquired virtue or talent, though it might be called the *gift* of the Holy Ghost, would ever be designated as the Holy Ghost himself abiding in a man. Neither was it the preventing [25] or assisting grace common to all Christian persons; for it was given to Timothy in particular by imposition of St. Paul's hands. It could only be, what the Church interprets it, apostolical or episcopal grace.

Apostolical, then, or episcopal grace is by God's ordinance the guardian of sound doctrine; the Spirit abiding in Timothy is to watch incessantly the deposit or trust of divine truth left in his charge: and where the one, the succession, fails, there, as this verse would lead us to expect, and as all church history proves, the other, the truth of doctrine, is immediately in imminent jeopardy.

Here, then, we seem to have arrived at one cardinal point at least, whereby we may shape our course in times and emergencies more than usually perplexing. We are to look before all things to the integrity of the good deposit, the orthodox faith, the creed of the apostolical Church, guaranteed to us by Holy Scripture, and by consent of pure antiquity.

25. [ED.] *I.e., gratia praeveniens.*

Present opportunities of doing good; external quietness, peace, and order; a good understanding with the temporal and civil power; the love and co-operation of those committed to our charge — these, and all other pastoral consolations, must be given up, though it be with a heavy heart, rather than we should yield one jot or one title of the faith once delivered to the saints.

And whereas the dangers to that faith vary according to the differences of times, interests, and opinions; and sometimes the scriptural, sometimes the traditionary safeguards of it appear to be more immediately threatened; both must be watched with jealous and impartial care, since comparative neglect of either is sure to be attended with ill consequences to both. Thus the reverence of the Latin Church for tradition, being applied unscrupulously, and without the necessary check from Scripture, to opinions and practices of a date comparatively recent, has led a large portion of Christendom to disuse and contempt, not of Scripture only, but of that real and sure tradition which they might and ought to have religiously depended upon. On the other hand, is there not reason to fear that the Holy Scriptures themselves are fast losing reverence, through the resolute defiance of tradition, which some affect, in conformity, as they suppose, with the maxim, that the Bible only is the religion of Protestants? Surely it is no rare nor unnatural result, if such as are trained to this principle, being left, as someone has said, alone with their Bibles,[26] use their supposed liberty of interpretation, first in explaining away the mysterious meaning, and afterwards in lowering or evading the supernatural authority, of the very Scriptures which at first they deferred to exclusively. And no wonder — since among the traditionary truths which they are taught to undervalue is the canon of Scripture itself, and the principle, also, that fundamental articles of belief must be sought for in Scripture. In short, the sacred building is so divinely, though invisibly, cemented, that, for aught we know, it is impossible to remove any portion, either of scriptural or traditionary truth, without weakening the whole arch. We, to whom the whole is committed, under the most solemn of all pledges, and with the actual gift of the all-sufficient Spirit to aid us in redeeming that pledge — let us, above all things, beware of the presumption of selecting for ourselves among the truths and laws of

26. [ED.] Hooker, *Ecclesiastical Polity*, Preface, 8 (*Works*, I, 185): "When they and their Bibles were alone together, what strange fantastical opinion soever at any time entered into their heads, their use was to think the Spirit taught it them."

the Most High, *which* we will retain and *which* we may venture to dispense with.

In the next place, let us beware of novelty: novelty, I mean, as compared with the apostolic age; not the mere appearance of novelty as compared with the current notions of our time. For it is self-evident that if in any age or country any portion of apostolical truth be lost, whenever it is revived it must for the time look new; and its maintainers will have to contend with the prejudice which constantly waits on the disturbers of things established. Not novelty, therefore, relative to us, but novelty relative to the primitive and original standard, is the thing above all to be deprecated in the whole of theology, by whatever plausible air of originality, ingenuity, completeness, it may seem to recommend itself.

Observe under what a fearful penalty, in a warning parallel to that of the text, St. Paul, writing to the Thessalonians, discourages every intrusion of speculative doctrine. The apostasy, he tells them, will come; the wicked one shall be revealed, actuated by Satan to deceive them that perish, "on whom God will send strong delusion, that they may believe a lie" [2 Thess. 2:11]. And then he proceeds: "Wherefore, brethren, stand fast, and hold the traditions which ye have been taught, whether by word or our epistle" [2 Thess. 2:15]. Is not this equivalent to saying that whoever is studious of novelty in religion is in a way to take part with Antichrist; that the only security against him, and the spirit which prepares the way for him, is to hold the apostolical doctrine, whether taught in word or in writing, and to exclude all additions, however tempting to human ingenuity and love of system, however acutely they may appear to be reasoned out, and to fall in with allowed principles?

Had this rule been faithfully kept, it would have preserved the Church just as effectually from the assertion of transubstantiation on the one hand, as from the denial of Christ's real presence on the other hand. The two errors in the original are perhaps but rationalism in different forms; endeavours to explain away, and bring nearer to the human intellect, that which had been left thoroughly mysterious both by Scripture and tradition. They would both turn the attention of men from the real life-giving miracle to mere metaphysical or grammatical subtleties such as our fathers never knew.

Observe, again, the phraseology of the apostle, how it is formed throughout upon the supposition, that in the substance of the faith there is no such thing as improvement, discovery, evolution of new truths; none of those processes, which are the pride of human reason and knowledge, find any place here. Here the one thing needful is to *"retain* the mystery of the faith" (1 Tim. 3:9); to *"abide* in the good instruction whereto we have already attained" (1 Tim. 4:6); to "teach no *other* doctrine" (1 Tim. 1:3); to be on our guard against those who resist the truth under pretence of "proceeding further" (2 Tim. 3:9), assured that such, although they seem to be "ever learning," shall never be able to "come to the knowledge of the truth" (2 Tim. 3:7); they will *"proceed"* indeed, but it will be from bad to worse. All these cautions, and others no less fearful, the Holy Spirit has left for our admonition, directed not against any positive wrong opinion, but in general against the fatal error of treating theology like any human science, as a subject in which every succeeding age might be expected to advance on the former.[27]

Nor is the warning less important, nor the application to our times less certain, where Timothy is enjoined to "keep that committed to his charge, turning away from profane, empty verbal discussions, and oppositions of knowledge falsely so called" (1 Tim. 6:20). The allusion was probably in the first instance to the low-minded empirical system of the Gnostics. But the words are not much less appropriate to that which may be called the *nominalism* of our days; I mean, the habit of resolving the high mysteries of the faith into mere circumstances of language, methods of speaking adapted to our weak understanding, but with no real counterpart in the nature of things.[28] Whoever takes this line must needs hold the tradition of antiquity cheap, since it is based altogether on the supposition which he rejects as unphilosophical.[29] Thus slighting tradition,

---

27. [ED.] Against this "fatal error" Keble quotes Vincent of Lérins, *Commonitorium*, 22 (*NPNF*[2], XI, 147; *PL*, L, 667), and cites Joseph Butler, *The Analogy of Religion*, Pt. II, chap. 3 (*Works* [Oxford, 1896], I, 234 f.).

28. [ED.] *Cf.* R. D. Hampden, *The Scholastic Philosophy Considered in Its Relation to Christian Theology*, 3d ed. (Hereford, 1848), 54 f.: "The Scripture intimates to us certain facts concerning the Divine Being: but conveying them to us by the medium of language, it only brings them before us darkly, under the signs appropriate to the thoughts of the human mind. And though this kind of knowledge is abundantly instructive to us in point of sentiment and action; teaches us, that is, both how to feel, and how to act, towards God — for it is the language that we understand, the language formed by our own experience and practice — it is altogether inadequate in point of Science. The most perfect reasonings founded on the terms of theological propositions, amount only to evidences of the various connexions of the signs employed."

29. [ED.] *Cf.* Blanco White, memorandum of April 7, 1839, in J. H. Thom, ed., *The Life of the Rev. Joseph Blanco White, written by himself; with portions of his Correspondence* (London, 1845), III, 55 f.: "God would not employ human language

and explaining away Scripture, there is no saying what pernicious heresy such a theorist may not fall into, if not happily guarded against himself by feelings and prejudices more reasonable than all his reasoning. Meantime the warning of Scripture is express: that they who "profess" such things may be expected to "err concerning the faith" [1 Tim. 6:21]. And it is plain that if at any time either the high places of the Church or the schools of theological knowledge should be left in such keeping, the guardians of the good deposit would be bound to direct especial attention that way, and not permit things to pass away, as in a dream, before men are aware.

This leads directly to the recollection of a third danger, to which the Church seems especially exposed at this moment; I mean, that which is commonly entitled *Erastianism;* the Church betraying to the civil power more or less of the good deposit which our Lord had put exclusively into her hands. This is a form of compromise with the world for which no occasion was given by the circumstances of the apostles: a trial peculiar to times like ours, when the governors of the world profess to have become the servants of our Lord and of his Christ. We cannot therefore look in the New Testament for literal instruction how to behave with regard to this delicate and dangerous part of our duty. The gospel affording no express rules or precedents, we are thrown first upon the many analogous cases which the inspired records of the Jewish history supply; and then upon the conduct and determinations of the Catholic Church, in those centuries of her establishment during which the primitive system existed in something like integrity, to guide her demeanour in her altered condition. Yet, undoubtedly the general rule, "Keep the deposit," affects our relations to the civil authorities more immediately than persons unversed in Church matters might imagine. If we are to understand by "the deposit" the faith once for all committed to Christians; and if the apostolical succession be the appointed guard of that faith; and if the charter of the succession, "As my Father hath sent me, even so send I you" [Jn. 20:21], convey the power of Church government as well as that of administering sacraments; then every undue sacrifice of the power of Church government to any earthly power is an infringement of the charter, and renders the deposit of the faith less

to say what, according to his laws, human language cannot express. This appears to me an unanswerable objection to the doctrines of the Trinity. But I am sure that few will understand it, for the simple reason that there are few among us who know any thing about the philosophy of language."

secure. For the sake therefore of the very foundation of sound doctrine, and not only for the sake of peace and order in the Church, ecclesiastical government, as well as the custody of the sacraments, should be jealously reserved in those hands to which Christ originally entrusted it. Nor do I see how it can be less than a sacred duty, however painful, and to human eyes unavailing, to protest, if we can do no more, against unauthorized intrusions on Church government, as everyone will readily allow we ought to protest against unauthorized administration of sacraments.

Such being the object for which we are set in defence, and such the enemies with whom we have to contend; such also the heavenly Assistant, dwelling in us and fighting on our side; it cannot be hard to perceive with what dispositions we ought to address ourselves to that holy warfare. It will not do to shrink from responsibility, or to be overscrupulous in calculating immediate results. Once let us be reasonably assured that we are in the way of our duty, really keeping the good deposit; and then, to use the words of the prophet, we may "set our faces like a flint, and need not be ashamed" [Is. 50:7]. Then, as often as misgivings and alarms come over us, we must "stir up the grace of God which is in us by imposition of apostolic hands." For "God hath not given us a spirit of cowardice, but of power, and of love, and of brotherly correction and reproof" [2 Tim. 1:6 f.]; a Spirit that brings with him an invisible but real *power*, to open and shut the kingdom of heaven in the name of our Lord Jesus Christ [Mt. 16:19]; a Spirit of never-failing *love* and *charity* to men's souls, to guide us in the exercise of that more than human power; and, lastly, a Spirit of kind and fatherly, yet, if need be, uncompromising and fearless *rebuke*.

Let us be only true to our sacred trust; let us put everything else by for the sake of handing down the whole counsel of God, our good deposit, entire as we received it; and who knows but we may by God's mercy be made instrumental in saving the English Church from ruin not unlike that which has fallen on Ephesus, Smyrna, or Sardis? At any rate, the Church Catholic, in one country or another, we are sure, will survive and triumph. As of old she has stood before kings and governors, and it turned to her for a testimony [Mt. 10:18], so now blessed are they whom divine providence shall choose and enable worthily to support her cause against popular delusion and tyranny. We, indeed, as priests of the second order, are but under-labourers in that most holy cause. Yet the least and lowest among us may look for his share of the blessing, as he has undoubtedly his share of the burthen and of the peril. Is there not a hope that by resolute self-denial and strict and calm fidelity to our ordination vows we may not only aid in preserving that which remains, but also may help to revive in some measure, in this or some other portion of the Christian world, more of the system and spirit of the apostolical age? New truths, in the proper sense of the word, we neither can nor wish to arrive at. But the monuments of antiquity may disclose to our devout perusal much that will be to this age new, because it has been mislaid or forgotten; and we may attain to a light and clearness, which we now dream not of, in our comprehension of the faith and discipline of Christ. We may succeed beyond what humanly appears possible in rekindling a primitive zeal among those who shall be committed to our charge. Even as Abraham, neglecting all earthly objects, "taught his children and his household after him, to keep the way of the Lord, to do justice and judgment" (Gen. 18:19); and one part of his reward was, that "God would not hide from Abraham the thing which he did" (Gen. 18:17); another, that he was made the glorious and favoured instrument for transmitting divine truth through a fallen and corrupt age.

PART THREE

❖

The Anglo-Catholic Revolution

❖ ❖ ❖ ❖ ❖ ❖ ❖ ❖
❖   ❖
❖   I   ❖
❖   ❖
❖ ❖ ❖ ❖ ❖ ❖ ❖ ❖

JOHN HENRY NEWMAN

Lectures on the Prophetical Office of the Church
(SELECTION)

Editor's introduction. By the end of 1833 no less than seventeen *Tracts for the Times* — about two-thirds of them written by Newman or Keble — had been published anonymously. At the beginning of January 1834 *Tract Eighteen: Thoughts on the Benefits of the System of Fasting Enjoined by our Church* appeared over the initials "E. B. P." Those three letters symbolize one of the decisive events in Tractarian history — the public identification of Edward Bouverie Pusey with the Oxford Movement.[1]

> He at once [Newman wrote] gave to us a position and a name. Without him we should have had no chance, especially at the early date of 1834, of making any serious resistance to the Liberal aggression. But Dr. Pusey was a Professor [2] and Canon of Christ Church; he had a vast influence in consequence of his deep religious seriousness, the munificence of his charities, his Professorship, his family connexions, and his easy relations with University authorities. . . . He was able to give a name, a form, and a personality to what was without him a sort of mob; and when various parties had to meet together in order to resist the liberal acts of the Government, we of the Movement took our place by right among them.[3]

Before long Pusey was influencing the theological program as well as the public relations of the Tractarian group.

1. In the popular mind this identification may well have gone further than Pusey intended at the time. *Cf.* H. P. Liddon, *Life of Edward Bouverie Pusey, D.D.*, 4th ed. (London, 1894–98), I, 279 ff.
2. Regius Professor of Hebrew at Oxford, 1828–82.
3. J. H. Newman, *Apologia pro vita sua* (Garden City, N.Y., 1956), 173 f.

I suspect [Newman tells us] it was Dr. Pusey's influence and example which set me, and made me set others, on the larger and more
careful works in defence of the principles of the Movement which
followed in a course of years — some of them demanding and receiving from their authors, such elaborate treatment that they did
not make their appearance till both its temper and its fortunes had
changed.[4]

The nature of Newman's first contribution to the new program was
determined by the pressure of circumstances.

I set about a work at once; one in which was brought out with
precision the relation in which we stood to the Church of Rome.
We could not move a step in comfort, till this was done. It was of
absolute necessity and a plain duty, to provide as soon as possible
a large statement, which would encourage and re-assure our friends,
and repel the attacks of our opponents. A cry was heard on all sides
of us, that the Tracts and the writings of the Fathers would lead us
to become Catholics, before we were aware of it.

To this cry Newman responded with his *Lectures on the Prophetical
Office of the Church, viewed relatively to Romanism and Popular
Protestantism,* published in 1837.[5]

Newman himself has clearly outlined the purpose of his first major
systematic treatise:

It attempts to trace out the rudimental lines on which Christian
faith and teaching proceed, and to use them as means of determining
the relation of the Roman and Anglican systems to each other. In
this way it shows that to confuse the two together is impossible,
and that the Anglican can be as little said to tend to the Roman, as
the Roman to the Anglican.[6] . . . But this Volume had a larger
scope than that of opposing the Roman system. It was an attempt

4. *Ibid.,* 175.
5. The lectures on which the book was directly based were given between 1834 and
1836, under Newman's novel scheme of public theological lectures at St. Mary's.
6. *Cf.* William Palmer, *A Narrative of Events connected with the Publication of
the Tracts for the Times,* 2d ed. (London, 1883), 141 f.: "The charge of Romanizing
tendencies, to which so many advocates of Church principles have been subjected,
notwithstanding their exertions in the field of controversy against Rome, did not
excite surprise or uneasiness amongst them, because they were well aware that the
imputation of Popery is the standing argument of those who have no other mode of
resisting the truth. . . . That any tendency to Romanism should ever exist amongst
themselves; that Church principles should ever become the path to superstition and
idolatry; that they or their disciples should ever become alienated from the English
Church, never entered their imaginations as possible."

at commencing a system of theology on the Anglican idea, and based upon Anglican authorities.[7]

For a succinct account of Newman's approach to his problem we may confidently turn to Dean Church's narrative:

The point which he chose for his assault was indeed the key of the Roman position — the doctrine of Infallibility. He was naturally led to this side of the question by the stress which the movement had laid on the idea of the Church as the witness and teacher of revealed truth: and the immediate challenge given by the critics or opponents of the movement was, how to distinguish this lofty idea of the Church, with its claim to authority, if it was at all substantial, from the imposing and consistent theory of Romanism. He urged against the Roman claim of Infallibility two leading objections. One was the way in which the assumed infallibility of the present Church was made to override and supersede, in fact, what in words was so ostentatiously put forward, the historical evidence of antiquity to doctrine, expressed by the phrase, the "consent of the Fathers." The other objection was the inherent contradiction of the notion of infallibility to the conditions of human reception of teaching and knowledge, and its practical uselessness as an assurance of truth, its partly delusive, partly mischievous, working. But he felt, as all deep minds must feel, that it is easier to overthrow the Roman theory of Church authority than to replace it by another, equally complete and commanding, and more unassailable. He was quite alive to the difficulties of the Anglican position; but he was a disciple in the school of Bishop Butler, and had learned as a first principle to recognise the limitations of human knowledge, and the unphilosophical folly of trying to round off into finished and pretentious schemes our fragmentary yet certain notices of our own condition and of God's dealings with it. He followed his teacher in insisting on the reality and importance of moral evidence as opposed to demonstrative proof; and he followed the great Anglican divines in asserting that there was a true authority, varying in its degrees, in the historic Church; that on the most fundamental points of religion this authority was trustworthy and supreme; that on many other questions it was clear and weighty, though it could not decide everything. This view of the "prophetical office of the Church" had the dialectical disadvantage of appearing to be a compromise, to many minds a fatal disadvantage. It got the name of the *Via Media;* a satisfactory one to practical men like Dr. Hook, to whom it recommended itself for use in popular teaching; but to others, in aftertimes, an ill-sounding phrase of dislike, which summed up the weakness of the Anglican case.

7. Newman, *Apologia*, 176.

Yet it only answered to the certain fact, that in the early and undivided Church there was such a thing as authority, and there was
no such thing known as Infallibility. It was an appeal to the facts
of history and human nature against the logical exigencies of a
theory. Men must transcend the conditions of our experience if
they want the certainty which the theory of Infallibility speaks of.[8]

❖   ❖   ❖   ❖

INTRODUCTION

So much is said and argued just at this time on the subject of the
Church, by those who use the word in different senses, and those who
attach to it little distinct sense at all, that I have thought it might be useful,
by way of promoting sound and consistent views concerning it, to consider it attentively in several of its bearings, and principally in its relation
to Romanism, which possesses the most systematic theory concerning it.
Unhappy is it that we should be obliged to discuss and defend what a
Christian people were intended to enjoy, to appeal to their intellects
instead of "stirring up their pure minds by way of remembrance" [2 Pet.
3:1], to direct them towards articles of faith which should be their
place of starting, and to treat as mere conclusions what in other ages
have been assumed as first principles. Surely life is not long enough
to prove everything which may be made the subject of proof; and,
though inquiry is left partly open in order to try our earnestness, yet it is
in great measure, and in the most important points, superseded by Revelation — which discloses things which reason could not reach, saves us the
labour of using it when it might avail, and sanctions thereby the *principle*
of dispensing with it in other cases. Yet, in spite of this joint testimony of
nature and grace, so it is, we seem at this day to consider discussion
and controversy to be in themselves chief goods. We exult in what we
think our indefeasible right and glorious privilege to choose and settle
our religion for ourselves; and we stigmatize it as a bondage to be bid
take for granted what the wise, good, and many have gone over and
determined long before, or to submit to what Almighty God has revealed.
   From this strange preference, however originating, of inquiry to belief,
we, or our fathers before us, have contrived to make doubtful what really
was certain. We have created difficulties in our path; we have gone out of

8. R. W. Church, *The Oxford Movement: Twelve Years, 1833–1845*, 3d ed. (London
1892), 210–12.

our way to find ingenious objections to what was received, where none hitherto existed; as if forgetting that there is no truth so clear, no character so pure, no work of man so perfect, but admits of criticism, and will become suspected directly it is accused. As might be expected, then, we have succeeded in our attempt; we have succeeded in raising clouds which effectually hide the sun from us, and we have nothing left but to grope our way by our reason, as we best can — our necessary, because now our only, guide. And as a traveller by night, calculating or guessing his way over a morass or amid pitfalls, naturally trusts himself more than his companions, though not doubting their skilfulness and goodwill, and is too intent upon his own successive steps to hear and to follow them, so we, from anxiety if not from carelessness, have straggled each from his neighbour, and are all of us, or nearly so, in a fair way to lose our confidence, if not our hope. I say, we, or others for us, have asserted our right of debating every truth, however sacred, however protected from scrutiny hitherto; we have accounted that belief alone to be manly which commenced in doubt, that inquiry alone philosophical which assumed no first principles, that religion alone rational which we have created for ourselves. Loss of labour, division, and error have been the threefold gain of our self-will, as evidently visited in this world — not to follow it into the next.

How we became committed to so ill-advised a course, by what unfortunate necessity, or under what overpowering temptation, it avails not here to inquire. But the consequences are undeniable; the innocent suffer by a state of things which to the proud and carnal is an excuse for their indifference. The true voice of Revelation has been overpowered by the more clamorous traditions of men; and where there are rivals, examination is necessary, even where piety would fain have been rid of it. Thus, in relation to the particular subject which has led to these remarks, that some one meaning was anciently attached to the word "church," is certain from its occurring in the creed; it is certain, for the same reason, that it bore upon some first principle in religion, else it would not have been there. It is certain moreover, from history, that its meaning was undisputed, whatever that meaning was; and it is as certain that there are interminable disputes and hopeless differences about its meaning now. Now is this a gain or a loss to the present age? At first sight one might think it a loss, so far as it goes, whatever be the cause of it; in the same sense in which the burning of a library is a loss, the destruction of a monument, the disappearance of an ancient record, or the death of an experimentalist or philosopher. Diminution from the stock of knowledge is commonly considered a loss in this day; yet strange to say, in the instance before us, it is thought far otherwise. The great mass of educated men are at once uneasy, impatient, and irritated, not simply incredulous, directly they are promised from any quarter some clear view of the original and apostolic doctrine, to them unknown, on any subject of religion. They bear to hear of researches into Christian antiquity if they are directed to prove its uncertainty and unprofitableness; they are intolerant and open-mouthed against them if their object be to rescue, not to destroy. They sanction a rule of philosophy which they practically refute every time they praise Newton or Cuvier. In truth, they can endure a positive theory in other provinces of knowledge; but in theology it becomes practical. They perceive that there, what in itself is but an inquiry into questions of fact, tends to an encroachment upon what they think fit to consider their Christian liberty. They are reluctant to be confronted with evidence which will diminish their right of thinking rightly or wrongly, as they please; they are jealous of being forced to submit to one view of the subject, and to be unable at their pleasure to change; they consider comfort in religion to lie in all questions being open, and there being no call upon them to act. Thus they deliberately adopt that liberty which God gave his former people in wrath, "a liberty to the sword, to the pestilence, and to the famine" (Jer. 34:17), the prerogative of being heretics or infidels.

It would be well if these men could keep their restless humours to themselves; but they unsettle all around them. They rob those of their birthright who would have hailed the privilege of being told the truth without their own personal risk in finding it; they force them against their nature upon relying on their reason, when they are content to be saved by faith. Such troublers of the Christian community would, in a healthy state of things, be silenced or put out of it, as disturbers of the king's peace are restrained in civil matters; but our times, from whatever cause, being times of confusion, we are reduced to the use of argument and disputation, just as we think it lawful to carry arms and barricade our houses during national disorders.

Let this be my excuse for discussing rather than teaching what was meant to be simply an article of faith. We travel by night; the teaching of the apostles concerning it, which once, like the pillar in the wilderness, was with the children of God from age to age continually, is in good measure withdrawn; and we are, so far, left to make the best of our way to the promised land by our natural resources.

In the following lectures, then, it is attempted, in the measure which such a mode of writing allows, to build up what man has pulled down in some of the questions connected with the Church; and that, by means of the stores of divine truth bequeathed to us in the works of our standard authors.

The immediate reason for discussing the subject is this: In the present day, such incidental notice of it as Christian teachers are led to take in the course of their pastoral instructions is sure to be charged with what is commonly called "Popery," and for this reason — that Romanists having ever insisted upon it, and Protestants neglected it, to speak of it at all, though it is mentioned in the creed, is thought to savour of Romanism.[1] Those then who feel its importance, and yet are not Romanists, are bound on several accounts to show why they are not Romanists, and how they differ from them. They are bound to do so, in order to remove the prejudice with which an article of the creed is at present encompassed; and on the other hand to prevent those who have right but vague ideas concerning it from deviating into Romanism because no other system is provided for them. Till they do more than they have hitherto done, of course they hazard, though without any fault of theirs, a deviation on the part of their hearers into Romanism on the one hand, a reaction into mere Protestantism on the other.

From the circumstances then of the moment, the following lectures

1. [ED.] Cf. the prophecy of Thomas Sikes, quoted by E. B. Pusey, *A Letter to His Grace the Archbishop of Canterbury on some circumstances connected with the present crisis in the English Church* (Oxford, 1842), 27–29: "Wherever I go all about the country I see amongst the clergy a number of very amiable and estimable men, many of them much in earnest, and wishing to do good. But I have observed one universal want in their teaching: the uniform suppression of one great truth. There is no account given anywhere, so far as I see, of the one Holy Catholic Church. . . . The doctrine is of the last importance, and the principles it involves of immense power; and some day, not far distant, it will judicially have its reprisals. And whereas the other articles of the Creed seem now to have thrown it into the shade, it will seem, when it is brought forward, to swallow up the rest. . . . And woe betide those, whoever they are, who shall, in the course of Providence, have to bring it forward. . . . They will be endlessly misunderstood and misinterpreted. There will be one great outcry of Popery from one end of the country to the other. It will be thrust upon minds unprepared, and on an uncatechized Church. . . . How the doctrine may be first thrown forward we know not; but the powers of the world may any day turn their backs upon us, and this will probably lead to those effects I have described."

are chiefly engaged in examining and exposing certain tenets of Romanism. But this happens for another reason. After all, the main object in a discussion should be, not to refute error merely, but to establish truth. What Christians especially need and have a right to require is a positive doctrine on such subjects as come under notice. They have a demand on their teachers for the meaning of the article of the Apostles' Creed which binds them to faith in "the Holy Catholic Church." It is a poor answer to this inquiry merely to enter into an attack upon Romanism and to show that it contains an exaggerated and erroneous view of the doctrine. Erroneous or not, a view it certainly does contain; and that religion which attempts a view, though imperfect or extreme, does more than those which do not attempt it at all. If we deny that Romanists speak the truth, we are bound in very shame to commit ourselves to the risk of a theory, unless we would fight with them at an unfair advantage; and in charity to our own people, lest we tempt them to error while we refuse to give them what is better instead of it. But at the same time it stands to reason that to do this effectually, we must proceed on the plan of attacking Romanism, as the most convenient way of showing what our own views are. It has preoccupied the ground, and we cannot erect our own structure without partly breaking down, partly using, what we find upon it. And thus for a second reason, the following lectures, as far as in their very form goes, are chiefly written against Romanism, though their main object is not controversy but edification.

Their main object is to furnish an approximation in one or two points towards a correct theory of the duties and office of the Church Catholic. Popular Protestanism does not attempt it at all; it abandons the subject altogether. Romanism supplies a doctrine, but, as we conceive, an untrue one. The question is, what is that sound and just exposition of this article of faith, which holds together, or is consistent in theory, and is justified by the history of the Dispensation, which is neither Protestant nor Roman, but proceeds according to that *via media* which, as in other things so here, is the appropriate path for sons of the English Church to walk in? What is the nearest approximation to that primitive truth which Ignatius and Polycarp enjoyed, and which the nineteenth century has virtually lost?

This is the problem which demands serious consideration at this day, and some detached portions of which will be considered in the following lectures. Leaving to others questions directly political and ecclesiastical,

I propose to direct attention to some of those connected with the pro-phetical office of the Church.

It is obvious to insist on certain supposed disadvantages of considering such a subject at this moment. In replying to the objections thence arising, which I shall now attempt to do, an opportunity will be given me to explain more at length the object contemplated.

It is urged, then, by conscientious and sensible men, that we have hitherto done sufficiently well without any recognized theory on the subject, and therefore do not need it now or in prospect; that certain notions, in whatever degree abstractedly correct, have become venerable and beneficial by long usage, and ought not now to be disturbed; that the nature and functions of the Church have been long settled in this country by law and by historical precedents, and that it is our duty to take what we find and use it for the best; that, to discuss the question of the Church, though under the guidance of our great divines, necessarily involves the unsettling of opinions now received; that, though the views which may be put forward be in themselves innocent or true, yet under the circum-stances they will lead to Romanism, if only because the mind, when once set in motion in any direction, finds it difficult to stop, and because the article of the Church has been accidentally the badge and index of that system; that the discussions proposed are singularly unseasonable at this day, when our Church requires support against her enemies, and must be defended by practical measures, not by speculations upon her nature and historical pretensions, speculations of a past day, unprofitable in themselves, and in fact only adding to our existing differences, and raising fresh parties and interests in our already distracted communion — speculations, it is urged, which have never been anything but specula-tions, never were realized in any age of the Church; lastly, that the pretended *via media* is but an eclectic system, dangerous to the religious temper of those who advocate it, as leading to arrogance and self-sufficiency in judging of sacred subjects. This is pretty nearly what may be said.

Now it is obvious that these objections prove too much. If they prove anything, they go to show that the article of the Holy Church Catholic should not be discussed at all, not even as a point of faith; but that in its most essential respects, as well as in its bearings and consequences, it may be determined and interpreted by the law of the land. This con-sideration in itself would be enough to show that there was some fallacy in them somewhere, even if we could not detect it. However, let us consider some of them in detail.

One of the most weighty of these objections, at first sight, is the danger of unsettling things established, and raising questions, which, whatever may be their intrinsic worth, are novel and exciting at the present day. When, for instance, the divinely intended office of Holy Scripture, or the judicial power of the Church, or the fundamentals of faith, or the legitimate power of the Roman see, or the principles of Protestantism are discussed, it is natural to object that since the Revolution of 1688 they have been practically cut short and definitely settled by civil acts and precedents. It may be urged that the absolute subjection of the bishops, as bishops, to the crown is determined by the deprivations of 1689; [2] the Church's forfeiture of her synodical rights by the final measure of 1717; [3] the essential agreement of presbyterianism with episcopacy by the union with Scotland in 1706–07; and our incorporation with Dissenters, on the common ground of Protestantism, by the proceedings of the Revolution itself. It may be argued that these measures were but the appropriate carrying out of the acts of the Reformation; that King William and his party did but complete what King Henry began; and that we are born Protestants, and though free to change our religion and to profess a change, yet, till we do so, Protestants, as other Protestants, we certainly are, though we happen to retain the episcopal form; that our Church has thriven upon this foundation in wealth, station, and usefulness; that being a part of the constitution, it cannot be altered without touching the constitution itself; and, consequently, that all discussions are either very serious or very idle.

To all this I answer that the constitution has already been altered, and not by us; and the mere question is, whether the constitution being altered, and the Church in consequence, which is part of it, being exposed to danger in her various functions, we may allow those who have brought her into danger to apply what they consider suitable remedies, without claiming a voice in the matter ourselves. Are questions bearing more or less upon the education of our members, the extension of our communion, and its relations to Protestant bodies, to be decided without us? Are

2. [ED.] The Convention Parliament of 1689 imposed on all ecclesiastics an oath of allegiance to William III and Mary II. The Archbishop of Canterbury and six other bishops (five English and one Irish) were deprived of their sees for refusing the oath.

3. [ED.] The Convocation (provincial synod) of Canterbury was prorogued by royal order in 1717, and did not meet again to transact business until 1852. The York Convocation was silent from 1698 to 1861.

precedents to be created while we sit by, which afterwards may be assumed as our acknowledged principles? It is our own concern; and it is
not strange if we think it will be better looked after by ourselves than
by our enemies or by mere politicians. We are driven by the pressure of
circumstances to contemplate our own position, and to fall back upon
first principles; nor can an age which prides itself on its powers of scrutiny
and research be surprised if we do in self-defence what it does in wanton-
ness and pride. We accepted the principles of 1688 as the Church's basis,
while they remained, because we had received them: they have been
surrendered. If we now put forward a more ancient doctrine instead of
them, all that can be said against us is that we are not so much attached
to them on their own account as to consent that persons, still more
ignorant of our divinely framed system than the statesmen of that era,
should attempt, in some similar or worse form, to revive them. In truth,
we have had enough, if we would be wise, of mere political religion;
which, like a broken reed, has pierced through the hand that leaned upon
it [Is. 36:6]. While, and in proportion as we are bound to it, it is our
duty to submit, as the duties of the Jews lay in submitting to Nebuchadnezzar, as Jeremiah instructed them [Jer. 27:6-14]. We will not side
with a reckless and destructive party, even in undoing our own chains,
where there is no plain call of duty to oblige us; nay, we will wear them,
not only contentedly but loyally; we will be zealous bondsmen while
the state honours us in our captivity. It has been God's merciful pleasure,
as of old time, to make even those who led us away captive to pity us
[Ps. 106:46]. Those who might have been tyrants over us have before
now piously tended on the Church, and liberated her, as far as was expedient, in the spirit of him who "builded the city, and let go the captives
not for price nor reward" (Is. 45:13). And while the powers of this world
so dealt with us, who would not have actively co-operated with them,
from love as well as from duty? And thus it was that the most deeply
learned and most generous-minded of our divines thought no higher
privilege could befall them than to minister at the throne of a prince
like our first Charles, who justified their confidence by dying for the
Church a martyr's death. And I suppose, in similar circumstances, any
one of those who afterwards became Nonjurors, or of such persons at
this day as have the most settled belief in the spiritual powers of the
Church, would have thought himself unworthy to be her son had he
not fallen in with a system which he had received and found so well
administered, whatever faults might exist in its theory. This is the view

to be taken of the conduct of our Church in the seventeenth century, which we do not imitate now only because we are not allowed to do so, because our place of service and our honourable function about the throne are denied us. And, as we should act as our predecessors were we in their times, so, as we think, they too would act as we do in ours. They, doubtless, at a time when our enemies are allowed to legislate upon our concerns, and to dispose of the highest offices in the Church, would feel that there were objects dearer to them than the welfare of the state, duties even holier than obedience to civil governors, and would act accordingly. It is our lot to see the result of an experiment which in their days was but in process, that of surrendering the Church into the hands of the state. It has been tried and failed; we have trusted the world, and it has taken advantage of us. While the event was doubtful, it was the duty of her rulers to make the best of things as they found them; now that it is over, though we must undergo the evil, we are surely not bound to conceal it.

These reflections would serve to justify inquiries far beyond the scope of the following lectures, such, I mean, as bear upon our political and ecclesiastical state; whereas those which will here come into consideration have more reference to religious teaching than to action — to the Church's influence on her members, one by one, rather than to her right of moving them as a whole. But the distinct portions of the general subject so affect each other that such points as Church authority, tradition, the rule of faith, and the like cannot be treated without seeming to entrench upon political principles, consecrated by the associations of the Revolution. It has ever required an apology, since that event, to speak the language of our divines before it; and such an apology is now found in the circumstances of the day, in which all notions, moral and religious, are so unsettled that every positive truth must be a gain.

But, in answer to a portion of the foregoing remarks, it is not uncommon to urge what at first sight seems to be a paradox: that our enemies, or strangers, or at least persons unacquainted with the principles of the Church, are better fitted than her proper guardians and ministers to consult for her welfare; that they are better friends to us than ourselves, and in a manner often defend us against ourselves; and the saying of a great and religious author is quoted against us, that "clergymen understand the least and take the worst measure of human affairs of all mankind that can write and read." [4] And so they certainly do, if their

4. *The Life of Edward, Earl of Clarendon* [Oxford, 1857], I, 74.

end in view be that which secular politicians imagine. If their end be the temporal aggrandizement of the Church, no greater or more intolerable visitation could befall us than to be subjected to such counsellors as Archbishop Laud. But, perchance the objects we have in view are as hidden from the man of the world, whether statesman, philosopher, or courtier, as heaven itself from his bodily eyes; and perchance those measures which are most demonstrably headstrong and insane, if directed towards a political end, may be most judicious and successful in a religious point of view. It is an acknowledged principle that the blood of martyrs is the seed of the Church; [5] and if death itself may be a victory, so in like manner may worldly loss and trouble, however severe and accumulated.

I am aware that professions of this nature increase rather than diminish to men of the world their distaste for the conduct they are meant to explain. The ends which are alleged to account for the conduct of religious men remove the charge of imprudence only to attach to them the more odious imputation of fanaticism and its kindred qualities. Pilate's feeling when he asked, "What is truth?" [Jn. 18:38] is a type of the disgust felt by men of the world at the avowal of Christian faith and zeal. To profess to act towards objects which to them are as much a theory and a dream as the scenes of some fairy tale, angers them by what they consider its utter absurdity and folly. "Miserable men!" said the heathen magistrate on witnessing the determination of the martyrs of Christ, "if ye will die, cannot you find precipices or halters?" [6] Nor is this feeling confined to infidels or scorners; men of seriousness and good intentions, and it is especially to the purpose to observe this, feel the same annoyance and impatience at certain parts of that ancient religion, of which the doctrine of the Church is the centre, which profligate men manifest towards moral and religious motives altogether. To take an instance which will be understood by most men: Should a man, rightly or wrongly, for that is not the question, profess to regulate his conduct under the notion that he is seen by invisible spectators, that he and all Christians have upon them the eyes of angels, especially when in church; should he, when speaking on some serious subject, exhort his friends as in their presence, nay, bid them attend to the propriety of their apparel in divine worship because of them [1 Cor. 11:10], would he not at first be thought to speak poetically, and so excused? next, when he

5. [ED.] Cf. Tertullian, *Apology*, 50 (*ANF*, III, 55; *CSEL*, LXIX, 120): "The blood of Christians is seed."

6. Tertullian, *To Scapula*, 5 [*ANF*, III, 107; *PL*, I, 783].

was frequent in expressing such a sentiment, would he not become tiresome and unwelcome? and when he was understood to speak literally, would not what he said be certainly met with grave, cold, contemptuous, or impatient looks, as idle, strained, and unnatural? Now this is just the reception which secular politicians give to religious objects altogether; and my drift in noticing it is this — to impress on those who regard with disgust the range of doctrines connected with the Church, that it does not at all prove that those doctrines are fanciful and are uninfluential because *they* are disgusted, unless indeed the offence which the infidel takes at the doctrine of the Cross be an argument that it also is really foolishness [1 Cor. 1:18–25]. These doctrines may be untrue and unreasonable certainly; but if the surprise of those who first hear them and have never acted on them be a proof that they are so, more will follow than would be admitted by any of us; for surely no disagreeable feeling which they can experience equals the scorn with which irreligious men hear of the blessed doctrine that God has become man, no surprise of theirs can equal the amazement and derision with which the pagans witnessed a saint contending even unto bonds and death for what they considered a matter of opinion.

It does not follow, then, that doctrines are uninfluential, when plainly and boldly put forward, because they offend the prejudices of the age at first hearing. Had this been true, Christianity itself ought not to have succeeded; and it cannot be imagined that the respectable and serious men of this day who express concern at what they consider the exaggerated tone of certain writers on the subject of the Church, are more startled and offended than the outcasts to whom the apostles preached in the beginning. Truth has the gift of overcoming the human heart, whether by persuasion or by compulsion, whether by inward acceptance or by external constraint; and if what we preach be truth, it must be natural, it must be seasonable, it must be popular, it will make itself popular. It will find its own. As time goes on, and its sway extends, those who thought its voice strange and harsh at first will wonder how they could ever so have deemed of sounds so musical and thrilling.

The objection, however, which has led to these remarks, takes another and more reasonable form in the minds of practical men, which shall now be noticed. A religious principle or idea, however true, before it is found in a substantive form, is but a theory; and since many theories are not more than theories, and do not admit of being carried into effect, it is

exposed to the suspicion of being one of these, and of having no existence
out of books. The proof of reality in a doctrine is its holding together
when actually attempted. Practical men are naturally prejudiced against
what is new, on this ground if on no other, that it has not had the opportunity of satisfying this test. Christianity would appear at first a mere
literature, or philosophy, or mysticism, like the Pythagorean rule or
Phrygian worship; nor, till it was tried, could the coherence of its parts
be ascertained. Now the class of doctrines in question as yet labours under
the same difficulty. Indeed, they are in one sense as entirely new as
Christianity when first preached; for though they profess merely to be
that foundation on which it originally spread, yet as far as they represent
a *via media*, that is, are related to extremes which did not then exist, and
do exist now, they appear unreal, for a double reason, having no exact
counterpart in early times, and being superseded now by actually existing
systems. Protestantism and Popery are real religions; no one can doubt
about them; they have furnished the mould in which nations have been
cast: but the *via media*, viewed as an integral system, has scarcely had
existence except on paper, it has never been reduced to practice but by
piecemeal; it is known, not positively but negatively, in its differences
from the rival creeds, not in its own properties; and can only be described
as a third system, neither the one nor the other, partly both, cutting
between them, and, as if with a critical fastidiousness, trifling with them
both, and boasting to be nearer antiquity than either. What is this but
to fancy a road over mountains and rivers, which has never been cut?
When we profess our *via media* as the very truth of the apostles, we
seem to bystanders to be mere antiquarians or pedants, amusing ourselves
with illusions or learned subtleties, and unable to grapple with things
as they are. They accuse us of tendering no proof to show that our view
is not self-contradictory, and if set in motion, would not fall to pieces
or start off in different directions at once. Learned divines, they say, may
have propounded it, as they have; controversialists may have used it to
advantage when supported by the civil sword against Papists or Puritans;
but, whatever its merits, still, when left to itself, to use a familiar term,
it may not "work." And the very circumstance that it has been propounded for centuries by great names, and yet not reduced to practice
as a system, is alleged as an additional presumption against its feasibility.
To take for instance the subject of private judgment, our theory here is
neither Protestant nor Roman, and has never been duly realized. Our

opponents ask, What is it? Is it more than a set of words and phrases, of exceptions and limitations made for each successive emergency, of principles which contradict each other?

It cannot be denied there is force in these representations, though I would not adopt them to their full extent; it still remains to be tried whether what is called Anglo-Catholicism, the religion of Andrewes, Laud, Hammond, Butler, and Wilson, is capable of being professed, acted on, and maintained on a large sphere of action and through a sufficient period, or whether it be a mere modification or transition-state either of Romanism or of popular Protestantism, according as we view it. It may be plausibly argued that whether the primitive Church agreed more with Rome or with Protestants, and though it agreed with neither of them exactly, yet that one or the other, whichever it be, is the nearest approximation to the ancient model which our changed circumstances admit; that either this or that is the modern representative of primitive principles; that any professed third theory, however plausible, must necessarily be composed of discordant elements, and when attempted must necessarily run into Romanism or Protestantism, according to the nearness of the attracting bodies, and the varying sympathies of the body attracted, and its independence of those portions of itself which interfere with the stronger attraction. It may be argued that the Church of England, as established by law and existing in fact, has never represented a certain doctrine or been the development of a principle, that it has been but a name, or a department of the state, or a political party, in which religious opinion was an accident, and therefore has been various. In consequence, it has been but the theatre of contending religionists, that is, of Papists and Latitudinarians, softened externally, or modified into inconsistency by their birth and education, or restrained by their interests and their religious engagements. Now all this is very plausible, and is here in place, as far as this, that there certainly is a call upon us to exhibit our principles in action; and until we can produce diocese, or place of education, or populous town, or colonial department, or the like, administered on our distinctive principles, as the diocese of Sodor and Man in the days of Bishop Wilson,[7] doubtless we have not as much to urge in our behalf as we might have.

This, however, may be said in favour of the independence and reality of our view of religion, even under past and present circumstances, that,

7. [ED.] Thomas Wilson (1663–1755), a great pastor whose theology was akin to that of the Nonjurors, was a hero of the Tractarians.

whereas there have ever been three principal parties in the Church of
England, the Apostolical, the Latitudinarian, and the Puritan, the two
latter have been shown to be but modifications of Socinianism and Calvinism by their respective histories when allowed to act freely, whereas
the first, when it had the opportunity of running into Romanism, did
not coalesce with it; which certainly argues some real differences in it
from that system with which it is popularly confounded. The Puritan
portion of the Church was set at liberty, as is well known, during the
national troubles of the seventeenth century; and in no long time pros-
trated the episcopate, abolished the ritual, and proved itself by its actions,
if proof was necessary, essentially Calvinistic. The principle of Latitude
was allowed considerable range between the times of Charles II and
George II, and, even under the pressure of the Thirty-nine Articles, possessed vigour enough to develop such indications of its real tendency, as
Hoadly [8] and his school supply. The Apostolical portion of the Church,
whether patronized by the court, or wandering in exile, or cast out of
their native communion by political events, evinced one and the same
feeling of hostility against Rome. Its history at the era of the Revolution
is especially remarkable. Ken, Collier,[9] and the rest, had every adventitious
motive which resentment or interest could supply for joining the Romanists; nor can any reason be given why they did not move on the one side,
as Puritans and Latitudinarians had moved on the other, except that their
creed had in it an independence and distinctness which was wanting in
the religious views of their opponents. If nothing more has accrued
to us from the treatment which these excellent men endured, this at
least has providentially resulted, that we are thereby furnished with
irrefragable testimony to the essential difference between the Roman
and Anglican systems.

But if this be so, if the English Church has the mission, hitherto un-
fulfilled on any considerable stage or consistent footing, of representing
a theology, Catholic but not Roman, here is an especial reason why her
members should be on the watch for opportunities of bringing out and

---

8. [ED.] Benjamin Hoadly (1676–1761), Bishop successively of Bangor, Hereford,
Salisbury, and Winchester, was one of the outstanding political and theological controversialists of his time. His Low Church views on the Church and the Eucharist
provoked strong opposition within the Church of England.

9. Thomas Ken (1637–1711), Bishop of Bath and Wells, was one of the "Seven
Bishops" imprisoned by King James II in 1688, but refused to take the oath of allegiance to William and Mary and was deprived of his see. Jeremy Collier (1650–1726),
also a Nonjuror, was an historian and liturgiologist.

carrying into effect its distinctive character. Such opportunities perhaps have before now occurred in our history, and have been neglected, and may never return; but, at least, the present unsettled state of religious opinion among us furnishes an opening which may be providentially intended, and which it is a duty to use. And there are other circumstances favourable to the preaching of the pure Anglican doctrine. In a former age, the tendency of mere Protestantism had not discovered itself with the fearful clearness which has attended its later history. English divines were tender of the other branches of the Reformation, and did not despair of their return to the entire Catholic truth. Before Germany had become rationalistic, and Geneva Socinian, Romanism might be considered as the most dangerous corruption of the gospel; and this might be a call upon members of our Church to merge their differences with foreign Protestantism and Dissent at home, as if in the presence of a common enemy. But at this day, when the connexion of foreign Protestantism with infidelity is so evident, what claim has the former upon our sympathy?[10] and to what theology can the serious Protestant, dissatisfied with his system, betake himself but to Romanism, unless we display our characteristic principles, and show him that he may be Catholic and Apostolic, yet not Roman? Such, as is well known, was the service actually rendered by our Church to the learned Prussian divine, Grabe, at the end of the seventeenth century, who, feeling the defects of Lutheranism even before it had lapsed, was contemplating a reconciliation with Rome when, finding that England offered what to a disciple of Ignatius and Cyprian were easier terms, he conformed to her creed, and settled and died in this country.[11]

Again: though it is not likely that Romanism should ever again become formidable in England, yet it may be in a position to make its voice heard, and in proportion as it is able to do so, the *via media* will do important service of the following kind. In the controversy which will ensue, Rome will not fail to preach far and wide the tenet which it never

10. [ED.] This negative assessment of Protestantism became a commonplace among the Tractarians and contributed largely to their aversion from the Protestant churches. Cf. John Medley, *The Union of the Members in Christ's Body* (Exeter, 1839), 19: "Unlike Rome, we are never, for the attainment of unity, to sacrifice truth; unlike Geneva, we are never to seek for truth to the neglect of unity; lest, as she has done, we let go both."

11. [ED.] Johannes Ernst Grabe (1666–1711), a distinguished Biblical and patristic scholar, settled in England in 1697, received Anglican orders, and became a close friend of leading Nonjurors.

conceals, that there is no salvation external to its own communion. On the other hand, Protestantism, as it exists, will not be behindhand in consigning to eternal ruin all who are adherents of Roman doctrine. What a prospect is this! two widely spread and powerful parties dealing forth solemn anathemas upon each other, in the name of the Lord! Indifference and scepticism must be, in such a case, the ordinary refuge of men of mild and peaceable minds, who revolt from such presumption, and are deficient in clear views of the truth. I cannot well exaggerate the misery of such a state of things. Here the English theology would come in with its characteristic calmness and caution, clear and decided in its view, giving no encouragement to lukewarmness and liberalism, but withholding all absolute anathemas on errors of opinion, except where the primitive Church sanctions the use of them.

Here we are reminded of one more objection which may be made to the discussion of such subjects as those contained in the following lectures; and with a brief notice of it I will conclude. It may appear, then, that there is that in the very notion of inquiries into a doctrine but partly settled and received, and in the very name of a *via media*, adapted to foster a self-sufficient and sceptical spirit. The essence of revealed religion is the submission of the reason and heart to a positive system, the acquiescence in doctrines which cannot be proved or explained. A realized system is presupposed as the primary essential, from the nature of the case. When, then, we begin by saying that the English doctrine is not at present embodied in any substantive form, or publicly recognized in its details, we seem to reduce religion to a mere literature, to make reason the judge of it, and to confess it to be a matter of opinion. And when, in addition to this, we describe it as combining various portions of other systems, what is this, it may be asked, but to sanction an eclectic principle, which of all others is the most arrogant and profane? When men choose or reject from religious systems what they please, they furnish melancholy evidence of their want of earnestness; and when they put themselves above existing systems, as if these were suited only to the multitude or to bigoted partisans, they are supercilious and proud; and when they think they may create what they are to worship, their devotion cannot possess any high degree of reverence and godly fear [Heb. 12:28]. Surely, then, it may be said, such theorizing on religious subjects is but to indulge that undue use of reason which was so pointedly condemned in the commencement of these remarks.

I would not willingly undervalue the force of this representation.

It might be said, however, in reply, that at the worst the evil specified would cease in proportion as we were able to realize that system which is wanting. But after all the true answer to the objection is simply this, that though Anglo-Catholicism is not practically reduced to system in its *fulness*, it does exist, in all its parts, in the writings of our divines, and in good measure is in actual operation, though with varying degrees of consistency and completeness in different places. There is no room for eclecticism in any elementary matter. No member of the English Church allows himself to build on any doctrine different from that found in our Book of Common Prayer. That formulary contains the elements of our theology; and herein lies the practical exercise of our faith, which all true religion exacts. We surrender ourselves in obedience to it; we act upon it; we obey it even in points of detail where there is room for diversity of opinion. The Thirty-nine Articles furnish a second trial of our humility and self-restraint. Again, we never forget that, reserving our fidelity to the creed, we are bound to defer to episcopal authority. Here then are trials of principle on starting; so much is already settled, and demands our assent, not our criticism. What remains to be done, and comes into discussion, are secondary questions, such as these: How best to carry out the rubrics of the prayer book; how to apply its services in particular cases; how to regard our canons of the sixteenth and seventeenth centuries; how to reconcile the various portions of the ritual; how to defend certain formularies, or how to explain others. Another series of unsettled difficulties arises out of the question of education and teaching: What are the records, what the rule, of faith? What the authority of the Church? How much is left to private judgment? What are the objects and best mode of religious training? and the like. The subject of Church government opens another field of inquiries, which are more or less unanswered, as regards their practical perception by our clergy. The Thirty-nine Articles supply another. And in all these topics we are not left to ourselves to determine as we please, but have the guidance of our standard writers, and are bound to consult them, nay, when they agree, to follow them; but when they differ, to adjust or to choose between their opinions.

Enough has now been said by way of explaining the object of the following lectures. It is proposed to offer helps towards the formation of a recognized Anglican theology in one of its departments. The present state of our divinity is as follows: the most vigorous, the clearest, the most fertile minds have through God's mercy been employed in the service of our Church — minds, too, as reverential and holy, and as fully imbued with ancient truth, and as well versed in the writings of the Fathers, as they were intellectually gifted. This is God's great mercy indeed, for which we must ever be thankful. Primitive doctrine has been explored for us in every direction, and the original principles of the gospel and the Church patiently and successfully brought to light. But one thing is still wanting: our champions and teachers have lived in stormy times; political and other influences have acted upon them variously in their day, and have since obstructed a careful consolidation of their judgments. We have a vast inheritance, but no inventory of our treasures. All is given us in profusion; it remains for us to catalogue, sort, distribute, select, harmonize, and complete. We have more than we know how to use; stores of learning, but little that is precise and serviceable; Catholic truth and individual opinion, first principles and the guesses of genius, all mingled in the same works and requiring to be discriminated. We meet with truths overstated or misdirected, matters of detail variously taken, facts incompletely proved or applied, and rules inconsistently urged or discordantly interpreted. Such indeed is the state of every deep philosophy in its first stages, and therefore of theological knowledge. What we need at present for our Church's well-being is not invention, nor originality, nor sagacity, nor even learning in our divines, at least in the first place, though all these gifts of God are in a measure needed and never can be unseasonable when used religiously, but we need peculiarly a sound judgment, patient thought, discrimination, a comprehensive mind, an abstinence from all private fancies and caprices and personal tastes — in a word, divine wisdom. For this excellent endowment, let us, in behalf of ourselves and our brethren, earnestly and continually pray. Let us pray that he who has begun the work for our Holy Mother with a divine exuberance will finish it as with a refiner's fire and in the perfectness of truth.

Merely to have directed attention to the present needs of our Church would be a sufficient object for writing the following pages. We require a recognized theology, and if the present work, instead of being what it is meant to be, a first approximation to the required solution in one department of a complicated problem, contains after all but a series of illustrations demonstrating our need, and supplying hints for its removal, such a result, it is evident, will be quite a sufficient return for whatever anxiety it has cost the writer to have employed his own judgment on so serious a subject. And, though in all greater matters of theology there is

no room for error, so prominent and concordant is the witness of our
great masters in their behalf, yet he is conscious that in minor points,
whether in questions of fact or of judgment, there is room for difference
or error of opinion; and while he has given his best endeavours to be
accurate, he shall not be ashamed to own a mistake, nor reluctant to
bear the just blame of it.

LECTURE I:

THE NATURE AND GROUND OF ROMAN AND PROTESTANT ERRORS

All Protestant sects of the present day may be said to agree with us,
and differ from the Romanists, in considering the Bible as the only
standard of appeal in doctrinal inquiries. They differ indeed from each
other as well as from us in the matter of their belief; but they one and
all accept the written word of God as the supreme and sole arbiter of
their differences. This makes their contest with each other and us more
simple; I do not say shorter — on the contrary, they have been engaged
in it almost three hundred years, as many of them, that is, as are so
ancient, and there are no symptoms of its ending — but it makes it less
laborious. It narrows the ground of it; it levels it to the intelligence of
all ranks of men; it gives the multitude a right to take part in it; it
encourages all men, learned and unlearned, religious and irreligious, to
have an opinion in it, and to turn controversialists. The Bible is a small
book; anyone may possess it; and everyone, unless he be very humble,
will think he is able to understand it. And therefore, I say, controversy
is *easier* among Protestants, because anyone can controvert; easier, but
not shorter; because though all sects agree together as to the *standard*
of faith, viz., the Bible, yet no two agree as to the *interpreter* of the Bible,
but each person makes himself the interpreter, so that what seemed at
first sight a means of peace, turns out to be a chief occasion or cause of
discord. It is a great point to come to issue with an opponent; that is, to
discover some position which oneself affirms and the other denies, and
on which the decision of the controversy will turn. It is like two armies
meeting and settling their quarrel in a pitched battle, instead of wandering to and fro, each by itself, and inflicting injury and gaining advantages where no one resists it. Now the Bible is this common ground
among Protestants, and seems to have been originally assumed in no small
degree from a notion of its simplicity in argument. But, if this was the
case in any quarter, the hope has been frustrated by this difficulty — the

Bible is not so written as to force its meaning upon the reader; no two
Protestant sects can agree together whose interpretation of the Bible is
to be received; and under such circumstances each naturally prefers his
own — his own "interpretation," his own "doctrine," his own "tongue,"
his own "revelation" [1 Cor. 14:26]. Accordingly, acute men among
them see that the very elementary notion which they have adopted, of
the Bible without note or comment being the sole authoritative judge in
controversies of faith, is a self-destructive principle, and practically involves the conclusion that dispute is altogether hopeless and useless, and
even absurd. After whatever misgivings or reluctance, they seem to
allow, or to be in the way to allow, that truth is but matter of opinion;
that that is truth to each which each thinks to be truth, provided he
sincerely and really thinks it; that the divinity of the Bible itself is the
only thing that need be believed, and that its meaning varies with the
individuals who receive it; that it has no one meaning to be ascertained
as a matter of fact, but that it may mean anything because it is said to
mean so many things; and hence that our wisdom and our duty lie in
discarding all notions of the importance of any particular set of opinions,
any doctrines, or any creed, each man having a right to his own, and in
living together peaceably with men of all persuasions, whatever our
private judgments and leanings may be. I do not say that these conclusions need follow by logical necessity from the principle from which
I have deduced them; but that practically they will follow in the long
run, and actually have followed where there were no counteracting
causes in operation. Nor do I allow that they will follow at all in our
own case, though we agree with Protestant sects in making Scripture the
document of ultimate appeal in matters of faith. For though we consider
Scripture a satisfactory, we do not consider it our sole informant in
divine truths. We have another source of information in reserve, as I shall
presently show. We agree with the sectaries around us so far as this, to
be ready to take their ground, which Romanists cannot and will not do,
to believe that our creed can be proved entirely, and to be willing to
prove it solely from the Bible; but we take this ground only in controversy, not in teaching our own people or in our private reading. We
are willing to argue with them with texts; they may feel the force of
these or not; we may convince them or not, but if such conviction were
a necessary criterion of good argument, sound reasoning is to be found
on no side, or else there would soon cease to be any controversy at all.
It is enough that we are able to convince and convert others by means

of their weapon, though not them; which proves its cogency in our use of it. We have joined issue with them, and done all that can be done. The case is not as if we were searching after some unknown and indefinite ground of proof which we were told they had, but were uncertain about, and could not ascertain or circumscribe. We know their greatest strength, and we discover it to be weakness. They have no argument behind to fall back upon: we have examined and decided against their cause.

And they themselves, as I have observed, have decided against it too; their adoption of the latitudinarian notion that one creed is as good as another, is an evidence of it. We on the contrary should not be perplexed at hearing their opposite interpretations of Scripture, were they ever so positive and peremptory in maintaining them. Nay, we should not waver even if they succeeded in weakening some of our proofs, taking the text of Scripture by itself, both as considering that in matters of conduct evidence is not destroyed by being impaired, and because we rely on antiquity to strengthen such intimations of doctrine as are but faintly, though really, given in Scripture.

Protestant denominations, I have said, however they may differ from each other in important points, so far agree, that one and all profess to appeal to Scripture, whether they be called Independents, or Baptists, or Unitarians, or Presbyterians, or Wesleyans, or by any other title. But the case is different as regards Romanists: they do not appeal to Scripture unconditionally; they are not willing to stand or fall by mere arguments from Scripture; and therefore, if we take Scripture as our ground of proof in our controversies with them, we have not yet joined issue with them. Not that they reject Scripture, it would be very unjust to say so; they would shrink from doing so, or being thought to do so; and perhaps they adhere to Scripture as closely as some of those Protestant bodies who profess to be guided by nothing else; but, though they admit Scripture to be the word of God, they conceive that it is not the whole word of God, they openly avow that they regulate their faith by something else beside Scripture, by the existing traditions of the Church. They maintain that the system of doctrine which they hold came to them from the apostles as truly and certainly as their inspired writings; so that, even if those writings had been lost, the world would still have had the blessings of a revelation. Now, they must be clearly understood if they are to be soundly refuted. We hear it said that they go by tradition, and we fancy in consequence that there are a certain definite number of statements ready framed and compiled, which they profess to have received from the apostles. One may hear the question sometimes asked, for instance, *where* their professed traditions are to be found, whether there is any *collection* of them, and whether they are printed and published. Now though they would allow that the traditions of the Church are in fact contained in the writings of her doctors, still this question proceeds on somewhat of a misconception of their real theory, which seems to be as follows. By tradition they mean the whole system of faith and ordinances which they have received from the generation before them, and that generation again from the generation before itself. And in this sense undoubtedly we all go by tradition in matters of this world. Where is the corporation, society, or fraternity of any kind, but has certain received rules and understood practices which are nowhere put down in writing? How often do we hear it said that this or that person has "acted unusually," that so and so "was never done before," that it is "against rule," and the like; and then perhaps, to avoid the inconvenience of such irregularity in future, what was before a tacit engagement is turned into a formal and explicit order or principle. The want of a regulation must be discovered before it is supplied; and the virtual transgression of it goes before its adoption. At this very time great part of the law of the land is administered under the sanction of such a tradition; it is not contained in any formal or authoritative code, it depends on custom and precedent. There is no explicit written law, for instance, simply declaring murder to be a capital offence; unless indeed we have recourse to the divine command in the ninth chapter of the book of Genesis [Gen. 9:6]. Murderers are hanged by *custom*. Such as this is the tradition of the Church; tradition is uniform custom. When the Romanists say they adhere to tradition, they mean that they believe and act as Christians have always believed and acted; they go by the custom, as judges and juries do. And then they go on to allege that there is this important difference between their custom and all other customs in the world; that the tradition of the law, at least in its details, though it has lasted for centuries upon centuries, anyhow had a beginning in human appointments; whereas theirs, though it has a beginning too, yet, when traced back, has none short of the apostles of Christ, and is in consequence of divine not of human authority — is true and intrinsically binding as well as expedient.

If we ask why it is that these professed traditions were not reduced to writing, it is answered that the Christian doctrine, as it has proceeded from the mouth of the apostles, is too varied and too minute in its details

to allow of it. No one you fall in with on the highway can tell you all
his mind at once; much less could the apostles, possessed as they were
of great and supernatural truths, and busied in the propagation of the
Church, digest in one epistle or treatise a systematic view of the revelation made to them. And so much at all events we may grant, that they
did not do so; there being confessedly little of system or completeness
in any portion of the New Testament.

If again it be objected that this notion of an unwritten transmission
of the truth being supposed, there is nothing to show that the faith of
today was the faith of yesterday, nothing to connect this age and the
apostolic, Romanists maintain, on the contrary, that over and above the
corroborative though indirect testimony of ecclesiastical writers, no
error could have arisen in the Church without its being protested against
and put down on its first appearance; that from all parts of the Church
a cry would have been raised against the novelty, and a declaration put
forth, as we know was the practice of the early Church, denouncing it.
And thus they would account for the indeterminateness on the one hand,
yet on the other the accuracy and availableness of their existing tradition
or unwritten creed. It is latent, but it lives. It is silent, like the rapids of
a river, before the rocks intercept it. It is the Church's unconscious habit
of opinion and feeling; which she reflects upon, masters, and expresses,
according to the emergency. We see then the mistake of asking for a
complete collection of the Roman traditions; as well might we ask for
a collection of a man's tastes and opinions on a given subject. Tradition
in its fulness is necessarily unwritten; it is the mode in which a society
has felt or acted during a given period, and it cannot be circumscribed
any more than a man's countenance and manner can be conveyed to
strangers in any set of propositions.

Such are the traditions to which the Romanists appeal, whether viewed
as latent in the Church's teaching, or as passing into writing and being
fixed in the decrees of the councils or amid the works of the ancient
Fathers.

Now how do we of the English Church meet these statements? or
rather, I should say, how do the Romanists prove them? For it will be
observed that what has been said hitherto does not prove that their
traditions are such as they aver, but merely that their theory is consistent with itself. And as a beautiful theory it must, as a whole, ever
remain. At the same time I do not deny that to a certain point it is
tenable: but this is a very different thing from admitting that it is so as

regards those very tenets for which the Romanists would adduce it. They have to show not merely that there was such a traditionary system, and that it has lasted to this day, but that their peculiarities are parts of it. Here then we see how under such circumstances we ought to meet their pretensions. Shall we refuse to consider the subject of tradition at all, saying that the Bible contains the whole of divine revelation, and that the doctrines professedly conveyed by tradition are only so far apostolic as they are contained in Scripture? This will be saying what is true, but it will be assuming the point in dispute; it will in no sense be meeting the Romanists. We shall only involve ourselves in great difficulties by so doing. For, let us consider a moment; a Christian does not like to dwell on the following question, but the Romanist will be sure to ask it, and we shall have to answer it; so we had better consider it beforehand. I mean, how do we know that Scripture comes from God? It cannot be denied that we of this age receive it upon general tradition; we receive through tradition both the Bible itself and the doctrine that it is divinely inspired. That doctrine is one of those pious and comfortable truths "which we have heard and known, and such as our fathers have told us," "which God commanded our forefathers to teach their children, that their posterity might know it, and the children which were yet unborn; to the intent that when they came up, they might show their children the same" (Ps. 78:3–7). The great multitude of Protestants believe in the divinity of Scripture precisely on the ground which the Romanists trust in behalf of their own erroneous system, viz., because they have been taught it. To deride tradition therefore as something irrational or untrustworthy in itself is to weaken the foundation of our own faith in Scripture, and is very cruel towards the great multitude of uneducated persons who are obliged to believe what their instructors tell them. If, however, it be said that pious Protestants have "the witness in themselves" [1 Jn. 5:10], as a sure test to their own hearts of the truth of Scripture, the fact is undeniable; and a sufficient and consoling proof is it to them that the *doctrines* in Scripture are true; but it does not prove that the very book we call the Bible was written, and all of it written, by inspiration; nor does it allow us to dispense with the external evidence of tradition assuring us that it is so.

But if, again, it be said that the New Testament is received as divine, not upon the present traditionary belief of Christians, but upon the evidence of antiquity, this too, even were it true — for surely the multitude of Christians know nothing about antiquity at all — yet this is exactly what the Romanists maintain of their unwritten doctrines also. They argue that their present creed has been the universal belief of all preceding ages, as recorded in the writings of those ages, still extant. Suppose, I say, we take this ground in behalf of the divinity of Holy Scripture, that it is attested by all the writers and other authorities of primitive times: doubtless we are right in doing so; it is the very argument by which we actually do prove the divinity of the sacred Canon; but it is also the very argument which the Romanists put forward for their peculiar errors; viz., that while received on existing tradition, they are also proved by the unanimous consent of the first ages of Christianity. If then we would leave ourselves room for proving that Scripture is inspired, we must not reject the *notion* and *principle* of the argument from tradition and antiquity as something in itself absurd and unworthy of Almighty wisdom. In other words, to refuse to listen to these informants because we have a written word is a self-destructive course, inasmuch as that written word is proved to be such mainly by these very informants which we reject as if to do honour to it. It is to overthrow our premisses with our conclusion. That which ascertains for us the divinity of Scripture *may* convey to us other articles of faith also, unless Scripture has expressly determined in the negative.

But the sacred volume itself, as well as the doctrine of its inspiration, comes to us by traditional conveyance. The Protestant of the day asks the Romanist, "*How* do you know your unwritten word comes from the apostles, received as it is through so many unknown hands through so many ages? A book is something definite and trustworthy; what is written remains. We have the apostles' writings before us; but we have nothing to guarantee to us the fidelity of those successive informants which stand between the apostles and the unwritten doctrines you ascribe to them." But the Romanist surely may answer by the counter inquiry, *how* he on his part knows that what he considers their writings are really such, and really the same as the Fathers possessed and witness to be theirs. "You have a printed book," he may argue; "the apostles did not write that; it was printed from another book, and that again from another, and so on. After going back a long way, you will trace it to a manuscript in the Dark Ages, written by you know not whom, copied from some other manuscript you know not what or when, and there the trace is lost. You profess, indeed, that it runs up to the very autograph of the apostles; but with your rigorous notions of proof, it would be more to your purpose to produce that autograph than to give probable reasons for the fidelity of the copy. Till you do this, you are resting on a series of unknown links as well as we; you are trusting a mere tradition of men. It is quite as possible for human hands to have tampered with the written as with the unwritten word; or at least if corruption of the latter is the more probable of the two, the difference of the cases is one of degree, and not any essential distinction." Now, whatever explanations the Protestant in question makes in behalf of the preservation of the written word will be found applicable in the *theory* to the unwritten. For instance, he may argue, and irresistibly, that a number of manuscripts of various, and some of very early times, are still extant, and these belonging to different places and derived from sources distinct from each other; and that they all agree together. If the New Testament were practised upon, this must have happened before all these families of copies were made; which is to throw back the fraud upon such very early times as are a guarantee for believing it to have been impracticable. Or he may argue that it was the acknowledged duty of the Church to keep and guard the Scriptures, and that in matter of fact her various branches were very careful to do so; accordingly, that it is quite incredible that the authentic text should be lost in spite of so many trustees, as they may be called, and an altered copy or a forgery substituted. Or again, he may allege that the early Fathers are frequent in quoting the New Testament in their own works; and that these quotations accurately accord with the copy of it which we at present possess.

Such as these are the arguments we as well as the ordinary Protestant use against the infidel in behalf of the written word, and most powerfully; but it must be confessed that they are applicable in their *nature* to traditionary teaching also; they are such as the Roman doctrines *might* possess, as far as the *a priori* view of the case is concerned.

How then are we to meet the Romanists, seeing we cannot join issue with them, or cut short the controversy, by a mere appeal to Scripture? We must meet them, and may do so fearlessly, on the ground of antiquity, to which they betake themselves. We followed the Protestant's challenge in arguing from mere Scripture in our defence; we must not, and need not, shrink from the invitation of the Romanist to stand or fall by antiquity. Truth alone is consistent with itself; we are willing to take either the test of antiquity or of Scripture. As we accord to the Protestant sectary that Scripture is the inspired treasury of the whole faith, but maintain that his doctrines are not in Scripture, so we agree with the Romanist in appealing to antiquity as our great teacher, but we deny that his doctrines are to be found in antiquity. So far then is clear: we do not deny the force of tradition in the abstract; we do not deny the soundness of the argument from antiquity; but we challenge the Romanist to prove the matter of fact. We deny that his doctrines are in antiquity any more than they are in the Bible; and we maintain that his professed tradition is not really such, that it is a tradition of men, that it is not continuous, that it stops short of the apostles, that the history of its introduction is known. On both accounts then his doctrines are innovations; because they run counter to the doctrine of antiquity and because they rest upon what is historically an upstart tradition.

This view is intelligible and clear, but it leads to this conclusion. The Bible indeed is a small book, but the writings of antiquity are voluminous; and to read them is the work of a life. It is plain then that the controversy with the Romanists is not an easy one, not open to everyone to take up. And this is the case for another reason also. A private Christian may put what meaning he pleases on many parts of Scripture, and no one can hinder him. If interfered with, he can promptly answer that it is his opinion, and may appeal to his right of private judgment. But he cannot so deal with antiquity. History is a record of facts; and "facts," according to the proverb, "are stubborn things." Ingenious men may misrepresent them or suppress them for a while; but in the end they will be duly ascertained and appreciated. The writings of the Fathers are far too ample to allow of a disputant resting in one or two obscure or ambiguous passages in them and permanently turning such to his own account, which he may do in the case of Scripture. For two reasons, then, controversy with Romanists is laborious; because it takes us to ancient Church history, and because it does not allow scope to the offhand or capricious decisions of private judgment.

However, it must be observed, for the same reasons, though more laborious, it is a surer controversy. We are more likely to come to an end; it does not turn upon opinions but on facts.

This may be put in somewhat a different point of view. You know that three centuries ago took place a great schism in the Western Church, which thenceforth divided into two large bodies, the Romanists on one hand, the Protestants on the other. On the latter side it is usual to reckon our own Church, though really on neither: from which after a time certain portions split off, and severally set up a religion and communion for themselves. Now supposing we had to dispute with these separated portions, the Presbyterians, Baptists, Independents, or other

Protestants, on the subject of their separation, they would at once avow the *fact*, but they would deny that it was a *sin*. The elementary controversy between us and them would be one of *doctrine* and *principle:* viz., whether separation was or was not a sin. It is far otherwise as regards the Romanists; they as well as ourselves allow, or rather maintain, the criminality of schism, and that a very great sin was committed at the Reformation, whether by the one party, or by the other, or by both. The only question is, *which* party committed it; the Romanists lay it at our door, we retort it, and justly, upon them. Thus we join issue with them on a question of *fact;* one which cannot be settled without a sufficient stock of learning on the part of the disputants. So again the Calvinistic controversy is in great measure dependent on abstract reasoning and philosophical discussion; whereas no one can determine by *a priori* arguments whether or not the Papacy be a persecuting power.[1]

On the whole, then, it appears from what has been said that our controversies with the Protestants are easy to handle but interminable, being disputes about opinions; but those with Romanists, arduous but instructive, as relating rather to matters of fact.

These last remarks throw some light on the characteristic difference of system between Protestantism and Romanism, as well as of argumentative basis. Our controversy with Romanists turns more upon facts than upon first principles; with Protestant sectaries it is more about principles than about facts. This general contrast between the two religions, which I would not seem to extend beyond what the sober truth warrants, for the sake of an antithesis, is paralleled in the common remark of our most learned controversialists, that Romanism *holds the foundation,* or *is the truth overlaid with corruptions.* This is saying the same thing in other words. They discern in it the great outlines of primitive Christianity, but they find them touched, if nothing worse, touched and tainted by error, and so made dangerous to the multitude — dangerous except to men of spiritual minds, who can undo the evil, arresting the tendencies of the system by their own purity and restoring it to the sweetness and freshness of its original state. The very force of the word *corruption* implies that this is the peculiarity of Romanism. All error indeed of whatever kind may be called a corruption of the truth; still we properly apply the term to such kinds of error as are not denials but perversions, distortions, or excesses of it. Such is the relation of Roman-

1. [ED.] On this point Newman calls attention to a section of an article on "Church Matters," *British Magazine,* IX (1836), 327 f.

ism towards true Catholicity. It is the misdirection and abuse, not the absence of right principle. To take a familiar illustration: rashness and cowardice are both faults, and both unlike true courage; but cowardice implies the absence of the principle of courage, whereas rashness is but the extravagance of the principle. Again, prodigality and avarice are both vices, and unlike true and wise liberality; but avarice differs from it in principle, prodigality in matters of detail, in the time, place, person, manner of giving, and the like. On the other hand, prodigality may accidentally be the more dangerous extreme, as being the more subtle vice, the more popular, the more likely to attract noble minds, the more like a virtue. This is somewhat like the position of Romanism, Protestantism, and Catholic truth, relatively to each other. Romanism is an unnatural and misshapen development of the truth; not the less dangerous because it retains traces of its genuine features, and usurps its name, as vice borrows the name of virtue, as pride is often called self-respect, or cowardice or worldly wisdom goes by the name of prudence, or rashness by that of courage. On the other hand, no one would ever call a miser liberal; and so no one would call a mere Protestant a Catholic, except an altogether new sense was put on the word to suit a purpose. Romanism has the principle of true Catholicism perverted; popular Protestantism is wanting in the principle. Lastly, virtue lies in a mean, is a point, almost invisible to the world, hard to find, acknowledged but by the few; and so Christian truth in these latter ages, when the world has broken up the Church, has been but a stranger upon earth, and has been hidden and superseded by counterfeits.

The same view of Romanism is implied when we call our ecclesiastical changes in the sixteenth century a Reformation. A building has not been reformed or repaired when it has been pulled down and built up again; but the word is used when it has been left substantially what it was before, only amended or restored in detail. In like manner, we Anglo-Catholics do not profess a different religion from the Romanists, we profess their faith *all but* their corruptions.[2]

Again, this same character of Romanism as a perversion, not a contradiction of Christian truth, is confessed as often as members of our Church in controversy with it contend, as they may rightly do, that it must be

2. [ED.] In a note Newman appeals to Canon 30 of 1604, according to which the English Church departed from "the Churches of Italy, France, Spain, Germany, or any such like Churches," *only* "in those particular points, wherein they were fallen both from themselves in their ancient integrity, and from the apostolical Churches, which were their first founders."

judged, not by the formal decrees of the Council of Trent, as its advocates are fond of doing, but by its practical working and its existing state
in the countries which profess it. Romanists would fain confine us in
controversy to the consideration of the bare and acknowledged principles of their Church; we consider this to be an unfair restriction; why?
because we conceive that Romanism is far more faulty in its details than
in its formal principles, and that councils, to which its adherents would
send us, have more to do with its abstract system than with its practical
working, that the abstract system contains for the most part *tendencies*
to evil, which the actual working brings out, thus supplying illustrations
of that evil which is really though latently contained in principles capable
in themselves of an honest interpretation. Thus, for instance, the decree
concerning purgatory [3] might be charitably made almost to conform to
the doctrine of St. Austin or St. Chrysostom, were it not for the comment
on it afforded by the popular belief as existing in those countries which
hold it, and by the opinions of the Roman schools.

It is something to the purpose also to observe that this peculiar character of Romanism, as being substantial truth corrupted, has tended to
strengthen the popular notion that it, or the Church of Rome, or the
Pope or Bishop of Rome, is the Antichrist foretold in Scripture. That
there is in Romanism something very unchristian, I fully admit, or rather
maintain; but I will observe here that this strange twofold aspect of the
Roman system seems in matter of fact to have been in part a cause of its
retaining that fearful title — and in this way. When Protestants have
come to look at it closely, they have found truth and error united in so
subtle a combination (as is the case with all corruptions, as with sullied
snow, or fruit overripe, or metal alloyed), they have found truth so
impregnated with error, and error so sheltered by truth, so much too
adducible in defence of the system, which, from want of learning or
other cause, they could not refute without refuting their own faith and
practice at the same time, so much in it of high and noble principle, or
salutary usage, which they had lost, and, as losing, were, in this respect,
in an inferior state, that for this very reason, as the readiest, safest,
simplest solution of their difficulties, not surely the fairest, but the
readiest, as cutting the knot and extricating them at once from their
position, they have pronounced Romanism to be the Antichrist; I say,
for the very reason that so much may be said for it, that it is so difficult
to refute, so subtle and crafty, so seductive — properties which are

3. [ED.] *I.e.*, the definition of the Council of Trent.

tokens of the hateful and fearful deceiver who is to come.[4] Of course I do not mean to say that this perplexing aspect of Romanism has originally brought upon it the stigma under consideration; but that it has served to induce people indolently to acquiesce in it without examination.

In these remarks on the relation which Romanism bears to Catholic truth, I have appealed to the common opinion of the world; which is altogether confirmed when we come actually to compare together the doctrinal articles of our own and of the Roman faith. In both systems the same creeds are acknowledged. Besides other points in common, we both hold that certain doctrines are necessary to be believed for salvation; we both believe in the doctrines of the Trinity, incarnation, and atonement; in original sin; in the necessity of regeneration; in the supernatural grace of the sacraments; in the apostolical succession; in the obligation of faith and obedience, and in the eternity of future punishment.

In conclusion I would observe that I have been speaking of Romanism, not as an existing political sect among us, but considered in itself, in its abstract system, and in a state of quiescence. Viewed indeed in action, and as realized in its present partisans, it is but one out of the many denominations which are the disgrace of our age and country. In temper and conduct it does but resemble that unruly Protestantism which lies on our other side, and it submits without reluctance to be allied and to act with it towards the overthrow of a purer religion. But herein is the difference of the one extreme from the other: the political Romanist of the day becomes such in spite of his fundamental principles; the political Protestant, in accordance with his. The best Dissenter is he who is least of a Dissenter; the best Roman Catholic is he who comes nearest to a Catholic. The reproach of the present Romanists is that they are inconsistent; and it is a reproach which is popularly felt to be just. They are confessedly unlike the loyal men who rallied round the throne of our first Charles, or who fought, however ill-advisedly, for his exiled descendants. The particular nature of this inconsistency will be discussed in some following lectures;[5] meanwhile I have here considered Romanism in its abstract professions for two reasons. First, I would willingly believe that in spite of the violence and rancour of its public supporters,

4. Cf. Edward Bickersteth, "Introductory Remarks on the Progress of Popery" [The Testimony of the Reformers, 1st ser. (London, 1836)], xvii–xx, lii.

5. [ED.] Cf. Lecture II below, and Lectures III–IV in J. H. Newman, Lectures on the Prophetical Office of the Church (London, 1837), 102–53.

there are many individuals in its communion of gentle, affectionate, and deeply religious minds; and such a belief is justified when we find that the *necessary* difference between us and them is not one of essential principle, that it is the difference of superstition, and not of unbelief, from religion. Next, I have insisted upon it, by way of showing what must be the nature of their Reformation, if in God's merciful counsels a Reformation awaits them. It will be far more a reform of their popular usages and opinions, and ecclesiastical policy, or a destruction of what is commonly called Popery, than of their abstract principles and maxims.

On the other hand, let it not be supposed because I have spoken without sympathy for popular Protestantism in the abstract, that this is all one with being harsh towards individuals professing it; far from it. The worse their creed, the more sympathy is due to their persons; chiefly to those, for they most demand and will most patiently suffer it, who least concur in their own doctrine, and are held by it in an unwilling captivity. Would that they would be taught that their peculiar form of religion, whatever it is, never can satisfy their souls, and does not admit of reform, but must come to nought! Would that they could be persuaded to transfer their misplaced and most unrequited affection from the systems of men to the one Holy Spouse of Christ, the Church Catholic, which in this country manifests herself in the Church commonly so called as her representative! Nor need we despair that as regards many of them this wish may yet be fulfilled.

Lecture II:
On Romanism as Neglectful of Antiquity [1]

We differ from the Romanists, as I have said, more in our view of historical facts than in principles; but in saying this, I am speaking, not of their actual system, nor of their actual mode of defending it, but of their professions, professions which in their mouths are mere professions, while they are truths in ours. The principles, professed by both parties, are at once the foundation of our own theology and what is called an *argumentum ad hominem* against theirs. They profess to appeal to primitive Christianity; we honestly take their ground, as holding it ourselves; but when the controversy grows animated, and descends into details, they suddenly leave it and desire to finish the dispute on some other

1. [ED.] Several passages (chiefly long quotations) are omitted from the text of this lecture, and Newman's longer notes are replaced by editorial summaries.

field. In like manner in their teaching and acting, they begin as if in the name of all the Fathers at once, but will be found in the sequel to prove, instruct, and enjoin simply in their own name. Our differences from them, considered not in theory but in fact, are in no sense matters of detail and questions of degree. In truth, there is a tenet in their theology which assumes quite a new position in relation to the rest, when we pass from the abstract and quiescent theory to the practical workings of the system. The infallibility of the existing Church is then found to be its first principle, whereas, before, it was a necessary, but a secondary, doctrine. Whatever principles they profess in theory, resembling or coincident with our own, yet when they come to particulars, when they have to prove this or that article of their creed, they supersede the appeal to Scripture and antiquity by the pretence of the infallibility of the Church, thus solving the whole question by a summary and final interpretation both of antiquity and of Scripture.

This is what takes place in the actual course of the controversy. At the same time it is obvious that, while they are as yet but engaged in tracing out their elementary principles and recommending them to our notice, they cannot assign to this influential doctrine the same sovereign place in their system. It cannot be taken for granted as a first principle in the controversy; if so, nothing remains to be proved and the controversy is at an end, for every doctrine is contained in it by implication, and no doctrine but might as fairly be assumed as a first principle also. Accordingly, in order to make a show of proving it, its advocates must necessarily fall back upon some more intelligible doctrine; and that is, the authority of antiquity, to which they boldly appeal, as I described in my last lecture. It follows that there is a striking dissimilarity, or even inconsistency, between their system as quiescent, and as in action, in its abstract principles, and its reasonings and discussions on particular points. In the Creed of Pope Pius not a word is said expressly about the Church's infallibility; it forms no article of faith there. Her interpretation, indeed, of Scripture is recognized as authoritative; but so also is the "unanimous consent of Fathers." [2] But when we put aside the creeds and professions of our opponents for their actual teaching and disputing, they will be found to care very little for the Fathers, whether as primitive or as concordant; they believe the existing Church to be infallible, and if ancient belief is at variance with it, which of course they do not allow, but if

2. [ED.] *Cf.* H. Denzinger, ed., *Enchiridion Symbolorum*, 23rd ed. (Fribourg, 1937), 346–49: "Professio fidei Tridentina."

it is, then antiquity must be mistaken; that is all. Thus Romanism, which even in its abstract system must be considered a perversion or distortion of the truth, is in its actual and public manifestation a far more serious error. It is then a disproportionate or monstrous development of a theory in itself extravagant. I propose now to give some illustration of it, thus considered, viz., to show that in fact it substitutes the authority of the Church for that of antiquity.

First, let us understand what is meant by saying that antiquity is of authority in religious questions. Both Romanists and ourselves maintain as follows: that whatever doctrine the primitive ages unanimously attest, whether by consent of Fathers, or by councils, or by the events of history, or by controversies, or in whatever way, whatever may fairly and reasonably be considered to be the universal belief of those ages, is to be received as coming from the apostles. This canon, as it may be called, rests upon the principle, which we act on daily, that what many independent and competent witnesses guarantee, is true. The concordant testimony of the Church Catholic to certain doctrines, such as the incarnation, is an argument in its behalf the same in kind as that for the being of a God, derived from the belief of all nations in an intelligent providence. If it be asked why we do not argue in this way from the existing as well as from the ancient Church, we answer that Christendom now differs from itself in all points except those in which it is already known to have agreed of old; so that we cannot make use of it if we would. So far, then, as it can be used, it is but a confirmation of antiquity; though a valuable one. Besides, the greater is the interval between a given age and that of the apostles, and the more intimate the connexion and influence of country with country, the less can the separate branches of the Church be considered as independent witnesses. In the Roman controversy, then, the witness of a later age would seldom come up to the notion of a Catholic tradition, inasmuch as the various parts of Christendom either would not agree together, or when they did, would not be distinct witnesses. Thus ancient consent is, practically, the only, or main kind of tradition which now remains to us.

The rule or canon which I have been explaining is best known as expressed in the words of Vincentius, of Lérins, in his celebrated treatise upon the tests of heresy and error; viz., that that is to be received as apostolic which has been taught "always, everywhere, and by all." [3] Catholicity, antiquity, and consent of Fathers, is the proper evidence of

3. [ED.] Cf. Vincent of Lérins, *Commonitorium*, 2. See p. 77, n. 16, above.

the fidelity or apostolicity of a professed tradition. Infant baptism, for instance, must have been appointed by the apostles, or we should not find it received so early, so generally, with such a silence concerning its introduction. The Christian faith is dogmatic because it has been so accounted in every church up to this day. The washing of the feet, enjoined in the thirteenth chapter of St. John [Jn. 13:14 f.], is not a necessary rite or a sacrament because it has never been so observed — did Christ or his apostles intend otherwise, it would follow (what is surely impossible) that a new and erroneous view of our Lord's words arose even in the apostles' lifetime, and was from the first everywhere substituted for the true. Again: fabrics for public worship are allowable and fitting under the gospel, though our Lord contrasts worshipping at Jerusalem or Gerizim with worshipping in spirit and truth [Jn. 4:21–24], because they ever have been so esteemed. The sabbatical rest is changed from the Sabbath to the Lord's Day because it has never been otherwise since Christianity was a religion.

It follows that councils or individuals are of authority when we have reason to suppose they are trustworthy informants concerning apostolical tradition. If a council is attended by many bishops from various parts of Christendom, and if they speak one and all the same doctrine, without constraint, and bear witness to their having received it from their fathers, having never heard of any other doctrine, and verily believing it to be apostolic — great consideration is due to its decisions. If, on the other hand, they do not profess to bear witness to a fact, but merely to deduce from Scripture for themselves, besides or beyond what they have received from their fathers, whatever deference is due to them, it is not of that peculiar kind which is contemplated by the rule of Vincentius. In like manner, if some great Christian writer in primitive times, of high character, extensive learning, and ample means of information, attests the universality of a certain doctrine and the absence of all trace of its introduction short of the apostles' age, such a one, though an individual, yet as the spokesman of his generation, will be entitled to especial deference. On the other hand, the most highly gifted and religious persons are liable to error, and are not to be implicitly trusted where they profess to be recording, not a fact, but their own opinion. Christians know no master on earth [Mt. 23:8–10]; they defer, indeed, to the judgment, obey the advice, and follow the example of good men in ten thousand ways, but they do not make their opinions part of what is emphatically called the faith. Christ alone is the Author and Finisher of faith [Heb.

12:2] in all its senses; his servants do but witness it, and their statements are then only valuable when they are testimonies, not deductions or conjectures. When they speak about points of faith of themselves, and much more when they are at variance with Catholic antiquity, we can bear to examine and even condemn the uncertain or the erroneous opinion. Thus Pope Gregory might advocate a doctrine resembling purgatory; St. Gregory Nyssen may have used language available in defence of transubstantiation; St. Ephraim may have invoked the Virgin; St. Austin might believe in the irrespective predestination of individuals; St. Cyril might afford a handle to Eutyches; Tertullian might be a Montanist; Origen might deny the eternity of future punishment; yet all such instances, whatever be their weight, from other circumstances, not professing to be more than expressions of private opinion, have no weight at all, one way or other, in the argument from Catholic tradition. In like manner, universality, of course, proves nothing if it is traceable to an origin short of apostolic, whether to existing influences from without, or to some assignable point of time. Whatever judgment is to be formed of a certain practice or doctrine, be it right or wrong, and on whatever grounds, at any rate it is not part or adjunct of the faith, but must be advocated on its intrinsic propriety, or usefulness, or, if tenable, is binding in duty only on particular persons or parties, ages or countries, if its history resembles that of the secular establishment of the Church, or of monachism, or of putting to death for religious opinions, or of sprinkling in baptism, or of the denial of the cup to the laity, or of ecclesiastical liberty, or of the abolition of slavery, subjects which I do not, of course, put on a footing with each other, but name together as being one and all external to that circle of religious truth which the apostles sealed with their own signature as the gospel faith, and delivered over to the Church after them.

But here it may be asked, whether it is possible accurately to know the limits of that faith, from the peculiar circumstances in which it was first spread, which hindered it from being realized in the first centuries in its complete proportions. It may be conjectured, for instance, that the doctrine of what is familiarly called "Church and King" is apostolic, except that it could not be developed while a heathen and persecuting power was sovereign. This is true; and hence a secondary argument is derivable from ancient consent in any doctrine, even when it does not *appeal* to traditionary reception; viz., on the principle that what an early age held universally must at least in spirit have been unconsciously transmitted from the apostles, if there is no reason against it, and must be the due expression of their mind and wishes, under changed circumstances, and therefore is binding on us in piety, though not part of the faith. The same consideration applies to the interpretation of Scripture; but this is to enter on a distinct branch of the subject, to which I shall advert hereafter.[4]

In the foregoing remarks I have not been attempting any systematic discussion of the arguments from antiquity, which is unnecessary for our present purpose, but have said just so much as may open a way for illustrating the point in hand, viz., the disrespect shown towards it by Romanists. In theory, indeed, and in their professions, as has already been noticed, they defer to the authority of the rule of Vincent as implicitly as we do; and commonly without much hazard, for Protestantism in general has so transgressed it that, little as it tells for Rome, it tells still more against the wild doctrines which go under that name. Besides, Romanists are obliged to maintain it by their very pretensions to be considered the one true Catholic and Apostolic Church. At the same time there is this remarkable difference, even of theory, between them and Vincentius, that the latter is altogether silent on the subject of the Pope's infallibility, whether considered as an attribute of his see, or as attaching to him in general council. If Vincentius had the sentiments and feelings of a modern Romanist, it is incomprehensible that, in a treatise written to guide the private Christian in matters of faith, he should have said not a word about the Pope's supreme authority, nay, not even about the infallibility of the Church Catholic. He refers the inquirer to a triple rule, difficult, surely, and troublesome to use, compared with that which is ready furnished by Romanism. Applying his own rule to his work itself, we may unhesitatingly conclude that the Pope's supreme authority in matters of faith is no Catholic or Apostolic truth because he was ignorant of it.

However, Romanists are obliged by their professions to appeal to antiquity, and they therefore do so. But enough has been said already to suggest that, where men are indisposed towards such an appeal, where they determine to be captious and take exceptions, and act the disputant and sophist rather than the earnest inquirer, it admits of easy evasion, and may be made to conclude anything or nothing. The rule of Vincent is not of a mathematical or demonstrative character, but moral, and re-

4. [ED.] Cf. J. H. Newman, *Lectures on the Prophetical Office of the Church* (London, 1837), Lecture XI: "On Scripture as the Record of Faith."

quires practical judgment and good sense to apply it. For instance: What is meant by being "taught *always*"? Does it mean in every century, or every year, or every month? Does "*everywhere*" mean in every country, or in every diocese? And does "the *consent of Fathers*" require us to produce the direct testimony of every one of them? How many Fathers, how many places, how many instances constitute a fulfilment of the test proposed? It is, then, from the nature of the case, a condition which never can be satisfied as fully as it might have been; it admits of various and unequal application in various instances; and what degree of application is enough must be decided by the same principles which guide us in the conduct of life, which determine us in politics, or trade, or war, which lead us to accept Revelation at all, for which we have but probability to show at most; nay, to believe in the existence of an intelligent Creator. This character, indeed, of Vincent's canon, will but recommend it to the disciples of the school of Butler, from its agreement with the analogy of nature; but it affords a ready loophole for such as do not wish to be persuaded, of which both Protestants and Romanists are not slow to avail themselves.

Here, however, we are concerned with the Romanists. For instance: if some passage from one of the Fathers contradicts their present doctrine, and it is then objected that what even one early writer directly contradicted in his day was not Catholic at the time he contradicted it, they unhesitatingly condemn the passage as unsound and mistaken. And then follows the question, is the writer in question to be credited as reporting the current views of his age, or had he the hardihood, though he knew them well, to contradict, yet without saying he contradicted them? — and this can only be decided by the circumstances of the case, which an ingenious disputant may easily turn this way or that. They proceed in the same way, though a number of authorities be produced; one is misinterpreted, another is put out of sight, a third is admitted but undervalued. This is not said by way of accusation here, though of course it is a heavy charge against the Romanists; nor with the admission that their attempts are successful, for, after all, words have a distinct meaning in spite of sophistry, and there is a true and a false in every matter. I am but showing *how* Romanists reconcile their abstract reverence for antiquity with their Romanism — with their creed and their notion of the Church's infallibility in declaring it; how small their success is, and how great their unfairness, is another question. Whatever judgment we form either of their conduct or its issue, such is the fact, that they extol the Fathers as a whole and disparage them individually; they call them one by one Doctors of the Church, yet they explain away one by one their arguments, judgment, and testimony. They refuse to combine their separate and coincident statements; they take each by himself, and settle with the first before they go on to the next. And thus their boasted reliance on the Fathers comes, at length, to this — to identify Catholicity with the decrees of councils, and to admit those councils only which the Pope has confirmed.

Such is that peculiarity of Romanism which is now to be illustrated; and with this purpose I will first quote one or two passages from writers of authority, by way of showing the abstract reverence in which Romanism holds the Fathers, and then show from others how little they carry it into practice.

Bossuet, in his celebrated *Exposition,* thus speaks:

> The Catholic Church, far from wishing to become absolute mistress of her faith, as it is laid to her charge, has, on the contrary, done everything in her power to tie up her own hands, and to deprive herself of the means of innovation; for she not only submits to the Scripture, but in order to banish for ever these arbitrary interpretations, which would substitute the whims of men for the word of God, she hath bound herself to interpret it, in what concerns faith and morality, according to the sense of the holy Fathers, from which she professes never to depart; declaring by all her councils, and by all her professions of faith, that she receives no dogma whatever that is not conformable to the tradition of all preceding ages.[5]

[Newman then proceeds to quote from John Milner (1752–1826), a popular Roman Catholic apologist, and from St. Robert Bellarmine (1542–1621), the great Jesuit controversialist.[6]]

Let us now proceed from the theory of the Roman Church to its practice. This is seen in the actual conduct of its theologians, some of whom shall here be cited as a sample of the whole.

First, I refer to the well-known occasion of Bishop Bull's writing his *Defence of the Nicene Faith.*[7] He was led to do so by an attack upon the orthodoxy of the Ante-Nicene Fathers from a quarter whence it was

5. [ED.] Jacques-Bénigne Bossuet, *Exposition de la doctrine de l'Eglise catholique sur les matières de controverse, Oeuvres* (Paris, 1877), I, 736.

6. [ED.] The passages quoted by Newman will be found in J. Milner, *The End of Religious Controversy* (London, 1843), 150, 168 (Letters XI–XII); and in R. Bellarmine, *De Verbo Dei,* III, 10; *De Purgatorio,* I, 15 (*Opera Omnia* [Naples, 1856–62], I, 114; II, 384).

7. [ED.] G. Bull, *Defensio Fidei Nicaenae* (Oxford, 1851–52).

at first sight little to be expected. The learned assailant was not an Arian, or Socinian, or Latitudinarian, but Petavius, a member of the Jesuit body. The tendency of the portion of his great work on *Theological Doctrines* [8] which treats of the Trinity is too plain to be mistaken. The historian Gibbon does not scruple to pronounce that its "object, or at least, effect," was "to arraign," and as he considers, successfully, "the faith of the Ante-Nicene Fathers"; [9] and it was used in no long time by Arian writers in their own justification. Thus, Romanist, heretic, and infidel unite with one another in this instance in denying the orthodoxy of the first centuries, just as at this moment the same three parties are banded together to oppose ourselves. We trust we see in this circumstance an omen of our own resemblance to the primitive Church, since we hold a common position with it towards these parties, and are in the centre point, as of doctrine, so of attack. But to return to Petavius. This learned author, in his elaborate work on the Trinity, shows that he would rather prove the early confessors and martyrs to be heterodox than that they should exist as a court of appeal from the decisions of his own Church; and he accordingly sacrifices, without remorse, Justin, Clement, Irenaeus, and their brethren to the maintenance of the infallibility of Rome. Or to put the matter in another point of view, truer, perhaps, though less favourable still to Petavius — he consents that the Catholic doctrine of the Holy Trinity should so far rest on the mere declaration of the Church, that before it was formally defined, there was no heresy in rejecting it, provided he can thereby gain for Rome the freedom of making decrees unfettered by the recorded judgments of antiquity. This it was which excited the zeal of our great theologian, Bishop Bull, whom I will here quote, both in order to avail myself of his authority, and because of the force and clearness of his remarks.

[A long quotation follows from Bull's vigorous attack, in the introduction to his *Defensio*, on Petavius' presumed "underhand purpose." [10]]

8. [ED.] The massive work of Dionysius Petavius (Denys Pétau), *De Theologicis Dogmatibus*, first published in 1644–50 and often reprinted, was a pioneering study of dogmatic history read in the light of a theory of development. Although Newman had studied Petavius, his own theory of doctrinal development, first advanced in a sermon on February 2, 1843 (Newman, *Fifteen Sermons Preached before the University of Oxford*, 3d ed. [London, 1872], 312–51), seems to have been worked out independently. *Cf.* O. Chadwick, *From Bossuet to Newman: The Idea of Doctrinal Development* (Cambridge, 1957), 122–24.

9. [ED.] E. Gibbon, *The History of the Decline and Fall of the Roman Empire* (London, 1909), II, 363 n.

10. [ED.] Bull, *Defensio Fidei Nicaenae*, I, 9–12 (abbrev.).

So remarkable an instance as this is not of every day's occurrence. I do not mean to say there have been many such systematic and profound attempts as this on the part of Petavius, at what may be justly called parricide. Rome even, steeled as she is against the kindlier feelings when her interests require, has more of tender mercy left than to bear them often. In this very instance, the French Church indirectly showed their compunction at the crime, on Bull's subsequent defence of the Nicene Anathema, by transmitting to him, through Bossuet, the congratulations of the whole clergy of France assembled at St. Germain's, for the service he had rendered to the Church Catholic. However, not even the Gallican Church, moderate as she confessedly has been, can side with Rome without cooling in loyalty towards the primitive ages; as will appear by the following remarks extracted from the Benedictine edition of St. Ambrose. The Benedictines of St. Maur are, as is well known, of a school of Romanism distinct from the Jesuits, to whom Petavius belonged. So much so that the Benedictine edition of Bossuet's works is accused of Jansenism, at least so I understand the English editor of his *Exposition,* who speaks of its being "infected with the spirit of that sect which disfigures everything that it touches." [11] Their learning and candour are well known; and one can hardly accuse those who spend their lives in an act of ministration towards the holy Fathers, of any intentional irreverence towards them. The following passage occurs in their introduction to one of the works of St. Ambrose, on occasion of that Father making some statements at variance with the present Roman views of the intermediate state:

> It is not indeed wonderful that Ambrose should have written in this way concerning the state of souls; but what seems almost incredible is the uncertainty and inconsistency of the holy Fathers on the subject, *from the very times of the apostles* to the pontificate of Gregory XI and the Council of Florence; that is, *for almost the whole of fourteen centuries.* For they not only differ from one another, *as ordinarily happens in such questions before the Church has defined,* but they are even inconsistent with themselves, sometimes allowing, sometimes denying to the same souls the enjoyment of the clear vision of the divine nature.[12]

It may be asked, how it is the fault of the Benedictines if the Fathers are inconsistent with each other and with themselves in any point; and

11. [ED.] Newman cites the long excursus on Jansenism in W. Palmer, *A Treatise on the Church of Christ,* 3d ed. (London, 1842), I, 244–63.
12. "Admonitio" on Ambrose, *De Bono Mortis* [PL, XIV, 561 f.].

what harm there is in stating the fact, if it is undeniable. But my complaint with them would be on a different ground, viz., that they profess to know better than the Fathers; that they, or rather the religious system which they are bound to follow, consider questions to be determinable on which the early Fathers were ignorant, and suppose the Church is so absolutely the author of our faith that what the Fathers did not believe, we must believe under pain of forfeiting heaven. Whether Rome be right or wrong, this instance contains an acknowledgment, as far as it goes, that her religion is not that of the Fathers; that her creed is as novel as those Protestant extravagancies from which in other respects it is so far removed.

[Newman turns next to Bellarmine, to whose ability and honesty he pays a generous tribute.[13] He summarizes two passages in which Bellarmine, while quoting twenty-two Fathers in support of the idea of a purgatorial fire, had noted the vagueness of the patristic teaching in comparison with the explicit statement of the Council of Trent.[14]]

Now, do I mean to accuse so serious and good a man as Bellarmine of wilful unfairness in this procedure? No. Yet it is difficult to enter into the state of mind under which he was led into it. However we explain it, so much is clear, that the Fathers are only so far of use in the eyes of Romanists as they prove the Roman doctrines; and in no sense are allowed to interfere with the conclusions which their Church has adopted; that they are of authority when they seem to agree with Rome, of none if they differ. But, if I may venture to account in Bellarmine's own person for what is in controversy confessedly unfair, I would observe as follows, though what I say may seem to border on refinement.

A Romanist then cannot really argue in defence of the Roman doctrines; he has too firm a confidence in their truth, if he is sincere in his profession, to enable him critically to adjust the due weight to be given to this or that evidence. He assumes his Church's conclusion as true; and the facts or witnesses he adduces are rather brought to receive an interpretation than to furnish a proof. His highest aim is to show the mere consistency of his theory, its possible adjustment with the records of antiquity. I am not here inquiring how much of high but misdirected moral feeling is implied in this state of mind; certainly as we advance

---

13. [ED.] Newman quotes several Protestant commendations of Bellarmine, including J. L. von Mosheim, *An Ecclesiastical History, Ancient and Modern* (London, 1819), IV, 222.

14. [ED.] Bellarmine, *De Purgatorio*, I, 10; II, 1 (*Opera Omnia*, II, 373, 385 f.).

in perception of the truth, we all become less fitted to be controversialists.

   If this be the true explanation of Bellarmine's strange error, the more
it tends to exculpate him, the more deeply it criminates his system. He
ceases to be chargeable with unfairness only in proportion as the notion
of the infallibility of Rome is admitted to be the sovereign and engross-
ing tenet of his communion, the foundation stone, or (as it may be
called) the fulcrum of its theology. I consider, then, that when he first
adduces the above-mentioned Fathers in proof of purgatory, he was
really but interpreting them; he was teaching what they ought to mean
— what *in charity* they must be supposed to mean — what they *might*
mean, as far as the very words went — *probably* meant, *considering* the
Church so meant — and might be taken to mean, even if their authors did
not so mean, from the notion that they spoke vaguely, and, as children,
that they really meant something else than what they formally said, and
that, after all, they were but the spokesmen of the then existing Church,
which, though in silence, certainly held, as being the Church, that same
doctrine which Rome has since defined and published. This is to treat
Bellarmine with the same charity with which he has on this supposition
treated the Fathers, and it is to be hoped with a nearer approach to the
matter of fact. So much as to his first use of them; but afterwards, in
noticing what he considers erroneous opinions on the subject, he treats
them not as organs of the Church infallible, but as individuals, and interprets their language by its literal sense, or by the context, and in
consequence condemns it. The Fathers in question, he seems to say, really
held as modern Rome holds; for if they did not, they must have dissented from the Church of their own day; for the Church then
held as modern Rome holds. And the Church then held as Rome holds
now, because Rome is the Church, and the Church ever holds the same.
How hopeless then is it to contend with Romanists, as if they practically agreed with us as to the foundation of faith, however much they
pretend to it! Ours is antiquity, theirs, the existing Church. Its infallibility is their first principle; belief in it is a deep prejudice quite beyond
the reach of anything external. It is quite clear that the combined testimonies of all the Fathers, supposing such a case, would not have a feather's
weight against a decision of the Pope in council, nor would matter at all,
except for the Fathers' sake who had by anticipation opposed it. They
consider that the Fathers ought to mean what Rome has since decreed,

and that Rome knows their meaning better than they themselves did. That venturesome Church has usurped their place, and thinks it merciful only not to banish outright the rivals she has dethroned. By an act, as it were, of grace, she has determined that when they contradict her, though not available as witnesses against her, yet as living in times of ignorance, they are only heterodox and not heretical; and she keeps them around her to ask their advice when it happens to agree with her own.

Let us then understand the position of the Romanists towards us; they do not really argue from the Fathers, though they seem to do so. They may affect to do so in our behalf, happy if by an innocent stratagem they are able to convert us; but all the while in their own feelings they are taking a far higher position. They are teaching, not disputing or proving. They are interpreting what is obscure in antiquity, purifying what is alloyed, correcting what is amiss, perfecting what is incomplete, harmonizing what is various. They claim and use all its documents as ministers and organs of that one infallible Church, which once forsooth kept silence, but since has spoken; which by a divine gift must ever be consistent with herself, and which bears with her, her own evidence of divinity.[15]

I have said enough perhaps to illustrate the subject in hand; yet various instances shall be added, which are noticed by our divines in the controversy. They are from such and so various quarters, as make them fair samples of the system.[16]

Cardinal Fisher, Bishop of Rochester, who suffered death during the troubles in King Henry VIII's reign, is a man, as readers of our history know, of no ordinary name. He is supposed to have assisted Henry in his work against Luther, and while in prison received a cardinal's hat from the Pope. He surely is as fair a specimen of the Roman controversialist as could be taken. Now in one of his works against Luther, he thus speaks on the subject of indulgences and purgatory:

15. A learned friend to whom I am indebted for other hints, has observed to me that in like manner, as regards the canon law, while Romanists give up, nay freely censure and even insinuate the appearance of dishonesty in Gratian's professed quotations from the Fathers [in his *Decretum*], they do not scruple to avail themselves of his authority when it suits their purpose, and to quote those decisions as valid which depend on the quotations they themselves have elsewhere surrendered.

16. [ED.] For quotations from Cardinal Cajetan, Maldonatus, and Bellarmine, Newman draws on Edward Stillingfleet, *A Rational Account of the Grounds of Protestant Religion* (Oxford, 1844), I, 233–35, and Jeremy Taylor, *A Dissuasive from Popery*, Pt. II, Introduction (*Works* [London, 1822], X, 320, 322).

There are many things, about which no question was agitated in
the primitive Church, which, by the diligence of posterity, when
doubts had arisen, have now become clear. No orthodox believer,
certainly, *now* doubts whether there be a purgatory. Whoever will
read the commentaries of the old Greeks, he will find *no mention*,
as I think, or as little as possible, concerning purgatory. Nor did
the Latins, all at once, and without effort, apprehend the truth of
this matter. For faith, whether in purgatory or in indulgences, was
not so necessary in the primitive Church as now. For then love so
burned, that everyone was ready to meet death for Christ. Crimes
were rare: and such as occurred, were avenged by the great severity of the canons. Now, however, a good part of the people
would rather burn Christianity itself, than bear the rigour of the
canons; so that it was not without the especial providence of the
Holy Spirit, that *after the lapse of so many years*, belief in purgatory and the use of indulgences was generally received by the
orthodox. As long as there was no care of purgatory, no one sought
for indulgences. For the consideration of indulgences depends entirely on it. If you take away purgatory, what is the use of indulgences? for we should not need these, but for it. By considering,
then, that purgatory was for some time unknown, and then believed by certain persons, *by degrees*, partly from revelations,[17]
partly from the Scriptures, and so at length, that faith in it became
firmly and generally received by the orthodox Church, we shall
most easily form our view of indulgences.[18]

[Newman then cites further instances of Roman Catholic criticism of
the Fathers, dwelling at some length on Miguel de Medina's charge that
Jerome and other Fathers followed Aerius in denying the essential distinction between bishops and presbyters.[19]]

It is not surprising, with these sentiments, that Romanists should have
undertaken before now to suppress and correct portions of the Fathers'
writings. An edition of St. Austin published at Venice contains the following most suspicious confession: "Besides the recovery of many passages by collation with ancient copies, we have taken care to *remove
whatever might infect the minds of the faithful* with heretical pravity,
or turn them aside from the Catholic and orthodox faith." [20] And a
corrector of the press at Lyons, of the middle of the sixteenth century,

---

17. [ED.] *E.g.*, the "revelations" of St. Catherine of Genoa (1447–1510).
18. John Fisher, *Assertionis Lutheranae Confutatio* [Antwerp, 1523], art. 18.
19. [ED.] Newman bases his account of Medina on Bellarmine, *De Clericis*, I, 15
(*Opera Omnia*, II, 171).
20. [ED.] *Cf.* Taylor, *Dissuasive from Popery*, Pt. II, Bk. I, 6 (*Works*, X, 497).

complains that he was obliged by certain Franciscans to cancel various passages of St. Ambrose, whose works he was engaged upon.[21]

The Council of Constance furnishes us with a memorable instance of the same disregard for antiquity, to which the whole Roman Communion is committed, in the decree by which it formally debars the laity from the participation of the cup in the Lord's Supper. There is no need here of entering into the defence put forward by Romanists, as if the Church had a certain discretion committed to her in the administration of the sacraments, and used it in this prohibition, as in the substitution of affusion for immersion in baptism. Even allowing this for argument's sake, the question simply is, whether the spirit of the following passage is one of reverence for antiquity.

> Whereas (says the council) in certain parts of the world, some temerariously presume to affirm, that the Christian people ought to receive the holy sacrament of the Eucharist, under both kinds of bread and wine, and do everywhere make the laity communicate not only in bread but in wine also, and pertinaciously assert that communion should take place after supper, or else not fasting, contrary to the laudable and reasonable custom of the Church, which they damnably endeavour to reprobate as sacrilegious, this present holy General Council of Constance, legitimately assembled in the Holy Ghost, being anxious to preserve the faithful from this error, after mature deliberation of persons most learned both in divine and human law, declares, decrees, and defines, that, though Christ instituted this venerable sacrament after supper and administered it to his disciples under both kinds of bread and wine, yet, notwithstanding this, the laudable authority of the sacred canons and the approved custom of the Church has observed and observes, that this sacrament should not be consecrated after supper, nor be received by the faithful unless fasting, except in case of infirmity or other necessity conceded or admitted by right or the Church; and in like manner, that *although in the primitive Church the sacrament was received by the faithful under both kinds*, yet for the avoiding some dangers and scandals, this custom has been reasonably introduced, that it be received by the consecrating persons under both kinds and by the laity only under the bread; since it is to be most firmly believed, and in no wise to be doubted, that the entire body and blood of Christ is truly contained as well under the bread as under the wine.[22]

21. [ED.] Cf. Taylor, *Dissuasive from Popery*, Pt. II, Bk. I, 6 (*Works*, X, 500).
22. [ED.] Council of Constance, Session XIII (J. D. Mansi, *Sacrorum Conciliorum Nova et Amplissima Collectio* [Florence-Venice, 1759-98], XXVII, 727).

The primitive Church, we can believe, has authority as the legitimate expositor of Christ's meaning; she acts not from her own discretion, but from Christ and his apostles. We communicate in the morning, not in the evening, though he did in the evening, because she, his work and pattern to us, was used to do so. For the same reason we baptize infants, and consider the washing the feet no sacrament, though his own words, literally taken, command the latter far more strongly than the former observance. But, what is to be thought of a theology which, on its own authority, on mere grounds of expedience, to avoid dangers and scandals, reverses what itself confesses to be the custom of that Church which came next to the apostles?

[Newman adds an extended reference to the defence of the decree of Constance by Nicholas of Cusa in the second of his *Epistolae ad Bohemos*.[23]]

Lastly, I quote the words of Cornelius Mussus, Bishop of Bitonto, who acted a conspicuous part at the Council of Trent: "I for my part, to speak candidly, would rather credit one Pope in matters touching the faith, than a thousand Augustines, Jeromes, or Gregories." [24]

Before concluding, I would briefly remark that instances such as the foregoing altogether expose the pretence of some Romanists, that the silence of antiquity on the subject of their peculiarities arises from a *disciplina arcani*, as it has been called, or rule of secrecy, which forbade the publication of the more sacred articles of faith to the world at large.[25] For it has now been seen that according to the avowed or implied conviction of their most eminent divines, there is much actually to censure in the writings of the Fathers, much which is positively hostile to the Roman system. No rule of secrecy could lead honest men to make statements diametrically opposite to their real belief, statements which are now the refuge of those who resist what the Romanists consider the real opinion of the men who made them.

I am led to this remark because apprehensions have been felt, I would say causelessly, lest those who admit the existence of this primitive rule, or rather usage, were thereby making some dangerous concession to the Romanists; which it cannot be, if, as the latter avow, the Fathers, not merely fail to mention, but actually contradict the Roman peculiarities.

---

23. [ED.] Cf. Taylor, *Dissuasive from Popery*, Pt. II, Bk. I, 5 (*Works*, X, 485 f.).
24. [ED.] Quoted from Stillingfleet, *Grounds of Protestant Religion*, I, 233.
25. [ED.] For a succinct outline of the history of this idea, *cf.* F. L. Cross, ed., *The Oxford Dictionary of the Christian Church* (London, 1957), 405 f.

But were they only silent respecting them, so as just to admit of the hypothesis of a rule of secrecy of such a nature as these apologists wish, at least this would be inconsistent with Bossuet's boast of the "conditions and restrictions" under which the Church has ever exercised her gift of infallibility. "Far from wishing," he says in a passage already quoted, but which will be now more justly estimated after the specimens since given of his Church's reckless conduct towards the primitive Fathers,

> far from wishing to become absolute mistress of her faith, as is laid to her charge, she has on the contrary *done everything in her power to tie up her own hands, and deprive herself of the means of innovation;* for she not only submits to Scripture, but in order to banish for ever those arbitrary interpretations, which would substitute the whims of man for the word of God, *she hath bound herself to interpret it,* in what concerns faith and morality, *according to the sense of the holy Fathers, from which she professes never to depart.*[26]

That is, she implicitly obeys an authority which, even on the more favourable supposition, says nothing for, and as the fact really is, earnestly protests against, the course which she ventures to pursue.

I make one remark more. Enough has been said to show the hopefulness of our own prospects in the controversy with Rome. We have her own avowal that the Fathers ought to be followed, and again that she does not follow them; what more can we require than her witness against herself which is here supplied us? If such inconsistency is not at once fatal to her claims, which it would seem to be, at least it is a most encouraging omen in our contest with her. We have but to remain pertinaciously and immovably fixed on the ground of antiquity; and, as truth is ours, so will the victory be also. We have joined issue with her, and that in a point which admits of a decision — of a decision, as she confesses, against herself. Abstract arguments, original views, novel interpretations of Scripture, may be met by similar artifices on the other side; but historical facts are proof against the force of talent, and remain where they were when it has expended itself. How mere Protestants, who rest upon no such solid foundation, are to withstand our common adversary, is not so clear, and not our concern. We would fain make them partakers of our vantage ground; but since they despise it, they must take care of themselves, and must not complain if we refuse to desert a position which promises to be impregnable — impregnable both as against Romanists and against themselves.

26. [ED.] *Cf.* above, p. 134.

JOHN HENRY NEWMAN

Tract Ninety:
Remarks on Certain Passages in the Thirty-nine Articles
(SELECTIONS) [1]

Editor's introduction.

I call the notion of my being a Papist absurd, for it argues an utter ignorance of theology. We have all fallen back from the time of the Restoration in a wonderful way. . . . True it is, every one who by his *own wit* had gone as far as I *from* popular Protestantism, or who had been taught from *without*, not being up to the differences of things, and trained to discrimination, might have been in danger of going further; but no one who either had learned his doctrine *historically* or had tolerable clearness of head could be in more danger than in confusing the sun and moon.

However, I frankly own that if, in some important points, our Anglican ἦθος differs from Popery, in others it is like it, and on the whole far more like it than like Protestantism. So one must expect a revival of the slander or misapprehension in some shape or other. And we shall never be free from it, of course.[2]

In the spring of 1837, when he spoke so confidently from the standpoint of his *Prophetical Office*, Newman seemed completely secure in his Anglican allegiance. In his new book, a trenchant criticism of "popular Protestantism" for its failure to recognize the just claims of Christian antiquity, and a no less forceful and more extended attack on "Romanism" for its practical subordination of the witness of antiquity to

1. The text is printed according to the first edition, but some of the more significant *additions* made in the second edition are given in the footnotes.
2. Anne Mozley, ed., *Letters and Correspondence of John Henry Newman during His Life in the English Church* (New York, 1911), II, 206 f. (Newman to Jemima Mozley, April 25, 1837).

the voice of the contemporary Church, had led to the vindication of the Anglican *via media* as the unique reincarnation of apostolic Christianity. Never, perhaps, had the distinctive *raison d'être* of Anglicanism been so clearly formulated in such exalted and exclusive terms. Yet within a decade the great prophet of the *via media* was to turn finally into another path. "This night," he wrote to the same correspondent on October 8, 1845, "Father Dominic, the Passionist, sleeps here. He does not know of my intention, but I shall ask him to receive me into what I believe to be the One Fold of the Redeemer."[3] Not a little of the interest of the *Tract Ninety* episode lies in its contribution to our understanding of Newman's painful pilgrimage between 1837 and 1845.

The idea of writing on the Thirty-nine Articles did not come abruptly to Newman at the beginning of 1841, but it was only then that the exigencies of controversy drove him to publish his "speculations" on the subject.[4] As long as he was (as he supposed) systematizing the teaching of the "classical" Anglican divines into the theory of the *via media,* he could not take seriously the suggestion that he might find insurmountable difficulties in the official Anglican formularies.[5] In 1839, however, his conviction of the peculiar rightness of the *via media* suddenly collapsed under Roman Catholic attack, and he found himself looking at the Thirty-nine Articles in a new light and seeing awkward problems in them.

Newman's ecclesiology of the *via media* had been founded on three points: "the principle of dogma, the sacramental system, and anti-Romanism."[6] Since he was prepared to admit that the first two points were more effectively safeguarded by Rome than by Canterbury, he obviously had to rest his Anglican apologetic on a comprehensive critique of Roman Catholicism. What happened in 1839 was that he lost confidence in the key principle of his anti-Roman polemic.

> The Anglican disputant [he wrote many years later] took his stand upon Antiquity or Apostolicity, the Roman upon Catholicity. The Anglican said to the Roman: "There is but One Faith, the Ancient, and you have not kept to it"; the Roman retorted: "There is but one Church, the Catholic, and you are out of it."[7]

Given this definition of the issue, Newman had long believed that the final word lay with the Anglican. "Of course," he says, "I contended that the Roman idea of Catholicity was not ancient and apostolic."[8] But

3. *Ibid.,* 419.
4. J. H Newman, *Apologia pro vita sua* (Garden City, N.Y., 1956), 186 f.
5. *Ibid.,* 187. 6. *Ibid.,* 221 f. 7. *Ibid.,* 210. 8. *Ibid.,* 211.

in August 1839 a skilful controversialist unexpectedly turned Newman's chosen weapon of antiquity against him.

"Since I wrote to you," Newman told Frederic Rogers on September 22, 1839, "I have had the first real hit from Romanism which has happened to me. . . . I must confess it has given me a stomach-ache." [9] The "hit" was Nicholas Wiseman's fateful *Dublin Review* article comparing the Church of the *via media*, in its complacent isolation from the rest of Christendom, with the Donatist sect of Roman Africa. In retrospect Newman doubted that the specific reference to Donatism had seriously disturbed him,[10] but it is clear that the implications of the comparison shook him badly. In his theory of the *via media* he had found a "distinctive plea for Anglicanism" [11] — a justification for its insular separation from the great Roman land-mass — in its peculiar purity as a representation of antiquity. But now, as he looked back at antiquity in a new perspective, he seemed to see the prototype of Anglicanism, not in the "great Church" of Saint Athanasius and Saint Leo, of the Nicene Creed and the Chalcedonian Definition, but among Monophysites and other dissidents, who in their own time and their own way had gloried in their distinctive position over against Rome and her allies. Once this comparison was admitted, Anglicans could hardly evade the consequences of Saint Augustine's anti-Donatist dictum that "the wide world is safe in its judgment" of divisiveness.[12] " '*Securus judicat orbis terrarum!*' By those great words of the ancient Father, the theory of the *via media* was absolutely pulverized." [13] "Antiquity," no less than "Catholicity," witnessed against the English Church.

Daunted, but not yet defeated, Newman began to work out another (and much more modest) apologetic for the Church of England. Very significantly, he still assumed that Anglicanism must necessarily be defined with reference to Rome,[14] but his new theory of Anglican-Roman relations was very different from the old. Rome, and not England, had turned out to be the true "Jerusalem," and England was to be vindicated, in so far as vindication was possible, by being cast in the role of "Samaria." [15] It followed that in the new apologetic the anti-Roman aspects

9. Mozley, *Letters and Correspondence of J. H. Newman,* II, 256.
10. Newman, *Apologia,* 218.   11. *Ibid.,* 221.
12. Augustine, *Contra Epistulam Parmeniani,* III, iv, 25 (PL, XLIII, 101).
13. Newman, *Apologia,* 219.
14. *Cf.* T. A. Lacey, *Catholicity* (London, 1914), Appendix B, "Securus Iudicat Orbis Terrarum," 135–49.
15. Newman, *Apologia,* 251.

of the Anglican tradition, of which the theory of the *via media* had made
so much, must be minimized and the basic compatibility of Anglican
with Roman teaching stressed. To that end, Newman undertook to spell
out his view of the history and meaning of the Thirty-nine Articles.

> I had in mind [he explained] to remove all such obstacles as were
> in the way of holding the Apostolic and Catholic character of the
> Anglican teaching; to assert the right of all who chose to say in
> the face of day, "Our Church teaches the Primitive Ancient faith."
> I did not conceal this: in Tract 90, it is put forward as the first
> principle of all, "It is a duty which we owe both to the Catholic
> Church, and to our own, to take our reformed confessions in the
> most Catholic sense they will admit: we have no duties towards
> their framers." [16]

It should be added that in his new enterprise Newman was not simply
concerned to safeguard his own position. His "first real hit from Romanism" coincided with the emergence of a new group of "Tractarians,"
for whose welfare he felt some responsibility.

> A new school of thought was rising, as is usual in such movements,
> and was sweeping the original party of the movement aside, and was
> taking its place. . . . This new party rapidly formed and increased,
> in and out of Oxford, and, as it so happened, contemporaneously
> with that very summer, when I received so serious a blow to my
> ecclesiastical views from the study of the Monophysite contro-
> versy. These men cut into the original Movement at an angle, fell
> across its line of thought, and then set about turning that line in its
> own direction. They were most of them keenly religious men, with
> a true concern for their souls as the first matter of all, with a great
> zeal for me, but giving little certainty at the time as to which way
> they would ultimately turn. [17]

It was above all for the sake of these men, among whom in fact a Rome-
ward tendency clearly predominated, that Newman published *Tract
Ninety*.

Nevertheless, in what he actually wrote he tried to serve the Oxford
Movement as a whole. The new school tended unequivocally to identify
the genuinely "Catholic" with the Roman, and Newman's own thought
was unmistakably moving in the same direction. [18] But there were others,

16. *Ibid.*, 232. Cf. *Tract XC* (Oxford, 1903), 83.   17. Newman, *Apologia*, 259 f.
18. Cf. W. Palmer, *A Narrative of Events connected with the Publication of the
Tracts for the Times*, 2d ed. (London, 1883), 150 n.: "I cannot but remark on the
improper manner in which this term [Catholic] has been used within the last two or
three years [before 1843]. It has become the fashion in some quarters to speak of everything Romish as *Catholic*."

such as Keble and Pusey, who, while they may never have followed Newman in his high-flown claims for the *via media*, were persuaded that the separate existence of the English Church was fully justified in the face of the Roman claims. Again, the new school tended to dismiss the Reformation, English as well as Continental, as an unmitigated disaster, and some early Tractarian opinion could be cited in support of this view.[19] But there were others, such as Pusey among the Tractarians themselves and Hook and Palmer among their conservative High Church friends, who more or less wholeheartedly defended the Reformers. When *Tract Ninety* appeared, on February 27, 1841, it was evident that Newman had tried to take account of these conflicting attitudes.

The result has been called inconsistent,[20] and it certainly was very complex. On the one hand, Newman argued as a matter of principle that the rule requiring a purely "literal and grammatical" interpretation of the Articles made it unnecessary to take the "known opinion of their framers" as a "comment upon their text." [21] On the other hand, he claimed that in fact the authors of the Articles meant to make room for "moderate reformers" who were essentially "Anglo-Catholics." [22] It is tempting to assume that in juxtaposing these arguments he was simply trying to cater to two conflicting schools of thought. It is at least possible, however, that he really knew what he was doing. Both arguments, after all, do point more or less clearly and accurately to aspects of Anglican history apart from which the Oxford Movement would have been inconceivable.

❖ ❖ ❖ ❖

INTRODUCTION

It is often urged, and sometimes felt and granted, that there are in the Articles propositions or terms inconsistent with the Catholic faith; or, at least, when persons do not go so far as to feel the objection as of force, they are perplexed how best to reply to it, or how most simply to explain

19. Cf. *Remains of the late Reverend Richard Hurrell Froude* (London-Derby, 1838–39), I, 393 f.: ". . . Why do you praise Ridley? Do you know sufficient good about him to counterbalance the fact that he was the associate of Cranmer, Peter Martyr, and Bucer?"

20. Cf. Francis Clark, S.J., *Eucharistic Sacrifice and the Reformation* (London, 1960), 27 ff.

21. *Tract XC*, 83.   22. *Ibid.*, 85.

the passages on which it is made to rest. The following tract is drawn up with the view of showing how groundless the objection is, and further of approximating towards the argumentative answer to it, of which most men have an implicit apprehension, though they may have nothing more. That there are real difficulties to a Catholic Christian in the ecclesiastical position of our Church at this day, no one can deny; but the statements of the Articles are not in the number; and it may be right at the present moment to insist upon this. If in any quarter it is supposed that persons who profess to be disciples of the early Church will silently concur with those of very opposite sentiments in furthering a relaxation of subscriptions, which, it is imagined, are galling to both parties, though for different reasons, and that they will do this against the wish of the great body of the Church, the writer of the following pages would raise one voice, at least, in protest against any such anticipation. Even in such points as he may think the English Church deficient, never can he, without a great alteration of sentiment, be party to forcing the opinion or project of one school upon another. Religious changes, to be beneficial, should be the act of the whole body; they are worth little if they are the mere act of a majority.[1] No good can come of any change which is not heartfelt, a development of feelings springing up freely and calmly within the bosom of the whole body itself. Moreover, a change in theological teaching involves either the commission or the confession of sin; it is either the profession or the renunciation of erroneous doctrine, and if it does not succeed in proving the fact of past guilt, it, *ipso facto,* implies present. In other words, every change in religion carries with it its own condemnation, which is not attended by deep repentance. Even supposing then that any changes in contemplation, whatever they were, were good in themselves, they would cease to be good to a church in which they were the fruits, not of the quiet conviction of all, but of the agitation, or tyranny, or intrigue of a few; nurtured, not in mutual love, but in strife and envying; perfected, not in humiliation and grief, but in pride, elation, and triumph. Moreover, it is a very serious truth, that persons and bodies who put themselves into a disadvantageous state cannot at their pleasure extricate themselves from it. They are unworthy of release; they are in prison, and Christ is the keeper. There is but one way towards a real

1. This is not meant to hinder acts of Catholic consent, such as occurred anciently, when the Catholic body aids one portion of a particular Church against another portion.

reformation — a return to him in heart and spirit, whose sacred truth they have betrayed; all other methods, however fair they may promise, will prove to be but shadows and failures.

On these grounds, were there no others, the present writer, for one, will be no party to the ordinary political methods by which professed reforms are carried or compassed in this day. We can do nothing well till we act "with one accord" [Acts 2:1]; we can have no accord in action till we agree together in heart; we cannot agree without a supernatural influence; we cannot have a supernatural influence unless we pray for it; we cannot pray acceptably without repentance and confession. Our Church's strength would be irresistible, humanly speaking, were it but at unity with itself: if it remains divided, part against part, we shall see the energy which was meant to subdue the world preying upon itself, according to our Saviour's express assurance that such a house "cannot stand" [Mk. 3:25]. Till we feel this, till we seek one another as brethren, not lightly throwing aside our private opinions, which we seem to feel we have received from above, from an ill-regulated, untrue desire of unity, but returning to each other in heart, and coming together to God to do for us what we cannot do for ourselves, no change can be for the better. Till we are stirred up to this religious course, let the Church sit still; let her [2] be content to be in bondage; let her work in chains; let her submit to her imperfections as a punishment; let her go on teaching with the stammering lips of ambiguous formularies,[3] and inconsistent precedents, and principles but partially developed. We are not better than our fathers; let us bear to be what Hammond was, or Andrewes, or Hooker; let us not faint under that body of death, which they bore about in patience; nor shrink from the penalty of sins, which they inherited from the age before them.[4]

But these remarks are beyond our present scope, which is merely to show that, while our Prayer Book is acknowledged on all hands to be of Catholic origin, our Articles also, the offspring of an uncatholic age, are, through God's good providence, to say the least, not uncatholic, and

2. [ED.] In the second edition, *her* is replaced by *us* throughout this sentence.

3. [ED.] In the second edition, the preceding seven words are modified to read "through the medium of indeterminate statements."

4. "We, thy sinful creatures," says the Service for King Charles the Martyr, "here assembled before thee, do, in behalf of all the people of this land, humbly confess, that they were the *crying sins* of this nation, which brought down this judgment upon us," *i.e.*, King Charles's murder.

may be subscribed by those who aim at being catholic in heart and doctrine. . . .

§ 2. JUSTIFICATION BY FAITH ONLY

Article XI. That we are justified by Faith only, is a most wholesome doctrine.

The Homilies add that Faith is the sole *means*, the sole *instrument* of justification. Now, to show briefly what such statements imply, and what they do not.

1. They do *not* imply a denial of *baptism* as a means and an instrument of justification; which the Homilies elsewhere affirm, as will be shown incidentally in a later section.[5]

> The instrumental power of Faith cannot interfere with the instrumental power of Baptism; because Faith is the sole justifier, not in contrast to *all* means and agencies whatever (for it is not surely in contrast to our Lord's merits, or God's mercy), but to all other *graces*. When, then, Faith is called the sole instrument, this means the sole *internal* instrument, not the sole instrument of any kind.
>
> There is nothing inconsistent, then, in Faith being the sole instrument of justification, and yet Baptism also the sole instrument, and that at the same time, because in distinct senses; an inward instrument in no way interfering with an outward instrument, Baptism may be the hand of the giver, and Faith the hand of the receiver.[6]

Nor does the sole instrumentality of Faith interfere with the doctrine of *Works* being a mean also. And that it is a mean, the Homily of Almsdeeds declares in the strongest language, as will also be quoted in Section 11.[7]

> An assent to the doctrine that Faith alone justifies, does not at all preclude the doctrine of Works justifying also. If, indeed, it were said that Works justify in *the same sense* as Faith only justifies, this would be a contradiction in terms; but Faith only may justify in one sense — Good Works in another — and this is all that is here maintained. After all, does not Christ only justify? How is it that the doctrine of Faith justifying does not interfere with our Lord's being the sole justifier? It will, of course, be replied, that

5. [ED.] *Cf. Tract XC* [Oxford, 1903], 45–49 (§ 7. The Sacraments).
6. [ED.] Newman is quoting from his *Lectures on Justification*, 2d ed. (London, 1840), 256 f., with minor verbal changes.
7. [ED.] *Cf. Tract XC*, 69–78 (§ 11. The Homilies).

our Lord is the *meritorious cause*, and Faith the *means;* that Faith justifies in a different and subordinate sense. As then, Christ only justifies *in the sense* in which he justifies, yet Faith also justifies in its own sense; so Works, whether moral or ritual, may justify us in their own respective senses, though in the sense in which Faith justifies, it alone justifies. The only question is, *What* is that sense in which Works justify, so as not to interfere with Faith only justifying? It may, indeed, turn out on inquiry, that the sense alleged will not hold, either as being unscriptural, or for any other reason; but, whether so or not, at any rate the apparent inconsistency of language should not startle men; nor should they so promptly condemn those who, though they do not use *their* language, at least use St. James's. Indeed, is not this argument the very weapon of the Arians, in their warfare against the Son of God? They said, Christ is not God, because the Father is called the "*Only God*" [*cf*. Jn. 17:3; Jude 4].[8]

2. Next we have to inquire *in what sense* Faith only does justify. In a number of ways, of which here two only shall be mentioned.

First, it is the pleading or impetrating principle, or constitutes our *title* to justification; being analogous among the graces to Moses' lifting up his hands on the Mount, or the Israelites eyeing the Brazen Serpent [9] — actions which did not merit God's mercy, but *asked* for it. A number of means go to effect our justification. We are justified by Christ alone, in that he has purchased the gift; by Faith alone, in that Faith asks for it; by Baptism alone, for Baptism conveys it; and by newness of heart alone, for newness of heart is the *sine qua non* life of it.

And secondly, Faith, as being the beginning of perfect or justifying righteousness, is taken for what it tends towards, or ultimately will be. It is said by anticipation to be that which it promises; just as one might pay a labourer his hire before he began his work. Faith working by love is the seed of divine graces, which in due time will be brought forth and flourish — partly in this world, fully in the next.

§ 5. GENERAL COUNCILS

Article XXI. General councils may not be gathered together without the commandment and will of princes. And when they be gathered together, forasmuch as they be an assembly of men, whereof all be not governed with the Spirit and Word of God, they

8. [ED.] Quoted from Newman, *Lectures on Justification*, 314 f., with slight verbal changes.

9. [ED.] Cf. *ibid.*, 325 f.

may err, and sometimes have erred, in things pertaining to God. Wherefore things ordained by them as necessary to salvation have neither strength nor authority, unless it may be declared that they are taken out of Holy Scripture.

That great bodies of men, of different countries, may not meet together without the sanction of their rulers, is plain from the principles of civil obedience and from primitive practice. That, when met together, though Christians, they will not be all ruled by the Spirit or Word of God, is plain from our Lord's parable of the net [Mt. 13:47–50], and from melancholy experience. That bodies of men, deficient in this respect, may err, is a self-evident truth — *unless*, indeed, they be favoured with some divine superintendence, which has to be proved before it can be admitted.

General councils, then, may err, *as such* — may err, *unless* in any case it is promised, as a matter of express supernatural privilege, that they shall *not* err; a case which lies beyond the scope of this Article, or at any rate beside its determination.

Such a promise, however, *does* exist in cases when general councils are not only gathered together according to "the commandment and will of princes," but *in the Name of Christ*, according to our Lord's promise [Mt. 18:20]. The Article merely contemplates the human prince, not the King of Saints. While councils are a thing of earth, their infallibility of course is not guaranteed; when they are a thing of heaven, their deliberations are overruled, and their decrees authoritative. In such cases they are *Catholic* councils; and it would seem, from passages which will be quoted in Section 11,[10] that the Homilies recognize four, or even six, as bearing this character. Thus Catholic or Ecumenical Councils are General Councils, and something more. Some general councils are Catholic, and others are not. Nay, as even Romanists grant, the same councils may be partly Catholic, partly not.

If Catholicity be thus a *quality*, found at times in general councils, rather than the *differentia* belonging to a certain class of them, it is still less surprising that the Article should be silent on the subject.

What those *conditions* are which fulfil the notion of a gathering "in the Name of Christ," in the case of a particular council, it is not necessary here to determine. Some have included among these conditions the subsequent reception of its decrees by the universal Church; others, a ratification by the Pope.

10. [ED.] Cf. *Tract XC*, 69–78 (§ 11. The Homilies).

Another of these conditions, however, the Article goes on to mention, viz., that in points necessary to salvation, a council should prove its decrees by Scripture.

[The three concluding paragraphs, which do not add to the main argument, are omitted.]

§ 12. The Bishop of Rome

Article XXXVIII. The Bishop of Rome hath no jurisdiction in this realm of England.

By "hath" is meant "ought to have," as the Article in the Thirty-sixth Canon [11] and the Oath of Supremacy show, in which the same doctrine is drawn out more at length. "No foreign prince, person, prelate, state, or potentate, hath, *or ought to have*, any jurisdiction, power, superiority, pre-eminence, or authority, ecclesiastical or spiritual, within this realm."

This is the profession which everyone must in consistency make, who does not join the Roman Church. If the Bishop of Rome has jurisdiction and authority here, why do we not acknowledge it, and submit to him? To use, then, the above words is nothing more or less than to say, "I am not a Roman Catholic"; and whatever reasons there are against using them, are so far reasons against remaining in the English Church. They are a mere enunciation of the principle of Anglicanism.

Anglicans maintain that the supremacy of the Pope is not directly from revelation, but an event in providence. All things may be undone by the agents and causes by which they are done. What revelation gives, revelation takes away; what providence gives, providence takes away. God ordained by miracle, he reversed by miracle, the Jewish election; he promoted in the way of providence, and he cast down by the same way, the Roman Empire. "The powers that be are ordained of God" [Rom. 13:1], *while* they be, and thereby have a claim on our obedience. When they cease to be, they cease to have a claim. They cease to be when God removes them. He may be considered to remove them when he undoes what he had done. The Jewish election did not cease to be when the Jews went into captivity; this was an event in providence; and what miracle had ordained, it was miracle that annulled. But the Roman power ceased to be when the barbarians overthrew it; for it rose by the sword, and it therefore perished by the sword. The Gospel Ministry began in Christ and his Apostles; and

11. [ED.] Canon 36 of the English Canons of 1604.

what they began, they only can end. The Papacy began in the exertions
and passions of man; and what man can make, man can destroy. Its jurisdiction, while it lasted, was "ordained of God"; when it ceased to be, it
ceased to claim our obedience; and it ceased to be at the Reformation. The
Reformers, who could not destroy a Ministry which the Apostles began,
could destroy a Dominion which the Popes founded.

Perhaps the following passage will throw additional light upon this
point:

> The Anglican view of the Church has ever been this: that its
> portions need not otherwise have been united together for their
> essential completeness, than as being descended from one original.
> They are like a number of colonies sent out from a mother-country.
> . . . Each Church is independent of all the rest, and is to act on
> the principle of what may be called Episcopal independence, ex-
> cept, indeed, so far as the civil power unites any number of them
> together. . . . Each diocese is a perfect independent Church, is
> sufficient for itself; and the communion of Christians one with
> another, and the unity of them altogether, lie, not in a mutual
> understanding, intercourse, and combination, not in what they do
> in common, but in what they are and have in common, in their
> possession of the Succession, their Episcopal form, their Apostolical
> faith, and the use of the Sacraments. . . . Mutual intercourse is
> but an *accident* of the Church, not of its essence. . . . Intercom-
> munion is a duty, as other duties, but is not the tenure of instrument
> of the communion between the unseen world and this; and much
> more the confederacy of sees and churches, the metropolitan, pa-
> triarchal, and papal systems, are matters of expedience or of natural
> duty from long custom, or of propriety from gratitude and rev-
> erence, or of necessity from voluntary oaths and engagements, or
> of ecclesiastical force from the canons of Councils, but not nec-
> essary in order to the conveyance of grace, or for fulfilment of the
> ceremonial law, as it may be called, of unity. Bishop is superior to
> bishop only in rank, not in real power; and the Bishop of Rome,
> the head of the Catholic world, is not the centre of unity, except
> as having a primacy of order. Accordingly, even granting, for ar-
> gument's sake, that the English Church violated a duty in the six-
> teenth century, in releasing itself from the Roman supremacy, still
> it did not thereby commit that special sin, which cuts off from it
> the fountains of grace, and is called schism. It was essentially com-
> plete without Rome, and naturally independent of it; it had, in the
> course of years, whether by usurpation or not, come under the su-
> premacy of Rome; and now, whether by rebellion or not, it is
> free from it: and as it did not enter into the Church invisible by
> joining Rome, so it was not cast out of it by breaking from Rome.

These were accidents in its history, involving, indeed, sin in individuals, but not affecting the Church as a Church.

Accordingly, the Oath of Supremacy declares "that no foreign prelate hath or ought to have any jurisdiction, power, pre-eminence, or authority within this realm." In other words, there is nothing in the Apostolic system which gives an authority to the Pope over the Church, such as it does not give to a bishop. It is altogether an ecclesiastical arrangement; not a point *de fide*, but of expedience, custom, or piety, which cannot be claimed as if the Pope *ought* to have it, any more than, on the other hand, the King could of Divine right claim the supremacy; the claim of both one and the other resting, not on duty or revelation, but on specific engagement. We find ourselves, as a Church, under the King now, and we obey him; we were under the Pope formerly, and we obeyed him. "Ought" does not, in any degree, come into the question.[12]

12. [ED.] J. H. Newman in *British Critic*, 4th ser., XXVII (Jan.–April 1840), 54–58.

III

WILLIAM GEORGE WARD

The Ideal of a Christian Church
Considered in Comparison with Existing Practice
(SELECTION)

Editor's introduction. Both at Oxford and in the larger world, the response to *Tract Ninety* was prompt and vigorous. In the university, the public attack opened with the letter of the "Four Tutors," [1] followed closely by a resolution of the Hebdomadal Board. On March 8, 1841, the "Four Tutors" wrote sharply (though in very general terms) to "the Editor of the *Tracts for the Times.*"

> We readily admit [they said] the necessity of allowing that liberty, in interpreting the formularies of our Church, which has been advocated by many of its most learned bishops and other eminent divines; but this tract puts forth new and startling views as to the extent to which that liberty may be carried. For if we are right in our apprehension of the author's meaning, we are at a loss to see what security would remain, were his principles generally recognised, that the most plainly erroneous doctrines and practices of the Church of Rome might not be inculcated in the lecture-rooms of the University, and from the pulpits of our churches.[2]

On March 15 the Heads of Houses, after noting the university's statutory requirement of subscription to the Articles, declared that

> the modes of interpretation, such as are suggested in the said Tract, evading rather than explaining the sense of the Thirty-nine Ar-

1. T. T. Churton, of Brasenose; H. B. Wilson, of St. John's (who was later, in the *Essays and Reviews* controversy, to have his own difficulties with the Anglican formularies); J. Griffiths, of Wadham; A. C. Tait, of Balliol (afterwards Archbishop of Canterbury).

2. *The Protest against Tracts for the Times, No. 90, Resolution of the Hebdomadal Board, and Mr. Newman's Letter to the Vice-Chancellor* (Oxford, 1841), 4 f.

ticles, and reconciling subscription to them, with the adoption of errors, which they were designed to counteract, defeat the object, and are inconsistent with the due observance of the above-mentioned Statutes.[3]

By this time, derogatory remarks had already been made in the House of Commons,[4] and before long a barrage of episcopal critiques opened.[5] Newman scarcely exaggerated when he spoke of "the universal storm of indignation with which the Tract was received on its appearance." [6]

He was not, of course, left without stalwart defenders. Surprisingly enough, *The Times* of London opened fire on the parliamentary critics of Tractarianism.[7] More predictably, Pusey and Keble rose to the defence of *Tract Ninety*.[8] For the moment, at least, even William Palmer and Walter Farquhar Hook, despite their enmity to "Popery," joined forces with Newman and his colleagues.

> It is a fact [Hook declared], an undeniable fact, that there are two Parties in the Church of England; the High Church Party and the Low Church Party. And the act of the Hebdomadal Board renders it absolutely necessary for us to range ourselves on the one side or on the other. That is to say, we must join that party with which in general principles we agree, and not desert it merely because we may think that a few individuals may have expressed themselves on some points incautiously, or have been hurried into acts which a colder and a calmer judgment may condemn. . . . On the publication of the Ninetieth Tract for the Times, I determined to point out in a pamphlet what I considered to be its errors. But the moment I heard that the writer was to be silenced, not by argument,

---

3. *Ibid.*, 6.

4. Cf. H. P. Liddon, *Life of Edward Boverie Pusey, D.D.*, 4th ed. (London, 1894-98), II, 165 ff.

5. Cf. J. H. Newman, *Apologia pro vita sua* (Garden City, N.Y., 1956), 239: "The bishops one after another began to charge against me." Episcopal criticism was deeply disturbing to Newman because of his "Apostolical" principles. Cf. "A Letter addressed to the Right Reverend Father in God, Richard, Lord Bishop of Oxford," in Newman, *The Via Media of the Anglican Church* (London, 1914), II, 398: "A Bishop's lightest word *ex Cathedrâ*, is heavy. His judgment on a book cannot be light."

6. Newman, *Apologia*, 195.

7. For excerpts from *The Times* of March 4 and March 6, 1841, *cf.* Liddon, *Life of Pusey*, II, 165 f.

8. Cf. E. B. Pusey, *The Articles treated of in Tract 90 reconsidered and their interpretation vindicated, in a Letter to the Rev. R. W. Jelf, D.D., Canon of Christ Church* (Oxford, 1841); J. Keble, *The Case of Catholic Subscription to the Thirty-nine Articles Considered, with especial Reference to the Duties and Difficulties of English Catholics in the Present Crisis: in a Letter to the Hon. Mr. Justice Coleridge* (privately printed, London, 1841).

but by a usurped authority, that moment I determined to renounce my intention: that moment I determined to take my stand with him; because, though I did not approve of a particular Tract, yet in general principles, in the very principle advocated in that Tract, I did agree with him: in a word, I was compelled by circumstances to act as a Party man. And in justice to one whom I am proud to call my friend, I am bound to say that Mr. Newman's explanatory Letter to Dr. Jelf is to my mind perfectly satisfactory.[9]

All things considered, during the first months of the *Tract Ninety* affair it was far from obvious that the Tractarian party was close to disaster.

Yet within five years the Oxford Movement, as a concerted and powerful movement within the English Church's great academic stronghold, was over. Its most brilliant leader had departed; the basic incompatibility of its teaching with Anglican principles was widely taken as demonstrated; and the long era of mutual suspicion between the Anglo-Catholic party and the greater part of the Anglican hierarchy was beginning. No doubt the weightiest single factor in the *débâcle* was Newman's withdrawal and eventual secession. But another noteworthy factor was the behaviour of one of the most uproarious bulls ever to invade a theological china-shop — William George Ward.

In his power of outrageous utterance, his love of disputation, and his particular dislike of the Reformers, Ward inevitably reminds us of Hurrell Froude, but he lacked Froude's deep-rooted attachment to the High Church tradition. Profoundly influenced in his way of thinking by the Utilitarianism of John Stuart Mill, he consistently measured ecclesiastical ideas and institutions in terms of their practical results in human life and ignored the historical considerations on which High Churchmen commonly laid great emphasis. (Of course, his supernaturalistic conception of human life sharply distinguished him from the philosophical Utilitarians, but that is another story.) Consequently, under the influence of Newman's preaching of supernatural holiness he managed to pass from an embryonic liberalism in the manner of Thomas Arnold to an advanced "papalism" without ever sharing Newman's feeling for the *via media*.

---

9. W. F. Hook, *Letter to the Right Reverend the Lord Bishop of Ripon, on the State of Parties in the Church of England* (London, 1841), 5 f. Newman's *Letter addressed to the Rev. R. W. Jelf, D.D., Canon of Christ Church, in Explanation of the Ninetieth Tract in the Series called the Tracts for the Times* (Oxford, 1841), completed on March 13, 1841, was perhaps his most effective defence of his position. For Palmer's attempt to get up a "Declaration" on behalf of the Tractarians, *cf.* Liddon, *Life of Pusey*, II, 204–08.

Three ideas were manifestly at the bottom of his attraction to Rome. One was that Rome did, and, he believed, nothing else did, keep up the continuous recognition of the supernatural element in religion, that consciousness of an ever-present power not of this world which is so prominent a feature in the New Testament, and which is spoken of there as a permanent and characteristic element in the Gospel dispensation. The Roman view of the nature and offices of the Church, of man's relations to the unseen world, of devotion, of the Eucharist and of the Sacraments in general, assumed and put forward this supernatural aspect; other systems ignored it or made it mean nothing, unless in secret to the individual and converted soul. In the next place he revolted — no weaker word can be used — from the popular exhibition in England, more or less Lutheran and Calvinistic, of the doctrine of justification. The ostentatious separation of justification from morality, with all its theological refinements and fictions, seemed to him profoundly unscriptural, profoundly unreal and hollow, or else profoundly immoral. In conscience and moral honesty and strict obedience he saw the only safe and trustworthy guidance in regard to the choice and formation of religious opinions; it was a principle on which all his philosophy was built, that "careful and individual moral discipline is the only possible basis on which Christian faith and practice can be reared." [10] In the third place he was greatly affected, not merely by the paramount place of sanctity in the Roman theology and the professed Roman system, but by the standard of saintliness which he found there, involving complete and heroic self-sacrifice for great religious ends, complete abandonment of the world, painful and continuous self-discipline, purified and exalted religious affections, beside which English piety and goodness at its best, in such examples as George Herbert and Ken and Bishop Wilson, seemed unambitious and pale and tame, of a different order from the Roman, and less closely resembling what we read of in the first ages and in the New Testament.[11]

It was from this standpoint that Ward undertook to prescribe for the ills of the English Church. "The Reformation," Froude had once remarked, "was a limb badly set — it must be broken again in order to be righted." [12] In article after article in the British Critic, which they had made their organ, Ward and his friends worked away at breaking the

10. [ED.] W. G. Ward, The Ideal of a Christian Church considered in Comparison with Existing Practice, 2d ed. (London, 1844), ix (slightly altered).

11. R. W. Church, The Oxford Movement: Twelve Years, 1833–1845, 3d ed. (London, 1892), 341 f.

12. Remains of the late Reverend Richard Hurrell Froude (London-Derby, 1838–39), I, 433.

crooked limb, in order to restore the Anglican body. As they worked, however, their confidence in the Anglican position steadily weakened.

> The whole course of [Ward's] writing in the *British Critic* may be said to have consisted in a prolonged and disparaging comparison of the English Church, in theory, in doctrine, in moral and devotional temper, in discipline of character, in education, in its public and authoritative tone in regard to social, political, and moral questions, and in the type and standard of its clergy, with those of the Catholic Church, which to him was represented by the mediaeval and later Roman Church. And in the general result, and in all important matters, the comparison became more and more fatally disadvantageous to the English Church. In the perplexing condition of Christendom, it had just enough good and promise to justify those who had been brought up in it remaining where they were, as long as they saw any prospect of improving it, and till they were driven out.[13]

To men in this frame of mind *Tract Ninety* inevitably seemed too moderate, and Ward set out to adapt its argument to his own purposes — partly, at least, in the hope of forcing Newman's hand.[14] Newman had relied heavily on an appeal to the "literal and grammatical sense" of the Articles; Ward now tried to show that more than one of the Articles demanded much more drastic treatment.

> Our twelfth Article [15] [he asserted] is as plain as words can make it on the "evangelical" side: . . . of course I think its natural meaning may be explained away, for I subscribe it myself in a non-natural sense: but I know no Article which "Romanizers" have to distort so much, as *all* "High-churchmen" have to distort this.[16]

As for the comprehensive outlook which Newman attributed to the compilers of the Articles, Ward declined to see anything more in it than an instance of political cynicism,[17] and he concluded that the product of unprincipled compromise need not — indeed, could not — be respected as a genuine statement of doctrine.

13. Church, *Oxford Movement*, 355 f.   14. Cf. *ibid.*, 363–65.
15. "Of Good Works."
16. Ward, *Ideal of a Christian Church*, 479.
17. Cf. *ibid.*, 481: "I am firmly convinced that no one clergyman of our Church, who will look honestly in the face the formularies which he is called on to subscribe, will be able to subscribe them *all* in a *natural* and *straightforward* sense. I attribute this fact to the utter want of fixed religious principles displayed by the leading Reformers. . . ."

If they are intended to teach doctrine, we discover their meaning by discovering *what* they teach; but if to include great varieties of opinion, we discover their meaning by discovering *how much* their wording will include. . . . I shall not fear to rest the whole of my case on a comparison between the manner in which the first five Articles were drawn up, and the rest. The first five relate to points of Catholic Faith, in which the then Church occupied herself merely in handing down what she had received; the remainder (to speak generally) to questions then in controversy: and the consideration to which I wish the attention of my brethren directed is this: are not the whole spirit and wording of the latter thirty-four, in every respect that which would be found in a document, the result of (I should say in parts disingenuous) compromise, and not that which would be found in a document intended to *teach* doctrines of whatever kind? [18]

Naturally enough, the opinions of Ward and his circle were coldly received in the Church at large — even by those who sympathized with Tractarianism in its earlier phases. Bishop Denison of Salisbury, for example, after speaking generously of the "distinguished individuals" associated with the *Tracts for the Times*, commented on the *British Critic* articles in these terms:

It savours of arrogance for men to presume to place themselves in a position extraneous to the Church to which they belong; and, fixing their critics' chair in the wide regions of Catholicism, from it boldly and irreverently to examine, to question, and to censure, if they do not finally condemn, that Church to which they owe, and, in general terms, profess to pay, loving obedience, and filial respect.[19]

Bishop Thirlwall of St. David's, in his perceptive and fair discussion of *Tract Ninety*, referred to the suspicions aroused by the language of the Ward faction.

That divines of our communion should speak of the Roman Church in terms not merely of indulgence, but of reverence, of tenderness, of affection, while they spoke harshly and disparagingly, not to say bitterly and contemptuously, of the Reformers, the Reformation, and Protestantism, was not only startling and offensive, but raised a suspicion, that where so much was said in spite of public opinion, and against the spirit of the times, still more might be meant, and

18. W. G. Ward, *Appendix to a Few More Words in Support of No. 90 of the Tracts for the Times, in Answer to Mr. Lowe's Pamphlet* (Oxford, 1841), 5 f.
19. *A Charge Delivered to the Clergy of the Diocese of Salisbury, by Edward, Lord Bishop of Salisbury, at his Second Visitation, September, 1842* (London, 1842), 17.

only reserved for a more favorable juncture. And this suspicion was of course greatly strengthened by expressions which fell from the same quarter, and which seemed to intimate a secret design of effecting some change of undefined extent in the character of our Church.[20]

William Palmer, for whom suspicion had become a certainty, undertook to produce an exposé, in the form of a *Narrative* of the Oxford Movement.

> The whole Tract [he wrote many years later] was governed by the then existing state of things . . . it was intended to meet the propagation of Roman Catholic sentiments in the *British Critic*, by men professing to be of the Church of England, but really hostile to her faith, and disbelieving in her ministry and valid administration of the sacraments.[21]

It was in direct reply to Palmer that Ward gathered his ideas together in a vast, shapeless *summa*, *The Ideal of a Christian Church*. Two points above all stand out clearly. First and foremost, in Ward's mind "spiritual benefits" are the real mark of the Church.

> Let us carry with us . . . this simple and obvious ideal of the Church's office (which, of course, like other ideals, is nowhere realised in perfection, but towards which indefinite progress may be made), that her one only object shall be to save the souls of those committed to her charge; and that the very proof which she offers to her children of her divine authority, shall be the sense entertained by them of the spiritual benefits she imparts; that her voice shall be as the Voice of God heard amidst the din of this restless and sinful world, guiding us in perplexities, soothing us in distresses, strengthening us in temptations, alarming the careless and worldly, cheering the contrite and humble of heart.[22]

Secondly, for Ward Roman Catholicism is the most complete embodiment of his "ideal," and the goal of all his efforts — and, indeed, the true end of the Oxford Movement — is complete "Romanizing."

> . . . The principles, which have been throughout the centre, rallying-point, and spring of the exertions that have been made — these have so fruitfully expanded and germinated in the mind of many

20. *A Charge to the Clergy of the Diocese of St. David's, by Connop, Lord Bishop of St. David's, Delivered at his Primary Visitation, October, 1842*, 2d ed. (London, 1842), 66.

21. William Palmer, *A Narrative of Events connected with the Publication of the Tracts for the Times*, 2d ed. (London, 1883), 81 f.

22. Ward, *Ideal of a Christian Church*, 11.

who had embraced them, that we find, oh most joyful, most wonderful, most unexpected sight! we find the whole cycle of Roman
doctrine gradually possessing numbers of English Churchmen; numbers even of those, who are as yet unconscious how much of truth
they hold, and may remain so, unless some sudden crisis call on them
to make an election and to take a side.[23]

Ward added that "the work going on among us . . . *has been done,
under God, by the inherent vitality and powers of our own Church,*"
but this confession seems to have made little impression on his critics.
What they did notice was his challenge on the next page:

Three years have passed, since I said plainly, that in subscribing the
Articles I renounce no one Roman doctrine: yet I retain my Fellowship which I hold on the tenure of subscription, and have received
no Ecclesiastical censure in any shape.[24]

His university hastened to oblige him, to the full extent of its powers.
At a dramatic meeting of Convocation in the Sheldonian Theatre on
February 13, 1845, the *Ideal* was condemned by 777 votes to 386, and
Ward was stripped of his university degrees by 569 votes to 511.[25]

A third resolution, censuring *Tract Ninety,* was prevented by the
proctors [26] from coming to a vote, but in any case Newman was beyond
caring what happened at Oxford. His reflections on the development of
Christian doctrine had finally shown him how to reconcile the Roman
"ideal" with his historical conscience, and on October 9, 1845, he was
received into the Roman Catholic Church. Ward and his bride of a few
months were already there.

❖ ❖ ❖ ❖

CHAPTER III:
IS IT UNDUTIFUL TO THE ENGLISH CHURCH TO AIM
AT SUCH AN IDEAL?

1. If it be maintained that an ideal of the Church, agreeing in substance with that drawn out in the last chapter,[1] is not the highest and the

---

23. *Ibid.,* 565 f.   24. *Ibid.,* 567.   25. Cf. Church, *Oxford Movement,* 381 f.
26. Guillemard of Trinity and Church of Oriel (the future historian of the Oxford
Movement).
1. [ED.] For a succinct summary, *cf.* W. G. Ward, *The Ideal of a Christian Church
considered in Comparison with Existing Practice,* 2d ed. (London, 1844), 11 (quoted
above, p. 163).

most fitting to be aimed at, there can be no fairer point on which to join issue; and any argument addressed to it shall meet with my most attentive consideration. All that concerns my present purpose, however, is to say that such was my own view during the time I wrote in the *British Critic*, and to submit (which will I think hardly be denied) that the conception of such an ideal is at least not extravagant nor irrational. But if anyone should acknowledge it to be higher than any which he can oppose to it, but should accuse me of disloyalty to my own Church because it is seen, on its very statement, to follow the Roman, not the English, pattern, I would beg such an one to reconsider the latter opinion, as it is a very important one in the argument. If on reconsideration he withdraw it, the charge of disloyalty, of course, falls with it: but if he repeat it (and I confess that it is an opinion in which I myself agree), then let me observe that it is he and not I who has given a most unassailable reason for preferring the Roman to the English system; a reason wholly untouched by any amount of *practical* corruption which so many Englishmen attribute to the Roman Church: viz., that Rome has preserved in the main, and we have not, what is so inestimably precious, the high and true *idea* of a Church; that whatever may be the present lukewarmness of her children (of which, for myself, I really cannot judge, nor have ever expressed an opinion), whenever zeal, energy, and piety revive, they can act immediately on the Church by *means* of the system they find, while among us they must begin by *attacking* the system they find. In no one of my articles have I expressed or implied any comparison more pointed than this; which yet, as I have shown, is necessarily implied in that very objection which is most certain to be brought. If this is to be disloyal to the English Church, the supposed objector is as disloyal as I. And I consider that Mr. Palmer should have attempted to prove this, not taken it for granted. He has shown, by unanswerable evidence, what I can hardly fancy anybody reading one of my articles without discovering, and what on one occasion I have asserted in terms, viz., that on a great number of points I conceive that the English Church would act wisely in making Rome her model; whereas he has merely assumed, what was the only real point at issue, that such an opinion argues want of patriotism in an English Churchman. Yet in parallel cases we find the very opposite held universally. No one would call an American of the present day unpatriotic because he very much indeed prefers the state of things which existed before the revolt, and because he is anxious to do his utmost in restoring, if possible, constitutional monarchy. An Englishman is not patriotic in that he believes and propagates the belief of one Englishman beating ten Frenchmen; but in that he makes England the one great sphere and centre of his energies; loves to study the feelings, habits, opinions of Englishmen, and brings whatever knowledge he possesses of other countries to bear upon this his favourite subject of thought; is more pained by the vices and more delighted by the virtues of Englishmen than by those of French, Germans, or Italians. I am not attempting to decide how far we are justified in allowing patriotism to supersede universal philanthropy: all acknowledge that we are in some degree, and all acknowledge that we are not entirely; but *so far forth* as we are patriotic, so far have we such sentiments as I just described. On the other hand, to intoxicate ourselves in insular pride, to hug ourselves in the thought of England's real and supposed excellences, to be blind to her failings, and to believe, even in the utmost simplicity of heart, that she is the envy of surrounding nations and eighth wonder of the world, this is no real patriotism; it is at bottom but base pride and vulgar nationality.

Again, to continue the same illustration, considering the tendency always and everywhere to national pride, there must ever be extreme danger in using habitually an inflated, boastful way of speaking concerning our country's greatness. But if the very besetting fault of our country, the very fault against which all our feelings of patriotism call us to contend, be that very national pride, how infinitely stronger the case becomes! And to speak plainly, believing, as I most firmly do, that ever since the schism of the sixteenth century the English Church has been swayed by a spirit of arrogance, self-contentment, and self-complacency, resembling rather an absolute infatuation than the imbecility of ordinary pride, which has stifled her energies, crippled her resources, frustrated all the efforts of her most faithful children to raise her from her existing degradation, I for one, however humble my position, will not be responsible for uttering one word, or implying one opinion, which shall tend to foster this outrageous delusion. The disease has been too deeply seated to yield to ordinary remedies: experience has shown that mere hints and implications, *especially when united with disclaimers of superior admiration for other systems*, have wholly failed in their objects: and even had the *British Critic* during its two last years performed no other service, it has at least succeeded in this; in impressing on the most careless and inobservant minds this fact, that certain members of the Church of England, be they more or fewer, do raise their voices in indignant protest against the system and spirit which so extensively energize within her, and do wish to raise the sympathies of her many holy and devoted children to some higher object than the maintenance and praise of that system.

Still, an objection has been taken to the *tone* in which my humble yet zealous protests have been made. A word has been used in a private communication, which I have not seen in print, but which, I suppose, expresses the sort of feeling: it has been said, then, that they appear couched not in sorrowful but in "spiteful" terms. I think I perceive what that element is in them, which has given rise to such a feeling, and I humbly trust that it is neither wrong nor unbecoming.

In the first place, most certainly it does not show that what appear to me the corruptions in question give me no pain. For years, consciously or not, and in various shapes not recognized by me at the time as modifications of the same symptoms, had my feelings been oppressed and (I may really say) tortured by this heavy, unspiritual, unelastic, prosaic, unfeeling, unmeaning Protestant spirit; all this time my ears were stunned with the din of self-laudation, with the words "pure and apostolical," "evangelical truth and apostolical order," and the like most miserable watchwords: those from whom I learned at one moment some high and elevating truth at the next crushed and overwhelmed me by some respectful mention of our existing system; with the single exception of Mr. Froude's work, no external response could I find to my ceaseless and ever-increasing inward repugnance against the habits of thought and action prevalent in our Church. At length I was able to fix, with some definiteness, on the particular cause of my annoyance; and soon afterwards (in writing two pamphlets[2] three years ago) I had the opportunity of speaking out. To say that the hearty and energetic tone with which I did speak out indicates my real feeling of sorrow to have been shallow and trifling is an allegation which I will meet by a parallel case. Let us suppose anyone to have been afflicted by some most painful illness for many weeks, but to have been compelled to restrain his outcries hitherto, because of dangerous illness in the next house: the impediment being removed, he cries out with no subdued tone, and with great relief of mind; on which he is accosted by a stranger with the observation, "Sir, your pain really cannot be very serious, or you would

---

2. [ED.] W. G. Ward, *A Few Words in Support of No. 90 of the Tracts for the Times, Partly with Reference to Mr. Wilson's Letter* (Oxford, 1841); *A Few More Words in Support of No. 90 of the Tracts for the Times* (Oxford, 1841).

not cry out with so good a heart, and with such evident satisfaction."

And, secondly, I trust that allowing myself to speak in such a tone was not in itself wrong or unbecoming. When the evils to which one desires to draw attention are facts whose existence has hitherto been unknown, all men's natural feelings conspire with the obvious rule of right, and the communication is made in a sorrowful and subdued spirit. But when the facts have been known from the first, but not recognized to *be* evils, then I conceive that words of zealous, indignant, declamatory remonstrance are generally allowable, and are often the most fitting of all possible methods.

2. It will be said, perhaps, that various things I have written have tended to cloud with perplexities many an humble and retiring spirit who wished but to know his duty and to do it; but was filled with misgiving and alarm at the strange and fierce denunciations he found in the *British Critic.*

[Ward quotes extensively from his own articles, to show that he has been aware of the danger and has tried to guard against it. He argues further that sharp criticism, which under other circumstances might be unjustifiable, is necessitated by the deep seated corruption of the English Church.]

But we shall see the whole matter in a clearer light by observing a mode of action which has ever obtained in the Catholic Church.

> The Church's system alone assigns its rightful place to intellect and practical ability: she uses them, hallows them in using, and yet assigns to them a place far lower than the highest. And for what great purpose has the Church always employed these two classes of character? For this: to guard in peace and tranquility from the world without (the one from its rude violence, the other from its restless questionings; the one by the barrier of spiritual power and the exercise of political wisdom, the other by that of well-digested, subtle, and deep statements of doctrine) the weak and uneducated poor in Christ; or again, the pure-minded and contemplative few, *whom their very protectors feel to be called to a higher and more heavenly lot than themselves.*[3]

Putting aside the question of ecclesiastical power, which does not here concern us, let us consider what will be the place held by thoughtful and argumentative Christians in a corrupt church, corresponding to that held by them in a pure one. It is evident that there is a certain class of

3. W. G. Ward, "The Synagogue and the Church" [*British Critic,* 4th ser., XXXIV (July–Oct. 1843)], 39.

men, called by their peculiar endowments to the office of sifting principles, classifying phenomena, analysing and deducing truths, and the
like. These may be considered as making up a certain community by
themselves, and separate from others; so that each one of them, in dealing with the rest, may do the most important service, by comparing
statements; putting forward plainly the ultimate ends he may wish; enforcing, by means of argument, the desirableness and practicability of
those ends; and, with those who agree with him, concerting plans for success in their joint desire. But the multitude of Christians is called to a
far nobler and more heavenly lot. Infinitely nobler surely it is, to believe
and act, and grow in faith and knowledge *by* action, than to criticize,
doubt, compare, argue. Let us call these two classes, for the present purpose and to make my reasoning clearer, by the respective names of the
"scientific" and the "favoured" class.

[Ward goes on to argue that, while the true vocation of the "scientific"
men is to work for the spiritual welfare of the "little ones of Christ,"
their own specialized services are indispensable to the Church. It should
be obvious, he says, that his articles in the *British Critic* were aimed at
"those who professed argument and analysis."]

It will not, I trust, be imagined, that I am either maintaining the intellect to be, even in the smallest degree, an independent judge of moral
and religious truth, or denying the disapprobation of a spiritually enlightened conscience to be a conclusive disproof of any alleged doctrine;
*supposing only that the doctrine be rightly understood, and the voice of
conscience rightly interpreted.* But then the right performance of these
two functions frequently requires an intellectual exercise of the greatest
complication and difficulty. Conscience reigns alone supreme in all
these matters; but when conscience has at its command a minister so
active, comprehensive, powerful, and versatile as the intellect, the range
of its judgments is infinitely enlarged, and the *external* value of its dictates
infinitely increased. So much as this indeed is implied in the very objection: for the objection which I am considering is not that the statements in the *British Critic* shock religious men who rightly understand
them (to *that* objection this whole work is my attempt to reply); but
that they shock large numbers of holy and humble men of heart who do
not profess that intellectual power which might enable them to appreciate
doctrines widely foreign to their moral experience, or expressions of
doctrine widely different from their traditionary expressions; and to
whom, in consequence, these statements cannot but appear harsh, para-

doxical, nay, profane. If, then, such a person should read these pages, I
would take the liberty of speaking to him plainly, yet with much reverence, as follows: You complain that you make no profession of argumentative powers; and that you have just reason for dissatisfaction if
expressions are put in your way which you cannot understand, which
do violence to early and holy associations, which perplex, alarm, shock
you. I ask, *who* put these expressions in your way? Not only were the
articles, which you criticize, written in a tone and language which might
have made it clear that they presupposed in the reader those very powers
which you disclaim in yourself; but also in almost every article, sometimes in almost every page, they enforce the duty incumbent on such
as you to confine your thoughts either to the doctrines you have been
taught or to those which gradually recommend themselves to your conscience in proportion to your spiritual development. Of course many
passages, written primarily with a controversial object, might contain
edification to like-minded Christians; and might well be a matter of interest if recommended to you by a teacher in whom you repose confidence. But when on your own responsibility you enter on the field of
controversy, and think of comparing doctrine with doctrine, argument
with argument, you descend from that high position in which God has
placed you: your proceeding is like that of some hitherto religious hermit
who should leave his peaceful desert and become candidate for an earthly
crown. You are called to a more heavenly course, you wilfully place
yourself in a more earthly course; you are called to the life of simple
obedience, you descend by your own act to the life of argument and
inquiry; and in one sense I am even glad, should the result of your free
inquiry be perplexity and confusion; because it may awaken you to a
sense of your misconduct, and teach you to value better the high and
noble privileges of your calling.[4]

3. Next, let me apply myself to the parallel objection which has been
raised: for frequently it has been said, not only that the *British Critic*
has scandalized the humble, but that it has encouraged the undutiful;
that it has sanctioned a spirit of wanton criticism, exercised on the system

4. I mentioned at starting that it is no business of mine to defend the works of
other writers; but I cannot forbear from adding here that the other articles in the
British Critic, almost without exception, seem to me so carefully and habitually defer-
ential towards our Church that I cannot fancy they would have been even accused of
an unsettling or disturbing tendency had they not been coloured, in the reader's mind,
by the tone or expressions of my own articles.

and formularies of our Church, or even has been an active instrument in fomenting such a spirit. Now that the claim of the English Church on our allegiance has not been a subject neglected in the *British Critic* is at once evident from the fact that, on looking over my own articles for the purpose, I find not so much as one in which that claim is not directly enforced; while in several I have gone to great length and detail in enforcing it. I am quite confident that the representation which follows is a fair exponent of the consistent and undeviating view on the matter which has been there maintained. I can perfectly understand, then, that a deeply religious person may, under present circumstances, entertain the most serious and anxious doubts whether he be not in duty bound at once to join the Roman Church. But I *cannot* understand that a religious person should, for any length of time, doubt that, if he do remain in our Church, he must remain as her faithful and attached son; not standing, as it were, with one foot in England and the other in Rome, but devoting himself with undivided loyalty to his immediate mother. And if it be asked what definite meaning can be attached to these words, let us, for example's sake, take such particulars as the following. (1) He will "fix his affections" immediately "on the Church wherein God has placed him," and only "*through* that, on the great Catholic community throughout the world": [5] the English Church will be to him the visible embodiment and channel of his Lord's presence. (2) Her morning and evening prayer will be the central points of his public and social devotions; he will offer up those prayers, not as one of the accidentally present congregation, nor yet as one of the Catholic Church; but more definitely, as a member of the English Church: through her, with her, and for her, will his addresses ascend to God day after day, in the language she has placed in his mouth. In like manner, should there be prayers for Catholic unity used by certain members of our own Church as such, and others used by Roman Catholics as such, he will unite in the former rather than in the latter. And (3) the sphere of his practical energies, the turning point of his hopes and fears, interests and disquietudes, the central position from which his view grows forth and expands, will be the Church through which he was regenerated, through which he has communion with the Body and Blood of Christ. He will be careful to make the most of all the salutary privileges she offers him; he will fight without

5. W. G. Ward, "Church Authority" [*British Critic*, 4th ser., XXXIII (Jan.–April 1843)], 222.

ceasing against any disposition to repine at the comparative paucity of means of grace; he will love to contemplate, with humble and affectionate veneration, the admirable patterns of holiness he may find within her pale, nor suffer any difference of opinion on a matter of minor importance to lessen his keen perception of their heavenly graces.

I would gladly add that he will accept the teaching of the English Church in the first instance, and should he become unable to accept it, leave her communion — if I could attach any sense whatever to those often-repeated words, "teaching of the English Church." That the phrase, "teaching of the Prayer Book," conveys a definite and important meaning, I do not deny: considering that it is mainly a selection from the Breviary, it is not surprising that the Prayer Book should on the whole breathe an uniform, most edifying, deeply orthodox spirit; a spirit which corresponds to one particular body of doctrine, and not to its contradictory. Again, that the phrase, "teaching of the Articles," conveys a definite meaning, I cannot deny; for (excepting the first five, which belong to the old theology) they also breathe an uniform, intelligible spirit. But then these respective spirits are not different merely, but absolutely contradictory: as well could a student in the heathen schools have imbibed at once the Stoic and the Epicurean philosophies, as could a humble member of our Church at the present time learn his creed both from Prayer Book and Articles. This I set out at length, in two pamphlets with an appendix, which I published three years ago; [6] and it cannot therefore be necessary to go again over the same ground: though something must be added, occasionally in notes, and more methodically in a future chapter.[7] The manner in which the dry wording of the Articles can be divorced from their natural spirit and accepted by an orthodox believer; how their prima facie meaning is evaded and the artifice of their inventors thrown back in recoil on themselves; this, and the arguments which prove the honesty of this, have now been for some time before the public. Others have not been equally open; and we can therefore form no judgment what the success of "Evangelicals" would be in showing how they give their full assent and consent to the Prayer Book. But it is plain, if there be force in the arguments used three years ago, that even *omissions* in the Prayer Book cannot be taken as any direct voice of the English Church; nor can it be said that prayers for the dead or invocations of

---

6. [ED.] Cf. above, p. 162, n. 18, and p. 167. n. 2.

7. [ED.] Cf. Ward, *Ideal of a Christian Church,* chap. VIII: "A Few Words on our Authoritative Formularies."

saints are condemned by her merely because she has dropped such addresses from her service.[8] For if those omissions were the result of a disingenuous compromise (as I endeavoured to show in my former pamphlet), and if the very men who made the omissions wished to include within our Church Christians who would have preferred their retention, it is plain that there can be no colour for the allegation that we are bound to withdraw from the English Church should we be led forward to such practices and devotions.

Having alluded to the subject of our Articles, it may be as well to add that so far has Mr. Palmer been from *arguing* against the *British Critic* on the ground of alleged inconsistency with those formularies, that he quotes as a part of his indictment a passage (not written by myself) in which Mr. Oakeley is quoted as having "proved historically that the Articles were not designed to exclude Roman Catholics," [9] and attempts no refutation whatever of the position.

But even were the formularies of our Church accordant instead of discordant, urgent instead of wavering, definite instead of vague, still, so long as her practical teaching is in the highest degree uncertain, conflicting, and contradictory; when members of our Church seem hardly to agree in one matter of positive opinion that can be named, except the purity of our Church; and when, even as to that, each party maintains that our Church would be most *im*pure if she taught doctrines which the other party strenuously contends she *does* teach; I can see no possible defence for the position,

> that her formularies, in their *primâ facie* bearing, demand implicit reception from her children. Surely, until she is able so far to invigorate her discipline, as that one and one only doctrine in essentials shall be taught within her pale, she can have no warrant in making this demand. How can that sacredness and divine authority, which attaches to our first instructors, be fairly claimed for the English formularies in their natural sense, when in point of fact they are *not* our first instructors? It is the creed of our parents which first introduces us to the creed of our Church, and colours the latter with its own hues. And when our moral development has compelled us to desert that creed, those do not fairly challenge our adherence, who give to our formularies their most *literal* sense, but those who

8. This has indeed been decided by the Ecclesiastical Court on the former subject [in the judgment of the Court of Arches in the case of Breeks v. Woolfrey, November 19, 1838].

9. [ED.] William Palmer, *A Narrative of Events connected with the Publication of the Tracts for the Times*, 2d ed. (London, 1883), 177.

give to them that sense which promises most fairly as a rest and satisfaction to that development.[10]

4. The two objections I have just considered are rather implied by Mr. Palmer, than distinctly stated. There is indeed only one passage, in all his pamphlet, which bears with it the profession of *reasoning* against the course adopted by the *British Critic:* [11] in all the remainder he merely expresses his own opinion, that such a course is undutiful and inexcusable. In the passage to which I refer, he proposes three exhaustive alternatives: of which I will proceed to quote that which concerns myself.

> If men are satisfied that it is a matter of duty to remain in the English Church, then I say, that it is wholly inconsistent with that duty to excite a spirit of doubt and dissatisfaction in the Church, and to tempt its members, in every possible way, to secede from its communion. Nothing can be more inconsistent than the practice of disregarding its authorities, encouraging disobedience and disrespect to its prelates, and discontent within the Church itself, as if the great mass of its members were engaged in measures hostile to the true faith. It is sinful even to contemplate the possibility of voluntarily separating from the Church under circumstances of persecution or obloquy. Notions of this kind tend to diminish the horror which every Catholic should feel at the very notion of schism.[12]

This, I say, is that part of the dilemma, proposed by Mr. Palmer, which includes my own case. I suppose indeed that, considering all the various proposals which have been made, and all the various measures which have been rumoured as in contemplation, and considering too *some* among the apparent tendencies of our existing condition, the number is very far from small of those who have had more or less misgiving, what at some future time might possibly *become* their duty. But I can most truly say that the very idea of leaving our Church has never been before my own mind as an immediately practical question; that my present feeling is (without for one moment judging others) that I should myself commit a mortal sin by doing so; and that it has been my uniform endeavour to divert my imagination from dwelling on such a contingency, even as a future possibility. It is very plain then that the paragraph I have quoted contains, if any part of the pamphlet contains, Mr. Palmer's

10. Ward, "Church Authority," 231 f.

11. Mr. Palmer's remarks on "development" shall be considered before I conclude [*cf.* Ward, *Ideal of a Christian Church,* 545–53]: but they are directed against the *truth* of opinions advocated in the *British Critic;* not against the legitimacy of English churchmen advocating such opinions. The latter is the point now in hand.

12. [ED.] Palmer, *Narrative of Events,* 178 f.

grounds for thinking that "the tone" of my articles "cannot be excused." [13]

First, then, is it wrong in me to "encourage" to the utmost of my humble power and opportunities "discontent with the Church itself, as if the great mass of its members" are "engaged in measures hostile to the true faith"? The answer to this must surely depend on the truth of the allegation. I willingly adopt Mr. Palmer's happy expression; I do believe that the "mass of our Church's members" are unconsciously and unintentionally, but most effectually, "engaged in measures hostile to the true faith"; this I believe, and hope before I end to prove. And believing this, it would surely be the strangest possible mode of showing loyalty to the English Church, were I to remain perfectly quiet, enjoying the proceeds of my fellowship, or (to use the ordinary language) "eating the bread of the Church," and abstain from drawing attention to evils which appear to me so imminent, so fearful, so destructive of the very life and essence of a church. Nor yet do I seek to encourage discontent with our Church herself, but only with that miserable system, to which, for three hundred years, she has been so unfortunately committed.

Secondly, is it wrong in me to "disregard the authorities of our Church"? This must surely depend on the dicta of those authorities. The Roman Catholics indeed generally say that Christians are, in matters of doctrine, bound to receive implicitly the decrees of St. Peter's Chair; but those who so think, think also that, by a divine promise, that Chair is infallibly saved from teaching error. But to reject the doctrine of the Church's infallibility as a figment, to proclaim as a great and glorious truth, that all bishops are but fallible men, and that the chief bishop on earth sanctions, nay, practises, idolatry; and at the same time to call for implicit deference and submission to the doctrinal statements of a certain small body of bishops, who are indefinitely at variance with each other, and who, according to Mr. Palmer's own theory, are separated off from the great body of the Catholic Church; [14] this is a flight of conservative extravagance, an assumption of spiritual despotism, which can find no parallel beyond the circle of Anglican "High-churchmen." My own sentiments on the subject I have already expressed, and find nothing to alter.

13. [ED.] *Ibid.*, 179.
14. [ED.] Ward is referring to the idea of the Catholic Church as divided into several "branches," elaborated by Palmer in his *Treatise on the Church of Christ.*

One of the many difficulties (I say) which press upon us in the present most unhappy state of our Church, is the question of the proper course to be pursued by Churchmen when a bishop delivers ex cathedrâ doctrines which are in fact heretical. There is no difficulty of course when the points at issue are short of fundamental articles of faith; for silent submission to his diocesan's will, supposing an injunction to have been laid upon him, is then the clergyman's plain duty; nor, again, in the case of fundamentals is the question one of principle; for learned persons tell us that, according to the uniform tradition of antiquity, even laymen have not the right only but the duty of contending for the faith openly and uncompromisingly, by whomsoever it may have been assailed, and under whatever circumstances. But the *when* and the *how* no doubt present matter for grave deliberation; and which perhaps at last must be decided in each case, as it separately arises, by reference to its own peculiar facts.[15]

Thirdly, is it right to "tempt" members of the English Church "in every possible way to secede from its communion"? Certainly not. That, for myself, it was in some sufficient measure impressed on my own mind, how serious responsibility on this head is incurred by all who express publicly their opinion on present circumstances, will, I hope, be evinced by the fact, which I lately mentioned, of my constant enforcement throughout my articles of our Church's claim on our allegiance. But fully acknowledging (which I do) that frank and bold protests against the English Reformation, and the system introduced by it, have an indirect and accidental tendency, in some cases, to hasten, or even to cause, a separation from our Church, I would still most fearlessly meet Mr. Palmer on his own ground and by his own theory; and I would ask him, whether in any age of the Church it would be thought even tolerable in individuals, to be in any way less diligent and energetic in their protests against heresy, deeply seated, subtly insinuating, and widely extending heresy, because such protests had the accidental effect of inducing one or two orthodox to join a foreign communion? My defence then entirely depends on the truth or falsehood of the views I hold as to the amount of corruption existing in and ruling our Church. If the evils be such as I suppose, I was justified in denouncing them as loudly as I did.

5. But although what I have said seems sufficiently to answer Mr. Palmer's observations, I feel deeply that there is a natural reason for great dislike and suspicion of statements such as I have made; and a

15. W. G. Ward, "Whately's Essays" [*British Critic*, 4th ser., XXXI (Jan.-April 1842)], 225.

reason far more serious, and requiring far greater deference of tone in meeting it, than any of the objections which have occurred to Mr. Palmer. It is thought that the most ordinary reverence and docility of mind would secure a willing reception of those principles under which one is born; and that to allow oneself in open dissatisfaction with, or even hatred to, those principles, must imply much holiness, or else little humility. "We do not augur much good," says a writer in the *British Critic*, "of any one, who does not in the first instance throw himself into the system under which he is born, accept the voices of the teachers, divines, and pastors, by whom he is providentially surrounded, as the voice of heaven, and identify their pattern and their faith with the holy doctrine which they have been the instruments of conveying to him." [16] This general principle, thus stated, is that very principle, *"the high sacredness of hereditary religion,"* which I singled out in the last chapter as all-important at the present moment; [17] and which it was the miserable sin of our Reformers so grievously to violate. In fact, I wrote an article in the *British Critic* (that on "Church Authority" [18]) with the main object of enforcing, illustrating, and vindicating this principle; in which article I extended it to its legitimate consequence, the case of Dissenters of whatever kind. Still, as the writer just quoted proceeds to say, "of course such implicit confidence cannot last in all cases, as time goes on; for there is but one truth whatever it is, whereas there are 'many kinds of voices in the world' [1 Cor. 14:10], and it is not to be anticipated that all minds, every where, as they grow, will just happen felicitously to concur with the system in which they find themselves." "It is the trial and mystery of our position in this age and country that a religious mind is continually set at variance with itself, that its deference to what is without *contradicts suggestions from within,* and that it cannot obey what is over it without *rebelling against what was before it."* And as to the origin, again, of such "suggestions from within," in the article of my own to which I just alluded, a passage occurs, quoted in the first chapter of this work, arguing with great earnestness, that "absolute and great defects of character" frequently occasion them.[19] Certainly, so far is it from being the case that the idea of corruptions within our Church was a congenial idea to my own mind, that I suffered innumerable troubles and perplexities before it even occurred to me to seek for their cause in

16. [ED.] *British Critic*, 4th ser., XXXI (Jan.–April 1842), 385.
17. [ED.] Ward, *Ideal of a Christian Church*, 44.
18. [ED.] Quoted several times in the present chapter.
19. Ward, "Church Authority," 225. [ED.] The passage is quoted at length in Ward, *Ideal of a Christian Church*, 6 f.

its true quarter; the radically corrupt and heretical nature of the system which I had been taught.

A sentiment is often expressed and often implied, not unlike the preceding, which, though substantially refuted by what has just been said, still deserves an explicit notice. We often hear admonitions of this kind, addressed to the "discontented young men" in the English Church: "Act up to the provisions of the Prayer Book; when you regularly attend morning and evening prayer, observe rigorously all the fasts in the calendar, and realize that type of character which the Prayer Book implies; then, if still dissatisfied with the English system, you may perhaps deserve a hearing; but not *till* then." Now I will not be betrayed, by the wish of defending myself, into any such concession, as that the English system *does* place before her children a sufficiently high standard, or that holy men, who shall have complied with the conditions above specified, will not be even more dissatisfied than they were before. But I will fully acknowledge that the Prayer Book puts before us a very high standard, and one indefinitely above my own humble aspirations or attainments: but so also, let it be carefully observed, did the Jewish law.

> To keep alive, throughout one nation at least, these truths (the perfection of God's law and our own miserable sinfulness) in all their native freshness and distinctness, to preserve man's conscience from becoming hardened, and his perception of religious truth deadened, over the whole world, was one especial cause, St. Paul seems to say, of the Jewish economy.[20]

> Ever since the Fall, man, viewed in himself, has remained knowing the law, but not doing it; admiring, not loving; assenting, not following; with the law not within him, but before him; not any longer in the heart, but departing from him and moving away and taking up its place, as it were, over against him, and confronting him as an enemy, accuser, and avenger.[21]

Christianity then was essentially and fundamentally a remedial religion; nor has it any object more closely connected with its whole scheme of doctrine and discipline than that of bringing our power to do right into some illimitably increasing proportion with our power to perceive it. To take a strong instance; the superiority itself of celibacy over marriage, I have confidently stated to be a dictate of the natural conscience: [22]

20. Ward, "The Synagogue and the Church," 28.
21. J. H. Newman, *Parochial and Plain Sermons* [London, 1908–18], V, 146 [abbrev.].
22. *Cf.* W. G. Ward, "Mill's Logic" [*British Critic*, 4th ser., XXXIV (July–Oct. 1843)], 406.

but the power of leading blamelessly a single life is one of the highest and most precious gospel gifts. Those then who hold such language as that above described, should in all consistency have held the same to the Jews also: Christ came to enable them to fulfil the law; but these objectors should have said, "fulfil the law first, and join Christ afterwards." Whether or no indeed the English Church *does* give such helps towards the most ordinary Christian life as frail and humble believers seek at her hands, is a question which will come under our consideration in a future chapter: [23] but unless she does so, though the character she held up for reverence and imitation were really the true evangelical pattern; though she encouraged her children to honour austerity, celibacy, voluntary poverty, as much as she in fact (practically at least, and in her authoritative teaching) encourages them to despise or revile those graces; even then there would not be so much as an approach to a proof that she even tolerably fulfils the very primary object for which the Church was founded; nor would her children have any reason for withholding their most bitter complaints if they meet not at her hands with that protection and support which shall shield them from the implacable enemies of their salvation.

6. "Granting, however, that our corruptions may be as grievous as the *British Critic* has represented, still," it may be asked, "why is Rome to be taken for our model in the needful task of reform and purification? Why not rather go back to more early and primitive times, than endeavour to place before the minds of Englishmen in such favourable colours a system which practically issues in the deep superstition and idolatry which we witness abroad?" Such will be the language of many members of our Church; and it certainly requires a reply. The inquiry indeed deserves most careful consideration, whether the Church of the fourth century (did we see it really reproduced amongst us, instead of being known to us through the less distinct and impressive media of historical documents) would appear on the whole much less idolatrous and superstitious than modern Rome herself. Waiving however this question (towards the elucidation of which something may be done in the next chapter [24]), and moreover without professing to give either, or even the principal, reasons, which lead me to consider the existing Church

23. [ED.] *Cf.* Ward, *Ideal of a Christian Church*, chap. VI: "On our Existing Practical Corruptions," where Ward lays great stress on "sacramental confession."
24. [ED.] *Ibid.*, chap. IV: "Does our Existing System Resemble that of the Early Centuries?"

abroad as the fit model to regard, those which follow will amply suffice
to support that opinion. It must be observed, however, that the idea of
introducing, as it were, bodily among us some foreign pattern, according
to the best conception we are able to form of it, would be absolute in-
sanity; to think of it would be most extravagant, even to attempt its
execution, absolutely impossible. No! the one principal object of our
observation must ever be *our own* Church; to study the nature and extent of her corruptions and the remedies for them which her present
resources are capable of supplying, this must be, beyond any comparison,
our principal task; the only question is, in what quarter are we to look
for the *suggestion* of appropriate remedies? And the Church abroad is
the point to which we are in duty bound first to turn our eyes, were it
only for the plain dictates of Christian love and charity. All our existing
most unhappy divisions cannot efface the obligation of that primary
gospel duty, which requires us to consider as brethren all who bear the
name of Christ, so only they be not heretical in some essential particular.
Now all English "High-churchmen" agree in denying that Roman
Catholics are so to be regarded; the plain duty then remains, to consult
first of all with our brethren in any difficulty wherein we may be placed;
and only in the event of failing to find in them what we seek, to turn our
thoughts in any other direction. Another reason which may be given is
the undoubted fact that great, as are the difficulties in either case, they
are incomparably less in the way of our rightly understanding a contemporary than an ancient system. Those innumerable details which,
small in themselves, go so very far, when taken together, in constituting
the real nature of an institution as a fact in history; and the knowledge
of which is so indispensably necessary in order to the practical working
of any imitation; all these we may study on the spot if we follow a living
example; but can by no possible efforts rescue from the abyss of time
when we desire to make the past our guide.

But over and above these considerations, there is another quite decisive on the subject. If our Church be so corrupt in her practical working as I have represented her, we should expect a priori, what we find
in fact, that we must look for the source of her corruptions in no less
vital part, but in the very foundation of all; her system, or rather her
total absence of system, of moral discipline. That this is the real truth,
it will be the main object of the following pages to show; and if it be
so, until this fountainhead of evil be closed up, the application of any
number of more superficial and external remedies will be wholly fruit-

less. Now it is plain at once that there is no subject in the whole range of theology which varies more indefinitely, according to the indefinite varieties of man's inward character (varies, that is, in every particular excepting the most general and fundamental principles), than this very subject. And this being so, considering how closely bound up in all the more essential features of their civilization (whatever important minor differences may exist) are all the countries of the great European family, to look for our guide, in the task of constructing a system of moral discipline for modern England, in the Church of fifteen centuries or even of five centuries since, when a Church exists before our eyes in modern France or modern Italy, this would be nothing short of absolute infatuation. To mention only one particular where very many might be mentioned; everyone knows that there is no more essential and important characteristic which distinguishes modern civilization from all former periods than the vast increase of what is called *subjectivity:* the very much greater portion of man's life and interest which is occupied in observation of his own thoughts, feelings, and actions; the very much less part which is occupied in action unaccompanied by self-consciousness, or uninterrupted contemplation of external objects. We might have been certain, then, beforehand that, supposing the ancient Church, which we regard, to have been really pure and efficient, the effect of appropriating its discipline to ourselves would be to lay far too much stress on outward action and devotion and far too little on the conscious regulation of the thoughts. This is perhaps a partial account of the accusation of formalism, so often brought against the Church by Protestants. They find much less said by early writers, than by Christians of the present day, on the inward life of the soul; and — failing to see that this was the necessary result of the habits and tendencies of the time, and that spiritual habits and desires do not the less exist because men do not contemplate, analyse, and describe them — they attribute it to something of a deadening and unspiritualizing character in the creed then professed. As though, from the time that *subjectivity* has obtained so complete an entrance, the works of any other writers could bear even a moment's most distant comparison with those of Roman Catholics, in profound acquaintance with the inmost recesses of the human heart.[25]

25. *Cf.* Ward, "Mill's Logic," 409 n.: "A sentiment is commonly found in Mr. [F. D.] Maurice's writings, which puzzles us more than any other of his sentiments; viz. that 'the truths, which constitute Protestantism, are those which concern man as a personal being, which assert his individual responsibility and relation to God, and

However, if antiquity is to be our guide in this matter, let us make it fairly and honestly our guide: let us look fully in the face those bodily privations and inflictions which to us seem so incredibly severe; and which nevertheless were not the choice of eminently holy men who had a special vocation and went on towards perfection, but were appointed as the ordinary lot of penitents, nay, in great measure, of all Christians. But if there appears small chance of introducing any approach to the like among ourselves, insomuch that the most sanguine can entertain no hope of its possibility (those even, I mean, who think their general introduction among us, in the abstract, desirable; a sentiment against which I most warmly protest); if this be so, we confess with our own lips that we cannot make the ancient Church our model in supplying our one primary deficiency; for we cannot hope to introduce that which was her very principal instrument in performing the work which *we* desire to be done. On the other hand, I know no more noble and wonderful event in the whole history of the Church than the mode in which the Roman Church has applied herself to meet this new and most conspicuous phenomenon which crossed her path. About the time when the Church of Christ was harassed, and outraged, and insulted, by the foreign Reformers, within the Church appeared the spiritual exercises of St. Ignatius; a work which all who have given deep and careful attention to it, and, far more, those who have used it practically, extol in terms of eulogy, which those who (like myself) have not done so, can hardly bring ourselves to believe is not exaggerated. On the basis of that miraculous work has been reared the whole scheme of occasional retreats, daily meditation, daily general examen of conscience, particular examen, and the rest, which is at present the very vital principle of the Roman religious system. This scheme it is from which we may really hope to derive remedies for our present need, of proved efficacy, and of the profoundest wisdom; not by the insane course of servile and literal imitation, but by bringing with us

---

provide that this responsibility and relation shall be realities, and not dreams.' We should not be more surprised than pleased, if Mr. Maurice could show us in Protestant writers any knowledge or realisation of these subjects, which can for very shame be *compared* with that displayed scientifically by St. Thomas and the moral theologians who have followed him; and practically by a hundred such works as 'The Spiritual Combat,' St. Francis de Sales's 'Love of God,' St. Alphonsus Liguori's Sermons, and 'Preparation for Death,' Salazar's 'Sinner's Conversion Reduced to Principles'; we may be allowed to add Mr. Newman's Sermons. We keep St. Ignatius's 'Spiritual Exercises' for a separate place, since the wonderful insight into such subjects which that work displays has led many to think it inspired, in a lower sense of the word."

to the study of that scheme a deep and habitual knowledge of the English feelings and habits of the day, and carefully adapting whatever proposals we may make to the exigencies of those feelings and habits.

It will be a great relief to many, who justly claim at our hands the deepest reverence and sympathy, when they are told that the name of St. Mary is so little prominent in these exercises, or generally in the whole scheme of discipline founded on them, that it hardly escapes omission. And I will say plainly that nothing, in my judgment, would be fraught with more omnigenous mischief, or would deservedly incur God's heavier displeasure, than any attempt to introduce generally among us at the present time any of those devotions to the Blessed Virgin which occupy so prominent a place in foreign churches. But having said this boldly, I will also say with equal boldness that this opinion implied no adverse criticism whatever on foreign systems as they exist. On this subject I have really seen no evidence which enables me to have so much as a bias one way or the other; nor indeed is it at all practically important that a member of our Church should have such a bias; we know our own duty, and we need know no more. If indeed some religious and unusually intelligent person were to live for a considerable time, say in some particular part of Italy; if he were able by a strong and sustained effort of the imagination, to realize and sympathize with the habitual emotions, desires, aspirations of the people; if he were to follow them into their retirement and their home, converse familiarly with them, and live almost as one of themselves; and if, after having done all this, his opinion were unfavourable, it would justly deserve the very greatest attention. But the mere random observations of those who go abroad mainly for recreation, and presume to pass judgment on a nation's religion by such mere external forms as a rapid passage through the country enables them to perceive, can surely have no weight whatever in the mind of any candid and reasonable inquirer. As to stories they hear, they are still less trustworthy than appearances they see; for it is well known that Italian guides continually invent false tales against their countrymen, with the view of obtaining better pay from the English traveller.

Observe, the question to be considered is this; not whether Roman Catholics address very frequent devotions to St. Mary (this is allowed on all hands), but whether those devotions tend to cloud or supersede in their minds the thoughts of their and her Creator; whether the form, as it were, in which she is habitually present to their imagination, is as kneeling with uplifted hands to her Son, praying for those favours which they beg from her; or, on the other hand, as scattering down on them those favours from her own treasury. If the former be the case, every invocation they address to her not only does not put her before their minds in the place of Christ, but imprints more deeply on their conscience and imagination her infinite inferiority to him. For instance, the Rosary, the use of which is continually thrown in their teeth, would most certainly tend very powerfully to this latter result. It consists in meditation on fifteen mysteries of St. Mary,[26] in all of which, except two, our Blessed Lord himself must be in the mind of those who meditate; and in almost all of these, must be so in their mind as forcibly to impress it with a sense of her infinite subordination to him. Indeed, it must not be supposed, notwithstanding the incalculable obstacles in the way of a fair judgment, on people so unlike ourselves in every particular, which is presented by all our prejudices of habit and education; it must not be supposed that the English are always unfavourably impressed with what they see abroad. When the Queen was in Belgium last year, even the newspaper reporters seemed struck by the peculiarly religious character of the people. And I have put down in an appendix several accounts, given by acquaintances of my own, of their personal experience, that it may be seen how much there is which presents itself even to Englishmen in a favourable light.[27]

However, it is continually supposed that a refusal to admit, without proof, the practical corruption of foreign systems, implies some desire of seeing those systems introduced here. Thus, for example, I have seen questions like this: "Is it possible that writers in the *British Critic* can desire the introduction among us of the state of things we witness in Belgium or Normandy — nay, in Naples or Palermo?" The very question points to the answer that must be given. The respective churches of Belgium, Normandy, Naples, Palermo, *differ from each other* in numberless matters of ceremonial and observance, of usage, discipline, ecclesiastical taste, nay, and in many minor points of religious opinion: which then of the four are we to adopt? What can be more preposterous than the fancy of our gravely endeavouring to imitate the external gestures, as it were, and demeanour of some foreign system, while all the habits

26. [ED.] Five "Joyful Mysteries" (of the Incarnation); five "Sorrowful Mysteries" (of the Passion); five "Glorious Mysteries" (including the Assumption and the Coronation of our Lady).

27. [ED.] Cf. Ward, *Ideal of a Christian Church,* 591–601.

of our mind, all our thoughts, feelings, and dispositions are in marked contrast with that system?

The only legitimate office of the external framework and constitution of a church is to be, first, the expression, mould, and protection of a certain given religious spirit; and, secondly, the mode by which this spirit is brought to bear upon a certain given condition of society; to pay any serious regard to it, on any other principles, is the certain road to the hollowest and most hideous formalism. First, then, let us endeavour to secure what *comes* first; let us learn, to the best of our power, to understand and appreciate the various exigencies, tendencies, tastes, capabilities of the modern English character: and in proportion as we succeed in our attempts, by help of such knowledge, to promote and forward the growth of this same Catholic spirit, the latter will clothe itself in whatever external envelopment may be found ready at hand, which it will quicken, enliven, and re-create, adopting it as the organ of its expression, and the minister of its will. What outward shape this envelopment will ultimately assume, in what degree Catholicism will modify our existing institutions, in what degree it will itself receive a colour *from* those institutions, and from our national character and dispositions; all this, and much more of the same kind, it is vain and useless to conjecture before the event. We must learn to content ourselves with what lies before us, and not dissipate our energies in barren and unprofitable speculations.

What *will* be the external manifestation of Catholicism in England is a question then which it is idle to ask; but we may be very certain what it will *not* be; it will not be the same with its manifestation in Belgium or Normandy, Naples or Palermo; much less, with that assumed by it in its conflicts with the expiring efforts of a paganism, powerful even in its decline; or in its attempts to humanize and soften the wild and lawless hordes, who at a later period became nominal adherents of the Church. Catholicism is something moral and spiritual, not formal, external, circumstantial; in doctrine, in sentiment, in principle, ever one and the same; but elastic and pliant to adapt itself to all conceivable circumstances, vigorous and full of life to cope with all conceivable emergencies. Take the case of an individual whose religion shall assume a more earnest or more orthodox character; we do not find that his recognizable identity of *mind* is affected, any more than of *body*. His numberless peculiarities of feeling and disposition, taste and imagination, intellectual cultivation and power, still remain undiminished in their native distinctness and energy; although at the same time a new and authoritative element has been introduced, which, to an illimitably increasing extent, controls, harmonizes, and colours those peculiarities. Let a number of serious and Catholic-minded men meet together: how very far will they be from exhibiting any artificial conformity to some external and partial standard! and yet for all this, a like-minded observer will very easily discern, by means of indications far too "subtle, delicate, indirect, and spiritual," to admit of analysis and formal expression, the essential oneness of principle which animates and informs those accidental diversities of character. What then would be thought of some disciple in the school who, being desirous of conforming more fully to the Catholic model, should copy the expressions and gestures, or even the argumentative methods and political opinions, of some one amongst their number, instead of attempting, by legitimate means, to lodge more deeply within his heart that essential principle which is common to them all? The application of this, from individuals to societies, is obvious.

Nor is it only external habits which are thus intimately connected with the inward principle; doctrines also, as I said in the last chapter,[28] are in many cases the spontaneous evolution, in all the appropriate correlative, of a certain moral character. This truth is the foundation of the *disciplina arcani* which existed in earlier ages;[29] and (whatever real and serious difficulties are in the way of its application on vital and fundamental articles of the Creed) when we are considering subordinate and accessory religious opinions, it is our one chief guide and protection. In proportion as any primary religious principle takes deep root in the mind, or any cardinal doctrine is realized, contemplated, and habitually appropriated, an indefinite number of minor opinions and practices start into existence: of which some are the simple and legitimate result of this doctrine or principle; but other some result, not from it as isolated and energizing by its own power, but as taken in connection with current opinions and feelings, which, however deeply and widely rooted in the popular mind, are peculiarities of a nation or of a period, and have an origin wholly independent of revelation.[30] We may apply this at once to that very class of doctrines and practices so lately mentioned. Nothing can be further from the truth than the supposition that the *British Critic*

---

28. [ED.] *Ideal of a Christian Church,* chap. II: "Of What Kind will be the Ideal of a Church in Circumstances like Ours?"

29. [ED.] *Cf.* above, p. 142, n. 25.

30. See this stated at somewhat greater length in Ward, "Church Authority," 218.

has ever advocated their introduction among ourselves. Speaking only for myself, in July last I say, "so far as later introductions are concerned, such as Images and Indulgences, and habitual Invocation of Saints, we should certainly be travelling out of our way to notice them." [31] In January: "Those who are pained and distressed by some circumstances in which the mediaeval system differs from antiquity, have a most legitimate satisfaction in the history of the early Church, which exhibits Catholic faith as truly active and energizing, at a time when such peculiarities (we allude, *e.g.* to the pointed and habitual invocations of the Blessed Virgin and Saints) are not prevalent." [32] In the previous October, in a passage quoted by Mr. Palmer, I go still further: "So long as an English churchman acts carefully up to the principles he has been taught, and *in* so acting feels himself in no way attracted towards these ways, *so long it would be a plain sin in him to resort to them.*" [33] Nay more; not only have I never expressed a wish (but the reverse), that these devotions should be generally practised by us at present, I have never even implied an opinion that, as popularly adopted, they are not mischievous and dangerous abroad; though neither have I, so at least I trust, implied the opposite opinion. What I *have* said is (and no greater proof can be given of our degraded and unchristian temper of mind, than that it is *necessary* to say what all ought to admit as a first principle), that *saints*, in using the high and glowing language which is found in their writings, have not made even the most distant approach to superstition or idolatry. Why I was called upon to say this will appear in the course of the work, when I hope to touch on the general subject with which it is connected; I mean, the authority of holy men on questions of religious truth.[34] Here I will only add so much as closely concerns the matter now in hand.

Roman Catholics say that it is impossible for the Church heartily to embrace and dwell upon the great and fundamental truths of our Lord's divinity, the indwelling of his Spirit in the souls of his disciples, and the importance of gaining to ourselves intercessors against his final judgment, without being led on in course of time to similar devotions. And certainly our experience in England does not enable us to deny this; for, as I shall presently have to urge, those great doctrines are either practically disbelieved or most insufficiently held by the great body of members of

31. Ward, "The Synagogue and the Church," 7.
32. Ward, "Church Authority," 215.
33. W. G. Ward, "St. Athanasius" [*British Critic*, 4th ser., XXXII (July–Oct. 1842)], 410.
34. [ED.] *Cf.* Ward, *Ideal of a Christian Church*, 517 ff.

our Church.[35] On the other hand, whether or no these devotions necessarily *spring* from fundamental doctrines, most certainly in themselves
they are *not* fundamental; as Roman Catholics themselves are forward in
assuring us. Let us then fairly and honestly try the experiment. "High-
churchmen" of all grades profess belief in the fundamental verities to
which I just now alluded; let them unite in the use of all such means as
are in our power, which, I hope to show in a future chapter,[36] are very
far from inconsiderable, to imprint these doctrines on the innermost hearts
of our fellow-churchmen, as living and absorbing realities; and let them
"leave the result with perfect calmness, contentment, and tranquillity of
heart in His hands, who, by His Apostle has praised Abraham's faith, in
that he went out, not knowing whither he went." [37] Should it be found
that the more deeply and practically English Christians embrace these
essential truths, so much the more powerfully they are attracted to such
usages and devotions as are now in question; no stronger proof can be
devised that those devotions are not injurious, but ministrative, to the
central and paramount doctrines of the gospel. Should the opposite be
found the case, I suppose there is no one member of our Church who
would desire their adoption: and the conclusion as to any given foreign
country would be that in its case either their use is attributable to particulars in the national history and character wherein it differs from
England; or else (which is of course perfectly conceivable) that it is a
real practical corruption, to which we may fitly desire that the Church
should apply a remedy.

It will be well, however, to enforce still further this very important
truth, that Catholicism (should it ever again exist actively in England)
will no more destroy English peculiarities of habit or opinion than it
does in the parallel case, which I put above, of an *individual* adopting a
more Catholic view of things. And the same considerations will also
show how utterly fallacious is that mode of judging as to the merits
of some religious system, which is founded on the superficial observation
of the various sentiments and practices, which are seen in some particular
country to be coexistent with it. Let it be observed then, that there is
not a single event which has happened to a nation in the earliest ages,
before Christianity had existence, which has not had its permanent and

35. [ED.] *Cf. ibid.*, 389 ff.
36. [ED.] *Ideal of a Christian Church*, chap. VII: "Additional Suggestions in the
Way of Remedy."
37. Ward, "Church Authority," 211.

abiding influence in constituting the nation's present character. Without refining however so much as to take this into account (though all this *must* be taken into account, if we desire a really accurate appreciation of the subject), such circumstances as the following are not permanent only but most essential, most fundamental, most vital elements, in the formation of that character: the race or mixture of races from which the nation has its origin: the climate; not only as affecting the mind directly, and disposing it to this vicious excess rather than that; but also as obliging the lower classes, when unemployed, to keep mainly within doors, or else allowing and alluring them to meet together in large bodies for recreation in the open air (the former leading to the more domestic, the latter to the more social life); as making a certain quantity of food and clothing more or less indispensable, and so giving or not giving an un-ceasing stimulus to labour; and so with other particulars: then again, the nature of the soil and the geographical position of the country, as directly fixing the principal employments pursued by the people, commercial, agricultural, or the like: the various other countries, with which, in times past, whether by war or by commerce, the nation has been brought into close contact; and the peculiar character of those countries: the nature of the civil government, past or present, and the degree in which it has made the people's welfare its principal object: the number of men gifted with great originality and genius who have flourished in the nation, and the respective bent of their minds; the number of saints and saintly men who have been raised up among them, and in what rank of life they have principally been. This list might be very much increased; but enough has been said to indicate the extreme complexity of any problem which proposes to derive a practical result from the observation of social and political facts in the concrete. Of these elements, the only one with which a religious system has any direct connection is the last; and even with the last its connection is very precarious: for we have no reason at all to believe (orthodoxy and Catholicity being supposed), that a practically pure church will be honoured by the presence of saints more often than one of an opposite character: rather, God raises up saints where he will, according to the inscrutable laws of his providence. Yet all of these elements, especially the two latter, have a very much — indeed more deep and intimate share in the form assumed even by religion itself, than, I suppose, anyone like myself, who has not deeply studied history, can at all realize.

And now, to see more clearly what it is which a religious system is called on to accomplish, let us conceive an imaginary hypothesis; let us suppose that these various causes had by themselves been operating for a long period, and issuing in those results which would follow their combined operation; and that then, for the first time, such a system were projected. It has to act on a large body of men, who are and have been exposed to certain most powerful influences, while *the very ministers, by whom it is obliged to act on them, have themselves been exposed to the same influences.* A system might be absolutely the very best possible, which yet, when acting under this double disadvantage, would present to those, who have themselves been governed by a lifelong bias of the most opposite character, an objectionable, not to say repulsive, appearance. And again, it is very plain that precisely the same religious system, acting on a people and by means of ministers, who, in all the particulars above specified, or nearly all of them, differ from that former nation, would wear an external dress so absolutely different also, that it would almost require a practised eye to recognize through that dress the same essential principles at work.

We shall the better understand this by fixing our ideas on one out of those numberless elements of a national character, and tracing in greater detail the degree of its influence; and there is more than one reason which induces me to select, for that purpose, the different effect caused by difference of *race*.

The division between the Teutonic and the Roman nations is, both in itself the most striking in modern Europe, and also acquires additional interest from the almost universal adoption of the Reformation by those of the former stock — its almost universal rejection by those of the latter. And if we examine the moral character of those nations, as they are exhibited in their most complete specimens; on the one hand in England and Germany, on the other hand in Spain and Italy; we shall find amidst the general resemblance which binds together all the parts of European Christendom, marked diversities, which cannot readily be ascribed to any other cause than their original difference of race. Of France it is the less necessary to speak, because the less strongly defined character of the French people, in the leading points which distinguish generally the Teutonic and Roman nations, is exactly what might be expected from a country in which the two elements were from the first most inseparably and equally blended; and exactly accords with the doubtful contest, there maintained so long, between the two contending principles of the sixteenth century, which in the other states of Europe so soon obtained mastery over the national mind.

It is not then too much to say, that the two great divisions, before mentioned, coincide as nearly as possible with two of the chief tendencies which divide the human race itself; and in which, so far as we can trace them back to their origin, we find on the one side the ideas of truth and justice, on the other side, those of beauty and love; which, when separated from each other, and exposed to evil influences, are liable to be corrupted, the one into selfish atheism, the other into a bloody and lying idolatry.[38] It will be sufficient for the present purpose, to dwell on the exemplification of these tendencies under their more favourable aspect, in each of these two great branches of the European commonwealth.

Long before the introduction of Christianity among the German races, Tacitus had contrasted their truthful and independent spirit with the servility of his own countrymen. The English, whilst they are often regarded in the East as a people without religion and without morality, are yet known emphatically as the truth-speaking nation. The Saxon race has been pronounced to be the only one in which veracity is regarded as an undoubted virtue. On the other hand, it is no less notorious that our very idea and standard of beauty has been derived from Italy — that whatever elements have been powerful in refining and softening the harshness of the northern nations, have been derived almost entirely from the south. How different would have been Shakespeare's mind, without the conception of the Italian atmosphere which breathes through Romeo and Juliet! How different would have been all the poetry of Christendom, had it not found its first voice in the immortal work of Dante!

In each of these two divisions, the best man will of course rise above the failings of his nation, and the worst will sink below its virtues; but the character of the mass must be judged by the ordinary temptations, and the ordinary standard of excellence, in the race to which they belong. The mere Englishman is conscious of no struggle when he tells the truth — the mere Italian is conscious of no victory when he burns with passionate enthusiasm. The mere Englishman will never be a treacherous assassin — the mere Italian will never be a drunken sot. No Englishman would have written Machiavelli's *Prince* — no Italian would have written Bentham's *Deontology*.[39]

It is no testimony to his religious system that an Englishman is veracious, nor yet that an Italian is ardent and reverential.

This consideration of the extensively important results, derived from

38. See the Preface to Dr. Arnold's fourth volume of Sermons [Thomas Arnold, *Christian Life, Its Course, Its Hindrances, and Its Helps*, 5th ed. (London, 1849), iv–v].

39. [ED.] The quoted passage, Ward informs us, "has been supplied me by a friend who understands the subject, which I do not."

one only among the numberless constituent elements of national character, will sufficiently show the extremely arduous nature, under any
circumstances, of the attempt to draw general lessons from social phenomena: and still more when those who observe them do not suddenly
descend from the moon, but are predisposed by their origin, and have
been strengthened in their predisposition by every early association,
either to undue sympathy, or undue antipathy. No one will at any time
be able to make real progress in such a study, to make way against the
unavoidable temptations, whether to overlenient or oversevere judgment,
unless he unite, in a very high degree, powers of mind seldom found
together in *any* degree; painful abstraction, vivid imagination, accurate
observation. But in the present, hardly even nascent, state of the social
science, no one, even so endowed to the uttermost extent, can derive any
general conclusions from these phenomena, except with extreme diffidence
and doubtfulness. No! the history of past ages and foreign countries is
not as yet productive of results, which may be separated, as it were, from
the concrete mass, and applied as general maxims for the guidance of a
nation or a national church. Its benefits are very considerable, but do not
amount to this. They are principally the two following. First, such
studies protect us against a certain pusillanimity and narrowness of mind,
incidental to merely personal experience; on the present subject, they
save us from that deep despondency which might otherwise bow us to
the earth, that oppressive and stifling fear lest it should be true that
Christian doctrines cannot, from their very nature, be the leaven and
animating principle of society; it saves us from this, by putting before
us in all their details, so as to satisfy our imagination and affections no
less than our understanding, the picture of those glorious ages when
religion was "a living power, kindling hearts, leavening them with one
idea, moulding them on one model, developing them into one polity;
when it was the life of morality, gave birth to power, wielded empire." [40]
And secondly, acquaintance with past ages or foreign countries may suggest to us, in abundant profusion, remedies for those unparalleled ir-
regularities and distresses which now surround us; remedies, however,
which it can only *suggest;* whose efficacy can be tested by reference to
no such merely external sources, but must be determined by the general
principles of human nature, and by a deep and penetrating insight, if it
be attainable, into men and things as they really exist in the midst of us.

40. Letters of Catholicus. [ED.] J. H. Newman, "The Tamworth Reading Room,"
in *Discussions and Arguments on Various Subjects* (London, 1918), 285 f. (abbrev.).

7. Thus, then, everything seems to throw us back on that course of action which feelings of natural affection would in themselves suggest; viz., the making our own Church our one great centre of thought, as it must inevitably be our one great sphere of action. We must learn to dismiss all otiose and unfruitful *contemplation* of external models, whether primitive or foreign, and apply ourselves to the more homely task of labouring, by their help, to introduce among ourselves that vital principle which has had so great a share in organizing those models. And just as we should encourage in our minds a warm and hearty affection for serious Christians throughout all the world (being confident of this, that so far forth as they are really serious, they have a true principle and sound faith, practically, even if unconsciously, energizing within them); so we should also cherish a regard in some respects even more especial and peculiar, to all serious Christians among ourselves, who join with us in affection to the English Church. All who seriously and unaffectedly desire to see that Church such in action as every Christian Church is in profession, and who are ready to devote their utmost energies to the accomplishment of that object, have, in point of fact — and should be made more and more to feel that they have — a very real bond of union and sympathy; however widely they may differ as to the means of that accomplishment. And if this be so, as it plainly is, even in cases where there is a radical contrariety of doctrinal profession, how much more will it be so, in cases where such profession is in fundamentals accordant!

> Numbers there are among ourselves, who fully agree in the profession of attachment to the early Church, and a real wish to conform to its standards; in the desire to lay far greater stress than heretofore on prayer, obedience, and self-denial; in zeal for the Sacraments and other Church ordinances; and a deep sense of the unspeakable blessings which God gives us through their channel. And how painful a reflection to any one, who has imbibed so much of the Catholic spirit, as to burn for union with all those who so much as bear the *name* of Christ (so far as truth and faithfulness will allow) — how painful to him the reflection that all this agreement is felt as yet to give no sufficient scope for genuine, hearty, unsuspicious sympathy, from the vivid perception we have of mutual differences, on points which, if less fundamental, are unhappily felt as even more obtrusive, and in a sense practical.
>
> On the primary points of doctrine we all agree [so far as conscious intention goes] [41] in reference to the same standard; yet little do we seem to feel how precious is this heritage of Catholic truth:

41. [ED.] Words in brackets inserted by Ward.

how constraining and intimate a bond of union it will supply, when cordially embraced, to all Catholic hearts throughout Christendom.[42]

It may appear paradoxical, but is certainly true, that my earnest sense of the importance of mutual confidence and sympathy is one principal reason of the great openness with which I am speaking in this publication. If there be in our Church at the present time one symptom of her deep-seated disease more distressing, more irritating, more ubiquitous, than another, it is the profound distrust between man and man: no one seems to know how much meaning may be concealed under the simplest sentence, or what ulterior projects may be meditated in the most profound silence. I am not saying that this could at all have been avoided; it may be a necessary law "with societies as with individuals, that sharp pangs and trials are in the way which leads from the lethargy of sloth and self-ignorance to the quiet and assured peace of an awakened conscience." When certain persons desire, by all allowable methods, to "unprotestantize the national Church," to supplant one dominant principle by its contradictory; granting the lawfulness of the desire (which is not the present question), it is very far from easy to discover what is and what is not the mode of proceeding likely to carry with it the least of permanent evil. Nothing in the whole world can be more unreasonable, however natural, than the respective complaints which are made. We use open and straightforward expressions; we are condemned loudly as hurrying persons forward prematurely, startling, alarming them, and the like; we write in a more reserved and cautious style; suspicions are insinuated of dishonesty, underhand dealing, nay, positive mendacity. The substance of what we advocate is so extremely displeasing to many around us that the manner really, I think, hardly receives the credit due to it. However, as I have reason to think from what I hear and see that few writings have perplexed and alarmed religious and excellent men more than my own articles in the *British Critic*, I do hope that it may tend to restore peace and quietness of mind if I state, with the utmost attainable openness, what I have meant (and do mean), and what I have not. Accordingly, if anything which follows shall appear unnecessarily uncouth and offensive to existing prepossessions, let it be attributed to my earnest desire of expressing myself frankly and intelligibly.

I have fully acknowledged, in the passage from which I quoted above, that these differences between "High-churchmen" "are certainly far

42. [ED.] Ward is quoting here and below from his article on "St. Athanasius," 407 ff.

more than merely formal or external, and correspond to a real difference of ethical character." Here is another benefit, which will possibly accrue from openness of speech; for by means of it, we may expect that these differences will be traced the more precisely to their ultimate elements: and all the world knows how much more nearly we are brought to the chance of agreement, when the points at issue are distinctly recognized. Further, even if such differences remain undiminished, I am still not without confident hope, that when we speak on matters of *immediate practice*, several suggestions, which I shall venture to make, may meet with the concurrence of many who widely differ from each other and from myself on the final objects they consider desirable. And lastly, since all serious persons have a much more certain knowledge of immediate duties than they can have of ultimate results, it will be made to appear from this that those measures on which even at present all "High-churchmen," in proportion as they may learn to apply rightly their *existing* principles, will tend closely to agreement, are those very measures of whose propriety they have the most certain conviction.

It will of course at once be asked: If this be so, why is it that so much has been said on these ultimate points? why is it that we have not been content with dwelling on points of agreement? why is it that the English Reformation has been so warmly attacked; monastic institutions, voluntary poverty, celibacy, and everything most plainly and directly opposed to the spirit of that Reformation, so warmly eulogized? I answer in the first place, speaking still only for myself, that I have not at all professed sympathy, even on matters of immediate practice, with *the course now adopted* by most "High-churchmen"; rather, I hope to establish that the principles they profess ought to lead them *to an extremely different course*. Since, then, it seems to me absolutely necessary, were it only with a view to most immediate and daily duties, to defend most earnestly and uncompromisingly the position that our Church, in her present practical working, is radically and vitally corrupt, I am not aware that I add materially to the odium necessarily incurred by such a statement when I go on to the further acknowledgment that I cannot but consider even the *professed* principles of most "High-churchmen" to be in some important respects, erroneous or deficient.

[Ward goes on to plead the cause of those ardent and self-sacrificing members of the English Church whose service of "their immediate Mother" is hindered by the common identification of Anglicanism with the "peculiarities" of the Reformation. He argues further that others, who at present are in no sense High Churchmen, will be attracted to the Catholic ideal once it is clearly presented in a pure form.]

But this is far from being even the most important answer that may be given. The points at issue between "High-churchmen," though not at this moment *externally* practical, must be at all times, as I have hinted above, *internally* so in a very high degree. Take, merely as instances, those particular opinions just now mentioned; the admiration of monastic institutions, of celibacy, of voluntary poverty. Is it not plain, on being once stated, that these opinions spring from real and important peculiarities of mind; from a far deeper sense than is now common among us of the supernatural character of Christian obedience, of the corrupting tendency of this world's goods, of the extreme arduousness of the path to heaven, of the peculiar beauty of virgin purity, of the inestimable value of habitual and abstracted spiritual contemplation? It cannot be of little moment, were it only for their own sakes, whether individuals do or do not entertain opinions such as these; for without them the Christian character is in a fair way to lose all that is most heavenly and most peculiar to itself. And believing, as we do most firmly, that in proportion as the Christian walks more steadily and consistently in the path of ordinary conscientiousness, he is likely to be attracted the more forcibly to these opinions, provided only they be fairly placed before him; it would be impossible to reconcile our conduct with the most obvious principles of duty were we parties to any compromise which might tend to withhold the knowledge of them from any who may be prepared to receive them. And the same considerations render it equally impossible to refrain from the most earnest and almost indignant disavowals of the language adopted by many "High-churchmen" towards Rome. A small, very small, knot of individuals, in using such language, intend only to attack certain modern developments of doctrine which they consider corruptions; but with the general body the case is very far different. "High-churchmen" of the present day are not in general (nor have any need to be) subtle and accurate theologians; in attacking Rome, they attack not this or that particular, but a certain general spirit to which Rome has ever most prominently and honourably witnessed; that very spirit of which I spoke above. It is a mere theory, refuted by the smallest practical experience, to suppose that these peculiarly Christian tempers of mind can ever be held in due honour and reverence, I do not say by a very few individuals, but by any numerous class, while such language towards Rome as that to which I allude receives encouragement or, indeed, tolerance. Nor in like manner can the all-important principles of dutifulness and faith be apprehended in their true colours so long as it is supposed to be an acknowledged fact that the English Reformation (which to me appears the very embodiment of the sins most opposed to those principles) is to be regarded with respect.

[Ward proceeds to plead for unity among High Churchmen, in the evident expectation that the views of his own school will ultimately prevail. He suggests that controversial issues can effectively be resolved "by discovering which alternative those adopt, who carry out into most earnest practice our points of agreement." Meanwhile, it is the urgent duty of High Churchmen to transcend their differences in "united efforts against the common foe."]

Let *our* zeal, accordingly, whether for the more Anglican or more Roman phase of doctrine, lead us not to barren and wasteful invectives; but to a fair trial of the experiment, which will give us the most effectual help in evangelizing our large towns, in promoting holiness of life, in restoring essential orthodoxy of faith.

8. In a word, then, if it be asked by "High-churchmen" of what are called more moderate opinions, on what grounds a person can feel real attachment to our Church, who should hold such opinions as those maintained in several parts of the *British Critic*, how he can defend himself for remaining in our Church, and in what course of action such attachment will display itself; the following answers may be given:

I. We feel attachment to our Church because through it we were born again, and because through its ordinances we obtain communion with Christ. I have never for one moment wavered in this conviction, from my first article in the *British Critic* to my last; and here is a marked difference between the attachment entertained by English churchmen to their Church, and that felt by Dissenters of various classes to *their* respective societies. If Dissenters enjoy communion with Christ (and I rejoice in believing that very many do enjoy it), it is not *through* their Church that they enjoy such communication, nor do they profess it to be so; but *our* Church is a channel of sacramental grace.

II. On the second head, an answer to the objectors is equally ready. The English Church, they are even forward in asserting, had not its origin in the Reformation, but has existed from far earlier times. Whereas then no one accuses *them* of disloyalty in preferring the seventeenth century to the nineteenth, what shadow of ground can there be for accusing *us* of disloyalty any more, in preferring the thirteenth century to either?

III. To the last question the foregoing pages, for some way back, have been one continued reply. In addition to the other demonstrations of attachment, specified in an earlier part of the chapter, we now see much more strongly, how great a scope her children have at the present time for indulging that sentiment: by fixing their thoughts mainly on the circumstances of her position; by studying foreign systems, past and present, with the one object of gathering from them what may be suitable to these circumstances; by endeavouring to obtain some little insight into that hitherto unexplored abyss, our doctrinal and practical corruptions; above all, by endeavouring to save her from that root of all other national and ecclesiastical sins which for three hundred years has been our peculiar note of disgrace, I mean *pride*.

PART FOUR

❖

The Heart of the Matter

EDWARD BOUVERIE PUSEY

Tract Sixty-seven:
Scriptural Views of Holy Baptism
(SELECTION)

Editor's introduction.

The [Tractarian] system has been uniform, and its several parts have held well together. . . . It has in all points been the direct opposite of what may be called the spirit of English protestantism of the nineteenth century: upholding whatever that spirit would depreciate; decrying whatever it would admire. A short statement of the principal views held by Mr. Newman and his friends will show this sufficiently.

"The sacraments, and not preaching, are the sources of divine grace." So it is said in the Advertisement prefixed to the first volume of the Tracts for the Times. . . . But the only security for the efficacy of the sacraments is the apostolical commission of the bishops, and under them, of the presbyters of the Church. . . . These two doctrines are the foundation of the whole system. God's grace, and our salvation, come to us principally through the virtue of the sacraments; the virtue of the sacraments depends on the apostolical succession of those who administer them. The clergy, therefore, thus holding in their hands the most precious gifts of the Church, acquire naturally the title of the Church itself; the Church, as possessed of so mysterious a virtue as to communicate to the only means of salvation their saving efficacy, becomes at once an object of the deepest reverence. What wonder if to a body endowed with so transcendent a gift, there should be given also the spirit of wisdom to discern all truth; so that the solemn voice of the Church in its creeds, and in the decrees of its general councils, must be received as the voice of God himself. Nor can such a body be supposed to have commended any practices or states of life which are not really excellent; and the duty either of all Christians, or of those at least who would follow the most excellent way. Fasting, therefore, and the state of celibacy, are the one a Christian obligation, the other, a Christian perfection. Again, being members of a body so exalted, and receiving our very salvation in a way altogether above reason, we must be cautious how we either trust to our individual conscience rather than to the command of the Church, or how we venture to exercise our reason at all in judging of what the Church teaches; childlike faith and childlike obedience are the dispositions which God most loves. What, then, are they who are not of the Church, who do not receive the sacraments from those who can alone give them their virtue? Surely they are aliens from God, they cannot claim his covenanted mercies; and the goodness which may be apparent in them, may not be a real goodness; God may see that it is false, though to us it appears sincere; but it is certain that they do not possess the only appointed means of salvation; and therefore, we must consider their state as dangerous, although we may not venture to condemn them.[1]

They who believe and realize the height of the gift of God in Baptism must, in the belief of the great things which God has done for them and His whole Church, have a source of solemn responsibility and deep awe, and humble amazement of God's graciousness, peculiar to themselves; and in proportion as they are penetrated with it, their preaching must be also raised. One may appeal safely on this point to the solid, subdued, but sublime eloquence of the early Church, or to those of our own who in older times most realize their baptismal gifts. Baptismal Regeneration, as connected with the Incarnation of our blessed Lord, gives a depth to our Christian existence, an actualness to our union with Christ, a reality to our sonship to God, an interest in the presence of our Lord's glorified Body at God's right hand, a joyousness amid the subduing of the flesh, an overwhelmingness to the dignity conferred on human nature, a solemnity to the communion of saints, who are the fulness of Him, who filleth all in all, a substantiality to the indwelling of Christ, that to those who retain this truth, the school which abandoned it must needs appear to have sold its birthright.[2]

These two passages — the one by a severe critic of Tractarian teaching,[3] the other by the Tractarian teacher who was to play the leading role in the ongoing drama of the Anglo-Catholic movement after the

1. Thomas Arnold, *Christian Life, Its Course, Its Hindrances, and Its Helps,* 5th ed. (London, 1849), xv–xvii.
2. E. B. Pusey, *Tract Sixty-seven: Scriptural Views of Holy Baptism,* 3d ed. (London, 1840), 12 f.
3. *Cf.* above, p. 61.

tragic episode of the secessions of 1845 [4] — when taken together clearly explain the connection between the outward and visible politics of the Tractarian party and that inward and spiritual concern without which Anglo-Catholicism could never have become a strong and enduring force in the Anglican Communion. If the Oxford Movement, from its earliest beginnings, stood so strongly for the authority of Church and hierarchy, the deepest reason (Arnold tells us) was the conviction that the efficacy of the sacramental means of grace rested on that authority. If the Anglo-Catholics are so intensely interested in sacramental efficacy, the point (Pusey adds) is that in the sacraments the wonder and the splendour of man's calling in Christ are powerfully manifested and almost tangibly embodied in the midst of man's world.

According to Newman, it was Pusey's "influence and example" that turned the Tractarians into serious theological authors rather than mere pamphleteers.[5] In its second edition,[6] at any rate, Pusey's *Tract Sixty-seven* was certainly a weighty example. But it was more than that. Apart from Newman's sermons at St. Mary's, whose cumulative effect was, according to all our witnesses, immense, it was the first massive expression of the spirituality of the Oxford Movement.

❖   ❖   ❖   ❖

CHAPTER II:

ON THE MEANING OF BAPTISMAL REGENERATION, AND THE PASSAGES OF HOLY SCRIPTURE WHICH SPEAK OF OR IMPLY THE GREATNESS OF BAPTISM

The passages of Holy Scripture which refer to baptism may naturally be divided under two heads: those which directly connect regeneration with it (Jn. 3:5; Tit. 3:5), and those which speak of its privileges in high indeed and glorious terms, but without the same precision and definiteness. Each class, in a different way, strengthens our faith; the one

4. In retrospect, Pusey's contribution to the whole Tractarian enterprise was to eclipse even Newman's, so that a Roman Catholic historian could describe Newman as "an adherent of Pusey's Oxford Movement." Cf. Martin Grabmann, *Die Geschichte der katholischen Theologie seit dem Ausgang der Väterzeit* (Freiburg, 1933), 279.

5. Cf. above, p. 94.

6. Pusey completed an extensive revision of *Tract Sixty-seven*, although he was unable to do the same for its sequels, *Tract Sixty-eight* and *Tract Sixty-nine*. The text printed below is from the definitive third edition, based on the second.

telling us what our privilege is, the other raising or illustrating our notions of that privilege by speaking of its accompaniments or results.

Before entering upon the consideration of these passages, however, some may wish to know the meaning here attached to the Scripture words "regeneration," or "new birth," and "birth from above." This was easy for practical purposes, by way of description, so as to set before ourselves the greatness of the gift by baptism bestowed on us; but it is not so easy by way of a technical definition. This arises from the very nature of the subject; for we can only accurately define that which we understand, not in its effects only but its cause. Things divine, even by describing, we are apt to circumscribe; much more, if we attempt strictly to define them: the depth of things divine cannot be contained within the shallowness of human words. The more carefully we express ourselves in the one way, the more escapes us in another. Thus, in the doctrine of justification by faith, a mind which should mainly fix itself on our being "accounted righteous" would by degrees lose sight of that other portion of it, the "having righteousness actually imparted, the being made righteous"; as, on the other hand, one who recently attempted to recover this last portion of the truth became so intent thereon as to do away the vividness of that former truth, that we are "judicially pronounced righteous or absolved for Christ's sake": what Christ worketh *in* us cast a shade over what he did and suffered *for* us.[1] So again, in many good persons, the desire to uphold (as they think) the doctrine of justification *by* faith practically obliterates the truth that our justification is imputed to us, not through the feelings, but *through* baptism; as on the other hand, there may be also a cold and exclusive recognition of the gift of God in baptism, without any vivid perception that by abiding faith only can that gift be retained. In all these cases, a portion of the truth has been taken for the whole, and has narrowed the whole. Neither again sufficeth it often that the whole truth should be really involved in the definition given. Thus in the words "justification by faith," all the Christian privileges and gifts are indeed included, since they are all part of the faith, bestowed on one who embraces the mercies of God in Christ and is through the sacraments made a member of him. It is justification by God's free grace in the gospel, as opposed to everything out of the gospel; yet when a person comes to look upon this as a definition, not as exhibiting the truth vividly upon one side only, he annexes restraining

1. [ED.] *Cf. Remains of Alexander Knox* [2d ed. (London, 1836–37), I, 282–300].

senses to the words, and goes on to substitute or oppose one portion of the truth — that most familiar to his own mind — to other portions likewise contained in it. Thus "justification by faith" came to be opposed [2] in men's minds to baptism, the means ordained by Christ himself for the remission of sin or for justification.

The like has happened with regard to baptism. Hence also it may be in part that the early Church has not fixed the language on this subject beyond the statement of the Nicene Creed (that there is "one baptism for the remission of sins"), and her teachers have, as occasion suggested, dwelt at different times upon the one or other portion of its blessings, but left no fixed form of speaking thereon. They have *described* not *defined* the gifts of God in baptism. Thus baptism may obviously be looked upon either with reference to the past or the future; as a passage *from* death or *to* life; as a deliverance *from* sin or a renewal *to* holiness; a death unto sin or a new birth unto righteousness; and men's minds might from circumstances be directed *prominently* to the one or other view. Again, they might look upon baptism as it was a *channel* of these blessings, in that the person baptized becomes thereby "a member of Christ" [3] (which one saying comprehends more than all which men's or angels' thoughts can conceive of blessedness); or they might look at the blessings of which it is the channel. Thus the Greek Fathers (who were harassed by no controversies connected with it) spoke principally of the blessedness whereof it makes us partakers. So St. Chrysostom:

> Blessed be God, who alone doeth wonders; who made all things, and changeth all. Behold, they enjoy the calm of freedom who a little before were held captives, they are denizens of the Church who were wandering in error, and they have the lot of righteousness who were in the confusion of sin. For they are not only free, but holy; not holy only, but righteous; not righteous only, but sons; not sons only, but heirs; not heirs only, but brethren of Christ; not brethren of Christ only, but co-heirs; not only co-heirs, but members; not members only, but a temple; not a temple only, but instruments of the Spirit. See how many are the largesses of baptism; and whereas some think that the heavenly grace consists only in the remission of sins, lo, we have recounted ten glories thereof. Wherefore we baptize infants, although they have no sins, that holiness,

2. Papers from the *Record*, 31, 33, etc. [ED.] It has not been possible to identify this reference more precisely. The *Record*, an aggressively Evangelical paper, began publication on January 1, 1828.

3. [ED.] Catechism, B.C.P. (1662).

righteousness, adoption, inheritance, brotherhood with Christ, may
be added to them; that they may become his members.[4]

It appears from this that some already had begun to restrict themselves
too rigidly to the words of the description given in the Creed of Constantinople. St. Augustine, on the other hand, living in the midst of the
Pelagian heresy, was compelled to take prominently this very line, which
St. Chrysostom regards as cold when taken exclusively: since the Pelagians denied all sin in infants, he was obliged very principally to insist
upon baptism as the remission of original sin.[5] In like manner, our Church
at first, in her Catechism, used the warm undefined language of the
Eastern churches, "wherein I was made a member of Christ, the child
of God, and an inheritor of the kingdom of heaven"; and afterwards
defined the benefits of baptism more after the manner of St. Augustine,
"a death unto sin, and a new birth unto righteousness; for being by
nature born in sin, and the children of wrath, we are hereby made the
children of grace." The two views, as above said, do in fact coincide, and
are only the same great truth looked upon on different sides; for neither
did St. Augustine regard the remission of original or actual sin as taking
place in any other way than through the union with Christ, nor doubted
he that this union infused actual righteousness and holiness, the seed of
immortality, and gifts in Christ far more than had been lost in Adam.[6]
On the other hand, the Greek churches, though chiefly dwelling upon
the blessings acquired, yet acknowledged baptism to be for the remission
of original, as well as actual sin.

The difficulty of explaining baptismal regeneration is twofold: first,
from its being a mystery; secondly, from men being in these days inclined to lower that mystery. Thus one should prefer speaking of it,
with our Catechism, as that whereby we were made "members of Christ";
but then, when people explain "members of Christ" to be "members

---

4. John Chrysostom, *Baptismal Instructions* [III, 5 f. (*ACW*, XXXI, 57)], quoted
by Augustine, *Against Julian*, I, vi, 21 [*FC*, XXXV, 25; *PL*, XLIV, 654 f.]. It is plain
(as St. Augustine remarks) that since St. Chrysostom speaks of children being free
from *sins*, he means *actual sins*, since original sin must always be spoken of in the
singular; so the Pelagians, to make the passage serve their end, substituted the singular
for the plural which St. Chrysostom used.

5. [ED.] *Cf.* E. R. Fairweather, "St. Augustine's Interpretation of Infant Baptism,"
in *Augustinus Magister* (Paris, 1954), II, 897–903.

6. [ED.] *Cf.* Augustine, *Opus imperfectum contra Iulianum*, II, 165 (*PL*, XLV,
1212): "That justification is not conferred merely by the remission of sins. . . . God
justifies the ungodly, not only by forgiving what he has done ill, but also by bestowing
charity."

of Christ's Church," and that to mean "members of his visible Church, or of the society of men called Christians," a description in itself the highest and most glorious, and the source of every other blessing, is made equivalent to "a mere outward admission into a mere outward assemblage of men." In either case, however, man is the author of his own difficulties; in the one, by lowering the fulness of Scripture truth; in the other, by carnally inquiring into the mode of the divine working. For a mystery presents no difficulty to belief; it becomes difficult only when we ask about the mode of its being. Nicodemus asked, "How can these things be?" [Jn. 3:9] and most of our questions about baptismal regeneration are Nicodemus questions. We know it in its author, God; in its instrument, baptism; in its end, salvation, union with Christ, sonship to God, "resurrection from the dead, and the life of the world to come." [7] We only know it not where it does not concern us to know it, in the mode of its operation. But this is just what man would know, and so he passes over all those glorious privileges, and stops at the threshold to ask how it can be. He would fain know *how* an unconscious infant *can be* born of God; *how* it can spiritually live; *wherein* this spiritual life consists; *how* baptism can be the same to the infant and to the adult convert; and if it be not in its visible and immediate and tangible effects, *how* it can be the same at all. Yet Scripture makes no difference; the gift is the same, although it vary in its application; to the infant it is the remission of original guilt, to the adult of his actual sins also; but to both by their being made members of Christ, and thereby partakers of his "wisdom and righteousness, sanctification and redemption" [1 Cor. 1:30]; by being made branches of the True Vine, and so, as long as they abide in him, receiving from him, each according to their capacities and necessities and willingness, nourishment and life; but if they abide not in him, they are cast forth like a branch, and withered [Jn. 15:1–6]. We can then, after all, find no better exposition than that incidentally given in our Catechism — "My Baptism, wherein I was made a member of Christ, the child of God, and an inheritor of the kingdom of heaven"; and with this statement we may well be content, as it expresses most our union with our Redeemer, the fountain of our gifts, and the ground of our hopes. One may then define *regeneration* to be that act whereby God takes us out of our relation to Adam and makes us actual members of his Son, and so his sons, as being members of his ever-blessed Son; "and if sons, then heirs of God through Christ" (Gal. 4:7). This is our

7. [ED.] Nicene Creed.

new birth, an actual birth of God, of water, and the Spirit, as we were actually born of our natural parents; herein then also are we justified, or both accounted and made righteous, since we are made members of him who is alone righteous; freed from past sin, whether original or actual; have a new principle of life imparted to us, since having been made members of Christ, we have a portion of his life, or of him who is our Life; herein we have also the hope of the resurrection and of immortality, because we have been made partakers of his resurrection,[8] have risen again with him (Col. 2:12).

The view, then, here held of baptism, following the ancient Church and our own, is, that we be engrafted into Christ, and thereby receive a principle of life, afterwards to be developed and enlarged by the fuller influxes of his grace; so that neither is baptism looked upon as an infusion of grace distinct from the incorporation into Christ, nor is that incorporation conceived of as separate from its attendant blessings.

The following sentences of Hooker express, is that great master's way, the view here meant to be taken:

> This is . . . the necessity of sacraments. That saving grace which Christ originally is or hath for the general good of his whole Church, by sacraments he severally deriveth into every member thereof. . . . By baptism therefore we receive Christ Jesus, and from him the saving grace which is proper unto baptism. . . . Baptism is a sacrament which God hath instituted in his Church, to the end that they which receive the same might . . . be *incorporated into Christ, and so* through his most precious merit obtain as well that saving grace of imputation, which taketh away all former guiltiness, as also that infused divine virtue of the Holy Ghost, which giveth to the powers of the soul the first disposition towards future newness of life.[9]

Two more observations must be premised on the Scripture evidence itself. First, whereas, confessedly, regeneration is in Scripture connected with baptism, there is nothing in Scripture to sever it therefrom. The evidence all goes one way. This, in itself, is of great moment. For if God, in two places only, assigns the means of his operations, and then in other places were to mention those operations apart from the means, we are not (as the manner of some is) to take these texts separately, as if they did not come from the same Giver, but to fill up what is not expressed in the one by what he teaches plainly in the other. Thus, when we have learnt that the "new birth," or "birth from above," is "of water and the

---

8. [ED.] *Cf.* Collect for Palm Sunday, B.C.P.

9. Richard Hooker, *The Laws of Ecclesiastical Polity*, Bk. V, chap. 57, 5–6; chap. 60, 2 [*Works* (Oxford, 1845), II, 258 f., 265 f.; italics Pusey's].

Spirit" (Jn. 3:5), then, where it is said, "who were born, not of blood, nor of the will of the flesh, nor of the will of man, but of God" (Jn. 1:13), we should, with the ancient Church, recognize here also the gift of God in baptism to "such as receive him" [Jn. 1:12].

But, secondly, not only is there nothing in Scripture to sever regeneration from baptism, but baptism is spoken of as the source of our spiritual birth, as no other cause is, save God: we are not said, namely, to be born again *of* faith, or love, or prayer, or any grace which God worketh in us, but to be "born *of* water and the Spirit" (Jn. 3:5), in contrast to our birth *of* the flesh (Jn. 3:6); in like manner as we are said to be born *of* God (Jn. 1:13): and in order to express that this our new birth *of* God is, as being of God, a deathless birth, it is described as a birth *of* seed incorruptible (1 Pet. 1:23), in contrast with our birth after the flesh, *of* corruptible seed through our earthly parents.[10] The immediate causes of our birth are not yet spoken of; only we are taught that it is *of* God, and in itself immortal, if men will but not part with it, or occasion God to withdraw it. Holy Scripture, indeed, *connects* other causes besides baptism with the new birth, or rather that one comprehensive cause, the whole dispensation of mercy in the gospel (for this, not the written or spoken word, is meant by the "word," the "word of truth" [Jas. 1:18]): but it at once marks, by the very difference of language, that these are only more remote instruments: we are not said to be born *of* them as *of* parents, but *by* or *through* them. They have their appointed place, and order, and instrumentality, *towards* our new birth, but we are not said to be born *of* them. Thus we are said to be "born" (as was noticed) "*of* seed incorruptible," *i.e.*, of an immortal birth, but only "*through* the word of God, which liveth and abideth for ever" (1 Pet. 1:23); "in Jesus Christ have I begotten you *through* the gospel" (1 Cor. 4:15); "of his own will begat he us by the word of truth" (Jas. 1:18); no other instrument being spoken of as having the same relation to our heavenly birth as this of water.[11] Had it even been otherwise, the mention of any other instru-

10. [ED.] In footnotes Pusey supplies the Greek text for each reference, emphasizing the use of the preposition ἐκ. He adds: "It has been a careless habit of interpretation which has here [1 Pet. 1:23] confounded words so distinct as ἐκ and διὰ, and then proceeded to identify ἡ σπορὰ here with the σπέρμα in our Lord's parable [presumably Lk. 8:11, though the word used is σπόρος — σπέρμα appears in another parable in Mt. 13:24]; and so, by this double mistake, inferred that St. Peter declared that 'the incorruptible seed, of which we are reborn,' is the 'preaching of the word.' . . ."

11. Hooker, *Ecclesiastical Polity*, Bk. V, chap. 60 [*Works*, II, 265]: "Unless as the Spirit is a necessary inward cause, so Water were a necessary outward mean to our regeneration, what construction should we give unto those words wherein we are said to be new-born, and that ἐξ ὕδατος, even of Water?"

ment in our regeneration could not of course have excluded the operation of baptism: as indeed in baptism itself, two very different causes are
combined, the one, God himself, the other a creature which he has
thought fit to hallow to this end. For then, as Christ's merits, and the
workings of the Holy Spirit, and faith, and obedience, operate, though
in different ways, to the final salvation of our souls, and yet the one
excludes not the necessity of the rest; so also the mention of faith, or of
the preaching of the gospel, as means towards our regeneration, would
not have excluded the necessity of baptism thereto, although mentioned
in but one passage of Holy Scripture. But now, as if to exclude all idea
of human agency in this our spiritual creation, to shut out all human
co-operation or boasting, as though we had in any way contributed to
our own birth, and were not only the creatures of his hands, no loophole has been left us, no other instrument named; our birth (when its
direct means are spoken of) is attributed to the baptism of water and
of the Spirit, and to that only. Had our new birth, in one passage only,
been connected with baptism, and had it in five hundred passages been
spoken of in connexion with other causes, still, because it was in that
one place so connected with baptism, no one who looked faithfully for
intimations of God's will would have ventured to neglect that one passage; the truth contained in Holy Scripture is not less God's truth because contained in one passage only; but now, besides this, God has so
ordered his word that it does speak of the connexion of baptism with our
new birth, and does not speak of any other cause in the like close union
with it.

These circumstances alone, thoughtfully weighed, would lead a teach-
able disposition readily to incline his faith whither God seems to point.
For although the privileges annexed to regeneration are elsewhere spoken
of, and the character of mind thereto conformable — our sonship and
the mind which we should have as sons, our new creation — yet these
are spoken of as already belonging to, or to be cultivated in, us, not as
to be begun anew in any once received into the body of Christ. There
are tests afforded whether we are acting up to our privilege of regeneration, and cherishing the Spirit therein given us, but there is no hint that
regeneration can be obtained in any way but by baptism, or if totally
lost, could be restored. We are warned that, having been "saved by
baptism through the resurrection of Jesus Christ, we should no longer
live the rest of our time in the flesh to the lusts of men but to the will
of God" (1 Pet. 3:21; 4:2); that, "having been born of incorruptible

seed, we should put off all malice, and like newborn infants desire the sincere milk of the word" (1 Pet. 1:23; 2:1 f.); that, "having been saved by the washing of regeneration and the renewing of the Holy Ghost, we should be careful to maintain good works" (Tit. 3:5–8); and again, those who had fallen in any way are exhorted to repentance; but men are not taught to seek for regeneration, to pray that they may be regenerate: it is nowhere implied that any Christian had not been regenerated, or could hereafter be so. The very error of the Novatians,[12] that none who fell away after baptism could be renewed to repentance, will approach nearer to the truth of the gospel than the supposition that persons could be admitted as dead members into Christ, and then afterwards, for the first time, quickened. Our life in Christ is, throughout, represented as commencing when we are by baptism made members of Christ and children of God. That life may through our negligence afterwards decay, or be choked, or smothered, or well-nigh extinguished, and by God's mercy again be renewed and refreshed; but a *commencement* of life in Christ after baptism, a death unto sin and a new birth unto righteousness, at any other period than at that one first introduction into God's covenant, is as little consonant with the general representations of Holy Scripture as a commencement of physical life long after our natural birth is with the order of his providence. Those miracles of God's mercy whereby he from time to time *awakens* souls from their lethargy, to see the reality of things unseen, and the extent of their own wanderings from the right way, no more indicate that they had had no life imparted to them before, than a man awaking from an unnatural slumber would that he had been physically dead. These analogies go but a little way; but the very terms "quickened," "awakened," "roused," and the like, wherewith men naturally designate the powerful interposition of God's Holy Spirit upon the hearts of men hitherto careless, convey the notion that the life was there before, although sunk in torpor, the gift there, although not stirred up, the powers implanted, although suffered to lie idle.

[Pusey goes on to criticize the metaphorical interpretation of the allusion to "water" in Jn. 3:5, advanced by certain Protestant authors. He piles up quotations from the Fathers and the ancient liturgies in

12. [ED.] *Cf.* H. P. Liddon, *Life of Edward Bouverie Pusey, D.D.*, 4th ed. (London, 1894–98), I, 352: "Pusey's statement of the effects of post-baptismal sin in his tract on baptism has often been exaggerated; he has even been accused of Novatianism. The truth is that, as faith in the grace of baptism had declined, so a sense of the grievousness of post-baptismal sin had been correspondingly lost."

support of his assertion that the universal consent of Christian antiquity applies the Johannine text to baptism.]

And now, let anyone who wishes to see the truth labour to lay aside prejudice, and without bias, to review this evidence. It relates to no insulated point, no bye or incidental question, which may be laid aside or assumed without affecting the rest. It lies, as is confessed, at the root of the whole system; as some say, a deadening doctrine; as the old Church found it, full of life; but, in either case, it is the point from which the two opposite systems, which divide the Church, diverge. Let a person, then, consider what the evidence is. Every vestige of Christian writing which God has preserved to us from the ancient Church that explains the words, "Except a man be born of water and the Spirit," assumes that they declare that in baptism we are born from above, through our Saviour's gift; every passage which speaks of the privileges of baptism at all implies the same; their whole system of theology presupposes it; every branch of the whole Church, independent as they may have been in their origin, engraft upon their baptismal liturgies (and in this sense) our Lord's words, "Except a man be born of water and the Spirit." The doctrine seems to militate against predestinarian views, yet St. Augustine, the author of those views, and his disciples, maintained and urged it; heretics, whose interest it was aforetime to deny it, retained, in their own sense, their belief in this; until, at last, after the Church had borne witness to it for fifteen centuries, one man arose and denied it.[13] Now, let anyone find any other instance in which the whole Church has thus uniformly held any doctrine which can be proved to be an error: if he cannot, let him ask himself what ground he has for supposing them to be in error on this, for setting a modern novelty against the consent of the whole Church, or how the supposition of such an error is consistent with the Saviour's promise never to forsake his Church.

But, combining this consent with our Lord's words, the argument becomes so strong that with one who loves his Saviour, and is not hindered by a long contrary bias, I would gladly rest the whole question of baptismal regeneration upon this one consideration. However men may think that the words do not *require* this interpretation, they will readily admit that it is *an* obvious, perhaps (apart from other considerations) *the more* obvious meaning; add, then, to this, that the Christian Church uniformly, for fifteen centuries, interpreted these his words of

13. [ED.] The reference is apparently to Zwingli; *cf.* E. B. Pusey, *Tract Sixty-seven: Scriptural Views of Holy Baptism*, 3d ed. (London, 1840), 29.

baptism; that on the ground of this text alone they urged the necessity of baptism; that upon it, mainly, they identified regeneration with baptism. If, then, this be an error, would our Saviour have used words which (since water was already used in the Jews' and John's baptism) must inevitably, and did, lead his Church into error, and which he, who knew all things, must at the time have known would lead his Church into error, and that, when, according to Zwingli's or Calvin's interpretation, his meaning had been as fully expressed, had it stood, "born of the Spirit," only? Rather, if one may argue from the result, one should think that our Saviour added the words "of water" (upon which, in his immediate converse with Nicodemus, he does not dwell) with the very view that his Church should thence learn the truth, which she has transmitted — that "regeneration" is the gift of God, bestowed by him, in this life, in baptism only. Indeed, the opposite exposition, invented by the Swiss teachers, was so manifestly a mere weapon by which to demolish a papal argument for the absolute necessity of baptism that it had hardly been worth commenting upon, but that no error ever stops at its first stage; mere repetition hardens, as well as emboldens; what is first adopted as an expedient is afterwards justified as being alone the truth — the mantle, which was assumed to cover shame, cleaves to us, like that in the fable, until it have sucked out the very life and marrow of our whole system. One text, misquoted in order to disprove the *absolute* necessity of baptism, has ended in the scarcely disguised indifference or contempt of an ordinance of our Saviour.

Not less peremptorily, however, do our blessed Saviour's words refuse to be bound down to any mere *outward* change of state, or circumstances, or relation, however glorious the privileges of that new condition may be. For this were the very opposite error; and whereas the former interpretation "dried up" [14] the water of baptism, so does this quench the Spirit therein. One may, indeed, rightly infer, that since the Jews regarded the *baptized* proselyte as a new-born child,[15] our Saviour would not have connected the mention of water with the new birth unless the new birth, which he bestowed, had been bestowed through baptism: but who would so fetter down the fulness of our Saviour's promises, as that his words should mean nothing more than they would in the mouth of

14. Hooker [*Ecclesiastical Polity*, Bk. V, chap. 59 (*Works*, II, 263)].

15. [ED.] On this point Pusey cites John Lightfoot, *Horae Hebraicae et Talmudicae* (Oxford, 1859), III, 265 f.; Richard Laurence, *The Doctrine of Baptismal Regeneration contrasted with the Tenets of Calvin* (Oxford, 1815), 28.

the dry and unspiritual Jewish legalists; or, because they, proud of the covenant with Abraham, deemed that the passing of a proselyte into the outward covenant was a new creation, who would infer that our Saviour spoke only of an outward change? Even some among the Jews had higher notions, and figured that a new soul descended from the region of spirits, upon the admitted proselyte.[16] And if it were merely an outward change — a change of condition only, wherein were the solemnity of this declaration, "Verily, verily, I say unto you, except a man be born again, he cannot see the kingdom of God" [Jn. 3:3]? for the "seeing" or "entering into" the kingdom of God, *i.e.*, the Church of Christ (first militant on earth, and then triumphant in heaven), was itself a change of state, so that the two sentences would have had nearly the same meaning. And who could endure the paraphrase, "unless a man be brought into a state outwardly different, he cannot enter into the kingdom"? But our Saviour himself has explained his own words. To be "born of the Spirit" stands opposed to the being "born of the flesh" [Jn. 3:6]. As the one birth is real, so must the other be; the agents, truly, are different, and so also the character of life produced by each: in the one case, physical agents, and so physical life, desires, powers; and, since from a corrupted author, powers weakened and corrupted: in the other, the Holy Spirit of God, and so spiritual life, strength, faculties, energies; still, in either case, a real existence; and, to the Christian, a new, real, though not merely physical beginning — an existence real, though invisible — and, though worked by an unseen Agent, yet (when not stifled) felt in its effects, like the energy of the viewless winds [Jn. 3:8].[17]

[In the remainder of the chapter, which continues to the end of *Tract Sixty-seven*, Pusey carries out an exhaustive study of other New Testament texts bearing on Christian baptism, of the meaning of Christ's own baptism by John, and of the Old Testament "types" of Christian baptism — all copiously illustrated from the Fathers and early liturgies.]

16. Cf. *ibid.*, 31 f.

17. [ED.] Pusey quotes Augustine, *Homilies on the Gospel of St. John*, XI, 6 (*NPNF*[1], VII, 77; *PL*, XXXV, 1478): "One [birth] is of the earth, the other of heaven; one of the flesh, the other of the Spirit; one of mortality, the other of eternity; one of man and woman, the other of God and the Church."

JOHN HENRY NEWMAN

Lectures on Justification
(SELECTION)

Editor's introduction.

Newman's "Lectures on Justification" of 1838, though they have not generally tempted his biographers to close study, form perhaps the chief theological document of the Oxford Movement, the most important attempt to find the theological expression of its piety. The book belongs to the golden age of *Via Media* and hence fights definitely on a double front, against Rome as much as against Wittenberg. Modern Roman moral theology, which was the object of Ward's undivided admiration, had no attraction to Newman in this his earlier phase; but in agreement with the leading idea of *Via Media*, he draws freely from the resources of the early Church, and if any form or system is visible in the background, it is especially that of St. Augustine: it is not the first time that we see the mighty shadow of the African Doctor fall across the path of the Oxford Movement.[1]

Newman tells us that a twofold concern moved him to prepare and publish his study of justification.

It was brought home to the writer from various quarters, that a suspicion existed in many serious minds against certain essential Christian truths, such as Baptismal Regeneration and the Apostolical Ministry, under the impression that they fostered notions of human merit, were prejudicial to the inward life of religion, and incompatible with the doctrine of justifying faith, nay, with express statements on the subject in our formularies; while confident reports were in circulation that the parties who advocated them, could not disguise even from themselves their embarrassment at those state-

1. Y. Brilioth, *The Anglican Revival: Studies in the Oxford Movement* (London, 1925), 282 f.

ments. Moreover, it was suggested, that though both these classes of doctrines had in matter of fact been continuously held by the great body of our divines for two centuries and more, yet historical considerations did not weigh with men in general against their own impressions; and that nothing would meet the evil but plain statements on the subject argued out from Scripture, — statements which, if not successful in convincing those who refused to trust Tradition and the Church, might at least be evidence to the world, that the persons so suspected, themselves honestly believed that the doctrines of our Articles and Homilies were not at variance with what they thought they saw in the Services for Baptism, Holy Communion, and Ordination, and in other forms contained in the Prayer Book.[2]

In the opening sentences of his first lecture, Newman sketches the theological issue as he sees it.

Two main views concerning the mode of our justification are found in the writings of English divines; on the one hand, that this great gift of our Lord's passion is vouchsafed to those who are moved by God's grace to claim it, — on the other, to those who by the same grace are moved to do their duty. These separate doctrines, justification by faith and justification by obedience, thus simply stated, are not at all inconsistent with one another; and by religious men, especially if not divines, will be held both at once, or indifferently either the one or other, as circumstances may determine. Yet, though so compatible in themselves, the case is altogether altered when one or other is made the elementary principle of the gospel system, — when professed exclusively, developed consistently, and accurately carried out to its limits. Then what seemed at first but two modes of stating the same truth, will be found, the one to be the symbol of Romanism, the other of what is commonly called Protestantism.

It shall be my endeavour in these lectures to take such a view of Justification, as may approve itself to those among us who hold whether the one or the other doctrine in an unsystematic way, yet falls in with neither when adopted as the foundation or "leading idea" of a theology. Justification by faith only, thus treated, is an erroneous, and justification by obedience is a defective view of Christian doctrine. The former is beside, the latter short of the truth. The former legitimately tends to the creed of the rigid Lutherans who opposed Melanchthon; the latter to that of Vasquez, and other extreme writers of the Roman school. That we are absolutely saved by obedience, that is, by *what we are*, has introduced the proper merit of good works; that we are absolutely saved by

2. J. H. Newman, *Lectures on Justification*, 2d ed. (London, 1840), v-vi.

faith, or by *what Christ is,* the notion that they are prejudicial to
our salvation.[3]

Newman proceeds to expound and contrast the ideas of justification
by faith and justification by obedience, as taught respectively by Luther
and St. Augustine. His conclusion is markedly anti-Lutheran:

> I conceive it will be found that the former [view] is false, and the
> latter is true, but that while the former is an utter perversion of
> the truth, the latter does in some respects come short of it. What is
> wanting to complete it, we learn from other parts of St. Austin's
> writings, which supply what Luther, not finding perhaps in the
> theology in which he had been educated, expressed in his own
> way. I say this, lest I should appear to be setting up any private
> judgment of my own against a Father of the Church, or to speak
> of him as I might speak of Luther. St. Austin doubtless was but a
> fallible man, and, if in any point he opposed the voice of the Catho-
> lic Church, so far he is not to be followed; yet others may be more
> fallible than he; and when it is a question of difference of opinion
> between one mind and another, the holy Austin will weigh more,
> even with ordinarily humble men, than their own thoughts. The
> Roman doctrine of justification is not complete, because St. Austin,
> and the other Fathers, go beyond it: the doctrine of the Continental
> Protestants is extravagant, because the Fathers interpret Scripture
> otherwise. What the Roman divines omit, St. Austin contains; but
> the Protestants in question distort it to the denial of other truth. St.
> Austin contemplates the whole of Scripture, and harmonizes it into
> one consistent doctrine; the Protestants, like the Arians, entrench
> themselves in a few favourite texts. Luther and the rest, men of
> original minds, spoke as no one before them; St. Austin, with no
> less originality, was contented to minister to the promulgation of
> what he had received. They have been founders of schools; St.
> Austin is a Father in the Holy Apostolic Church.[4]

Newman is now ready to advance his own thesis.

> Enough [he writes] has now been said to make it appear that
> the controversy concerning justification, agitated in these last
> centuries, mainly turns upon this question, whether Christians are
> or are not justified by observance of the moral law. I mean, this
> has been in matter of fact the point in dispute; whether, or how far
> it has been a dispute of words, or went to the root of the question
> doctrinally, or ethically, are considerations which I do not now
> dwell upon, but mention by way of explaining my meaning. That
> in our *natural* state, and by *our own* strength, we are not and cannot

3. *Ibid.,* 1 f.   4. *Ibid., 66* f.

be justified by obedience, is admitted on all hands, agreeably to St. Paul's forcible statements; and to deny it is the heresy of Pelagius. But it is a distinct question altogether, whether *with* the presence of God the Holy Ghost we can obey unto justification; and, while the received doctrine in all ages of the Church has been, that through the largeness and peculiarity of the gift of grace we can, it is the distinguishing tenet of the school of Luther, that through the incurable nature of our corruption we cannot. Or, what comes to the same thing, one side says that the righteousness in which God accepts us is inherent, wrought in us by the grace flowing from Christ's Atonement; the other says that it is external, reputed, nominal, being Christ's own sacred and most perfect obedience on earth, viewed by a merciful God as if it were ours. And issue is joined on the following question, whether justification means in Scripture *counting* us righteous, or *making* us righteous; — as regards, that is, our *present* condition; for that pardon of *past* sins is included under its meaning, both parties in the controversy allow.

Now, in the last Lecture [II], in which I stated what I consider as, *in the main*, the true doctrine, two points were proposed for proof: first, that justification and sanctification were substantially the same thing; next, that viewed relatively to each other, justification *followed upon* sanctification. The former of these statements seems to me entirely borne out by Scripture; I mean, that justification and sanctification are there described as parts of one gift, properties, qualities, or aspects of one; that renewal cannot exist without acceptance, or acceptance without renewal; that Faith, which is the symbol of the one, contains in it Love, which is the symbol of the other. So much concerning the former of the two statements; but as to the latter, that justification *follows* upon sanctification, that we are first renewed, and then and therefore accepted, this doctrine, which Luther strenuously opposed, is true in one sense, but not true in another, — true in a *popular* sense, not true in an *exact* sense. Now, in the present Lecture [III], I propose to consider the exact relation of justification to sanctification, in regard to which our Church would seem to consider Luther in the right: in the next Lecture [IV], the *popular* and *practical* relation of the one to the other, which St. Austin and other Fathers set forth: and in the Sixth and following, what has partly been the subject of the foregoing Lecture [II], the *real connexion* between the two, or rather *identity*, in matter of fact, however we may vary our terms, or classify our ideas.[5]

❖   ❖   ❖   ❖

5. *Ibid.*, 68–70.

LECTURE VI:
ON THE GIFT OF RIGHTEOUSNESS

2 Cor. 6:16. Ye are the temple of the living God; as God hath said, I will dwell in them, and walk in them.

Justification, being an act of divine mercy exerted towards the soul, does not leave it as it found it — cannot but make it what it was not before, as has been shown at length. It stands to reason that a soul that is justified is not in the same state as if it had not been justified — is not in the state of others which are not justified. No one would assert that one who is justified is in all respects the same as another who is not; even a professed antinomian will generally allow that he has certain spiritual feelings, as he falsely calls them, or experiences, or an assurance, or the consciousness of renouncing merit, to distinguish him from those who remain in a state of wrath.

We know well what that state of wrath consists in, or what is the formal character and condition of those who are in it: disobedience, an evil heart of unbelief [Heb. 3:12], hatred of the truth, guilt, fear of judgment to come, hardness of heart; such as these are the constituting parts of that state, and go to make up or define it. Now, on the other hand, what is the state of a justified man, or in what does his justification *consist?* This is the question which is now more exactly to be treated, as was proposed in a former place; and it is one of no small importance.

As far as the *name* is concerned, there is a general agreement among all parties; it is called "righteousness." But this is not the question; nor, again, what the *meaning* of the name is, which all allow to be equivalent to acceptableness, or acceptable obedience, though one school of opinion puts a second sense upon that word, and understands it also to mean an obedience which is short of acceptable, or a righteousness of sanctification. Nor is it now the question what is meant by justification, which some take for accounting, others, for being made, righteous. But the question is, what is *that* which is *named* righteousness; what is that object or thing, what is it in a man, which God seeing there, therefore calls him righteous; what is the state in which a justified person is, or that which constitutes him righteous in God's sight; just as one might ask what is really meant when it is said that a man is alive, what is the thing denoted by Scripture in saying that God "breathed into Adam the *breath of life*" [Gen. 2:7], the sense of the word *breath* being indisputable.

Now Luther, as we have seen, considers it to be Christ's obedience imputed; the Roman schools consider it to be the new and spiritual principle imparted to us by the Holy Ghost. But before entering upon the subject, I wish to insist that there really must be, as I had said, some such token or substance of his justification; I insist upon it, because many persons will try to slip away from so plain a truth. They so greatly dread our priding ourselves on anything that is good in us, that one cannot assert that there are distinctions between the justified state and the state of nature without being at once accused of treating these as meritorious causes; therefore, I will insist on the point at the hazard of being tedious.

It is certain, then, that all men are not justified; some are, some are not; what is it they differ in? To justify is to *account* or *declare* righteous; this is God's act; this is a movement of the divine mind, and altogether external to the *subject* of that justification. If the only real difference between a justified man and a man unjustified be Almighty God's thoughts concerning him, then those who are justified are justified from eternity, for God sees the end from the beginning. They are in a justified state even from the hour of their birth; before their conversion, while they are wallowing in all sin and unholiness, they are justified, if justification be an act of the divine mind and nothing more — a conclusion which has before now been admitted. Yet, unless we go these lengths, we must allow that there is a certain distinctive state of soul to which the designation of righteousness belongs. What, then, is the criterion within us which God sees there (his giving surely, but still given), the seal and signature of his elect, which he accepts now, which he will acknowledge at the last day?

In asking, then, what is our righteousness, I do not mean what is its *original source*, for this is God's mercy; nor what is its *meritorious cause*, for this is the life, and above all the death, of Christ; nor what is the *instrument* of it, for this (I would maintain) is holy baptism; nor what is the *entrance* into it, for this is regeneration; nor what the *first privilege* of it, for this is pardon; nor what the *ultimate fruit*, for this is everlasting life. I am not inquiring about anything past, or anything future, or anything on God's part, but of something present and inward. We should not say that animal life consisted in being born, or in having parents, or in breathing, or in sensation, or in strength, or in a certain period of years, or in God's will, or in God's attributes, or in God's knowledge of us. We should feel that nothing past, or to come, or external, could be a fit account of that which we call animal life, and that all answers so framed were beside the mark. It would be intelligible, for instance, to say that life consisted in the presence of the soul; but whether we said this or anything else, in any case we should fix on something in us, not out of us. And in like manner, when I ask what is that, called righteousness, which God first clothes us with as a robe, then looks upon and accepts, I do not ask why God so looks upon it, but *what* it is he looks upon.

1. This being the case, we may pronounce that Luther's answer to the question, viz., that Christ's obedience imputed to us is our righteousness, is in itself no answer at all, and needs explanation before it will apply. Properly speaking, I suppose it means, not that Christ's obedience imputed, but that the imputation of his obedience, is our righteousness. Christ's obedience in the days of his flesh centuries since, must be brought near to the soul of the individual; therefore that present applying or imputing of his obedience must be meant, when it is called our righteousness, not what is past. But that applying or imputing is the act of God; and the question now before us is, not what is God's act in justifying, but what the state of the justified soul. It is perfectly intelligible to say that Christ's obedience is the procuring, or the meritorious cause, of our righteousness; but to say that our state of righteousness is Christ's having obeyed the law eighteen hundred years since, if literally taken, is like saying that our animal life consists in the creation of Adam, or that the pangs of guilt consist in the fall of Satan, which are words without meaning.

For the same reason, it is no answer to the present question to say that a state of justification consists in the forgiveness of sins, or in acceptance, or in adoption, all these being God's acts, and as little in point here as if I said that obedience was divine aid.

Again: if it be laid down that our justification consists in union with Christ, or reconciliation with God, this is an intelligible and fair answer; and then the question will arise, what is *meant* by union with Christ. It may or may not be possible to explain it; if we consider Scripture to be silent on this point, then we shall say that justification consists in an *unknown, unrevealed, mysterious* union with Christ; if we do not allow that there is a mystery, then we shall be bound to say what that union does consist in.

For the same reason, to say with Roman divines that justification consists in spiritual renovation, whether correct or incorrect, is perfectly intelligible. It is a real answer.

And those who say that it is Christ's obedience seem to have felt this; for when pressed, they have sometimes said that faith is the discriminating mark of justification, or that in which it consists. But for the most part only *when* they were pressed; for though such an answer, whether correct or not, is clear and apposite, yet they seem to have feared that it was all one with saying that faith had merit or an intrinsic expiatory power in the remission of sins. At the same time, this has not hindered others from so resolving the question; [1] and as it is the only serviceable answer which I can find on the Lutheran side of the question, I shall make use of it.

These then are the two views which at first sight come into consideration, whether our state of justification, or righteousness in God's sight, consist in faith or in renovation.

Now, however intelligible each of these answers may be, neither will be found sufficient and final. I mean, without giving judgment between them, they do not seem to pursue, and, I conceive, they do not pursue, the inquiry so far as they might; they do not trace up the criterion of a justified state to its simplest and most elementary form. When faith is said to be the inward principle of acceptance, the question rises, what gives to faith its acceptableness? Why is faith more acceptable than unbelief? Cannot we give any reason at all for it, or can we conceive unbelief being appointed as the token, instrument, state, or condition (it matters not here which word we use) of justification? Surely not; faith is acceptable as having a something in it which unbelief has not; that something, what is it? It must be God's grace if God's grace act *in* the soul and not merely externally, as in the way of providence. If it acts in us and has a presence in us when we have faith, then the having that grace or that presence, and not faith, which is its result, must be the real token, the real state of a justified man.

Again: if we say that justification consists in a supernatural quality imparted to the soul by God's grace, as Roman writers say, then, in like manner, the question arises, is this quality all that is in us of heaven? does not the grace itself, as an immediate divine power or presence, dwell in the hearts which are gifted with this renovating principle? It may or it may not; but if it does, then surely its possession is really our justification, and not renewal, or the principle of renewal.

And thus by tracing farther back the lines of thought on which these

1. [ED.] Here and below a number of footnotes, containing long illustrative quotations, are omitted.

apparently discordant views are placed, they are made to converge; they converge, that is, supposing there to be vouchsafed to us an inward divine presence, of which both faith and spiritual renovation are fruits. If such a presence be not vouchsafed, then certainly faith on the one hand, renovation, on the other, are the ultimate elements to which our state of righteousness can be respectively referred in the two theologies. But if it be, neither Protestant nor Romanist ought to refuse to admit, and in admitting to agree with each other, that the presence of the Holy Ghost shed abroad in our hearts, the Author both of faith and of renewal, this is really that which makes us righteous, and that our righteousness is the possession of that presence.

2. So much is gained from the views of the contending parties; next, I observe, in corroboration of the conjectural inference to which they have led us, that justification actually *is* ascribed in Scripture to the agency of the Holy Spirit, and that immediately, neither faith nor renewal intervening. For instance, St. Peter speaks of our being "elect through sanctification," or consecration "of the Spirit, *unto*," that is, in order to "obedience and *sprinkling of the blood* of Jesus Christ" (1 Pet. 1:2), that is, the Holy Ghost is given us unto, or in order to renovation and justification. Again: we are said by St. Paul to be "washed, sanctified, and *justified*, in the name of the Lord Jesus, and by the *Spirit of our God*" (1 Cor. 6:11). The same apostle says, "Ye have not received the spirit of bondage again to fear, but ye have received the *Spirit of adoption*, whereby we cry, Abba, Father" (Rom. 8:15). Again: "The law of the *Spirit of life* hath made me free from the law of sin and death" (Rom. 8:2). Again: Christ says, "It is the *Spirit* that giveth life" (Jn. 6:63), *life* being the peculiar attribute or state of "the *just*," as St. Paul, and the prophet Habakkuk before him, declare [Rom. 1:17; Hab. 2:4]. These passages taken together, to which others might be added from a former lecture,[2] show that justification is wrought by the power of the Spirit, or rather by his presence within us. And this being the real state of a justified man, faith and renewal are both present also, but as fruits of it — faith, because it is said, "We through the Spirit wait for the hope of righteousness *by faith*" (Gal. 5:5); and renewal, because in another passage, "*renewal* of the Holy Ghost" is made equivalent to "being justified by his grace" (Tit. 3:5–7).

Such is the doctrine of Scripture, which our Church plainly acknowledges, as is evident from the following passages from her formularies.

2. [ED.] *Cf.* J. H. Newman, *Lectures on Justification*, 2d ed. (London, 1840), 101 ff.

In the Thirteenth Article, for instance, which I have already cited,[3] what in the title are called "works before justification," are in what follows called "works done before the *grace* of Christ, and the *inspiration of his Spirit*"; that is, justification may fitly be called an "inspiration of the Spirit of Christ," or a spiritual presence. Again, in the Baptismal Service: in which we pray God that the child to be baptized may "receive remission of his sins,"[4] which surely implies justification, "*by spiritual regeneration*," which is as surely the gift of the Spirit. The Homilies are in accordance; in which we are told, by way of comment upon St. Paul's words, "who rose again for our *justification*" [Rom. 4:25], that Christ "rose again to send down *his Holy Spirit* to rule in our hearts, *to endow us with perfect righteousness*"; and that in this way David's words in Ps. 85:11 are fulfilled, "Truth hath sprung out of the earth, and righteousness hath looked down from heaven," in that "from the earth is the everlasting Verity, God's Son, risen to life, and *the true righteousness of the Holy Ghost*, looking out of heaven, and in most liberal largess dealt upon all the world."[5] Justifying righteousness, then, consists in the coming and presence of the Holy Ghost within us.

3. But further, Scripture expressly declares that righteousness is a definite inward gift, while at the same time it teaches that it is not any mere quality of mind, whether faith or holiness; as I shall now proceed to show.

By a gift I mean a thing given. Now, there are four words[6] used in Scripture to describe the special abiding gift of the gospel, which either is, or at least includes, justification, nay, is expressly said to be justification, and they all signify a thing given, not a mere giving — not a favour (as if we should say, "it is a great *mercy* we are saved," that is, an act, display, proof of mercy), but, as indeed the word gift means in English, a possession; as when you say a man has the gift of languages, it is a faculty in him; whereas you would not say that popularity was a gift, which is something external, but rather the talent of becoming popular, or influence, is the gift; nor would you say acceptance was a gift, but acceptableness.

For instance, in Rom. 5:17 we read, "They that receive the abundance

---

3. [ED.] *Cf. ibid*, 92 f.

4. [ED.] The Ministration of Holy Baptism, B.C.P. (1662) actually reads: "receive remission of sin."

5. [ED.] "An Homily of the Resurrection of our Saviour Jesus Christ," *Certain Sermons or Homilies appointed to be read in Churches* (London, 1864), 464 f.

6. χάρισμα, δῶρον, δωρεά and δώρημα.

of grace, and of the *gift* [7] of righteousness, shall reign in life by one, Jesus Christ." The word *gift* here used certainly must mean a thing given; implying that the righteousness of justification, whatever it turn out to be, is a real and definite something in a person, implanted in him, like a talent or power, and not merely an act of the divine mind externally to him, as the forgiveness of sins may be.

But the preceding verses contain a still more convincing statement, on which indeed one might not be unwilling to rest the whole question. St. Paul says, "Not as the offence, so also is the *gift*.[8] . . . The *gift* is of many offences unto justification" [Rom. 5:15 f.]. Here, observe, he distinctly declares that justification is the result of a *gift*. Now the word used for "gift" in the original is the very word used elsewhere for extraordinary gifts, such as of healing, of tongues, and of miracles; that is, a definite power or virtue committed to us. Nowhere else does the word occur in Scripture without this meaning; indeed, it necessarily has it from its grammatical form. For instance, St. Paul says, he "longs to see" the Romans, "that he may impart unto them *some spiritual gift*" (Rom. 1:11); again, that "the *gift* of God is eternal life" (Rom. 6:23). He enumerates as gifts, prophecy, ministry, teaching, exhortation, giving, ruling, and showing mercy (Rom. 12:6–18). Speaking of continence, he says, "Every man has his proper *gift* from God" (1 Cor. 7:7). He says, there are "diversities of *gifts*, but the same Spirit" (1 Cor. 12:4). He exhorts Timothy "not to neglect the *gift* that was *in him*," but to stir up, to rekindle "the gift of God which was in him" (1 Tim. 4:14; 2 Tim. 1:6). St. Peter, too, speaks of our "ministering" our gifts "as good stewards" (1 Pet. 4:10).

If, then, by a gift is meant a certain faculty or talent, moral, intellectual, or other, justification is some such power. It is not a mere change of purpose or disposition in God towards us, or change of state in us, or a liberty, privilege, or (as it may be called) citizenship, but a something lodged within us.

To the same effect is St. Paul's intimation that righteousness is *ministered* or *dispensed* by the Spirit (2 Cor. 3:8 f.); for surely the idea of dispensing, as well as the general office of the gracious Dispenser, lead us to conclude that the righteousness dispensed is a thing, and not a name.

To these passages we shall be right in adding a number of others which speak of the gospel gift, though not calling it justification. For they speak as if there was *one* great benefit given to us under the gospel; and

7. δωρεᾶς.   8. χάρισμα.

so great and essential is justification, that it must be either this or included in it.

For instance; our Lord says to the Samaritan woman, "If thou knewest the *gift* of God, and who it is that saith to thee, Give me to drink, thou wouldst have asked of him, and he would have given thee living water" (Jn. 4:10). The water was a real thing to be given and received.

Again: St. Peter says to the multitude, "Repent and be baptized every one of you in the name of Jesus Christ, for the remission of sins, and ye shall receive the *gift* of the Holy Ghost" (Acts 2:38); can we doubt that this is identical with the abundance of grace and of the *gift* of righteousness of which St. Paul speaks?

Again: the same apostle alludes elsewhere to "those who were once enlightened and have tasted of the heavenly *gift*" (Heb. 6:4). Will it be said this means sanctification? Then is sanctification represented as greater than justification; else why is not justification mentioned in a passage which is expressly speaking of a case in which a second justification is pronounced to be impossible? The contrast surely requires that justification should be mentioned; yet unless included in "the heavenly gift," it is not. We may add such passages as the following: "The water that I shall give him shall be *in him* a well of water springing up into everlasting life" (Jn. 4:14). "He that believeth on me, as the Scripture hath said, out of his belly shall flow rivers of living water" (Jn. 7:38). With such compare the words in the prophet: "Then will I sprinkle clean water upon you, and ye shall be clean; from all your filthiness, and from all your idols, will I cleanse you" (Ezek. 36:25). This means justifying purification, for renewal is not mentioned till the next verse: "A new heart *also* will I give you and a new spirit will I put within you." By water, I say, is typified justification, which accordingly is a something applied and communicated, not a change in the divine mind merely.

The same doctrine is implied in the sacrament of baptism, which certainly typifies the justifying gift. But if so, that gift is not an act merely on God's part, but something, proximate and individual, undergone, received, embraced by us.

Once more: whatever be the more precise meaning of the words, does not the "bread of life" which is to be "eaten" [Jn. 6:48 ff.] typify an *inward* gift, not merely an imputation? Yet who can deny that that gift carries with it the application of Christ's merits to the soul, that is, justification?

Moreover, these passages show that this gift, whatever it is, is not any moral excellence or grace, or merely a renewed state. For instance, to recur to the last instance, faith is but the *recipient* of the heavenly bread, and therefore cannot be identical with it.

Thus an examination of the promises made us in Scripture bears out the conclusion we had already drawn on other grounds, that the righteousness, on which we are called righteous, or are justified, that in which justification results or consists, which conveys or applies the great gospel privileges, that this justifying principle, though *within* us, as it must be if it is to separate us from the world, yet is not *of* us, or *in* us, not any quality or act of our minds, not faith, not renovation, not obedience, not anything cognizable by man, but a certain *divine* gift in which all these qualifications are included.

4. Now to proceed a step further. We have seen that, whereas justification is the *application of Christ's merits* to the individual, that application is the imparting of an *inward* gift; in other words, justification is a real and actual communication to the soul of the atonement through the ministration of the Spirit. With whatever degree of confidence we might thus infer from the foregoing considerations, at least they avail in confirmation of such a doctrine, supposing it be otherwise and directly stated in Scripture, that there is such a wonderful communication vouchsafed to us. Now in truth a privilege is most explicitly promised us in Scripture which accurately answers to this description, as being at once the special fruit of Christ's sacrifice and also an inward gift possessed and residing within us; I mean the *habitation* in us of God the Father and the Word Incarnate through the Holy Ghost. If this be so, we have found what we sought: *This* is to be justified, to receive the divine presence within us and be made a temple of the Holy Ghost.

God is everywhere as absolutely and entirely as if he were nowhere else; and it seems to be essential to the existence of every creature, rational and irrational, good and evil, in heaven and hell, that in some sense or other he should be present with them and be their life. Thus we are told concerning mankind, that "in him we live, and move, and have our being" [Acts 17:28]. And he who lives in all creatures on earth in order to their mortal life, lives in Christians in a more divine way in order to their life immortal; and as we do not know how the creation exists and lives in him as a Creator, and use words about it beyond our comprehension, so much more (were not comparison out of the question) are we ignorant of the mode or nature of that life of God in the soul, which is the wellspring of the Christian's sanctity and the seed of everlasting happiness.

If this notion of the literal indwelling of God within us, whether in the way of nature or of grace, be decried as a sort of mysticism, I ask, in reply, whether it can possibly be but that his presence is in us if he is everywhere; and whether the same tone of reasoning which denies that it is, does not also tend to deny the doctrine of his literal omnipresence. So much in behalf of the general doctrine of God's presence in all his works. And if he is everywhere and dwells in all, there is no antecedent objection against taking Scripture literally, no difficulty in supposing that the truth is as Scripture says — that as he dwells in us in one mode in the way of nature, so he is in us in another in the way of grace; [9] that his infinite and incomprehensible essence, which once existed by and in itself alone, and then at the creation so far communicated itself to his works as to sustain what he had brought into existence, and that according to the different measures of life necessary for their respective perfection, may in the Christian Church manifest itself in act and virtue in the hearts of Christians, as far surpassing what it is in unregenerate man as its presence in man excels its presence in a brute or a vegetable. And those who without any antecedent difficulty still refuse to accept the literal interpretation of Scripture, should be reminded that since the promise expressly runs that we shall be made one *as* the Father and the Son are one [Jn. 17:11], we are necessarily led either to think highly of the union of the Christian with God, or to disparage that of the Father and the Son; and that such schools of religion as maintain that the former is but figurative, will certainly be led at length to deny the real union of our Lord with his Father, and from avoiding mysticism, will verge and fall upon what is called Unitarianism.

With these thoughts, let us turn to the review of the texts in which this awful promise is made to us.

Our Saviour, then, thus speaks of our communion with the Father and the Son: "At that day ye shall know that I am in my Father, and ye in me, and I in you" (Jn. 14:20). "He that loveth me, shall be loved of my Father; and I will love him, and will manifest myself to him. . . . My Father will love him, and we will come unto him, and make our abode with him" (Jn. 14:21, 23). Again he prays to his Father that his disciples "all may be one, as thou, Father, art in me and I in thee, that they also

---

9. The angelic appearances in the Old Testament, to which divine titles are given and divine honours paid, may be taken as an instance of such a presence of Almighty God in a created nature.

may be one in us: . . . I in them and thou in me, that they may be made perfect in one" (Jn. 17:21, 23).

Accordingly St. John says in his General Epistle that "if we love one another, God dwelleth in us, and his love is perfected in us. . . . He that dwelleth in love, dwelleth in God, and God in him. . . . He that keepeth his commandments, dwelleth in him, and he in him" (1 Jn. 4:12, 16; 3:24). "We are in him that is true, even in his Son Jesus Christ" (1 Jn. 5:20). "Truly our fellowship is with the Father, and with his Son Jesus Christ" (1 Jn. 1:3).

Further, this fellowship with the Son, and with the Father in the Son, is made through the Spirit. "Hereby we know that we dwell in him and he in us, because he hath given us of his Spirit" (1 Jn. 4:13). Hence St. Paul speaks of the "fellowship of the Holy Ghost" (2 Cor. 13:14); and that "we are the temple of God, and that the Spirit of God dwelleth in us" (1 Cor. 3:16); and that "our body is the temple of the Holy Ghost which is in us, which we have of God, and we are not our own" (1 Cor. 6:19). Agreeably to which are our Saviour's words, who, when he promised the indwelling of Father and Son in his followers, said also, "I will pray the Father, and he shall give you another Comforter that he may abide with you for ever, even the Spirit of truth. . . . He dwelleth in you, and shall be in you." And then he adds: "I will not leave you comfortless, I will come to you" (Jn. 14:16–18).

Moreover, this indwelling had been promised as the *distinguishing* grace of the gospel. St. Paul declares both the prophecy and its fulfilment in the text: "Ye are the temple of the living God; as God hath said, I will dwell in them, and walk in them; and I will be their God, and they shall be my people" (2 Cor. 6:16). Again, in our Saviour's words, "He that believeth on me, as the Scripture hath said, out of his belly shall flow rivers of living water; but this spake he of the Spirit, which they that believe on him should receive; for the Holy Ghost was not yet given, because that Jesus was not yet glorified" (Jn. 7:38 f.). Accordingly, in some of the texts just quoted, he who dwells in Christians is called "he that is *true*," and the Comforter is "the Spirit of *Truth*"; grace and *truth* being the characteristics of the New Covenant.

And further let it be remarked that the divine presence vouchsafed to us, besides being that of the Holy Trinity, is specially said to be the presence of Christ; which would seem to imply that the "Word made flesh" is in some mysterious manner bestowed upon us. Thus he says:

"If any man hear my voice, and open the door, I will come in to him, and will sup with him, and he with me" (Rev. 3:20). This allusion to a feast is conveyed in still more sacred and wonderful language in the following passage, to which I have already alluded: "I am the living bread which came down from heaven; if any man eat of this bread, he shall live for ever, and the bread that I will give is my flesh, which I will give for the life of the world. . . . He that eateth my flesh and drinketh my blood, dwelleth in me and I in him" (Jn. 6:51, 56). Again: "We are members of his body, from his flesh and from his bones" (Eph. 5:30; *cf.* 2 Pet. 1:4). Such, as far as the words of Scripture go, is the great gift of the gospel which Christ has purchased for all believers; not many words are necessary to connect it with justification. I observe then:

1. First, this indwelling accurately answers, as I have already said, to what the righteousness which justifies has already been shown to consist in; an inward gift conveying the virtue of Christ's atoning blood. The coincidence of one and the other in such a definition proves their identity; if to justify be to impart a certain inward token of our personal redemption, and if the presence of God within us is such a token, our justification must consist in God's coming to us and dwelling in us. It were the same to maintain, though knowing that God lives in us in the way of nature, that our mortal life does not consist in that indwelling, as to allow that he dwells in us Christians in a supernatural and singular way, yet deny that our new life of privilege and blessing depends on that mystical presence — to believe that we are temples of God, yet are not justified thereby. On the other hand, since this great gift is the possession of all Christians from the time they become Christians, whatever measures of increase it admits, justification as certainly presupposes it, as it involves justification. In a word, what is it to have his presence within us, but to be his consecrated temple? What to be his temple, but to be set apart from a state of nature, from sin and Satan, guilt and peril? What to be thus set apart, but to be declared and treated as righteous? And what is this but to be justified?

2. Next, it may be remarked that whatever blessings in detail we ascribe to justification, are ascribed in Scripture to this sacred indwelling. For instance, is justification *remission of sins?* The gift of the Spirit conveys it, as is evident from the Scripture doctrine about baptism: "One Baptism for the remission of sins." [10] Is justification *adoption* into the family of God? In like manner the Spirit is expressly called the

10. [ED.] Nicene Creed.

Spirit of adoption, "the Spirit whereby we cry, Abba, Father" [Rom. 8:15]. Is justification *reconciliation* with God? St. Paul says, "Jesus Christ is in you, unless ye be reprobates" [2 Cor. 13:5]. Is justification *life?* The same apostle says, "Christ liveth in me" [Gal. 2:20]. Is justification given to *faith?* He also prays "that Christ may dwell in" Christians' "hearts by faith" [Eph. 3:17]. Does justification lead to holy *obedience?* Our Lord assures us that "he that abideth in him, and he in him, the same bringeth forth much fruit" [Jn. 15:5]. Is it through justification that we rejoice *in hope of the glory* of God [Rom. 5:2]? In like manner "Christ in us" is said to be "the hope of glory" [Col. 1:27]. Christ then is our righteousness by dwelling in us by the Spirit: he justifies us by entering into us, he continues to justify us by remaining in us. *This* is really and truly our justification, not faith, not holiness, not (much less) a mere imputation; but through God's mercy, the very presence of Christ.

3. It appears, moreover, that this inward presence is sometimes described as God's presence or communion; sometimes that of Father and Son; sometimes of the Holy Ghost; sometimes of Christ the incarnate Mediator; sometimes "of God through the Spirit" [Eph. 2:22]; sometimes of Christ, of his body and blood, of his body in "flesh and bones" [Eph. 5:30], and this through the Spirit. Different degrees or characteristics of the gift are perchance denoted by these various terms, though to discriminate them is far beyond our powers. What is *common* to all Christians, as distinguished from good men under other dispensations, is that, however the latter were justified in God's inscrutable resources, Christians are justified by the communication of an inward, most sacred, and most mysterious gift. From the very time of baptism they are temples of the Holy Ghost. This, I say, is what is common to all; yet it is certain too, that over and above what all have, a still further communication of God's glory is promised to the obedient, and that so considerable as sometimes to be spoken of as the special communication, as if there were none previously. "He that loveth me," says our Lord, "shall be loved of my Father, and I will love him, and will manifest myself to him" [Jn. 14:21]; and: "Blessed are the pure in heart, for they shall see God" [Mt. 5:8].

4. Further, we here see in what sense it is true that justification admits of increase, and in what not. The fact that we are the temple of God does not admit of more or less; the words have no meaning when applied to it. Righteousness then, considered as the state of being God's temple,

cannot be increased; but, considered as the divine glory which that state implies, it can be increased, as the pillar of the cloud which guided the Israelites could become more or less bright. Justification being acceptable-ness with God, all beings who are justified differ from all who are not, in their very condition, in a certain property, which the one have and the other have not. In this sense it is as absurd to speak of our being more justified, as of life, or colour, or any other abstract idea increasing. But when we compare the various orders of just and acceptable beings with one another, we see that though they all are in God's favour, some may be more "pleasant," "acceptable," "righteous," than others, that is, may have more of the light of God's countenance shed on them; as a glori-fied saint is more acceptable than one still in the flesh. In this sense, then, justification does admit of increase and of degree; and whether we say justification depends on faith or on obedience, in the same degree that faith or obedience grows, so does justification. And again (to allude to a point not yet touched on), if justification is conveyed peculiarly through the sacraments; as Holy Communion conveys a more awful presence of God than Holy Baptism, so must it be the instrument of a higher justification. On the other hand, those who are declining in their obedience, as they are quenching the light within them, so are they diminishing their justification.

5. And this view of the subject enables us to understand how infants may be regenerate, though they give no indications of being so. For as God dwelt secretly in his material temple, ever hallowing it, yet only in season giving sensible evidences of what was there, so may he be present with their souls, rescuing them from Satan, and imparting new powers, manifesting new objects, and suggesting new thoughts and desires, without their being conscious, or others witnesses, of his work.

6. Moreover, if justification be the inward application of the atone-ment, we are furnished at once with a sufficient definition of a sacrament for the use of our Church. The Roman Catholic considers that there are seven; we do not strictly determine the number. We define the word generally to be an "outward sign of an inward grace," [11] without saying to how many ordinances this applies. However, what we do determine is that Christ has ordained two special sacraments as *generally necessary to salvation*. This, then, is the characteristic mark of those two, separating them from all other whatever; and what is this but saying in other words

11. [ED.] *Cf.* the Catechism, B.C.P.: "A sacrament is an outward and visible sign of an inward and spiritual grace given unto us. . . ."

that they are the only *justifying* rites, or instruments of communicating the atonement, which *is* the one thing necessary to us? Ordination, for instance, gives *power*, yet without making the soul *acceptable* to God; confirmation gives light and strength, yet is the mere completion of baptism; and absolution may be viewed as a negative ordinance removing the barrier which sin has raised between us and that grace which by inheritance is ours. But the two sacraments "of the gospel," as they may be emphatically styled, are the instruments of inward life, according to our Lord's declaration, that baptism is a new *birth*, and that in the Eucharist we eat the *living* bread.

7. Lastly. We now may see what the connexion really is between justification and renewal. I have said above that God's declaring us righteous renews us, as in the beginning he spake the word, and the world was created;[12] but *how* renewal followed on justification did not appear. Of course, all that is said on this subject must be mystery after all; yet so much we may now say, that if the justifying word be attended by the spiritual entrance of Christ into the soul, justification is perfectly distinct from renewal, with which the Roman schools identify it, yet directly productive of it, which strict Protestants deny. The latter say that renewal is a collateral result with justification from faith; the former say that it precedes justification. Rather Christ's sacred presence, which shines forth in the heart straight upon the word of justification, creates a renewal there as certainly as a light involves illumination, or fire, heat. And on the other hand, since quenching this renovating presence necessarily leads to its departure, renewal may be considered the condition on our part as well as the result of justification. The first blessing runs into the second as its necessary limit; and the second being rejected, carries away with it the first. And the one cannot be separated from the other except in idea, unless the sun's rays can be separated from the sun, or the power of purifying from water. I shall resume the subject in the next lecture.

LECTURE VII:

THE CHARACTERISTICS OF THE GIFT OF
RIGHTEOUSNESS

Is. 61:10. He hath clothed me with the garments of salvation, he hath covered me with the robe of righteousness, as a bridegroom

12. [ED.] Cf. Newman, *Lectures on Justification*, 89 ff.

decketh himself with ornaments, and as a bride adorneth herself with her jewels.

It is not uncommon in Scripture, as all readers must have observed, to represent the especial gift of the gospel as a robe or garment, bestowed on those who are brought into the Church of Christ. This in the text the prophet speaks of being "clothed with the garments of salvation, covered with the robe of righteousness," as with a rich bridal dress. A passage was quoted in a former place from the prophet Zechariah to the same purport; in which Almighty God takes from Joshua the high priest his filthy garments, and gives him change of raiment, and a mitre for his head [Zech. 3:4 f.]. In like manner, when the prodigal son came home, his father put on him "the best robe . . . , and a ring on his hand, and shoes on his feet" [Lk. 15:22]; agreeable to which is St. Paul's declaration that "as many as have been baptized into Christ, have *put on* Christ" [Gal. 3:27].

Now such expressions as these in Scripture are too forcible and varied to be a mere figure denoting the *profession of Christianity;* as if our putting on Christ were a taking on us the name and responsibilities of a Christian; as I shall take for granted. It is much the same kind of evasion or explaining away to say that by God's clothing us in righteousness is only meant his *counting* us as if righteous; all the difference being that in the former interpretation the clothing is made to stand for our calling ourselves, and in the latter, for God's calling us, what really we are not.

Nor, again, can these expressions be very well taken to mean newness of life, holiness, and obedience; for this reason, if for no other, that no one is all at once holy, and renewed, in that full sense which must be implied if the terms be interpreted of holiness. Baptized persons do not so put on Christ as to be forthwith altogether different men from what they were before; at least this is not the rule, as far as we have means of deciding. Thus there is a call on the face of the matter for some more adequate interpretation of the text and like passages than is supplied either by the Roman or the Protestant schools; and this surely is found in the doctrine of the last lecture. If that doctrine be true, the robe vouchsafed to us is the inward presence of Christ, ministered to us through the Holy Ghost; which, it is plain, admits on the one hand of being immediately vouchsafed in its fulness, as a sort of invisible Shekinah, or seal of God's election, yet without involving on the other the necessity of a greater moral change than is promised and effected in baptism.

With this, too, agrees what is told us of our own duties towards this sacred endowment, which are represented as negative rather than active; I mean, we are enjoined *not* to injure or profane it, but so to honour it in our outward conduct that it may be continued and increased in us. For instance, our Lord says, "Thou hast a few names even in Sardis, which have not *defiled* their garments; and they shall walk with me in white, for they are worthy" (Rev. 3:4). Such words are more naturally interpreted of an inward gift than of a mere imputation; and scarcely admit of being explained of a moral condition of heart, attained (under grace) *through* our own exertions. They are parallel to St. Paul's warning against "grieving the Spirit of God" [Eph. 4:30]; which may just as reasonably be interpreted of mere moral excellence, as in some heretical schools has been done. Of the same character are exhortations such as St. Paul's, not "to defile the temple of God" [1 Cor. 3:17]; to recollect that we are the temple of God, and that the Holy Ghost is in us [1 Cor. 6:19].

Moreover, it may throw light on the meaning of the text to observe that, whereas we have gained under the gospel what we lost in Adam, and justification is a reversing of our forfeiture, and a robe of righteousness is what Christ gives, perchance such a robe is what Adam lost. If so, what is told us of what he lost will explain what it is we gain. Now the peculiar gift which Adam lost is told us in the Book of Genesis; and it certainly does seem to have been a supernatural clothing. He was stripped of it by sinning as of a covering, and shrank from the sight of himself. This was the sign of his inward loathsomeness; and, accordingly, all through Scripture we find stress is laid on one especial punishment, which is hereafter to result from sin, of a most piercing and agonizing character, the manifestation of our shame. When we consider what our feelings are now as connected with this subject, we may fancy what an inexpressibly keen anguish is thus in store for sinners when their eyes shall be opened [Gen. 3:7], who at present "glory in their shame, and mind earthly things" [Phil. 3:19]. Such then was Adam's loss in God's sight, as visibly typified; and, therefore, such as what he lost is the nature of the gospel gift, so far as it is a return to what he lost. And as such our Lord speaks of it in the Apocalypse, warning us, as of our natural destitution, so of his power and willingness to remedy it. "I counsel thee," he says, "to buy of me gold tried in the fire, that thou mayest be rich; and white raiment, that thou mayest be clothed, and that the shame of thy nakedness do not appear" (Rev. 3:18). And again, "Blessed is he that watcheth, and keepeth his garments, lest he walk naked, and they see his shame" (Rev. 16:15). Christ then clothes us in God's sight with something over and above nature, which Adam forfeited.

Now that Adam's supernatural clothing was not a mere imputed righteousness need not formally be proved; it was a something, of the loss of which he was himself at once conscious, which he could not be of acts passing in the divine mind. Nor was it actual inherent holiness; at least we may so conjecture from this circumstance, that such a gift is the result of practice and habituation, and as it would be attainable but gradually, so when attained, it would scarcely yield at once to external temptation. But whether or not we may trust ourselves to such arguments, the early Church supersedes the need of them by explaining that what Adam lost on sinning was a supernatural endowment, and agreeably with the view of justification already taken, nothing less than the inward presence either of the divine Word, or of the Holy Ghost.

The Catholic Fathers, as Bishop Bull has collected their testimony, teach that the principle of sanctity in Adam, to which was attached the gift of immortality, was something distinct from and above his human nature.[1] That nature, indeed, did look towards such a perfection, but could not in itself reach it. Without this heavenly possession, man was not able to keep the law according to the covenant of life, but with it he could serve God acceptably, and gain the reward set before him.

This interpretation of the Scripture account of man's original nature and fall is confirmed by various passages of St. Paul. For instance; he speaks of man as being by mere creation what he calls a *soul:* "The first Adam was made a living *soul*" (1 Cor. 15:45); now just before, he has used a derived form of the same word, though in our version it does not appear. He says "there is a *natural* [2] body," that is, "a body with a *soul*" [3] (1 Cor. 15:44). Elsewhere he says, "the *natural* man," that is, the man with a *soul*, "receiveth not the things of the Spirit of God" (1 Cor. 2:14). Human nature, then, viewed in itself, is not spiritual, and that neither in soul nor body. Accordingly, St. Paul contrasts with this mere natural state that which is spiritual, which alone is pleasing to God, and which alone can see him. "The natural man receiveth not the things of the Spirit of God; for they are foolishness unto him, neither can he know

---

1. [ED.] Newman quotes a long passage from George Bull, "The State of Man before the Fall," in *Works* (Oxford, 1816), II, 338–40, in support of the idea of a *donum superadditum naturae*. Bull was Newman's major Anglican source on the problem of man, sin, and grace. His *Harmonia Apostolica* (1669–70) was an attempt to reconcile the Pauline teaching on justification with the Epistle of James.

2. [ED.] ψυχικόν.   3. [ED.] ψυχή.

them, because they are *spiritually* discerned; but he that is *spiritual* discerneth all things" (1 Cor. 2:14 f.). In like manner, after saying there
is a natural, he adds, "there is a *spiritual* body" (1 Cor. 15:44); and after
saying that Adam in himself was but a living soul, he adds that Christ,
the beginning of the new creation, is "a quickening Spirit" (1 Cor. 15:45).
In accordance with this distinction, in another epistle he prays for his
disciples, that their "whole *spirit,* and *soul,* and body may be preserved
blameless"(1 Thess. 5:23).

Whatever else, then, Adam had by creation, this seems to have been
one main gift, or rather that in which all others were included, the
presence of God the Holy Ghost in him, exalting him into the family and
service of his Almighty Creator. This was his clothing; this he lost by
disobedience; this Christ has regained for us. This, then, is the robe of
righteousness spoken of in the text, to be bestowed in its fulness hereafter,
bestowed partially at once; less at present than what Adam had in point
of completeness, far greater in its nature; less in that he had neither
decaying body nor infected soul, far more precious in that it is the
indwelling and manifestation in the heart of the Incarnate Word. For
what in truth is the gift even in this our state of humiliation, but a
grafting invisibly into the Body of Christ; a mysterious union with him,
and a fellowship in all the grace and blessedness which is hidden in him?
Thus it separates us from other children of Adam, is our badge and
distinction in the presence of the unseen world, and is the earnest of
greater good in store. It is an angelic glory which good spirits honour,
which devils tremble at, and which we are bound reverently to cherish,
with a careful abstinence from sin, and with the sacrifice of good works.
Well then may prophets and apostles exult in it as the great gift of divine
mercy, as the rich garment of salvation, and the enjewelled robe of
righteousness; as linen clean and white [Rev. 19:8], or, as it is elsewhere
expressed, as "Christ in us" [Col. 1:27], and "upon us" [Gal. 3:27], and
around us; as if it were a light streaming from our hearts, pervading the
whole man, enwrapping and hiding the lineaments and members of our
fallen nature, circling round us, and returning inward to the centre from
which it issues. The Almighty Father, looking on us, sees not us, but this
sacred presence, even his dearly beloved Son spiritually manifested in
us; with his blood upon our doorposts, in earnest of that final abolition
of sin which is at length to be accomplished in us.

Such is the great gift of the gospel conveyed to us by the ministration
of the Spirit, partly now, fully hereafter, and to it a number of passages

in the New Testament seem to refer. I shall now proceed to consider it under two chief designations which are there given to it; by attending to which we shall conceive more worthily of our privilege, and gain a deeper insight into the sacred text; I mean *glory* and *power*.

[Newman quotes 1 Cor. 15:43 f.; Eph. 3:16–18; Col. 1:11 f.; Heb. 6:4–6; where "glory" (or "light") and "power" appear together.]

Let us then consider this great gift, first as it is *glory*, then as it is *power*.

1. Besides the usual sense which the word *glory* bears in Scripture in relation to our duties to Almighty God, as when we are told to "do all to the glory of God" [1 Cor. 10:31]; it has besides, I need hardly say, in a number of places a mysterious sense, denoting some attribute, property, virtue, or presence of the divine nature manifested visibly. Thus we read of the glory of the Lord appearing over the tabernacle [Ex. 40:34 ff.], and entering into the temple [1 Kings 8:11]; and in like manner of the glory of the Lord shining round about the shepherds [Lk. 2:9]. Cases of this kind must occur to every attentive reader of the Scriptures. In the places just referred to it seems to mean a presence of God; but sometimes it stands for his moral attributes. Moses gained leave to see the skirts of his glory, and the permission was conveyed in these words, "I will make all my *goodness* pass before thee" [Ex. 33:19]. Accordingly Almighty God was proclaimed, as he passed by, as "the Lord, the Lord God, merciful and gracious, long-suffering, and abundant in goodness and truth" [Ex. 34:6].

Now as long as Scripture uses the word glory to denote the general awfulness attendant on the presence of Almighty God, there is nothing to surprise us, for everything that attaches to him is mysterious: but it becomes remarkable when we find, as in other passages, the same mysterious attribute, which belongs to him, ascribed to us.

In pursuing this point, it is obvious first to mention our Saviour's words to his Almighty Father in his prayer before his passion: "The glory which thou gavest me, *I have given them*" (Jn. 17:22).

What is this glory which has passed from Christ to us? It is some high gift which admits of being transferred, as is evident. What it was in Christ, we see in some degree by the following words of St. Paul: "Like as Christ was raised up from the dead by *the glory of the Father*, even so we also should walk in newness of life" (Rom. 6:4). Whatever else it was, it appears hence that it was a presence or power which operated for the resurrection of his body. In this connexion it may be well to direct attention to a passage which, otherwise, with our present notions, we should explain (what we call) more naturally. Before Christ raises Laza-rus, he says to Martha, "Said I not unto thee, that if thou wouldest be-lieve, thou shouldest see the *glory* of God?" (Jn. 11:40). What he *had* said before to her was simply that he was the resurrection and the life [Jn. 11:25].

[To illustrate the meaning of God's glory as "granted to us," Newman quotes Col. 1:11; Eph. 3:16; 1:18; 2 Pet. 1:3; 1 Pet. 4:14; 2 Cor. 3:18 (which shows that the gift is "habitual; both permanent and increasing"); Eph. 5:8, 14; 2 Cor. 4:4; Rom. 3:23.]

Lastly, these mentions of glory are distinctly connected with the gift of "righteousness." St. Paul speaks indifferently of the "ministration of the Spirit," and of the "ministration of righteousness, exceeding in glory" (2 Cor. 3:8 f.).

Now without knowing at all what "glory" means, all these passages seem to show that it is a gift intimately existing in God's nature, and intimately united to the Christian. Here then is additional evidence that an endowment is bestowed upon us distinct from any moral gift, or any mere external title or imputation; and that this endowment thus distin-guished is nothing else than our righteousness.

2. The same general conclusion will follow from considering it as *power*.

Properly speaking, the word "power" denotes a divine attribute or prerogative. As glory seems to designate the inherent perfection of Almighty God from eternity (as, for instance, when the Son is called "the brightness of God's glory" [Heb. 1:3]), so "power" is a character-istic of that perfection as manifested in time. Creation is the offspring of his *power;* again, he "upholds all things by the word of his *power*" [Heb. 1:3].

Next, it is used to denote the particular attribute manifested in the economy of redemption and in the person of the Redeemer; for instance: "The *power* of the Highest" (Lk. 1:35) overshadowed the Blessed Virgin in order to the Incarnation. "Jesus returned in the *power* of the Spirit into Galilee" (Lk. 4:14). Christ was "declared to be the Son of God with *power*, according to the Spirit of holiness, by the resurrection from the dead" (Rom. 1:4). St. Paul speaks of "knowing him and the *power* of his resurrection" (Phil. 3:10). "Jesus immediately perceived that virtue," or *power* (for the word is the same in the original), "had gone out of him" (Mk. 5:30). "There went *power* out of him and healed them all" (Lk. 6:19). "Mighty works do show forth themselves in him" (Mk.

6:14), that is, "virtues or *powers* do energize, act, live, or work, in him."

Next, let it be observed that this virtue or power was given to his disciples, and then in our version the word is commonly translated *miracle*. It is true, it does sometimes mean precisely the miraculous act or work; but it often means, not the work, but, as the word *virtue* implies, the faculty or gift of power within the agent which effects it. For instance: "He gave them *power* and authority over all devils, and to cure diseases" (Lk. 9:1). "Ye shall receive the *power* of the Holy Ghost coming upon you" (Acts 1:8). "My speech, and my preaching, was not with enticing words of man's wisdom, but in demonstration of the Spirit and of *power*" (1 Cor. 2:4). In like manner Simon Magus, when he bewitched the Samaritans, was called by them "the great *power*" or virtue "of God" (Acts 8:10).

Further, the effects of this indwelling gift in the apostles are described as similar to those which our Lord allowed to appear in himself; I mean, it showed itself as a virtue going out of them, so as to take away all pretence of its being considered a mere act of the power of God, external to themselves, accompanying their word or deed, and not an effect through them and from them. Thus of St. Paul it is said that "God wrought special miracles by the hands of Paul, so that *from his body* were brought unto the sick handkerchiefs and aprons, and the diseases departed from them, and the evil spirits went out of them" (Acts 19:11 f.).

Again: "By the hands of the apostles were many signs and wonders wrought among the people; insomuch that they brought forth the sick into the streets, and laid them on beds and couches, that at least the *shadow* of Peter passing by might overshadow some of them" (Acts 5:12–15). The instance of the virtue of Elisha's bones in raising the dead [2 Kings 13:21] is another remarkable instance of the inward gift of the Spirit, and anticipates gospel times.

St. Paul's ministerial power is spoken of as a similar inward gift — "whereof," he says, that is, of the gospel, "I was made a minister, by the gift of the grace of God, which was given to me by the *inward working of his power*" (Eph. 3:7).[4] Again, he speaks of his "striving according to his working, *which worketh in me* mightily" (Col. 1:29).

And, lastly, such in kind, though not miraculous (in the common sense of the word), is the gift bestowed upon the Christian Church and its members. The same word being used, we may well believe that it is an inward yet not a moral gift, but a supernatural power or divine virtue.

4. [ED.] Note Newman's insertion of *inward*.

Thus, for instance, our Lord speaks of it as being in the body or Church; and says, on one occasion, that there were some about him, "who should not taste of death, till they had seen the kingdom of God come *with power*" [Mk. 9:1]. The gospel is said to be "the *power* of God unto salvation" [Rom. 1:16]; Christ, "unto the called, both Jews and Greeks," is "the *power* of God and wisdom of God" [1 Cor. 1:24]. Now here, even though we were not elsewhere told that a divine indwelling is vouchsafed to us, nor were guided by the meaning of the word "power" in the foregoing texts, in what true or reverent sense could Christ be said to be power or virtue to us, unless he literally is so? If he has really condescended to become the principle of our spiritual life, then he may suitably be designated as what he is; but else who shall presume in words to degrade him to such a ministrative office We know that the (so called) Unitarians would destroy a testimony of the Psalmist's to our Lord's divinity by reading, instead of, "Thy throne, O God" [Ps. 45:6; Heb. 1:8], "God is thy throne for ever and ever." And it is usual in reply to object that, whether or not the grammatical construction bears them out, still it is most improbable antecedently that an inspired writer would be so familiar with the thought of God as to call him (as they allege) the throne on which a creature reigns.

Calvinists thus argue, and rightly; but if they pursued the argument to its legitimate results, they would surely cease to be Calvinists. "We read," says a modern writer of their school, "that heaven is God's throne, and earth his footstool, but who can conceive God himself to be the throne, on which a creature should reign to eternity?" [5] Now God's condescension in his dealings with us has been so unutterably great that no communication made in Scripture can surprise us concerning it; only let us be certain of this, that his word never outstrips his deed; and that if strong words are used, they are no mere figure, but are used with a purpose. As, then, we shrink from going beyond the doctrine of Scripture in what we attribute to God's condescension, so let us shrink from coming short of its letter; as we should fear to call God the throne of the creature, since so bold a word is nowhere sanctioned, so when he does call himself our inward life, let us fear by a false humility to reject it. Let us consider God's word and deed to run together, and then, while we cease to be Socinians, we shall cease also to be Calvinists. The same disposition which leads us to believe that divine attributes are really

5. [ED.] Thomas Scott, *Essays on the Most Important Subjects in Religion* (Philadelphia, 1821), 98 (very slightly altered).

Christ's, because they are said to be his, will lead us to consider that divine gifts are really ours, because they are said to be ours, or in other words, that they cannot be imputed to us in Scripture without being imparted. If Christ is said to be in us, or "a power of God to us" [1 Cor. 1:24], let us believe that he is what he says he is. He condescends to wash our feet; let us tremble with amazement, yet suffer it.

[Newman proceeds to quote, and argue from, 2 Cor. 12:9; Rev. 7:15; Phil. 4:13; Eph. 1:18–20; 3:20; Phil. 3:10; 2 Thess. 1:11; 2 Tim. 1:8; Heb. 7:16; 1 Pet. 1:5; 2 Pet. 1:3.]

Here then, as before, I conclude that an endowment is vouchsafed to us, not moral, yet internal, so as fitly to answer and corroborate the description I have already given of "the gift of righteousness."

However, certain as this is, I do not at all deny that by the gift of righteousness is sometimes meant in Scripture an inherent quality of mind, or holiness, just as justification has already been shown to stand for a renewal as well as an imputation. How this is, I shall now in conclusion explain; and in so doing may perhaps throw some additional light on that parallel mode of speaking also.

The sacred presence, then, which is our justification in God's sight, sanctifies the while, as a light illuminating a room; and as the room is called light from that which enlightens it, so the soul, as being renewed, inherits the titles of the gift which renews it. Thus, for instance, the figure in the text, which properly belongs to Christ's inward glory, is applied by himself to our inherent righteousness in the parable of the wedding garment [Mt. 22:11 ff.]. In like manner the words truth, life, light, and many more, are transferred from him to his work in us; or in other words, justification is ascribed, not to him, but to what we become through him.

Now the principle of such alleged confusion (for so men speak, not of course meaning to include Scripture under their censure, though they do), the principle on which this transference takes place is merely this: the gift of righteousness, not being a gift till it is given, cannot be separated, in our speaking of it, from its giving, that is from its entrance and admission into us, and its occupation of our nature. It cannot come to us except by forcing a way in, overcoming pride and sloth, penetrating and securing to itself a portion of us, and extending itself beyond itself; so that as it is really found in the soul, it cannot be viewed distinct from these realized effects, which in other words are renewal, and thus our renewal comes into the idea of our justification.

Here some illustrations may be useful. For instance, to take that in the text: the garment of salvation put on us is such as to cleave to us and to tend to become part of us; what was at first a covering merely, becomes our flesh. The glory of the divine nature, of which St. Peter says we are partakers [2 Pet. 1:4], first hides our deformity, then removes it.

Again: our Saviour asked the brother apostles whether they were able to drink of his cup and to be baptized in his baptism [Mk. 10:38]. Can a draught be separated from the drinking it, or a bath from being bathed in it? In like manner the gift of righteousness, which is justification as given, is renewal as received.

Or again: the seal, mould, or stamp with which our souls are marked as God's *coin*, impresses his *image* upon them [Mk. 12:16 f.]. He claims them as his own by the signature of holiness; or he justifies us by renewing. How natural this continuance is of the one idea into the other is shown in the literal sense of the words which I am using figuratively. The word *mark* stands both for the instrument marking, and the figure which it makes. So again, the word *copy* sometimes stands for the pattern, sometimes for the imitation. In like manner, *image* sometimes means the original, sometimes the duplicate or representation. Thus in one text, man is said to be formed *"after* the image of God" [Col. 3:10]; in another he is said to *be* "the image of Christ" [Rom. 8:29].[6] And in like manner, though the inward law commonly stands for the new creature, yet it may be said to justify, as standing also for that archetype of which the new creature is the copy. And again, we may be said to be "saved" by the "ingrafted Word" [Jas. 1:21], that is, the Word which *is* ingrafted, but which, for all that, does not cease to be what it was when first imparted, the presence of Christ.

The following passage in the Book of Wisdom well illustrates, in the case of the attribute from which it takes its name, what I would enforce — the indivisible union between the secret gift of righteousness imparted to us and viewed as propagated in us as renewal.

All men (says the writer) have one entrance into life, and the like going out. Wherefore I prayed, and understanding was given me; I called upon God, and the spirit of wisdom came to me. I preferred her before sceptres and thrones, and esteemed riches nothing in comparison of her. Neither compared I unto her any

6. Perhaps there is some difference in the sense of these two phrases. *Cf.* Petavius, *De Opificio sex Dierum,* II, 2 [*Dogmata Theologica* (Paris, 1866), IV, 222 ff.].

precious stone, because all gold in respect of her is as a little sand, and silver shall be counted as clay before her. I loved her above health and beauty, and chose to have her instead of light; for the light that cometh from her never goeth out. All good things together came to me with her, and innumerable riches in her hands. And I rejoiced in them all, because wisdom goeth before them; and I knew not that she was the mother of them. I learned diligently and do communicate her liberally; I do not hide her riches; for she is a treasure unto men that never faileth, which they that use *become the friends of God*, being commended for the gifts that come from learning (Wisd. of Sol. 7:6–14).

Now, if this were all that were said on the subject, unbecoming complaints would be uttered in some schools of religion, that in this passage an internal gift, called wisdom by the writer, was considered to make us "friends of God," or to justify; and a tendency to Pelagianism would be freely imputed, and an ignorance that justification was God's act, in spite of the strong expression which occurs of the spirit of wisdom *coming* to the writer, which surely implies a divine Agent, not an implanted excellence, and in spite of our Lord's plain declaration that we *are* his friends if we do what he commands us [Jn. 15:14]. However, as the description proceeds, it will be found that the wisdom spoken of is no created gift, no inward renewal, but none other than the eternal Word himself, who afterwards took flesh, in order thus mysteriously to be imparted; and who was announced beforehand in terms which inspired apostles in due time adopted. The sacred writer, then (for so surely he may well be called, considered what he says[7]), proceeds as follows:

In her (Wisdom) is an understanding spirit, holy, *only-begotten*, manifold, subtle, lively, clear, undefiled, plain, incorruptible, a lover of good, keen, free to act, beneficent, kind to man, steadfast, sure, free from care, *all-powerful, all-surveying*, and pervading all intellectual, pure, and subtle spirits. For wisdom is more moving than any motion; she passeth and goeth through all things because of her pureness. For she is the *breath of the power of God*, and a *pure effluence from the glory of the Almighty;* therefore can no defiled thing fall into her. For she is the *brightness of the everlasting light*, the *unspotted mirror of the power of God*, and *the image of his goodness*. And being but one, she can do all things; and *remaining in herself*, she *maketh all things new;* and in all ages *entering into holy souls* she maketh them friends of God and prophets (Wisd. of Sol. 7:22–27).

7. [ED.] Newman has in mind the limited authority conceded by the Thirty-nine Articles to the Old Testament "Apocrypha."

One more illustration shall be adduced; justification is the setting up of the cross within us. That cross, planted by almighty hands, is our safeguard from all evil; dropping grace, and diffusing heavenly virtue all around, and hallowing the spot where before there was but strife and death. It is our charm against numberless dangers, ghostly and bodily; it is our refuge against our accusing and seducing foe, our protection from the terror by night and the arrow by day [Ps. 91:5], and our passport into the Church invisible. But how does this cross become ours? I repeat, by being given; and what is this giving, in other words, but our being marked with it? Let us see what this implies. We know that in baptism a cross is literally marked on the forehead. Now suppose (to explain what I mean) we were ordered to mark the cross, not with the finger, but with a sharp instrument. Then it would be a rite of blood. In such a case justification and *pain* would undeniably go together; they would be inseparable. You might separate them in idea, but in fact they would ever be one. One act would convey both the one and the other. If the invisible presence of the justifying cross were conveyed to you *in* marking it visibly, you could not receive the justification without the pain. Justification would involve pain. Now it is in this way that justification actually does involve a spiritual circumcision, a crucifixion of the flesh, or sanctification. The entrance of Christ's sacred presence into the soul, which becomes our righteousness in God's sight, at the same time becomes righteousness in it. It makes us travail and be in pangs with righteousness, and work with fear and trembling. Such is the account given of it by the son of Sirach; who uses the same image of Wisdom already referred to.

> If a man (he says) commit himself to her, he shall inherit her, and his generation shall hold her in possession. For at the first she will walk with him *by crooked ways,* and *bring fear and dread* upon him, and *torment him with her discipline,* till she may trust his soul, and try him by her laws (Ecclus. 4: 16 f.).

Now it is very necessary to insist upon this, for a reason which has come before us in other shapes already. It is the fashion of the day to sever these two from one another, which God has joined, the seal and the impression, justification and renewal. You hear men speak of glorying in the cross of Christ, who are utter strangers to the notion of the cross as actually applied to them in water and blood, in holiness and pain. They think the cross can be theirs *without* being applied — without its coming near them — while they keep at a distance from it, and only gaze

at it. They think individuals are justified immediately by the great atonement — justified by Christ's death, and not, as St. Paul says, by means
of his resurrection [Rom. 4:24 f.] — justified by what they consider
looking at his death. Because the brazen serpent in the wilderness healed
by being looked at [Num. 21:8 f.; Jn. 3:14 f.], they consider that Christ's
sacrifice saves by the mind's contemplating it. This is what they call casting themselves upon Christ — coming before him simply and without
self-trust, and being saved by faith. Surely we ought so to *come* to Christ;
surely we must believe; surely we must look; but the question is, in what
form and manner he *gives* himself to us; and it will be found that, when
he enters into us, glorious as he is in himself, pain and self-denial are his
attendants. Gazing on the brazen serpent did not heal; but God's invisible
communication of the gift of health to those who gazed. So also justification is wholly the work of God; it comes from God to us; it is a power
exerted on our souls by him, as the healing of the Israelites was a power
exerted on their bodies. The gift must be brought *near* to us; it is not like
the brazen serpent, a mere external, material, local sign; it is a spiritual
gift, and, as being such, admits of being applied to us individually.
Christ's cross does not justify by being looked at, but by being applied;
not by being gazed at in faith, but by being actually set up within us,
and that not by our act, but by God's invisible grace. Men sit, and gaze,
and speak of the great atonement, and think this is appropriating it; not
more truly than kneeling to the material cross itself is appropriating it.
Men say that faith is an apprehending and applying; faith cannot really
apply the atonement; man cannot make the Saviour of the world his
own; the cross must be brought home to us, not in word, but in power,
and this is the work of the Spirit. This is justification; but when imparted
to the soul, it draws blood, it heals, it purifies, it glorifies.

    With one or two passages from St. Paul in behalf of what I have said,
I will bring this lecture to an end. We shall find from the apostle that
the gift of the justifying cross as certainly involves an inward crucifixion
as a brand or stamp causes sharp pain, or the cure of a bodily ailment
consists in a severe operation.

    [Newman quotes (or paraphrases) and comments briefly on Gal.
6:12–17; 2:16, 20; 5:24; Mk. 8:34; Rom. 6:4; 13:14; 2 Cor. 4:10 f.]

    The cross, then, in which St. Paul gloried was not (what the word will
literally mean, and which Romanists sometimes seem to make it mean)
the *material* cross on which Christ suffered — as little is it (what persons
among ourselves would take it to be, without even the plea of being

literal) the actual *sacrifice* on the cross, but it is that sacrifice coming in power to him who has faith in it, and converting body and soul into a sacrifice. It is the cross, realized, present, living in him, sealing him, separating him from the world, sanctifying him, afflicting him. Thus the great apostle clasped it to his heart, though it pierced it through like a sword; held it fast in his hands, though it cut them; reared it aloft, preached it, exulted in it. And thus we in our turn are allowed to hold it, commemorating and renewing individually, by the ministry of the Holy Ghost, the death and resurrection of our Lord.

But enough has been said on the matter in hand. On the whole, then, I conclude as follows: that though the gift which justifies us is, as we have seen, a something distinct from us and lodged in us, yet it involves in its idea its own work in us, and (as it were) takes up into itself that renovation of the soul, those holy deeds and sufferings, which are as if a radiance streaming from it.

LECTURE VIII:
RIGHTEOUSNESS VIEWED AS A GIFT AND AS A QUALITY

Gal. 2:20. I am crucified with Christ, nevertheless I live, yet not I, but Christ liveth in me.

I now propose to contrast the view of justification which has been drawn out in the last lectures with that to which certain Romanists consider themselves committed by the wording of the Tridentine Decree, to which they would fain confine the Fathers, into which some of our own writers have virtually fallen, and which, moreover, is unfairly imputed to many of our standard divines. As to the Protestant doctrine, on the other hand, which was a third in the discussion, I cannot go more deeply into what seems to me a system of words without ideas, and of distinctions without arguments. If I am told, in reply, that such a view of it arises from want of spiritual perception — such persons as discern not heavenly objects, not understanding heavenly words — I answer that, though undoubtedly divine words express divine things, and divine things are hidden from all but divinely enlightened minds, yet this will not account for a man's stumbling at words which are not divine. Luther's words are his own, reasoned out from Scripture, which every one of us has equal right to do. If I receive the doctrine of the Church Catholic as divine, it is as guaranteed by many concordant witnesses, which converge to one place and one time, the day of Pentecost, when the apostles were with one

accord assembled in one place [Acts 2:1]. And if I bow to some individual teacher, as Irenaeus or Augustine, it is not from a notion of his
infallibility, but on the ground of his representing the whole Church, or
from a sense of the authority of men of holy and mortified lives in religious matters. But what binds me to yield a submission to the sixteenth
century, which I withhold even from the second? to measure spiritual
discernment in myself and others by our apprehension, not of Scripture,
but of comparatively modern treatises? to accept terms and distinctions
which, over and above their human origin, have no internal consistence
— no external proof — no part or lot in antiquity; which, in short, have
but a praiseworthy object for their excuse, the overthrow of Roman
error? Surely the reverse of wrong is not right; yet this doctrine mainly
rests its pretensions upon the errors of a rival doctrine, assumes itself true
because it is serviceable, proves itself scriptural by proving Romanism
unscriptural, flatters itself that it has a meaning viewed out of Romanism,
and thinks to live and flourish though Romanism come to an end.

On these grounds, of the three doctrines above drawn out — of the
righteousness of Christ imputed only, imparted only, and both imputed
and imparted by his real indwelling — I omit the first in the comparison
between them, which now naturally follows, as being partly negative,
partly extravagant. It is a negative statement to say that justification
is not by works; it is extravagant to say that it is by faith as the primary
and sole instrument. Whether one says nothing positive, or nothing
literal, in neither case is there room for discussion, which claims to touch
and handle, to sift, to weigh, to adjust, to distribute. There is nothing
precise, nothing to grapple with, when we are told, for instance, that
faith justifies independent of its being a right and good principle — that
it justifies as an instrument, not as a condition — that love is its inseparable
accident, yet not its external criterion — that good works are necessary,
but not to be called so in controversy or popular preaching; and that
nothing in us constitutes our being justified. Such a doctrine is, what it
makes justification to be, a shadow.

I proceed, then, to suggest some points of contrast between the two
other views of justification mentioned, the doctrine of the justifying
presence and that of justifying obedience, and the latter, as found among
ourselves; for there certainly has been a school of divines in our Church,
who by a very different road have practically approached the doctrine
of Rome on this subject. What Rome has done by exalting the effects of
grace, some among ourselves have done by disparaging its sacramental

means. Rome raises man to the capacity, they have reduced him to the necessity, of being justified by his obedience. It is unnecessary to mention names; but I allude to a school of divines who rose in Charles the Second's time, and have exercised an extensive influence in our Church since 1688.[1] Those who conceive duly of the gift of justification, exalt the sacramental instruments of possessing it, as feeling that nothing short of means ordained of God can convey what is so much above them. Thus their glowing language about the sacraments is but the measure of their estimation of their spiritual privileges. And if they go on to say that obedience justifies, it never occurs to them to suppose that they can be taken to be speaking of anything but *the state of soul* in which the heavenly gift resides, and by which it is retained, not that which really causes, or procures, or effects it. Thus the high doctrine of the sacraments is a safeguard against the Tridentine Decree, as ordinarily interpreted; nay, perhaps, even in the case of persons who unhappily feel themselves committed to it. But they who see nothing supernatural and mysterious in the gift, though in words they refer it to the sacraments, yet practically associate it with that which they do see, and which seems to them naturally connected with it, their own obedience. Not believing in any true sense that they are temples of the Holy Ghost, inhabited by Christ, and members of his Body, they consider their justification properly to consist in works, because they do not discern, they do not believe in, anything else in which it can consist. Justification by obedience, then, is their distinguishing tenet; doubtless it is also the doctrine of the English Church, as it is of St. James; but it and much more besides. To put a parallel case, one man might say that our bodily *life* consisted in *organization,* or in a certain state of the nerves, or in the circulation of the blood; and another might ascribe it to *the presence of the soul.* The latter doctrine is the former and something besides; but the former by itself is defective. He who holds the former is not wrong, but he who holds only the former. Religious men may ascribe life to the heart, and thought to the brain; but those who say these are the only constituting causes of life and thought are materialists. In like manner St. Austin and others who, though they place justification in renewal, refer renewal to the indwelling presence of the Holy Ghost, are not to be compared with those who enlarge on what is seen, and explain away the mystery. This analogy holds in many other points; but I confine it to what is before

---

1. [ED.] Newman is referring to the "Latitudinarian" school, of which John Tillotson, Gilbert Burnet, and Benjamin Hoadly were prominent representatives.

us. I say, then, justification by obedience is anyhow true; it is sound doctrine if we hold another doctrine, too; it is defective if we omit it; it becomes erroneous if we deny it.

When it is held exclusively among ourselves, it often takes the following shape: that God accepts our sincere obedience as if it were everything; or that God will save us if we do our part; or that God has done his part in baptism, and now we must do ours. Such statements are most true and scriptural, if they are not meant to deny (what may be called) our sacramental life, the fount of grace which holy baptism has stored within us, and the awful realities of holy communion, those invisible facts (as I may call them) in which we stand, in which we breathe, on which we feed. For if our life be verily and indeed hid with Christ in God [Col. 3:3], it follows that though we are bound to do our part and work with him, such co-operation is the condition, not of our acceptance, or pardon, but of the continuance of that sacred presence which is our true righteousness, as an immediate origin. I believe this distinction is no matter of words, but real and practical, as a few remarks will show.

Now, when you teach as follows, that Christ's atoning death, eighteen hundred years since, and our individual baptism in our infancy, so changed our state in God's sight once for all that henceforth salvation depends on ourselves, on our doing our part in the covenant — that those gracious events put us indeed on a new footing, wiped out what was passed, set us off fair, and are still operative as gaining for us heaven, if obedient, and present aids if believing, but that faith and obedience are the conditions of grace and glory — true as all this is to the letter, yet if nothing more is added, we shall seem, in spite of whatever we say concerning the atonement and the influences of the Holy Ghost if duly sought, to be resting a man's salvation on himself, and to be making him the centre of the religious system. All has been done for him ages ago, or when he was an infant; and all that *has* been done seems as though a condition of his existing at all, as benefits on which he cannot be said to repose his mind because they are presupposed in his being himself, which do not come to him from without, nor admit of being viewed by him objectively. I would not say that this doctrine will so affect men of high religious attainments; but that, viewed as the multitude will view it, it does not come up to the idea of the gospel creed as contained in Scripture, does not fix our thoughts on Christ in that full and direct way of which Scripture sets the pattern, as being not only the Author of salvation to the whole race, but the Saviour of each of us individually through every stage of our Christian course, and in every act of our lives. This seems to be the real meaning of the popular saying that "Christ ought to be preached," and of the anxiety felt by a portion of the community to maintain the supremacy and all-sufficiency of his righteousness.[2]

Hence the charge, not unfounded as regards popular Romanism, that it views or tends to view the influences of grace, not as the operations of a living God, but as a something to bargain about, and buy, and traffic with, as if religion were, not an approach to things above us, but a commerce with our equals concerning things we can master. And this is the cause of the suspicions entertained in many quarters against those who in any sense teach that obedience justifies, as if it implied we had something in ourselves to rely upon; whereas if, as I would maintain, the presence of Christ is our true righteousness, first conveyed into us in baptism, then more sacredly and mysteriously in the Eucharist, we have really no inherent righteousness at all. What seems to be inherent may be more properly called *adherent*, depending, as it does, wholly and absolutely upon the divine indwelling, not ours to keep, but as heat in a sickly person, sustained by means external to himself. If the presence of Christ were to leave us, our renovation would go with it, and to say we are justified by renovation only means that we are interested in him from whom it flows, that we dwell beneath the overshadowing power of him who is our Justifier.

And further, it is not near such a consoling yet awful doctrine to say that we *have* had mercy and *shall* have reward, and are at present in some measure in a middle state, expected to move and promised grace upon moving, as to know, which I conceive is the full truth of the gospel, that that perfection, which is as yet but begun in our natures, is anticipated, pledged, and in one sense realized within us by a present gift, and that the centre on which our thoughts must be fixed, and the foundation from which our exertions must proceed, are not ourselves, but his presence, in whom "we live, and move, and have our being" [Acts 17:28]. And though it is most necessary to exhibit to men the severer side of the gospel, and dwell on their duties, and responsibilities, and the conditions on which grace is given, yet this is but one side; and when it is exclusively presented to Christians, as it is in the school of divinity in question, a complaint will not unfairly arise against it as cold and narrow,

2. [ED.] Newman is speaking of the "Evangelical" school, both within the English Church and beyond.

and unlike what it is popular to call "the freeness and fulness" of the gospel.

And here I am reminded of another objection which may be urged against this same school of theology, viz., that it disparages certain doctrines which are very prominent in Scripture, those of predestination and election. The gospel is a free gift; it comes to the unworthy, to those who have done nothing to earn it, who can do nothing right towards God before he shows mercy towards them. That spontaneous mercy is abundantly taught in the doctrine of the atonement itself and the ordinance of baptism; but, these being past events in our own case, and as if conditions of our existence rather than objects presented to us, the covenant of God's unsearchable grace becomes one of man's free election; and man has rather to choose heaven than heaven, man. The great mercies of God are done and over; and we have now to act, if we would receive additional benefits. Thus, in this view of the gospel, there is a tendency, which in our Church has been realized, to put out of sight the doctrines of election and sovereign grace; a circumstance which by itself would separate it, in spite of partial resemblance, from the teaching of St. Austin, who is known to have laid an unprecedented stress on those doctrines, and to have given them a new direction.

Moreover, it is no slight evil in the mode of teaching here censured, that by withdrawing a portion of truth, countenance is given to those false Protestant views now so popular among us. Truth always avenges itself; and if kept in bondage, it breaks forth irregularly, burying itself with the strong man in the overthrow of its oppressors [Judg. 16:23–30]. And so, if our Church has at any time forgotten the living presence conveyed in the sacraments, an opening has been at once made for the meagre and artificial doctrine of a nominal righteousness. So many passages are there which speak of the atonement as still living in Christians, that if we will not enforce them literally, we must be content to hear them explained of an imputation of it in God's dealings with us, or a contemplation of it by our faith.

I say, the view of justification taken by a school of divines in the Roman Church and among ourselves tends to fix the mind on self, not on Christ, whereas that which I have advocated as scriptural and Catholic buries self in the absorbing vision of a present, an indwelling God. And as so doing, it is a more awakening and fearful doctrine even, than that mode of teaching which insists mainly and directly on our responsibilities and duties. For to what does it point as the great and immediate condition of justification? to faith and holiness of our own? or, on the other hand, to the mere title of righteousness, which cannot be literally approached or profaned by us? no — but to the glorious Shekinah of the Word Incarnate, as to the true wedding garment in which the soul must be dressed. Does not such a view far increase, instead of diminishing, our responsibilities? Does it not make us more watchful and more obedient, while it comforts and transports us? Surely it takes our minds off ourselves in order to fill us with triumph, awe, and godly fear at what our state is, and what we hold within us. When are we the more likely to dread sinning, when we know merely we ought to dread it, or when we see the exceeding peril of it? When are we the more likely to keep awake and be sober, when we have a present treasure now to lose, or a distant reward to gain? Is it not more dreadful when evil thoughts assail us, more elevating and ennobling in affliction, more kindling in danger and hardship, to reflect (if the words may be said) that we bear God within us, as the martyr Ignatius expresses it,[3] that he is grieved by us or suffers with us according as we carry or renounce his cross — I say, has not this thought more of persuasiveness in it to do and suffer for him than the views of doctrine which have spread among us? Is it not more constraining than that which considers that the gospel comes to us in name, not in power; deeper, and more sacred than a second, which makes its heavenly grace a matter of purchase and trade; more glowing than a third, which depresses it almost to the chill temperature of natural religion?

Such are some of the doctrinal respects in which what I consider the scriptural view of justification recommends itself to the Christian mind. It is open, however, at first sight to one objection, which some persons may think not inconsiderable; but which I believe, when examined, will be found rather to be an additional argument in its favour. To this I shall now direct attention.

It may be said, then, that the doctrine of righteousness in the indwelling presence of Christ labours under this difficulty, that, supposing it true, the word justification has different senses in the Old and New Testament. If under the gospel it consists in the inward manifestation of the Incarnate Word, therefore, this gift being peculiar to the gospel, Abraham (for instance), who was justified, was justified some other way; whereas St. Paul certainly does liken the one justification to the other, as

3. [ED.] At the opening of each of his genuine epistles St. Ignatius of Antioch describes himself as "God-bearer."

if whatever the word meant in the Old Testament, such it meant in the New. For instance, it is said that faith "was imputed to Abraham for righteousness; now it was not written for his sake alone that it was imputed to him, but for us also, to whom it shall be imputed" [Rom. 4:22–24]. Here, it may be objected, that faith is said to justify us, *as* it justified Abraham; which it is supposed to do both in the system of the Romanists and of the Protestants, but not in that which has been here explained. Whether faith be taken as a mere instrument, as the Lutherans say, or for a sanctifying element, as the Romanists, in either case right-eousness means a state of divine acceptance; whereas (it may be objected), if it consists under the gospel in being a temple of Christ, this could not be Abraham's state, who lived before the Son became the Christ; and then the question arises, what did Abraham's justification consist in, and why is it compared to ours?

As far as this objection relates to an interpretation of Scripture, I do not consider it requires much notice; since all that St. Paul says is that righteousness, or acceptableness, is imputed to Abraham and us on faith, which I take as literally as Romanist or Lutheran; the distinction between Abraham and us relating to a further point, viz., *what* this righteousness is under the gospel; or *in what way* this acceptableness is conveyed, whether by mere act of God's will, or by a positive gift on his part. There is nothing contrary to St. Paul's argument in supposing that that same blessing which was conveyed before Christ came in one way, should under the gospel come to us in another and more precious way. For instance, animal life belongs to men and to brutes; but, whatever be the mode of its existence in the case of the latter, in the former it lies in the special gift of a rational soul. However, let us consider the state of the case more attentively.

Now this circumstance, which at first sight seems a difficulty, that the attribute of righteousness, however conveyed to the old saints, should since Christ's coming be the attendant on a divine gift, even his own sacred presence, will in truth be found, as I have said, an argument in favour of the doctrine. For such a transformation of shadows into sub-stances, and human acts into divine endowments, far from being anoma-lous, is the very rule of the New Covenant. Christ came for this very purpose, to gather together in one all the elements of good dispersed throughout the world, to make them his own, to illuminate them with himself, to reform and refashion them into himself. He came to make a new and better beginning of all things than Adam had been, and to be a fountainhead from which all good henceforth might flow. Hence it is said that "in the dispensation of the fulness of times" Almighty God "gathered together in one all things in Christ, both which are in heaven and which are on earth" (Eph. 1:10). How he became a new commencement to things in heaven, we know not; nor know we adequately in what way he recapitulated or ordered anew things on earth. But this we know, that, the world being under the dominion of Satan, and truth and goodness in it being but as gems in the mine, or rather as metal in the ore, he came to elicit, to disengage, to combine, to purify, to perfect. And, further than this, he came to new-create — to begin a new line, and construct a new kingdom on the earth; that what had as yet lain in sin might become what it was at the first, or more than that. In his incomprehensible mercy he designed that man, instead of being a child of wrath, should be quickened and impregnated with divine life; and sooner than this should not be (as the Creed says), he was made man. He took on him our nature, that in God that nature might revive and be restored; that it might be new born, and after being perfected on the cross, might impart that which itself was, as an incorruptible seed, for the life of all who receive it in faith, till the end of time. Hence he is called in Scripture the Beginning of the creation of God [Rev. 3:14], the First-begotten of the dead [Col. 1:18], the Firstfruits of the resurrection [1 Cor. 15:23].

If this be so, we see how wide and essential a difference there is, there must be, in this life, between good men before his coming and good men after. Whatever they were, however high in God's favour, however influenced by God's secret aids, they could not, while here below, be partakes of that which as yet did not exist; the body and blood of the Incarnate Son. God had his favoured servants then as afterwards, and had his own inscrutable ways both of blessing them at the time and of incorporating them afterwards into his Christ. But taking a general view of human nature, and not dwelling on exceptions, we may say that its highest piety and devotion, out of him, though the fruit (as it surely is) of divine assistance, is but the poor effort after that righteousness which it never can really reach, and which he is. Its services at best are but an imitation, not a likeness, of him. They do not tend to that perfection which they testify; like the moonlight which never rivals, though it comes from the radiance of the sun. They may be shadows and auguries of God's merciful purposes; but they cannot rise out of their feeble selves, or claim to be his work, not man's. Such is human nature in its fallen state; but at length its Redeemer came. He left his Father's courts, he was manifested, he spake; and his voice went out into all lands. He has taken to himself his great power and reigned [Rev. 11:17]; and whereas an enemy is the god and tyrant of this world, as Adam made it, so, as far as he occupies it, does he restore it to himself. Henceforth he is the one principle of life in all his servants, who are but his organs. The Jewish Church looked towards him; the Christian speaks and acts from him. What is behind him is dark, but all that is after him is illuminated. The Church, before his coming, offered to him material elements "which perish with the using" [Col. 2:22]; but now he has sent his Spirit to fill them all with himself, and to make them living and availing sacrifices to the Father. Figures have become means of grace, shadows are substances, types are sacraments in him. What before were decent ordinances and pious observances have now not only a meaning but a virtue. Water could but wash the body in the way of nature; but now it acts towards the cleansing of the soul. "Wine which maketh glad the heart of man," and "bread which strengthens man's heart," nay, the "oil which maketh him a cheerful countenance" [Ps. 104:15], henceforth are more than means of animal life, and savour of him. Hands raised in blessing, the accents of the voice of man, which before could but symbolize the yearnings of human nature, or avail for lower benefits, have now become the "un-utterable intercessions" [Rom. 8:26] of the Spirit and the touch and breath of the Incarnate Son. The Church has become his Body, her priests, his delegates, her people, his members.

This is what Christ has done by his coming; but observe, *while* he did all this for his Church, he claimed all he did *as* his own. Henceforth whatever is done is his doing, and it is called what it is. As he is the unseen Source, so must he be acknowledged as the Agent, the present Object of worship and thanksgiving in all that is done; and his instruments are not even so much as instruments, but only the outward linea-ments of him. All is superseded by him, and transmuted into him. Before he came, there were many masters, but henceforth only one [Mt. 23:10]; before he came, many fathers, but he is the one Father of the coming age, as the prophet styles him [Is. 9:6]; [4] before he came, all to whom the word of God came were called gods [Jn. 10:35], but he is the one God manifested in the flesh [1 Tim. 3:16]; before he came, there were many angelic appearances with the name of God on them, but now the great Angel of the Covenant [Mal. 3:1] is alone to be worshipped; before he came, there were many priests who had infirmity, offering sacrifices

---

4. [ED.] Vulgate: "*pater futuri saeculi.*"

year by year continually [Heb. 7:28; 10:1], but now there is but one
High Priest, "who is set on the right hand of the throne of the Majesty
in the heavens, a minister of the sanctuary, and of the true tabernacle,
which the Lord pitched, and not man" (Heb. 8:1 f.); before, there were
innumerable sacrifices of bulls and calves which could never perfect the
worshippers [Heb. 10:1–4], now one immaculate Lamb [1 Pet. 1:19]
who taketh away the sin of the world [Jn. 1:29]; before, there were
judges, kings, and rulers of various ranks, but now there is but one King
of kings, and Lord of lords [Rev. 19:16], in his kingdom. Those former
kings, prophets, priests, and sacrifices, those masters, teachers, and fathers,
not being from him, were not claimed by him as his; they were ordained
according to the old constitution of nature; they were but little glorious,
yet, what they were, they were in themselves, and had a sort of substantive existence, and gained some benefit by their functions. Their
priests were real priests, sacrificing real propitiations, and gaining thereby
real blessings, namely temporal. Their cities of refuge were really sanctu-
aries, and saved from death of the body. Their kings were real representatives of God, and suffered and wrought for the real good of their people.
There were mediators many, and prophets many, and atonements many.
But now all is superseded by one, in whom all offices merge, who has
absorbed into himself all principality, power, might, and dominion, and
every name that is named [Eph. 1:21]; who has put his holy and fearful
Name upon all, who is in and through all things, and without whom
nothing is good. He is the sole self-existing principle in the Christian
Church, and everything else is but a portion or declaration of him. Not
that now, as then, we may not speak of prophets, and rulers, and priests,
and sacrifices, and altars, and saints, and that in a far higher and more
spiritual sense than before, but that they are not any of them such of
themselves: it is not they, but the grace of God that is in them [1 Cor.
15:10]. There is under the gospel but one proper Priest, Prophet, and
King, Altar, Sacrifice, and House of God. Unity is its characteristic
sacrament; all grace flows from one Head, and all life circulates in the
members of one Body. And what is true of priests and sacrifices is true
of righteous and holy men. It is their very privilege thus to be taken into
Christ, to exist in Christ, as in their mortal life they already "have their
being" in God [Acts 17:28]. They had indeed before what was more
their own than they have now; but to what did it tend, and how far did
it aspire? It aspired to earthly blessings, and it tended to an earthly end.
Better surely to be the mere stones of the everlasting pavement than the

head of the corner in the Jewish temple. Better to be the least in the Kingdom of Heaven, even than the greatest before it of all that were born of women [Mt. 11:11]. Far better surely than Solomon in all his glory [Mt. 6:29] is that chosen generation, that royal priesthood, that holy nation, that peculiar people [1 Pet. 2:9], whose life is hid with Christ in God [Col. 3:3], who live because he lives in them, who are blessed because he is blessed, who are the fragrance of his breath, the myrrh, aloes, and cassia from his garments [Ps. 45:8]; nay, are one spirit with him [1 Cor. 6:17], as his dove, "his undefiled one," "his sister and spouse," "coming up from the wilderness leaning upon her beloved" [Song 5:2; 4:10; 8:5].

Now to apply these remarks to our immediate subject, unless this has been sufficiently done in the course of them. If in other things Christ changed the application of words, it is surely but fitting and natural that he should have in a similar way changed the application of the words righteousness and justification. Priests, I have said, offered sacrifices under the law: Christian ministers also offer sacrifices, but it is their privilege to know that those sacrifices are not independent of Christ, or complete in themselves, but continuations, as it were, of his sacrifice, and shadows cast from his cross; and that though distinct as visible and literal acts, yet as being instinct with that which they commemorate, they are absorbed and vivified in it. And so in like manner the inherent righteousness of a true Christian, viewed as distinct from Christ's inward presence, is something real, and doubtless far higher than that of a Jew; but why should we so degrade ourselves, so disparage our own high privilege, as to view it separately, to disjoin it from him through whom we do it, to linger in the thought of it instead of tracing it back to that which is its immediate source; as if a man were to praise the daylight, yet forget the sun? No, whatever might be the righteousness of the Jews, we certainly know what is ours; and it is what they could not have had; it is "Christ," our propitiation, "within us"; on it we rely, not on ourselves. It is our boast thus to retreat from the extreme manifestations of life, which is our sanctification, upon that glory within us, which is its fount, and our true justification. It is our blessedness to have our own glory swallowed up in Christ's glory, and to consider our works and our holiness to avail merely as securities for the continuance of that glory; not as things to be dwelt upon and made much of for their own sake, but as a sort of sacramental rite addressed to him, for the sake of which he may be pleased still to illuminate us, as tokens that his grace is not in vain. And after all, what we are, whatever it is, could not avail were it tried in the balance for more than this, to prove our earnestness and diligence. Even what is acceptable in us is still so imperfect that the blood of Christ is necessary to complete what his Spirit has begun; and as his regenerating grace has infused sweetness into what was bitter, so must his mercifulness overlook the remaining bitterness in what he has infused of sweetness.

In this way, then, let me reply to what seems at first sight a specious argument, against what I consider to be the Catholic doctrine. It is a more simple theory, doubtless, to say that righteousness should be to the Christian what it was to the Jew; as it is a more simple theory that we should have real priests, sacrifices, and altars now. But those who believe that Christ has set up a new creation in unity, and that he himself is the one principle in his Church of all grace and truth, will not be surprised to find that he has superseded the righteousness, as he has abolished the victims, of the ancient time; and that as the grace of the Holy Eucharist is the presence of Christ crucified, so the justification of those who approach it is the indwelling of Christ risen and glorified.

[Newman completes his work with discussions of "Christ's Resurrection the Source of Justification" (Lecture IX), "Justification by Faith Only" (X), "The Nature of Justifying Faith" (XI), "Faith Viewed Relatively to Rites and Works" (XII), "Preaching the Gospel" (XIII), and "The Formal Cause of Justification" (Appendix).]

III

ISAAC WILLIAMS

Tract Eighty-seven:
On Reserve in Communicating Religious Knowledge
(Conclusion)
(SELECTION)

Editor's introduction.

Isaac Williams, if any man, represented in the movement the moderate and unobtrusive way of religious teaching. But it was his curious fate to be dragged into the front ranks of the fray, and to be singled out as almost the most wicked and dangerous of the Tractarians. He had the strange fortune to produce the first of the Tracts which was by itself held up to popular indignation as embodying all the mischief of the series and the secret aims of the movement.[1]

The title of the Tract [2] was enough: the very word "reserve" suggested keeping back part of the counsel of God. It showed, so its foes declared, the real spirit of the Movement — its love of secret and crooked ways, its Jesuitical spirit. Bishops at once denounced it. One of the prelates (the Bishop of Gloucester) apparently had never read the Tract, which of course gave him the greater freedom. The Tract, then, in itself both true and beautiful, roused the suspiciousness already stirred by Froude's *Remains,* and these suspicions were never again allayed.[3]

Isaac Williams's work was in fact a sustained attack on the preaching of "cheap grace."

1. R. W. Church, *The Oxford Movement: Twelve Years, 1833–1845,* 3d ed. (London, 1892), 76.
2. [ED.] *On Reserve in Communicating Religious Knowledge* actually occupied both *Tract Eighty* (1837) and *Tract Eighty-seven* (1840).
3. S. L. Ollard, *A Short History of the Oxford Movement,* 2d ed. (London, 1932), 70 f.

The principle developed and established in these Tracts is directed
against a religious system which is adopted by the majority of
Dissenters, and also certain within the Church, whose doctrines and
sympathies, though nominally within the Church and many of them
exercising spiritual functions in it, are almost wholly on the side of
Dissent. The chief characteristics of this system may be said to be
the following: Instead of the whole counsel of God, as revealed in
Scripture — instead of the whole body of doctrine, as held by the
Church in its various proportions, and as exhibited in the Prayer
Book, to take one doctrine, and a part only of this, as a centre
around which to form a human system, and to give an undue (relative) prominence to this one, to the exclusion of others with which
it is always either preceded or accompanied in Holy Scripture.
The doctrine thus selected is that of the Atonement, which is made
the beginning, middle, and end of all their teaching, disjoined entirely from the future judgment, repentance, humility, self-denial,
mortification, in fact all practical obedience; and this not from over-
sight, as it seems, but as a *principle*, as though to enjoin or practise
them were to lay a burden on men's shoulders, and to impose a law
utterly at variance with the free grace of the Gospel. Likewise to
urge this doctrine, not only without these adjuncts, but without any
regard to the circumstances or condition of the persons addressed,
urging it alike on the repentant and impenitent — the bruised reed
and hardened rock — the religiously-disposed and worldly-minded;
as though it were the first, and last, and only truth, requiring no
preparation of the heart to receive it with profit, if not without
danger, no previous conviction of sin, whereby its transcendent
value and blessedness might be duly felt, without mention of righteousness, temperance, and judgment to come, placing feeling before faith, or rather as a substitute for it; virtually discountenancing
that practical holiness which is at once its fruit and the evidence of
its acceptance in the heart.[4]

Despite the insistence of leading Evangelicals that such a shallow
antinomianism, far from representing their own teaching, was a controversial invention of the Tractarian party, it seems clear enough that a
good deal of popular Evangelical preaching matched the Tractarian description only too closely. Bishop Thirlwall's dispassionate judgment
commands respect.

If it were true [he wrote] that such a system as this had been introduced into the Church, and was making progress, there can be no
doubt that those who undertook to expose and combat it would

4. H. A. Woodgate, *A Brief Analysis of the Tracts on Reserve in Communicating
Religious Knowledge, in the Series called Tracts for the Times: with Remarks on the
Same* (Oxford, 1842), 9 f.

be entitled to our sympathy, even though we might not agree with them in all their principles, or approve of all the remedies they proposed for the evil. But though it is certain that one of the parties in the controversy represents itself as contending against such a system, several of their opponents have not only indignantly disclaimed all connexion with it, but have seemed altogether to deny its existence, and to treat it as a mere fiction, with which their antagonists have either deceived themselves, or endeavoured to impose upon others: and which tends in its effect, if not in its design, to check the growth of vital religion, by casting undeserved obloquy on a portion of the Church, which is more especially distinguished by its close adherence to the principles of the Gospel, even if it be not entitled to a name, which imports that it is in the exclusive possession of them. There would indeed be just ground for the indignation which has been expressed on this subject, if the system above described had ever been imputed to the individuals who have disavowed it. But it seems perfectly consistent with the highest respect for them, and with the fullest admission of every thing they have asserted with regard to their own consciousness, practice, experience, and observation, to believe, that the evil is not so purely imaginary as they have represented it. It is a question of fact, on which no man ought to accept another's assertion as proof. But in the absence of what can never be given — a proof of the negative — it seems no more than common charity requires, to believe that those who profess to be setting themselves against such a system are sincerely convinced of its reality. As little can I doubt, that this conviction has been shared by numbers beside, and that this has been a main cause of the acceptance which writings directed against the system have met with. My own opinion on such a point can have no more weight than that of any other person, who has been used to pay attention to such subjects. But I must avow that the result of my observation has been a very strong impression both of the reality, and of the extensive prevalence of the evil.[5]

Once in his lifetime Williams ventured into the arena of theological controversy — and there (as we have seen) he caused no small stir. But it was in his preaching, and still more in his poetry, that he bore witness through the years to his religious ideals.

Isaac Williams wrote a great deal of poetry. . . . It was in a lower and sadder key than the *Christian Year*, which no doubt first inspired it; it wanted the elasticity and freshness and variety of

5. *A Charge to the Clergy of the Diocese of St. David's, by Connop, Lord Bishop of St. David's, Delivered at his Primary Visitation, October, 1842*, 2d ed. (London, 1842), 43 f.

Keble's verse, and it was often careless in structure and wanting in concentration. But it was the outpouring of a very beautiful mind, deeply impressed with the realities of failure in the Church and religion, as well as in human life, full of tenderness and pathetic sweetness, and seeking a vent for its feelings, and relief for its trouble, in calling up before itself the images of God's goodness and kingdom of which nature and the world are full. . . . Newman thought it too soft. It certainly wanted the fire and boldness and directness which he threw into his own verse when he wrote; but serious earnestness and severity of tone it certainly did not want.[6]

Indeed, it would be hard to find a more moving expression of the vigilant and awestruck piety of the Oxford Movement than the lines from Williams's *Hymns on the Catechism* (1842), which have become a familiar Anglican hymn:

> Be thou my Guardian and my Guide,
>   And hear me when I call;
> Let not my slippery footsteps slide,
>   And hold me lest I fall.
>
> The world, the flesh, and Satan dwell
>   Around the path I tread;
> O, save me from the snares of hell,
>   Thou Quickener of the dead.
>
> And if I tempted am to sin,
>   And outward things are strong,
> Do thou, O Lord, keep watch within,
>   And save my soul from wrong.
>
> Still let me ever watch and pray,
>   And feel that I am frail;
> That if the tempter cross my way,
>   Yet he may not prevail.[7]

❖ ❖ ❖ ❖

PART V:

THE PRINCIPLE OPPOSED TO CERTAIN MODERN RELIGIOUS OPINIONS

4. Danger in forming a plan of our own different from that of Scripture

Surely we know not what we do when we venture to make a scheme and system of our own respecting the revelations of God. His ways are

6. Church, *Oxford Movement*, 78.   7. *The English Hymnal*, No. 369.

so vast and mysterious that there may be some great presumption in our taking one truth, and forming around it a scheme from notions of our own. It may not be the way to arrive at even that truth; and also it may counteract some others, which it is equally important that we should be impressed with. The very idea of forming such a scheme arises from a want of a due sense of the depth and vastness of the divine counsels, as if we could comprehend them. It is with states of society as with individuals; those whose thoughts and knowledge are most superficial are most apt to systematize; and it is very little considered what awful things in the economy of God may be thus habitually kept out of sight — kept out of sight, perhaps, by many quite unconsciously; for the secret influence of these opinions is more extensive than they are aware of, who are subject to them. It is not an uncommon thing to hear sermons which are throughout specious and plausible, which seem at first scriptural, and are received as such without hesitation, and yet, on a little consideration, it will appear that they are but partial views of the truth, that they are quite inconsistent with the much forgotten doctrine of a future judgment. What effect, therefore, must this system have upon an age and whole nation?

Nor is it only in its not supporting the analogy of the faith that this system is opposed to Scripture; but its spirit and mode of teaching is quite different. It may be observed in this, that this scheme puts knowledge first, and obedience afterwards: let this doctrine, they say, be received, and good works will necessarily follow. Holy Scripture throughout adopts the opposite course.[1] In many and extensive senses, the language it adopts, and the plan it pursues, is on the principle that "the law is the schoolmaster, to bring us to Christ" [Gal. 3:24]; that "he who will do the will shall know of the doctrine" [Jn. 7:17]; whereas this teaching is, "receive only this doctrine, and you will do the will." The kind of secondary way, and as it were in the background, in which the necessity of obedience is put in this system, is the very opposite to

---

1. One instance in Scripture has been applied otherwise, "Make the tree good and his fruit good; or else make the tree corrupt and his fruit corrupt" [Mt. 12:33]; but this passage bears quite a different meaning; the obvious purport being that hypocritical, bad actions, like those of the Pharisees, flowed from a bad principle in the heart, that the whole heart needed to be amended. Is it not a very overstrained interpretation to apply this to the doctrine of the atonement, on the supposition that the infinite and incomprehensible love of God manifested therein will, on being published, powerfully affect men's minds, and, on being heard, regenerate their souls? Is there any sanction whatever for this in Holy Scripture?

scriptural teaching. Scripture ever introduces the warning clause, "If ye keep the commandments" [Deut. 28:9]; they, on the contrary, "If ye do not think of them too much."

And again, is there not an extraordinary confusion and perplexity raised, which has the effect of entangling men's minds with words and phrases? Are there not frequently logical fallacies, couched in verbal inaccuracies, which will appear, on a little consideration, to be mere confusions of expression, yet ever leave a false impression? Christian repentance is spoken of as something not only separate from, but opposed to Christ. The effect of Christian good works is treated as having a tendency to puff us up with pride and selfishness: works, that is, of humility and charity, exercised in secret, purely with the desire of pleasing God, for of course such only are good works which could be insisted on (though of course what they mean must be bad works, those of hypocrisy). Or again, that religious services weaken our dependence on the good Spirit; or, in other words, that frequent and constant prayers to God for his assistance diminish our reliance on God. Or again, that the deep and awful sense of judgment to come derogates from Christ's atonement, as if the most earnest consideration of the former did not most impress the unspeakable worth of the latter. Or again, that to insist on the value of the sacraments is to derogate from Christ; for when it is considered that there is no value whatever supposed in those sacraments, excepting from Christ's presence in them, and his atoning blood communicated through them, this is precisely the same as if the same charge were brought against attaching too high a value to the Holy Scriptures; for it might be said that we put the Scriptures in the place of Christ. It is very painful thus to be obliged to speak of these things. To answer them, we must come to plain first axioms in morals, such as the following.

5. Statement of the case from plain moral principles

Religious doctrines and articles of faith can only be received according to certain dispositions of the heart; these dispositions can only be formed by a repetition of certain actions.[2] And therefore a certain course

2. This is simply founded on the account which Bishop Butler gives of the formation of moral habits. [Cf. Joseph Butler, The Analogy of Religion, Pt. I, chap. 5 (Works [Oxford, 1896], I, 105–37).] It is, moreover, curious to observe how entirely Aristotle's system in this respect coincides with Holy Scripture, which makes our salvation to depend both on our mode of life, and also on our accepting certain articles of faith. For, according to Aristotle, the perception of any moral truth depends on the

of action can alone dispose us to receive certain doctrines; and hence it is evident that these doctrines are in vain preached unless these actions are at the same time practised and insisted on as most essential.

For instance, charitable works alone will make a man charitable, and the more anyone does charitable works, the more charitable will he become; that is to say, the more will he love his neighbour and love God; for a charitable work is a work that proceeds from charity or the love of God, and which can only be done by the good Spirit of God: and the more he does these works, therefore, the more will he love his neighbour and love God: and he who does not (in heart and intention at least) perform these works, will not be a charitable man, i.e., will not love God or his neighbour: and those are not charitable works which have not this effect; for no external act, such as the giving away of money, is necessarily a work of charity, but only such as consists in the exercise of the principle of charity. He therefore will, most of all, love God and love Christ, who does these works most; and he will most bring men to Christ, who most effectually, with God's blessing, induces them to do these works in the way that God hath required them to be done.

Or again, he only will be humble in heart who does humble actions; and no action is (morally speaking) an humble action but such as proceeds from the spirit of humility; and he who does humble actions most will be most humble; and he who is most humble will be most emptied of self-righteousness, and therefore will most of all value the cross of Christ, being least of all sensible of his own good deeds: and the more he does these works, the more will the Holy Spirit dwell with him, according to the promises of Scripture, and the more fully will he come to the knowledge of that mystery which is hid in Christ. That teacher, therefore, who will most induce men to do these works, will most of all bring men unto Christ, though he speaks not most fully and loudly of his ever-blessed atonement.

Or again, good works consist especially in prayers. He who does most

---

life which a person leads. He says that it depends, not on intellect itself, as in pure science; but that the understanding must have combined with it a certain desire, love, or motive (ὄρεξις or ἕνεκα τοῦ); but this desire or motive depends on the mode of life (ἠθικὴ ἕξις), and is given by it [Aristotle, *Nicomachaean Ethics*, VII, 8, 1151a11–19]. In another place he says, that which is truly good does not appear but to him who leads a good life; and at another time, that a man must be brought up well to understand morals; and that the faculty of discerning truth, vice destroys. From which it would follow that if any article of the creed is less received than another, it is owing to some peculiarity in the life and conduct, either of an individual or an age, that rejects it.

of these good works, *i.e.*, he who prays most, seeks most of all for an assistance out of, and beyond, himself, and therefore relies least of all on himself and most of all upon God; and the more he does these good works, the more does he rely upon God's good Spirit, for which he seeks. He, therefore, who, by preaching the judgment to come, or by recommending alms and fasting, or by impressing men with a sense of the shortness of life and the value of eternity, or by any such practical appeals which the occasion suggests, will lead men most to pray, will do most towards leading them to lean on God's good Spirit, although he may not repeat in express words the necessity of aid from that good Spirit, without whom we cannot please God.

To say, therefore, that such works, which alone are good works, tend to foster pride, and are a seeking for expiations beyond the one great atonement, conveys a most dangerous fallacy; when the works which are intended, if the words can be applied to anything worthy of condemnation, must be bad works, those of ostentation, of hypocrisy, or superstition, and the like, which, of course, the oftener they are repeated, the more do they make men ostentatious, hypocritical, or superstitious; and so do take them from the cross of Christ. They are sins against which we cannot warn men too much; sins repeatedly condemned by Christ, who never condemns or disparages good works, but insists upon them always and throughout most earnestly. Let hypocrisy, in all its shapes, be condemned as Scripture condemns, and we shall fully understand such teaching. Or again, consider the case morally with regard to the teaching of repentance. For instance, take the deceivable sin of covetousness, of which we are all in danger. A covetous man is he who trusts in riches; and so far as anyone trusts in riches, in that degree he cannot trust in God, and therefore can have no saving sense of the atonement of Christ, or dependence on the good Spirit of God. And if his feelings are excited on the subject of these doctrines while he is under the influence of this vice, it cannot be anything better than a mere delusion of the fancy; and therefore that teacher who will most of all lead men to abandon and get rid of covetousness will render their minds most open to receive these two great doctrines of the gospel; as seen in the case of Zacchaeus, when salvation came to his house as a true child of faith [Lk. 19:9]; and in our Lord's advice to all to sell and give alms [Lk. 12:33]. The same inference may be drawn with regard to the love of praise, in which case it may likewise be shown that it follows as a plain moral consequence, what our Lord has declared, that they cannot "believe who receive honour one of another" [Jn. 5:44]. So also with respect to impurity of heart; for a man of impure heart may be very sensibly affected by these touching and vital doctrines of the gospel; and yet it is certain that he cannot receive them rightly; for the pure in heart alone can see God [Mt. 5:8]; and therefore can alone see, so as rightly to understand, those doctrines in which God is manifested. That minister, therefore, who, by preaching the terrors of the judgment day, or by any other scriptural means, induces men to repent of these crimes, will necessarily, and by a plain moral consequence, open their eyes, their ears, their heart, to receive the high saving principles of the gospel; though he speaks not explicitly of them any more than the Baptist did, or our Lord, or his apostles. So palpably absurd, even on the plain grounds of moral principles, is it to speak of the teaching of repentance being opposed to the preaching of Christ.

This is an explanation of some obvious reasons why Holy Scripture should connect our own cross with the cross of Christ, as it so often does, and emblematically typified of the Church, in him who bore the cross after Christ; for it is said to us all, "whosoever doth not take up his cross and come after me cannot be my disciple" [Lk. 14:27]. Now there can be no repentance, and no progress in religious duties, without self-denial. These duties, therefore, are a bearing of our own cross, which will alone bring us to a right sense of the cross of Christ. It is not setting aside the cross of Christ, nor disparaging it; it is only showing the mode by which alone we may be brought to know its inestimable value.

He who most of all practises these duties will be most of all brought, by a necessary and moral consequence, to value the cross of Christ; and he who is brought to embrace that doctrine with most affection will speak of it with most reserve; he cannot speak of it as these persons require. Nor can there be any reasonable apprehension, as it is sometimes said, that the teaching of the Church, which keeps the doctrine of the atonement in the reserve of Scripture, will lead men to despair. Did anyone ever know an instance of this, of a Christian, in sound health of mind, brought to a state of despair from the fear of God and his judgments? There is a mistake in this use of the word despair, which rather means a careless, hopeless indifference to the anger of the Almighty, which is so common, than an excessive fear of his judgments. Such a fear brings with it abundant consolation and hope; and therefore the true knowledge of this saving doctrine of the atonement is expressed in such words as these, that "the salvation of God is nigh unto them that fear him" [Ps. 85:9]; that the Lord looks to him who "trembles at his word" [Is. 66:2]; that he "revives the spirit of the contrite" [Is. 57:15]; or that "whoso is wise will ponder these things; and they shall understand the loving-kindness of the Lord" [Ps. 107:43].

We must again return to and repeat this point; good works, being nothing else but the exercise of a good principle, will make a good man (as far as, humanly speaking, a man can be called good), and those are not good works which will not make a man good; and he is not a good man who does not love God with all his heart, and depend on the aid of the blessed Spirit, and trust in Christ. He, therefore, who most of all induces men to practise good works, under the awful sense of their condition as baptized Christians, brings them most of all to the cross of Christ; and he who, by his teaching, leads men to think that such works are of minor importance, and speaks slightingly of them, *i.e.*, works of charity, of humiliation, and prayer, teaches men false and dangerous doctrine, flattering to human indolence but opposed to Scripture, opposed to the Church, opposed to the first principles of our moral nature; and therefore it is said emphatically, "Whosoever shall break one of the least of these commandments, and shall teach men so, shall be called the least in the kingdom of heaven; but whosoever shall do and teach them, the same shall be called great in the kingdom of heaven" [Mt. 5:19]: that is to say, he who treats slightingly these good works shall obtain least of all the blessings of Christ's spiritual kingdom at present, the gracious gifts which are in the atonement of Christ, and by consequence be the lowest in his kingdom hereafter. By using high words of doctrine, without the inculcation of these commands, we lead men to trust to a vain shadow, instead of the Rock of their salvation. Doing the works or not it is which makes the entire difference between the house built on the sand, and that which is founded on a rock, though outwardly they appear alike; as our Lord has warned, he who "heareth these words *and doeth them*, I will liken to a wise man, who built his house on a rock"; and "everyone who heareth them and *doeth them not*," is outwardly the same, perhaps, but has no foundation [Mt. 7:24, 26]. And what is the rock on which he is built, but Christ? His very works are built on this Rock, otherwise they are not good works [1 Cor. 3:11]. It is not as if Christ was the end only (as they who disparage baptism would imply); not as if the atonement were a thing to be arrived at at last; but Christ is the way also [Jn. 14:6], the beginning and the end, the Author and the Finisher [Heb. 12:2], the Alpha and Omega [Rev.

1:8]. It is through the blood of Christ alone we are able to think or do what is good. It is through his blood alone that such thoughts and deeds are accepted. It is not simply that by bearing our cross we are brought to his; but we are in him, and he in us; our cross is his cross, and his cross is our cross. When we humble ourselves, we partake of the virtue going forth from his humiliation; it is he that is drawing us nearer to himself. When we pray, it is not our prayer, but his Holy Spirit within us that leads us unto himself. When we do works of charity, it is to him in his brethren: it is his compassionate bowels yearning in us towards them: it is the virtue of his ineffable charity through us, his members, again flowing forth to all mankind. To check, therefore, such works by any misstatements, by half admonitions and half encouragements, is to keep men from him. It is like stopping the mouths of the blind men, who have no way to approach him but by prayer, that he may open their eyes; for unless we practise these works of obedience and repentance, we shall assuredly have no eyes to see him; for it is "the commandment of the Lord" which "giveth light unto the eyes" [Ps. 19:8]. It is putting away the little children, the babes in Christ, because they are not of full stature. It is casting stumbling blocks in the way of weak men. It is very true that in the gospels the consolations of Christ may be more imparted to persons who were opprobriously designated "sinners" [Mt. 9:10–13]; and some of whom may have fallen into grievous sin; that "the publicans and harlots enter into the kingdom before the Pharisees" [Mt. 21:31]: but why? not because they were worse, but because they were far better than the Pharisees; as the poor and despised are perhaps generally found wiser and better than those in higher station.

EDWARD BOUVERIE PUSEY

Entire Absolution of the Penitent
(SELECTION)

Editor's introduction.

The first observation . . . that will naturally suggest itself to persons on comparing some of Dr. Pusey's present [1] with his past works, is the greater severity of the former, which the latter have softened. Without any literal opposition between the two in doctrine, the former exhibit certainly a more unqualified view than the latter do. . . . In Dr. Pusey's teaching the severe has prepared the way for the mild. There was something of what appeared, to many, over-austere in his first religious works: his last show anything but this. Here is then a difference before us which some will be inclined to call an inconsistency; others, only a natural consecutiveness. . . . But whatever we may call this change or this modification in Dr. Pusey; that it has taken place on a most natural principle, and has been in him only the legitimate development of one line of thought, is quite clear. There has been essential unity, consistency, sequence in his course of teaching, though that unity has come out in successive sides, and not appeared at once as a whole. It has only unfolded itself, in agreement with the religious wants of the times, in having a former as well as a latter stage: and it has been the more serviceable and effective from having come out thus successively and by parts.

Dr. Pusey has devoted himself to one main line of thought in his religious teaching. He has devoted himself to the consideration of Sin; its awful nature; its antagonism to God; its deep seat in our nature; the remedy provided for it by our Lord's meritorious sufferings and death, and the application of that remedy in the ordinance of Baptism. The subject of Baptism winds up the line of thought. . . . Baptism is a new birth, an entrance into a new world, the communication of a new nature. And Sin is in Baptism pardoned:

1. [ED.] These lines were written in 1846.

271

we are washed and made clean; and the evil is met and provided for. So far is clear, and the subject appears to close. But then comes the fact that men live after Baptism. Sin comes up again, and has to be dealt with again. Deadly sin after Baptism has the guilt and misery of a relapse over and above that of sin simply, and those sad and fearful thoughts come over us which are suggested by the passage in the Epistle to the Hebrews [6:4–6]: "It is impossible for those who were once enlightened, and have tasted the heavenly gift, and were made partakers of the Holy Ghost, and of the powers of the world to come; if they shall fall away, to renew them again unto repentance." There is no absolute renewal provided after that of Baptism has been received and has been fallen from. Here the easy way to peace ends, and a rough and difficult one begins. The first state is past, and any subsequent state of favour must be a hard-earned one. Innocence is over, and repentance follows. True, the mercy of God has not left us desolate even in this last and most forlorn state. For His Church is endowed with a power, though not an absolute and complete one, of restoration; and the sinner is allowed, after sincere repentance and a course of self-mortification, after much self-revenge and humiliation, to enter into the re-enjoyment, though not so entire a one as that which he has lost, of baptismal privileges. But that repentance must appear in solid form; it must have proved itself to have gone through difficulties, made real sacrifices, and shown itself in deeds, and not in words only. Till this is done, the judgments of God are alone before us, and we have no right to be easy or comfortable. Here then is a stage in the progress up to spiritual life in which we are upon indefinite ground, and have no fixed standard to go by. Some minds will be more severe, others more lenient, in their view of repentance. One age of the Church has given a harder, another a milder standard. . . . Different tempers will more or less differ, and the same person will have a different feeling on the subject at one time of his life from what he had at another. . . .

It is true, then, that Dr. Pusey's first publications do exhibit a more severe and less qualified mode of dealing with the sinner than his later ones do. But he has followed in such a course the natural progress of thought in a real spiritual mind, and taken those successive steps which the religious atmosphere around him naturally and fitly called for and elicited.[2]

Pusey's study of "Christian repentance,"[3] designed to complement his treatment of baptism, took the form of a course of sermons on "Com-

2. J. B. Mozley, *Essays Historical and Theological*, 3d ed. (London, 1892), II, 157–60.

3. H. P. Liddon, *Life of Edward Bouverie Pusey, D.D.*, 4th ed. (London, 1894–98), I, 352.

forts to the Penitent." He began his course on May 14, 1843, with a sermon on the Eucharist.

> It is [he said] part of the manifold wisdom of God, that His gifts, in nature and grace, minister to distinct, and, as it often seems, unconnected ends; manifesting thereby the more His own Unity, as the secret cause and power of all things, putting Itself forward in varied forms and divers manners, yet Itself the one Cause of all that is. . . . It is, then, according to the analogy of His other gifts, that His two great Sacraments have in themselves manifold gifts. Baptism containeth not only remission of sin, actual or original, but maketh members of Christ, children of God, heirs of heaven, hath the seal and earnest of the Spirit, the germ of spiritual life; the Holy Eucharist imparteth not life only, spiritual strength, and oneness with Christ, and His Indwelling, and participation of Him, but, in its degree, remission of sins also. As the manna is said to have "contented every man's delight and agreed to every taste" (Wisd. of Sol. 16:20), so He, the Heavenly Manna, becometh to every man what he needeth, and what he can receive; to the penitent perhaps chiefly remission of sins and continued life, to those who have "loved Him and kept His word" [Jn. 14:23], His own transporting, irradiating Presence, full of His own grace and life and love; yet to each full contentment, because to each His own overflowing, undeserved, goodness.[4]

"I chose the Holy Eucharist," Pusey later explained, "as the subject at which [people] would be less likely to take offence than at Absolution." [5] In keeping with his aim of comforting and encouraging the fearful, his sermon was completely uncontroversial in tone, while its contents were largely derived from the preaching of Chrysostom, Augustine, and other great Fathers. Nevertheless, a heated controversy followed.[6] Pusey's sermon was denounced to the vice-chancellor of the university, and on June 2, 1843, after a good deal of undercover skirmishing, the statutory commission of "Six Doctors" declared that its teaching was contrary to the doctrine of the English Church. The ensuing sentence of suspension from preaching within the university for two years was enforced by the vice-chancellor in the face of many vigorous protests, and it was not until February 1, 1846, that Pusey was able to preach the first of two sermons on "Entire Absolution of the Penitent." [7]

❖ ❖ ❖ ❖

4. E. B. Pusey, *The Holy Eucharist a Comfort to the Penitent* (Oxford, 1843), 1 f.
5. Liddon, *Life of Pusey*, II, 307.
6. For a full account, cf. *ibid.*, 306–69.   7. Cf. *ibid.*, III, 51–69.

Jn. 20:21–23. Then said Jesus unto them again, Peace be unto you. As my Father hath sent me, even so send I you. And when he had said this, he breathed on them, and saith unto them, Receive ye the Holy Ghost. Whose soever sins ye remit, they are remitted unto them; and whose soever sins ye retain, they are retained.

[Pusey begins by referring to his suspension and recapitulating the chief ideas of the condemned sermon. He goes on to speak of absolution, first discussing the teaching of the Anglican formularies on the power of the keys, and then commenting on the Biblical and early Christian witness to the forgiveness of post-baptismal sin. He turns next to the Church's commission to absolve.]

There are two distinct commissions conveyed to the apostles, and through them to the Church — authority to baptize, and authority to remit sins to the baptized; the first not only remitting all sin, but changing the whole man, making him another self: before out of Christ, now in Christ; new-born, new-created, a member of Christ, a Son of God, new-formed "after the image of him who created him" [Col. 3:10]. Such a re-creation there cannot again be. In baptism, a man becomes a new self, and being another man, has no more to do with his former sins than if they had been committed by another,[1] except to love and thank God who had freed him from them; by absolution, pardon is given, life is renewed, but the penitent is the same as the sinner. In baptism, sins are suddenly and painlessly blotted out through grace; deep sins after baptism are forgiven, but upon deep contrition which God giveth: and deep contrition is, for the most part, slowly and gradually worked into the soul, deepening with deepening grace, sorrowing still more, as, by God's grace, it more deeply loves; grieved the more, the more it knows him whom it once grieved, and through that grief and love inwrought in it by God, the more forgiven. So then, by the very order of God with the soul (except when he leads it in some special way, and by the cross and his own overflowing love blots out the very traces of past sin and its very memory), continued sorrow is not only the condition of continued pardon, but the very channel of new graces, and of the renewed life of the soul. Sorrow, as it flows on, is more refined, yet deeper. To part with sorrow and self-displeasure would be to part with love; for it grieveth, and is displeased because it loves. Again, sins before baptism

1. [ED.] Here and below several footnotes, containing illustrative quotations or references, are omitted.

come not into judgment at all; they belonged to one who is not; in baptism he was buried and died, and a new man, with a new life and a new principle of life, was raised through the resurrection of Christ. Grievous sins after baptism are remitted by absolution, and the judgment, if the penitent be sincere, is an earnest of the judgment of Christ, and is confirmed by him. Yet the same penitent has yet to appear before the judgment seat of Christ, that, according to his sincerity, the Lord may ratify or annul the judgment of his servants.

Yet with these limitations, the pardon upon penitence is as absolute as in baptism itself. Indeed, the commission to set free from sins, has by ancient Fathers [2] been thought, in a secondary way, to include the power of baptism; it is one power, and one pardon, and one blood diversely applied.[3]

This commission, upon which the authority of the Church rests, as it has ever been understood by the Church itself, was given, in part in different words, at three different times. Before the resurrection, first to St. Peter, as a type of unity: "I give unto thee the keys of the kingdom of heaven, and whatsoever thou shalt bind on earth shall be bound in heaven, and whatsoever thou shalt loose on earth shall be loosed in heaven" [Mt. 16:19]; and then, in the same words, to all the apostles [Mt. 18:18] — both these in promise; and then to all in fulfilment, in that solemn inauguration, the commencement of their apostolate, with the visible token that the Comforter, who proceeded from him, came upon them: "As my Father hath sent me, even so send I you" [Jn. 20:21]. Full of majesty and awe is the commission, full of instruction. The greatness of the power entrusted to man might well exceed our belief, and make us tremble to execute it, and almost doubt, as men have doubted, whether they had it.

What angel in Heaven (says our own Hooker) could have said to man as our Lord did to Peter, "Feed my sheep: Preach: Baptize: Do this in remembrance of me: Whose sins ye retain, they are

2. [ED.] Pusey cites Cyril of Alexandria, *Commentarius in Ioannem*, XII (*PG*, LXXIV, 721); Cyprian, *Epistle* 73, 7 (*ANF*, V, 381; *CSEL*, III/2, 783 f.); Firmilian, *ap.* Cyprian, *Epistle* 75, 16 (*ANF*, V, 394 f.; *CSEL*, III/2, 821); Pacian, *Epistula 1 ad Sympronianum*, VI (*PL*, XIII, 1057); Ambrose, *On Repentance*, I, viii, 36 (*NPNF²*, X, 335; *PL*, XVI, 497); Gregory the Great, *Morals on the Book of Job*, XXVIII, xviii, 38 (*LF*, XXIII, 292 f.; *PL*, LXXVI, 470 f.).

3. [ED.] Pusey quotes Jerome, *Against Pelagius*, I, 33; II, 7 (*NPNF²*, VI, 465, 467; *PL*, XXIII, 550, 568).

retained: and their offences in heaven pardoned whose faults you
shall on earth forgive"? What think we? Are these terrestrial
sounds, or else are they voices uttered out of the clouds above? [4]

So then our Lord premises his commission with those full brief words,
conveying at once both the extent of the commission, and a rule and
guidance in it. "As my Father hath sent me, even so send I you." The
very words are beforehand a comfort to the penitent. For to whom was
our Lord sent, but to the lost sheep of the house of Israel [Mt. 15:24], to
seek and to save that which was lost [Lk. 19:10], to "those who needed
a physician" and knew their need, to "call not the righteous but sinners
to repentance" [Mk. 2:17]?

> He sets forth at once (says St. Cyril) the dignity of the apostolate
> and the incomparable glory of the power given them, and suggests,
> as it seems, the path of apostolic offices. For if he deemed right so
> to send his own disciples as the Father sent him, how must not they
> who are to be followers of them, needs have in view, to what end
> the Father sent the Son? Comprehending then in few words the
> apostolic office, he said that he sent them as the Father sent him,
> that they might thence know that they ought to call sinners to re-
> pentance, to heal the sick in body or in spirit, in all the orderings of
> their doings not to seek anyhow their own will; and, as far as was
> possible, by their doctrine to save the world.[5]

And as he himself was "anointed by the Spirit to bind up the broken-
hearted, to proclaim liberty to the captives, and the opening of the prison
to them that are bound" [Is. 61:1; Lk. 4:18], so when he sent them in
his stead, he imparted to them the Comforter, who being from himself
as from the Father, was to replace himself. "When he had said this, he
breathed upon them, and saith unto them, Receive the Holy Ghost."
As an earnest at once of the gift to be bestowed at the day of Pentecost,
and a gift of sanctification for this immediate office, and to show that
the Holy Spirit, who should come from above, is from him also, and

4. Richard Hooker, *The Laws of Ecclesiastical Polity*, Bk. V, chap. 77, 1 [*Works* (Oxford, 1845), II, 455 f.]. Hooker continues in the fervid passage so well known: "The power of the ministry of God translateth out of darkness into glory; it raiseth men from the earth, and bringeth God himself down from heaven; by blessing visible elements it maketh them invisible grace; it giveth daily the Holy Ghost; it hath to dispose of that flesh which was given for the life of the world, and that blood which was poured out to redeem souls; when it poureth malediction upon the heads of the wicked, they perish; when it revoketh the same, they revive. O wretched blindness, if we admire not so great power, more wretched if we consider it aright, and, notwithstanding, imagine that any but God can bestow it!"

5. Cyril of Alexandria [*Commentarius in Ioannem*, XII (PG, LXXIV, 709)].

consubstantial from himself, and that he who created man in his own image [Gen. 1:27], breathing into his nostrils the breath of life [Gen. 2:7], was now about to re-create them in a more divine and perfect way by union with himself, "he breathed upon them," and imparted to them the Holy Ghost. And then he saith to them the solemn words, "Whose soever sins ye remit, they are remitted unto them; and whose soever sins ye retain, they are retained" [Jn. 20:23]. . . .

[Pusey goes on to discuss the power of the keys as related to, yet distinct from, the baptismal remission of sins. He then begins to consider the scope of absolution.]

But when we understand our blessed Lord in the plain meaning of his words, of a power lodged in his Church to forgive sins in his Name, then the very words themselves express the fulness of the pardon. As our Lord sent his apostles in the same way in which the Father had sent him, so the word by which he expresses the power to forgive is the very word by which he himself forgave. "Whose soever sins ye forgive, they are forgiven unto them" (ἀφέωνται), is the blessed echo of his own words: "Son, be of good cheer, thy sins are forgiven thee (ἀφέωνται)" (Mt. 9:2) — the very word by which he prayed for his murderers and all penitents upon the cross (Lk. 23:34), and teaches us in his own prayer, when we pray, to ask for forgiveness (Mt. 6:12); the very word under which he declared that "all sins and blasphemy shall be forgiven unto men" (Mt. 12:31); spake of the entire forgiveness by our heavenly Father to those who forgive (Mt. 6:12, 14 f.; Lk. 6:37); for the fulness of which the scribes disputed his authority — "Who is this that forgiveth sins also?" (Lk. 7:49); by which he claimed that power to himself — "That ye may know that the Son of Man hath power on earth to forgive sins" (Mt. 9:6); and now in the same words he leaves it to those whom he left in his Name to carry on his work on earth. But if any would restrain this to the apostles only, "why," as St. Pacian says, "do they not in the like way restrain baptism also?"[6] Either both were confined to the apostles only, or both were committed to that Church with which our Lord promised to be "always to the end of the world" [Mt. 28:20]; by baptism, to remit all sin original or actual; by absolution, to remit all which, by the frailty of our nature, any may afterwards contract; by baptism to bring into his fold, by absolution to restore those who had wandered from it.

What sins then may there be remitted? All which are not excepted;

6. Pacian, *Epistula I ad Sympronianum* [VI (PL, XIII, 1057), paraphrased].

and these are none. "He saith," says St. Pacian, " 'whatsoever ye shall loose.' He excepted nothing whatever. 'Whatsoever,' he says, great or small." [7]

> God (saith St. Ambrose) maketh no distinction, who promised his mercy unto all, and without any exception granted to his priests the power of loosing. Only whoso hath heaped up sin, let him heap up penitence; for greater sins are washed away with greater tears.[8]

All may be forgiven, for which God puts into the heart the desire to be forgiven. The unpardonable sin is therefore alone not forgiven (St. Augustine says), because the sinner asks not for forgiveness.[9]

Nothing can be more absolute than the words, "Whose soever sins ye remit, they are remitted unto them." No sin then is excepted for its greatness; none for their multitude. He saith, "Whatsoever ye loose on earth shall be loosed in heaven" [Mt. 18:18]; no sinner is excepted, however deeply ingrained by old, inveterate, accumulated sins; though his sins be upon him and weigh him down that he be not able to look up [Ps. 40:12], and defile his memory, and cloud his faith, and destroy the power of other ordinances, and chill the heart, and weaken the will, or even bring on him relapses, let him, with earnest purpose, lay down his sin at our dear Lord's feet, hating them for his love's sake who has so loved him; and he has said, "Whose soever sins ye remit, they are remitted unto them."

Nor again doth he put us off for that forgiveness to a distant day. The effects of sin upon the soul may often be to be worked out by sorrow and toil; the forfeited crown and larger favour of Almighty God to be gained by subsequent self-denial or suffering for him or devoted service. But we have the very craving of our hearts. Our sins, when we are fit to receive the blessed words, are forgiven at once. "They *are*," our gracious Lord says, "forgiven unto them (ἀφέωνται)"; as though he would express the swiftness of his pardon, in the same way as it is promised in the prophet, "Thou shalt call and the Lord shall answer; thou shalt cry and he shall say, Here I am" [Is. 58:9]; so now, so soon as his priest has, in his Name, pronounced his forgiveness on earth, the sins of the true penitent are forgiven in heaven. "Whose soever sins ye remit, they *are* remitted unto them."

---

7. [ED.] Pacian, *Epistula III ad Symproniamum* [XII (*PL*, XIII, 1071)].

8. Ambrose, *On Repentance*, I, iii, 10 [*NPNF*², X, 331; *PL*, XVI, 489].

9. [ED.] Pusey quotes Augustine, *Enchiridion*, 83 (*NPNF*¹, III, 264; *PL*, XL, 272), and cites Fulgentius, *De remissione peccatorum*, I, 24 (*PL*, LXV, 547).

All then combines to induce us to receive unhesitatingly the heavenly gift. Everything in and around our blessed Lord's words, the solemn investment of the apostles with his own power, "As my Father sent me, even so send I you": the imparting of the Holy Spirit for this office, which is the work of the Spirit; the solemn simplicity and absolute distinct meaning of his words, which, taken plainly, cannot fall short of the sense in which the Church has ever understood them; the unvarying agreement of the Church in so understanding them, assure our faith that he hath not left us comfortless, but hath left others with his authority, to convey to sinners in his Name the forgiveness of their sins. And with this key, all which we might have doubted about or feared as to other Scripture is opened to us. The fulness of the words with which our Lord gives power to remit sins is the very antidote to the heresy of Novatian; and those awful passages which shut out some sin, cannot exclude any sin which *can* sue for pardon, since he has said: "Whose soever sins ye remit." We see that the parables of our Lord's love for sinners apply to those too who have anew perished, since he has himself provided for the restoration of penitents; we see that they may be at once forgiven, and so to us too belong those promises of the swift forgiveness of our sins; and we may take boldly David's words, "I said, I will confess my sins unto the Lord, and so thou forgavest the wickedness of my sins" [Ps. 32:5]. He provides for their complete, absolute remission; so to us also are said the comfortable words of the prophet, "Though thy sins be as scarlet they shall be as white as snow" [Is. 1:18]. The word ἀφέωνται contains in one a whole gospel of forgiveness — a whole volume, filled within and without, and traced by the finger of our God and Saviour Jesus Christ, all that the penitent's heart craves for, full, present, absolute, universal forgiveness and release.

PART FIVE

❖

Discerning the Lord's Body

I

ROBERT ISAAC WILBERFORCE

*The Doctrine of the Incarnation of Our Lord Jesus Christ
in Its Relation to Mankind and to the Church*
(SELECTION)

Editor's introduction. In 1828 Newman and Froude, already tutors of
Oriel College, gained a new and congenial colleague in the person of
Robert Isaac Wilberforce, a member of the college since 1820 and a
fellow since 1826. The second son of the great Evangelical philanthro-
pist William Wilberforce, and elder brother of Samuel Wilberforce,
Bishop of Oxford (1845–69) and of Winchester (1869–73), and chief
prototype of the "new model" of pastoral episcopacy in the Church of
England, Robert Wilberforce had been drawn into the nascent Tractarian group as early as 1823, when, with Froude and Isaac Williams, he
spent the "Long Vacation" in Keble's company. Since he left Oxford in
1831, on the termination of his tutorship, and from 1832 to 1854 served
as a parish priest, first in Kent and then in Yorkshire, he was not directly
involved in the events which stirred the university between 1833 and
1845, but both in his preaching and in his extensive writings he consistently upheld the ideas and aims of the Oxford Movement. Indeed, his
work for the Tractarian cause was of such a calibre that one judicious
commentator could call him "the greatest philosophical theologian of
the Tractarians." [1]

One notable feature of Wilberforce's thought, as compared with most
Tractarian theology, is his greater openness to what we should now call
the "ecumenical dialogue." It is true that Pusey, at any rate, also looked
with interest at non-Anglican theology and piety. His first major publica-

1. A. T. Lyttelton, "Tractarianism and the Bible," *The Pilot*, III (1901), 362.

tion was a sympathetic study of German Protestant theology,[2] which he had come to know during his studies in Germany, while his later literary output included many adaptations of Roman Catholic devotional writings and several discussions of Roman-Anglican reunion. But he soon turned his back on German Protestantism as a form of "liberal" heresy, and he does not seem to have been affected by the fresher intellectual tendencies in contemporary Roman Catholicism. Wilberforce, on the contrary, worked in fruitful contact with foreign theology. On the Protestant side, he studied Schleiermacher, he relied heavily on Dorner's history of Christology, he made extensive use of the exegetical work of Olshausen. On the Catholic side, he was strongly influenced by the thought of Möhler and was even acquainted with the work of Günther.[3] Moreover, he showed a lively interest in the "Mercersburg theology" — the "catholicizing" tendency fostered by the work of Nevin and Schaff among the German Reformed in America.[4] He particularly admired Nevin's writings.

> You take so much interest in the course of opinions [he wrote to Gladstone] that I wish you might fall in some day with the works of a remarkable school which is growing up among the German Protestants in Pennsylvania. It is founded on a study of Primitive Antiquity, and of Mediaeval History, as given in German writers. Its chief writer is a Dr. Nevin, who has contributed many essays of great ability to the Mercersburg Review. He takes the highest tone in maintaining Church Authority, the Sacramental Theory, and all the points, for which we are contending in this country; and in ability as well as learning exceeds I think the American Episcopalians, whom I have met with.[5]

It was no accident that Wilberforce singled out "Church authority" and the "sacramental theory" for special mention in these comments. These central themes of the Oxford Movement had long concerned him deeply, and since 1850 they had been inseparably linked in the "Gorham controversy" — an ecclesiastical crisis which was also the climactic

---

2. E. B. Pusey, *An Historical Enquiry into the Probable Causes of the Rationalist Character lately Predominant in the Theology of Germany* (London, 1828–30).

3. Wilberforce refers both to Johann Adam Möhler, *Die Einheit der Kirche* (1825), and to his *Symbolik* (1832), as well as to Anton Günther, *Vorschule zur spekulativen Theologie* (1828–29).

4. Cf. J. H. Nichols, *Romanticism in American Theology* (Chicago, 1961), 228–31.

5. R. I. Wilberforce to W. E. Gladstone, November 5, 1853, British Museum Add. Ms. 44,376 (Gladstone Papers, Vol. 291), fol. 135.

crisis of Wilberforce's own life.[6] In the Gorham Judgment of March 8, 1850, the Judicial Committee of the Privy Council, by ordering the Bishop of Exeter to institute the somewhat eccentric Evangelical George Cornelius Gorham to a living in his diocese despite his conviction that Gorham's views on baptismal grace were incompatible with Anglican orthodoxy, seemed to Anglo-Catholics to be at once an assault on the Church's faith and a challenge to episcopal authority. A wave of secessions to Rome, comparable only to the secessions of 1845, followed the Gorham Judgment. Wilberforce held out, despite his growing conviction that the English Church was fatally compromised by its bondage to the state,[7] until November 1, 1854, when he submitted to Rome — in Paris, to avoid embarrassment to his episcopal brother at Oxford. In less than three years he was dead.

The Doctrine of the Incarnation, published in 1848, is both Wilberforce's finest theological work and one of the most distinguished pieces of nineteenth-century Anglican divinity. Indeed, with the exception of Frederick Denison Maurice's *Kingdom of Christ*, published ten years earlier, it is hard to find another English theological production from the first half of the nineteenth century that shows a comparable grasp of the basic pattern of Christian doctrine. Even Newman's systematic works, for all their insight and their moments of brilliance, seem rather casual beside Wilberforce's *magnum opus*. To say nothing more, *The Doctrine of the Incarnation* is unquestionably the great synthesis of Tractarian teaching.

In a sermon preached on March 10, 1850, Wilberforce intimates that the fundamental and distinctive idea of Christianity (and therefore of his own theological work) is "the doctrine . . . of *Mediation*." [8] This doctrine appears repeatedly, in various contexts, in his preaching and his official utterances.

> Here then [he declares] is the main truth of the Gospel — the renewal of fallen nature in that Divine Man, from whom the gifts of pardon and grace are transmitted to His brethren. . . . There

6. Cf. J. C. S. Nias, *Gorham and the Bishop of Exeter* (London, 1951).

7. As early as February 11, 1848, Wilberforce wrote to Gladstone: "I am afraid you don't estimate at quite so high a rate as I do what it is worthwhile to do and suffer in order to be free from our present bondage" (British Museum, Add. Ms. 44,367 [Gladstone Papers, Vol. 282], fol. 76).

8. R. I. Wilberforce, *The Sacramental System: A Sermon Preached at St. Mary's Church, before the University of Oxford, on Sunday, March 10th, 1850* (London, 1850), 4.

are persons who suppose that they can be joined to God by the mere exercise of their thoughts. . . . Yes, brethren, this *is* the natural way in which man may approach his Maker, and if we could be saved by *nature*, this were all, doubtless, which could be required. But then by the course of nature there shall no flesh be saved. . . . Men cannot apply Christ's merits to themselves by their private will unless He first applies His merits to them from without by His public ministry. Else would the first movement towards their recovery be internal and spontaneous, as the Pelagians teach, instead of resting on that efficacy of the New Head of our race, which implies the existence of a Church, and the influence of an external Saviour. Hence the need of sacramental rites, and of the perpetual sacrifice, and of a ministry of reconciliation, and of an earthly absolution. All these depend upon the truth that the Inter-cession of the one great High Priest is a *reality* which we cannot appropriate to ourselves by the mere exercise of our thoughts, but which He must bestow upon us through some actual channel of intervention. Let us have but a deep sense of the greatness of that loss which was entailed upon us by the fall, of the immensity of that interval which separates us from God, and of the absolute necessity of *His* gracious interference, through whom only we are reunited to our offended Creator, and we shall be in no danger of supposing that we can dispense with those means whereby He joins us to Himself. . . . To deem highly of the means of grace is to attach great weight to the presence and efficacy of the New Head of humanity.[9]

As God created the sun to rule in the sky, and made it the source of light to all men, so the man Christ Jesus was made the centre and source of all life to all generations of mankind. . . . He had accomplished His service on the cross, He had finished the work which was given Him to do. But might He cast off the raiment of His humanity, as if its purposes were altogether fulfilled? Then how could we have gained that inward grace, of which His mediation was the only channel? Since the very thing we need is that renew-ing influence by which our will is to be brought into union with the will of God, the continual presence of such a Divine helper is as necessary to us as that one sacrifice which He offered for us on the bloody tree.[10]

Christianity is the doctrine of grace. It is the substitution of the system of Mediation for the system of nature. It is built upon the truth that all heavenly gifts were first received by the manhood of

9. R. I. Wilberforce, *Sermons on the New Birth of Man's Nature* (London, 1850), 215–21.
10. *Ibid.*, 178 f.

the Church's Incarnate Head, that from Him they might flow forth
into all its members. Thus are divine blessings received by His servants through Sacramental grace, because they pertained to Him by
oneness of nature. And hence we see how close is the union between
a Christian education, and all those means of grace, whereby we
maintain our union with the Lord's Mystic Body. . . . Is it alleged,
then, that the Church's system of education interferes with the full
development of the intellectual faculties of men, that daily devotions, and a lengthened service, and full attention to the doctrinal
teaching of our Holy Mother, abstract too much of that time which
is required for the increasing demands of a cultivated age; we answer that too great prominence *cannot* be given to the highest of
all sources of knowledge. . . . Shall we go back from Mediation
to nature: having begun in the spirit, shall we be made perfect by
the flesh? [11]

. . . His Manhood was designed to supersede all those means of
intercourse which the mercy of God had hitherto opened to mankind. Instead of the Voice which had spoken to Adam, or the Shape
which had appeared to Abraham, or the tabernacle round which the
tribes of Israel worshipped, we have that better Temple, which was
fashioned by the power of the Holy Ghost in the Virgin's womb.
. . . Why do we assemble on the first day of the week, in place of
that which had been devoted to the remembrance of the creation,
but because the raising of Christ's Body from the earth was a
second and more glorious act than the very rearing of a world? [12]

The Church system . . . supposes the first movement to come
from God, when, in the person of the Word, He united to Himself
man's nature. Its primary principle is that those spiritual gifts which,
but for sin, would have been the original inheritance of man's
nature, were embodied in the humanity of the Word made flesh, that
from Him they might be communicated to His brethren. In this
manner did grace find its way from heaven to earth, diffusing itself
through the body of the Church, and extending to all its members.
That which dwelt first in Christ in that He was full of grace and
truth by nature, was to be extended as a gift to His servants.[13]

All this must true faith realize and accept. It must look to Christ
as a personal Mediator, and from His man's nature accept the gifts
which shall regenerate ours. It must seek to discern the Lord's
Body. It must wait upon Him in the ordinances of His love, with

11. *Ibid.*, 194–96.
12. R. I. Wilberforce, *Sermons on the Holy Communion* (London, 1854), 164 f.
13. R. I. Wilberforce, *The Evangelical and Tractarian Movements: A Charge to
the Clergy of the East Riding, Delivered at the Ordinary Visitation, A.D. 1851*
(London, n.d.), 12 f.

firm persuasion that from Him there issues sufficient grace for the salvation of a world.[14]

❖   ❖   ❖   ❖

CHAPTER XI:
CHRIST IS PRESENT WITH MEN IN HIS CHURCH OR BODY MYSTICAL

The nature and importance of Christ's presence has been exhibited in the preceding chapter.[1] He is present with his people through his man's nature; not however by material contact, but by spiritual power. And through this presence does he act as the Head of the renewed race — as the second Adam of restored humanity. The question which next suggests itself is, by what means man may profit through this great blessing; how each individual may obtain a part in that work of mediation which was wrought in expiation on the cross; which is still discharged by intercession in heaven; and whose sphere of operation is as extensive as that presence upon earth, which the God-Man vouchsafes through spiritual power. For this end something is wanting plainly on our part, as well as something on the part of God. But the qualifications which are required on our part — the efficacy of faith, the importance of love — will not be touched upon in this place, because they belong to a different inquiry. For these pertain to man, who is the subject in whom religious feelings exist; though they be God's gift, yet they are a gift which exists within and not without us; their nature and importance follow from consideration of our inward constitution. On the circumstance that each man has a true personal existence, and that to each is committed the awful power of choosing or refusing Christ, depends the necessity of individual faith and love for each man's salvation. But on this question we are not at present occupied: what is said here refers to what is done without, not to what is done within us; to Christ as a real being external to our thoughts, as the object of our faith who exists outside of our minds. For it was at first proposed to treat the *objective* not the *subjective* part of religion;[2] not to inquire what changes were necessary in man, who is the *subject* of religion, but to show that there was an *object*

---

14. R. L. Wilberforce, *The New Birth of Man's Nature*, 280.

1. [ED.] Cf. R. I. Wilberforce, *The Doctrine of the Incarnation of Our Lord Jesus Christ* (London, 1848), chap. X: "Our Lord's Spiritual Presence as Mediator with Men."

2. [ED.] Cf. *ibid.*, 5–8.

above and around man, the reality of whose existence it was essential to believe. This object is Christ our Lord: "Christ who died, yea rather who is risen from the dead, who is also at the right hand of God, who also maketh intercession for us" [Rom. 8:34]. And since his intercession and the presence of his man's nature are realities existing outside of ourselves — not mere fancies, but actual objects external to us — it is necessary to ask in what way these general advantages are so consigned to individuals that they may be the separate portion of single souls. The question is, not what is necessary on our part, whether faith or love, but what is the condition or quality in these external realities themselves, which renders them available for our individual apprehension.

Now, on this subject it may be said in general that our union with the manhood of Christ, or our participation in his presence, is brought about in our union with the Church, which is his body mystical. It is not that one of these is a means or channel through which we approach the other, but that since the two processes are identical, it is impossible to divide them. For that which joins men to Christ's mystical body the Church is their union with his man's nature; and their means of union with his man's nature is bestowed in his Church or body mystical. This will become more evident when it is shown that the sacraments, which are the means of binding us to the mystical body of Christ, derive their efficacy from the influence of his body natural. And hence the impossibility of answering a question which is sometimes asked, whether men are joined to Christ by being joined to his Church, or joined to his Church by being joined to him. It would be a parallel question to ask, whether we were sharers in Adam's nature because we were men or men because we were sharers in Adam's nature. The two relations hang inseparably together. By the mystical body of Christ is meant the whole family of those who by the Holy Ghost are united in Church ordinances to his man's nature. Our real union with each is what gives us a part in the other.

This intimacy of union between Christ and the Church may be gathered in the first place from the direct words of Scripture. Why should the Church be called a body, and especially why should it be called the body of Christ, did not some relation bind it to that body of Christ, which came into existence at his Incarnation? It may be answered, that the Church is spoken of as a body, because thought of as a whole through the abstracting power of reason. Yet why should it be called the body of the Lord? The subjects of an earthly prince might be spoken of as making up together the body of his realm, but who would call them the body of their king? Yet such language is repeatedly employed, and under various forms, respecting Christians in Holy Scripture. The very harmony of its metaphorical expressions implies that they rest upon some real relation. When Christ declares himself the vine, and his people the branches [Jn. 15:5], this is because the trees of the field have an organized life. If the Church is his bride,[3] this is because the marriage bond savours so strongly of an actual union. So that a real, and not merely a metaphorical, conjunction must be designed when we read, "Ye are the body of Christ, and members in particular" [1 Cor. 12:27].

Now, since the mention of "body" leads us plainly to the human part of our Lord's being (for God is a spirit [Jn. 4:24]), therefore whatever relation is implied in the application of this term to the Church must plainly connect it with our Lord's human nature. And the manner in which St. Paul transfers what is applicable to our Lord's actual body to his body mystical implies that the one of these is truly dependent on the other. Thus does the natural affection which each man bears to himself pass on into our Lord's affection to his people: "No man ever yet hated his own flesh, but nourisheth and cherisheth it, even as the Lord the Church. For we are members of his body; of his flesh, and of his bones. . . . This is a great mystery, but I speak concerning Christ and the Church" [Eph. 5:29 f., 32]. And, therefore, he is "the Head, from which all the body by joints and bands" has "nourishment ministered" [Col. 2:19]. And so identified is the man Christ Jesus and his spiritual members that the name which belongs individually to him is used for them in their collective character. Hence he who, as the apostle tells us, "gave gifts unto men," was himself, as the psalmist expresses it, their receiver [Eph. 4:8; Ps. 68:18]. When St. Paul is arguing that the promise to Abraham was not pledged to all the races which descended from him, but to one only of the families of which he was parent, he comprehends the spiritual progeny of Abraham under the name of Christ:[4] "For as the body is one and hath many members, and all the members of that one body being many are one body, so also is Christ" [1 Cor. 12:12]. It seems unquestionable, therefore, that some real relation must bind together that body natural which he took by his Incarnation, and his body mystical

---

3. [ED.] *Body* in the original edition is a misprint, corrected in the 2d ed. (1849).

4. [ED.] *Cf.* Wilberforce, *Doctrine of the Incarnation*, 23. Here and below a number of Wilberforce's footnotes are abridged or omitted.

the Church, so that our union with the one must be a ground of union with the other.[5]

The intimate connexion by which the natural body of Christ is bound to his body mystical becomes still more evident if we advert to one peculiar characteristic, which the one derives from the other. What is the cause and import of that unity of the Church which is directly asserted in Holy Writ, and which has been delivered to us as so fundamental a doctrine of our faith as to be made an Article of the Creed? "There is one body and one Spirit, even as ye are called in one hope of your calling" [Eph. 4:4]. Unless St. Paul's word are to go for nothing, there must plainly be some reason why this unity in the Church's external form is put forth in so emphatic a manner. Or again, "we, being many, are one body in Christ" [Rom. 12:5]. And this unity of the Church's body has in all ages been esteemed essential to Christian belief. The assertion of it, as an original Article of the Creed, is the testimony of that universal community, which Christ our Lord promised to guard from fatal error. It would have been to corrupt the principles of the gospel if the collective voice of Christians had proclaimed among its fundamental verities what was either false or futile. Yet if the unity of the Church were nothing but that those who bear the same name may be classed together, as we bestow the name of Platonists on those who followed the disciple of Socrates, its assertion as a doctrine would be altogether unmeaning. But suppose that something further is designed: on what can it be dependent? Was it merely an arbitrary rule, imposed as a technical restraint upon the extension of the Christian body? Could it be meant to shackle its advance by subjecting it to such restricting conditions as at present interfere with the growth of the Church of Christ, in many countries where it receives state assistance? If such a thing could be thought possible, yet the absence of any original rules for the Church's general government shows that it was not attempted. By a noiseless and simultaneous growth did it spring up like Solomon's temple [1 Kings 6:7] in the beauty of holiness, till it filled the mighty precincts of the Roman Empire. For three centuries at least there was no reference for purposes of government to any earthly head, while yet the Church's body seemed as though it were instinct with a single soul. From whence could come this marvelous co-operation? Its inconsistency with the acts of men bespeaks at once its divine parentage.

5. [ED.] Wilberforce quotes Richard Hooker, *The Laws of Ecclesiastical Polity*, Bk. V, chap. 56, 7 (*Works* [Oxford, 1845], II, 250).

The Church is *one* because it is the body of Christ, and because it is quickened by his spiritual presence. Through spiritual life does his body natural act upon mankind, and become germinant of that which is called his body mystical, from its relation to himself. It was predicted that "he shall see his seed, he shall prolong his days, and the pleasure of the Lord shall prosper in his hand. He shall see of the travail of his soul, and shall be satisfied" [Is. 53:10 f.]. In this manner it was that he should "divide the spoil with the strong" [Is. 53:12]. Thus has God made him "the first-born among many brethren" [Rom. 8:29]. Christ's humanity, that stone cut out of the mine of man's nature without his co-operation, has swelled up into a mountain. Its cementing principle is that quickening influence of the second man, by which he lives in all his members. Thus do they trace to Christ's manhood their spiritual life, as to Adam their natural parentage.

We need not wonder then that the Church's unity is declared to be a fact, and that its confession is a fundamental doctrine. That the Church is one body results from organization, not from enactment; it is Christ's body, wrought out through the sacrifice of that manhood, which he offered on the cross. From the oneness of his body which is slain results the oneness of his body which is sanctified. Neither is the profession of the Church's unity the mere admission of an external appearance, but the belief in an inward verity. It is to recognize the presence of that spiritual power which spreads itself from Christ our Lord throughout all members of his mystical body. In this presence consists their life: "If any man have not the Spirit of Christ, he is none of his" [Rom. 8:9]. "But if the Spirit of him that raised up Jesus from the dead dwell in you, he that raised up Christ from the dead shall also quicken your mortal bodies by his Spirit that dwelleth in you" [Rom. 8:11]. From this central source, then, flows all the life of renewed humanity. And that its being and harmony might have their origin in the highest of all perfections, and be truly the reflection upon earth of what is heavenly and divine, therefore its principle of connexion is a counterpart here below of that primary union which existed before all creation, and which is the grand type and cause of concord and law. For the Mediator promised to be in his servants, even as he himself is the seat of that mysterious indwelling of the Eternal Father, whereby the whole Blessed Trinity is united in the never-ending perfection of an actual oneness: "I in them, and thou in me, that they may be made perfect in one" [Jn. 17:23]. And again, "that they all may be one; as thou, Father, art in me, and I in thee, that they also may be one in us" [Jn. 17:21]. Not, of course, that we can speak of that union in which men partake, as the same with that ineffable union which binds together those three blessed persons who are numerically one. We can affirm only that the union in Christ which exists among men has borrowed something from the ineffable union of the divine nature. As the perfection of God's being is the true cause and source of everything perfect which the world exhibits, so in the oneness of the renewed family in Christ we discern traces of that mysterious unity which underlies all things. "At that day ye shall know that I am in my Father, and ye in me, and I in you" [Jn. 14:20]. And therefore "our fellowship is with the Father, and with his Son Jesus Christ" [1 Jn. 1:3]. For the whole three persons of the Blessed Godhead take part in that work of mercy for which the Mediator became incarnate. For the Holy Ghost, as St. Augustine expresses it, "acts through the whole Church, as the soul in all the members of one body." [6] And "the Father himself loveth you" [Jn. 16:27]; while the Son is "Head over all things to the Church, which is his body, the fulness of him that filleth all in all" [Eph. 1:22 f.]. Thus does unity stoop down from the higher to the lower nature, and the Church on earth is the true and real manifestation of the kingdom of heaven. Not that our union in spirit with God has superseded or taken the place of that personal oneness, whereby in Christ our Lord the manhood is united to God. This were the Sabellian heresy, which would represent the Deity as manifesting himself only in three relations, whereof each succeeded and superseded its predecessor. For the union of Godhead with manhood in Christ is a real, perfect, and lasting union, of which the union of Christ with men is the appointed effect. So that these mysterious relations are cumulative and not consequent only, leading us down by successive steps to things on earth from things in heaven.[7]

6. Augustine, *Sermo* 267, 4 [PL, XXXVIII, 1231].

7. This wonderful chain of connexion is set forth by Lord Bacon in his Confession of Faith: "The Word did not only take flesh, or was joined to flesh, but was made flesh, though without confusion of substance or nature: so as the Eternal Son of God and the Ever-Blessed Son of Mary was one Person — so one, as the Blessed Virgin may be truly and catholically called *Deipara*, the Mother of God — so one, as there is no unity in universal nature, not that of the soul and body of man so perfect; for the Three Heavenly Unities, whereof that is the second, exceed all natural unities; that is, the unity of the Three Persons in the Godhead; the unity of God and man in Christ; and the unity of Christ and the Church — the Holy Ghost being the worker of both these latter unities; for by the Holy Ghost was Christ Incarnate, and quickened in flesh; and by the Holy Ghost was man regenerated, and quickened in the spirit" [ED.] Francis Bacon, *Works* (New York, 1869), XIV, 52 f.

Thus does the impulsive wave of heavenly concord extend itself to the race of man, from its primary source in the bosom of incommunicable Godhead. To assert the truth of Christ's presence — the reality of that union which binds the whole mystic body of his Church to the manhood of the Incarnate Word — is to maintain the reality of his mediation, and the absolute necessity of that bond by which heaven and earth are united. For it is a necessary result of the cardinal truth of the Christian system — the truth, *i.e.*, that all gifts and blessings are introduced into our race through the intervention of that nobler member, who connects it with the Almighty. And herein is the Christian scheme of mediation opposed to that theory of rationalism, which rests upon the capacities of nature. The principle of rationalism is, that man's improvement may be effected through those gifts which God bestowed upon him by creation, inasmuch as sufficient means of intercourse with the Supreme Spirit were provided by the law of his nature. Whereas the Church deals with man as a fallen race, whose original means of intercourse with God have been obstructed, and which needs a new and supernatural channel for the entrance of heavenly gifts. And this channel has been provided through the Man Jesus Christ. In his person did Godhead enter manhood, that through this one perfect type of humanity it might "leaven the whole lump" [1 Cor. 5:6]. Thus does the law of grace supersede the law of nature. If man had never fallen, to inherit the nature of the first Adam had been a sufficient means of communion with God. But because the natural means of communication have been cut off, that supernatural union is requisite which we obtain by participating the nature of the second Adam. Now, it is for the diffusion of this renewed and renewing manhood that those media have been provided whereby the Son of Man communicates himself to his brethren. All the ordinances of the Church, its hallowed things, places, and persons — its worship and sacraments — are a series of instruments whereby the sanctified manhood of the Mediator diffuses itself as a life-giving seed through the mass of humanity. Thus does he continue to effect that work through his man's nature, which he avowed to be the very object of his earthly being: "For their sakes I sanctify myself, that they also might be sanctified through the truth" [Jn. 17:19]. And for this office are external media as requisite, as were body and limbs to the truth of his human being. As he could not be a man without that substantial existence which revealed him to the senses of mankind, so he could not be the Head of the body mystical without the use of those actual media of intercourse whereby he unites his living members to himself.

The importance, then, of external ordinances results from that fact on which Christianity is dependent, that through the Incarnation of the Mediator, the corrupted race of man has been regenerated by a heavenly nature. Yet this gracious provision is often received with repugnance by those for whose benefit it is intended. Many who are called Christians, and who profess to value above all things the mediation of Christ, consider themselves actually injured because this "new and living way" has been opened to them "through the veil, that is to say his flesh" [Heb. 10:20]. The opportunity of approaching God through the Man Christ Jesus, which is given to them through the ordinances of his mystic body, seems an encroachment on that right of access which they before had, through the free exercise of their own thoughts. Before a country is marked out by roads, anyone may make his way through woods and over commons to the royal dwelling; but the institution of highways abridges the previous liberty of approach. This seems to be the feeling of many in regard to the mediation of Christ. They wish to approach God in their own way, as mind speaks to mind, without resorting to that circuitous method which requires their union with the Church. But the appointment of a Mediator with the Father does not diminish men's means of access, unless the opportunity of approach, which existed before, is denied them. Now, since the gospel is offered only to those to whom it is communicated (for "how shall they hear without a preacher" [Rom. 10:14]?), the condition of persons to whom mediation is unknown remains unaffected by its announcement. Wherever graces appear in the children of men, we know that they come down only from the "Father of Lights" [Jas. 1:17], and we rejoice that

> Light can find its way
> To regions furthest from the fount of day.

Such influence was visible in former times among men who were blinded by ignorance, and it may be found at present among men who are blinded by prejudice. And yet it is impossible to deny that those who reject the doctrine of mediation, now that it is revealed, are in danger of rejecting Christ. For what is their conduct in reality, but the very crime which is forbidden in the Second Commandment? The First Commandment inhibited the substitution of other gods, Baal or Ashtaroth, in place of Jehovah. The Second forbade to worship Jehovah in other ways than that which was "ordained by angels in the hand of a mediator" [Gal. 3:19]. It was the place of this mediator, Moses, which the golden calf was intended to supply [Deut. 9:16]. The crime of Israel was that when the Most High had appointed a mode of access, men thought that they could approach him better through their own inventions. And what else is the result, when men think that they can reach over the God-Man, the one channel of intercourse between earth and heaven, and address themselves by a shorter and more direct approach to God? This course may be adopted without professed disbelief in Christ if men neglect that channel of approach which he has opened to the Father. For the notion of communing with God, the Eternal and Infinite Spirit, through the immediate action of our own spirits, independently of that mode of coming to him which has been provided through the manhood of Christ, tends to a denial of the whole principle of his mediation. What does it matter whether men call the object of their worship Christ, and profess belief in him, if the only thing to which they direct their thoughts is the ultimate and incommunicable Godhead? What more remarkably distinguishes the Mediator from the Father and the Holy Ghost than that they are *not*, whereas he *is*, personally united to manhood? So that in approaching him, we cannot overpass his man's nature — it is our natural channel of communion with him. What is addressed directly by man's spirit to the Ultimate Spirit of the universe is not addressed to Christ, or if addressed to him in name, it is not addressed to him as Mediator, but only through his general participation in the nature of Godhead.

Here then lies the error of those who, like the Quakers, reject or at least undervalue those external means whereby the Son of Man unites himself to his spiritual members. The disuse of sacraments is only one point in that general system, which looks rather to the actings of our own mind than to the agency of an incarnate Mediator. Now, without judging individuals, who must stand or fall to their own master, it may safely be affirmed that the ultimate tendency of this system, however it may retain the phraseology of the gospel, is to substitute natural religion for revealed. Our irresistible conviction respecting the acting of spirits leads us to conclude that the thought, wish, and conviction of our own minds is at all times present as an object to the all-wise Spirit of God. Do our souls then desire to hold intercourse with the great primary Spirit of the universe, there needs, so far as nature tells us, no intervening link: what exists as an intellectual reality in us is a real object to the knowledge of the Most High. But to build on such intercourse as this, is to rest only on those principles which belong to us by creation. It is to employ mere natural means for intercourse with God. So that to make it an objection against the Church system, that its media of communion are not simple, natural, and immediate — that they do not commend themselves to human judgment, but tax our faith, and introduce something external between us and God — is in reality to complain that the system of nature has been superseded by the system of mediation. For when Christ's manhood was made a bridge between heaven and earth, whereby the purity and exaltation of the divine nature might be brought into contact with the infirmity and defilement of ours, an external channel of communication was substituted for the immediate intercourse of mind with mind. So long as man's mind speaks immediately to the Universal Mind which pervades all things, its inner actions are realities in themselves, which are contemplated at once by the Supreme Essence; but if there be a Being external to us, through whom all intercourse must pass — a single Being, characterized by all the reality which depends on material existence — then must something be superadded to those mere inward actions of faith and love which are all that nature could point out as the means of intercourse between one spirit and another. This new medium of intercourse, this channel of communication between earth and heaven, has been provided exclusively by *his* gift, who of his free mercy undertook to be Mediator between God and man. The road of access which is opened to us in the system of the Church's ordinances is not in any degree of our making: we need to use, but we do not contribute at all to prepare it. The work of mediation is Christ's work from beginning to end: when he took our nature, he did it by actual union — when he joins his members to himself, they are really, though by immaterial and spiritual influence, engrafted into his purified humanity. His members have actually "put on the new man" [Eph. 4:24], and "as many as have been baptized into Jesus Christ have put on Christ" [Gal. 3:27].

It would be unjust, of course, to attribute to the whole body of Quakers any conscious design of rejecting Christ: their notion no doubt is that he is present to their thoughts, and in this way they suppose that they make him their means of access. But this is to forget that the principle of his mediation is not that his man's nature is the ultimate object of worship, but that it is the sole road of approach to the Father. His

manhood is "the door" [Jn. 10:9] through which we are admitted to
his Godhead. When the Church system is opposed to rationalism, the
actions of his manhood are in reality opposed to those of our own spirits.
The channel of union which has been provided through grace is opposed
to that which existed by nature. What is needed, therefore, is some real
agency on his part, whereby this merciful intervention may be effected.
He must actually stretch forth the hand of his humanity towards us
before we can effectually stretch forth the hand of faith towards him.
Adam is not merely an object to men's thoughts, like the angels of God;
he is bound to his descendants by the true but unknown tie of paternity:
if Christ our Mediator be the second Adam, there must be as real an
influence, by which all his members must hold to *his* man's nature. And
if this union is not brought about, as rationalists suppose, through those
means which had their existence through creation, it must be effected
through media which are beside and foreign to nature. That spiritual
power, whereby his humanity becomes the seminal principle of his body
mystical, must act through such supernatural agency as it pleases him to
adopt. So that the ancient writers, as Bishop Taylor says, speak of "the
Blessed Sacrament" as "the extension of the Incarnation." [8] No wonder,
then, that in the palmy days of the Quaker sect, when its principles were
fully developed, their denial of those ordinances whereby the God-Man
discharges his office of mediation should have led them into expressions
inconsistent with any belief in his real existence.[9] The characteristic
doctrine of the gospel, that God and man were permanently made one
in the person of Christ, was superseded by a dreamy notion of the abstract intercourse between the minds of faithful men and the governing
Mind of the universe. The tendency of such a system is to substitute
rationalism for the gospel; in place, that is, of the revelation through
a Mediator, to fall back upon the universal revelation of nature. And
since the doctrine of the Incarnation for the first time revealed the personal character of God, rationalism itself is but the entrance to that
deeper abyss of pantheism, towards which the rejection of the sacramental system has a tendency to conduct.

8. [ED.] Jeremy Taylor, *The Worthy Communicant*, Bk. I, chap. 2 (*Works* [Lon-
don, 1822], XV, 420).
9. [ED.] Wilberforce quotes Charles Leslie's *The Snake in the Grass*, sec. 10 (*The
Theological Works of the Rev. Charles Leslie* [Oxford, 1832], IV, 131): "And G. Fox
says, that if there be any other Christ but he that was crucified within, he is the false
Christ — this Christ that was risen and crucified within, 'devils and reprobates make
a talk of him without.'"

The custom, therefore, of putting inward acts of faith and love in place of those external means whereby Christ vouchsafes to join men to his manhood is in reality to make these the channel of mediation instead of him; it is to set up idols in our hearts, and thank them for our deliverance from the house of bondage. Those who do not go so far as directly to abandon the appointed means of grace must be on their guard lest a measure of the same evil should be incurred by undervaluing them.[10] For whatever derogates from the sacramental system has the effect of depreciating that union with God which we have by grace, and therefore of casting us on that union which existed by nature. This is the virtual tendency when inward seriousness — the necessity of which in itself cannot be too earnestly maintained — is supposed to dispense with those external means whereby Christ allies himself to his members. The remark applies of course not to those who are debarred the use of such means, but to those by whom they are deemed superfluous. It was a sublime exhortation of the ancient Platonist, "to fly to the solitary Deity in the solitude of our own spirit." But that which in a heathen was a pious reaching forth after light would be an impious

---

10. An instance may be afforded by the ordinance of confirmation. Among its benefits must be ranked the opportunity afforded, at a most critical period of life, for confirming the promises of childhood. Such an act, conscientiously discharged in the presence of many witnesses, has no little tendency to strengthen good resolutions; and since all good acts must be suggested as well as favoured by God, we may safely speak of the inward resolution as dependent on his spiritual succour. Now, this account of confirmation, if regarded as a partial view of the service, would be fitting enough; but if considered to be the whole of its benefits, it would resolve an ordinance of the gospel into a mere rationalistic act. For, according to this view of things, the candidates come to confirm themselves in the bishop's presence (or, perhaps, to confirm the bishop in the belief of their good intentions), instead of being brought, as the prayer book directs, "to be confirmed by him." The sole object is the ratification of their vows; the added assurance of their intention to perform what at baptism was promised. The efficacy of the service rests altogether upon the acceptableness of their previous prayers, and the sincerity of their present purpose, which, according to God's natural mode of dealing with men, are met by a corresponding blessing. What converts this act of natural religion into a Christian rite is that through the instrumentality of his minister, the New Head of man's race receives his younger members into closer union, and confirms those graces which at baptism have already flowed into them from himself. Thus is a natural mode of converse with God exalted into a means of supernatural union. Unless this truth be admitted, unless Christ be discerned to be truly present through the agency of his servants, to bless in the laying on of hands, and to communicate through external means that supernatural life of which his humanity is the source, wherein does this act differ from any other whereby responsible agents pledge themselves to serve God, and what especial benefit is there in Christian confirmation?

rejection of it in a Christian. For what renders man's responsibility so great is the greatness of the gift which is offered to his acceptance. To careless men this is the great argument against the Church system: they would rather live at a lower stage of accountableness — they shrink with horror from the real indwelling of this Holy God. But it will be otherwise with devout minds. Let them once feel the reality of Christ's presence, and they will not again take up with a religion of shadows. All which is needful for such persons is to understand that to admit the Church, or sacramental, system is only to believe the reality of those acts whereby the God-Man discharges his work of mediation. However jealous they are of the formalism of their own hearts, and however watchful against spiritual carelessness, they cannot be afraid of resting too much on the mediation of Christ, and of esteeming too highly his presence by the Spirit. For the Holy Ghost, as he came at Pentecost with power, and as his dealings by grace are discriminated from the general actings of the Great Spirit of the universe, has a peculiar function and office in the Gospel Covenant. And since it has been his will that those gracious strivings whereby he renews all hearts should be consequent on the mediation of Christ, therefore to leave out of account that perfect manhood whereby the new Head of our race acts upon his members is to dispense also with the specific operations of the Blessed Comforter. So that the whole system of mediation would be passed by in this method of approach, as though the spirit of man could by direct, self-originating, immediate impulse commune with the Almighty. If men say that what they trust is not their own spirit, but something bestowed upon them by God, yet still it is something within themselves — something,

> Which if heaven gave it, may be termed their own.

For they look to some chain of intercourse which, starting from themselves, communicates directly with the Most High. What is this in truth but to fall back upon those endowments of man's spirit which he has by creation — upon the natural powers of the soul — and thus to pass by Christ the Mediator in our access to God?

> There were of the old Valentinian heretics (says Hooker) some, which had knowledge in such admiration, that to it they ascribed all, and so despised the sacraments of Christ, pretending that as ignorance had made us subject to all misery, so the full redemption of the inward man, and the work of our restoration, must needs belong unto *knowledge* only. They draw very near unto this error who, fixing wholly their minds on the known necessity of faith,

imagine that nothing but faith is necessary for the attainment of all grace.[11]

We are to believe and acknowledge that as God the Father doth neither forgive nor vouchsafe reconciliation, but for the merits and satisfaction of his only Son; so neither will he vouchsafe to convey this or any other blessing unto us, which his Son hath purchased for us, but only through his Son: not only through him as our Advocate or Intercessor, but through him as our Mediator — that is, through his humanity, as the organ or conduit, or as the only bond by which we are united and reconciled unto the divine nature.[12]

The views of these two great writers, always esteemed among the highest authorities in the English Church, have been strikingly illustrated since they wrote, by some circumstances in the history of the sect which has been referred to. In the case of the Quakers, whose opinions were avowed with greater consistency than is found in many of their partisans, may be seen by what sure steps a forgetfulness of our Lord's office as Mediator, and of those sacramental ordinances whereby he unites men to himself, leads persons who least design it to errors respecting his nature. If this result is not always reached, it is because those who live in the atmosphere of a Christian country derive a large portion of their opinions from the standard which obtains around them. No one seems to have less anticipated such consequences than George Fox, when he first yielded to the impulse to head a party. It was among the fermentations which issued in the Great Rebellion, when, as he complained in his last moments, "the outward Christians" were "broken up into many sects," [13] that he was impelled to look within himself for the principle of unity. The times peculiarly inclined earnest men to such a course. Never was religion more overlaid by hypocrisy, or truth more lost in contentiousness. The Puritan divines had explained away the meaning of gospel ordinances, while they insisted zealously on their formal observance. Now, it is so contrary to the genius of Christianity to attach primary weight to what is purely technical that Fox can hardly be censured for supposing that if the sacraments and public worship were merely forms, they could not be essentials of the gospel. Is it less unlikely

---

11. Hooker, *Ecclesiastical Polity*, Bk. V, chap. 60, 4 [*Works*, II, 267].

12. Thomas Jackson, *Commentaries on the Creed*, XI, 3, 12 [*The Works of Thomas Jackson, D.D.* (Oxford, 1844), X, 40].

13. W. Sewel, *The History of the Rise, Increase and Progress of the Christian People Called Quakers* [5th ed. (London, 1811)], II, 492.

that the command to observe the Eucharist should be metaphorical, than the ordinance itself? Doubtless this earnest man did not discern that his teaching would turn men away from Christ, or interfere with the "one Mediator between God and men" [1 Tim. 2:5]. Yet that such was the real tendency of his system is apparent even from the report of his friendly historian, whose object is to show that he maintained the common truths, which are received among Christians. The basis of his instruction is stated to have been, "that every man is enlightened with the Divine Light." [14] And in corroboration of this assertion (though their real proof could be only their own inward consciousness), he and his followers perpetually referred to the declaration, "that was the true light, which lighteth every man, that cometh into the world" [Jn. 1:9].[15] This passage, which refers in reality to the Incarnation of Christ, and consequently to the gifts bestowed upon his brethren through participation in him as Mediator, they interpreted of an immediate indwelling of Godhead in the whole body of mankind. But the true light, which at the creation of man's race had bestowed on Adam the perfect light of his own image, the faint remains of which make up that light of nature which has shown since in every man's bosom, had, in the fulness of time, come personally into the world, the Son of God. To confound this peculiar gift, which was bestowed on humanity through the Incarnation of Christ, with that general influence of the Divine Spirit, which all men inherit from their creation, is virtually a form of rationalism. For it is to merge the gifts of grace in the gifts of nature. But suppose that to escape this danger the name of the Holy Ghost is introduced; that *his* present influence is represented as the fulfilment of God's general promises to humanity. Yet even then, unless the manhood of the one Mediator is regarded as the fountain and well-head of those gifts, which the Comforter distributes to Christ's members, rationalism is only disguised under the kindred heresy of Sabellianism. For in this case the work of the Holy Ghost is represented as something which supersedes the work of Christ, as though the same Being, who once dwelt in Christ's manhood, dwells *instead thereof* in the manhood of individual Christians. The doctrine of our Lord's mediation is, that through the communication of his human nature, its quickening gifts are bestowed according to their measure upon his members below: to suppose these gifts therefore to be obtained by God's immediate indwelling, without such

14. *Ibid.*, II, 575.

15. [This text] might be more exactly rendered, "the true light which lighteth every man, was coming into the world."

communication, is to pass him by in our approach to God. This is the exact result of the Sabellian heresy, which usually represents the Almighty as having had three successive modes of dwelling upon earth: first, in his ancient worship, then in the humanity of Christ, and, that mode of dwelling being terminated, in the minds of men. These are supposed by the Sabellians to be three successive economies; three several temples, as it were, in which the same Person has been pleased to display himself. Thus is the real action of the three persons in the Blessed Trinity explained away, and the mystery of the Godhead evaporates in three successive relations of the same Being towards mankind. On this principle, the sacraments, as Fox asserted, may well be dispensed with, "because Christ the substance" is "come": [16] the purpose, that is, of his Incarnation, is supposed to be completed, and the dispensation of the Spirit is alleged to leave nothing for his man's nature to perform. Neither need we wonder at what otherwise would seem the strange delusion, that James Naylor should declare himself to be actually Christ, and that many of his brethren should so regard him. There seems little reason for doubting that the opinions, a few years later attributed to them by Leslie, were not uncommon among the early Quakers.

> The Quakers (he asserts) say Christ took flesh, but no otherwise, as they explain it, than as angels assumed bodies, or as he (Christ or the Word) did inspire or dwell in prophets or holy men of old; though they allow (not always) that Christ did inspire the person of that man Jesus in a higher measure than other men. But they deny any proper incarnation of Christ, that is, that he was made flesh, or that he and Jesus were one person. Yet they allow Jesus to be called Christ, from the dwelling of Christ in him; but for the same reason they take the name of Christ to themselves, and say that it belongs to them as well as to Jesus.[17]

These statements show that the Quakers had already adopted the Sabellian hypothesis respecting our Lord's nature; and the prevalence of avowed Socinianism among them in later days is still more manifest indication of the result which attends the abandonment of the sacramental system.

The example of the Quakers shows by what inevitable sequence the neglect of our Lord's office as Mediator leads to heresies respecting his

16. Sewel, *The History of the Rise, Increase and Progress of the Christian People Called Quakers*, II, 580.

17. Leslie, *The Snake in the Grass*, sec. 10 [*Works*, IV, 130 f.].

nature. Two writers of the present age, each the head of a theological school, may be cited as an evidence that inadequate views respecting his nature have a corresponding connexion with a low estimate of the gifts of grace. The sentiments of Professor Schleiermacher are apparent from a statement, for which its antithetical form probably has gained the wider acceptance, that

> Catholicism is that system which represents the relation of the individual to Christ to be dependent on his relation to the Church; Protestantism that which represents the relation of the individual to the Church to be dependent on his relation to Christ.[18]

This contrast is put forward by Schleiermacher as containing the characteristic distinction between the two leading parties who call themselves Christians. But the very statement of such a contrast involves a virtual denial of the spiritual nature of the Church. For if the Church be really Christ's "body, the fulness of him, that filleth all in all" [Eph. 1:23], then its spiritual or invisible action is inseparable from the right use of its visible ordinances, and it becomes impossible to contrast things which are actually identical. It would be an analogous question, as was observed, to ask whether we were men by being joined to Adam, or were joined to Adam by being men. It is Christ's manhood which binds men through sacraments to his mystic body. So that to give effect to this contrast, the Church must be supposed to be only a human system, devised for the more convenient working of religion among men, and not the presence of Christ's manhood, acting spiritually on all who are engrafted into himself. How is it then that a writer who enters so deeply into some parts of the Christian system, and is regarded as their chief authority by a large portion of what are considered the more orthodox Germans, should have adopted a principle which implies a complete denial of the spiritual life of the Church? The answer may be learned from the account of Schleiermacher's opinions given by his countryman, Dorner. Schleiermacher, he says, finds fault with the expression that the Son of God has taken man's nature into the unity of his person. For this would be to make the personality of Christ dependent on the personality of the second person in the Divine Godhead, and consequently on the doctrine of the Trinity. Such a notion accordingly would be inconsistent with the Sabellian theory.[19]

---

18. [ED.] *Cf.* Friedrich Schleiermacher, *The Christian Faith* (Edinburgh, 1928), 103.
19. [ED.] *Cf.* I. A. Dorner, *History of the Development of the Doctrine of the Person of Christ* (Edinburgh, 1878), Div. II, III, 187 f.

Here, then, we see clearly to what we must attribute Schleiermacher's low estimate of the spiritual nature of the Church. He could not suppose it to be the mystical body of the Eternal Son, united by spiritual presence to his glorified humanity, because there was wanting in his system that substratum for such a doctrine, which the truth of the Trinity could alone supply.[20] If the same tendency is to be found in the teaching of Archbishop Whately, his probity and public spirit, as well as his high station, are a sufficent guarantee that it is not from any intentional rejection of the authorized declarations of the Church. Neither does the writer pretend to conjecture how far the Archbishop may be conscious of the tendency of that system, the results of which are visible in his works. But though it would be unfair to charge individuals with holding the logical consequence of their assertions, there can be no injustice in showing how one peculiarity in a school or writer involves another as its natural complement. This may be seen in the case of Archbishop Whately, whose views of the Church are in exact accordance with what might be anticipated from his opinions respecting the Blessed Trinity, and respecting Christ our Lord. For the word person, as used in respect to the Blessed Trinity, means merely, according to the Archbishop, some new relation or character assumed by the same Being.[21] He says accordingly, that "in respect of the sacrifice of Christ, and of the spiritual gifts poured out on the disciples, it was the same thing in *relation* to *them* as if there had been really three distinct Beings." [22] And again, "Our Lord took care to indicate that the Comforter the disciples are to expect is no other than Himself under another character." [23]

It is not here inquired how far these assertions accord with the statements of Scripture, or the teaching of the Church of England. But they account clearly enough for the view which is adopted by Archbishop Whately respecting the Church of Christ. His respect for the declarations of Scripture leads him to assert strongly its claim to authority: what is wanting in his system is a due estimate of its ordinances as means of grace. Now, if God's presence as Mediator has been succeeded by his presence as the Holy Ghost, the Church can no longer be characterized by its relation to Christ, as his mystic body united by the spiritual action

20. [ED.] Cf. Wilberforce, *Doctrine of the Incarnation*, 168.

21. [ED.] Wilberforce illustrates this statement by quoting from Richard Whately, *Sermons on Various Subjects* (London, 1835), 203, and his *Elements of Logic* (London, 1826), 292.

22. Whately, *Sermons on Various Subjects*, 201 f.   23. *Ibid.*, 197 [slightly altered].

of his man's nature to himself. So that those who do not, as did the Quakers, deny its existence, are thrown upon the fact that it is a social system for the advance of religion, established under God's sanction, and conducive in various ways to those purposes of improvement, for which God bestows his help on individuals among men. Thus is the present action of the one common Mediator lost sight of, and the Church, instead of being a means of grace, becomes simply a scheme of government. The consequence when men are led, like Archbishop Whately, by the plain words of Scripture to take a high view of Church authority,[24] is to infuse harshness and technicality into the gospel system. The kingdom of Christ seems as though it was designed to limit the gifts of his grace rather than to extend them. The Church assumes the austerity of a Sabine mother rather than the affectionate loving-kindness of the daughter of Zion. Since its ordinances are not coincident with the means of grace, but something besides and beyond them, the question naturally arises, "Is not the life more than meat and the body than raiment?" [Mt. 6:25]. So that men's natural instinct testifies against the maintenance of authority, while the precepts of Scripture forbid its abolition.

Such are some of the evils of forgetting the real nature of the Church's being — our union, namely, with the manhood of Christ in his mystic body, together with his true presence and continued mediation. These doctrines, it may be observed in conclusion, are also our right security against substituting the Church as a formal system in place of its Head; and they afford the best answer to the intricate questions respecting Church communion and Church obedience. So long as the Church is regarded as an external system, based on certain laws and administered by certain leaders, it can never fail to enlist a measure of that party spirit which belongs to man's nature, and thus to draw away attention from the holy purposes for which it was instituted. The only safeguard against this danger is the due subordination of its external framework to its internal principle; and the constant recognition that its life depends, not on the gifts of government but on the gifts of grace. If the essence of the Church's existence be that certain men have a right to rule, and teach, and minister, whether they be chosen by the free voice of the congregation, imposed by government, or delegated by the apostles, there is such large opening for cabal and dispute that love and peace and Christ's presence will soon be lost in the din of party strife. The

24. [ED.] Cf. Richard Whately, *The Kingdom of Christ* (New York, 1842), 123, 186 f.

presbyterian platform offers as good footing to the spirit of partisanship as the system of episcopacy; and the Pilgrim fathers of Massachusetts were as ready to persecute as Boniface or Hildebrand. But let the essence of the Church's existence be felt to be Christ's presence — let it be remembered that his manhood is the true seed of the renewed race, and that through spiritual presence it bestows its life-giving power on all the members of his mystic body — let every other question be dependent upon these — let them take their place as of subordinate importance, and as merely contributing to this great result — and what room is there for discord between Christ and the Church, when the Church is Christ himself manifest in his mystic body? "For no man ever yet hated his own flesh, but nourisheth and cherisheth it, even as the Lord the Church" [Eph. 5:29]. The theorist may be unvisited by the sun's warmth while he discusses its nature, or the poet while he describes its brilliancy; but how can we lose sight of his glorious beams by going forth to walk in the sunshine? And so long as this divine principle is kept fully in view, it can hardly fail to soften and elevate those whom it influences. So that if the harshness of party spirit be not cured, it may at least be abated.

There are those indeed who forget that by Christ is meant that "one Mediator between God and men" [1 Tim. 2:5], who unites these two natures, and is to be approached therefore through that manhood, whereby he allies himself to our race. Their wish is for such communing with the Spirit of the universe as may be maintained by each individual spirit in the separate temple of the heart. To set forth Christ the Mediator as our only road of access to the Most High is supposed by them to encumber our approach. This is to renounce Christianity for rationalism, and to prefer the system of nature to the system of grace. For if the doctrine of mediation be accepted at all, the results which it involves must be accepted also. And, therefore, to maintain that the outward means of grace, whereby we are united to the manhood of Christ, are not less necessary than those emotions of our own, which have their seat within, is not to put the Church instead of Christ, but to protest against men's putting themselves in the place of their Redeemer. To speak of inward seriousness as necessary is only to testify the truth of each man's separate responsibility; but to speak of it as superseding outward means is to do away with the office of the "one Mediator." The individual life of each man's spirit, as opposed to the carelessness of a thoughtless walk, is the very treading down of Satan under our feet;

but to contrast it with the value of gospel ordinances is to deny Christ — to depose him from his office of a Mediator — and to set up idols of intercession in our own hearts.

Again, the recollection that Christ's spiritual presence is the Church's life is the answer to all questions respecting Church Communion. For the Church's being depends on union with him; its well-being, on union with all its members. The latter is as essential to its perfect state as that holiness of life, which Christ likewise entreated for all his members; the Church's completeness, therefore, cannot be attained without both the one and the other. But as we see holiness of life to be too often wanting in its present season of warfare, so also is the perfect unity of the whole Christian body. That which cannot be dispensed with — the loss of which would be its death — is that union with Christ on which depends its claim to be the Lord's body. While this continues, the several members of Christ are in truth united to one another, whether they discern it or no; because they are united to the common Head of the body. So that "if one member suffer, all the members suffer with it; and if one member rejoice, all the members rejoice with it" [1 Cor. 12:26]. And the same principle must be our guide respecting all questions of Church obedience. For Church obedience depends on the authority to bless, not on the power to govern. Its rule is not coercive, but parental; it stands on the communication of gifts, not the enactment of penalties. This is what makes persecution alien to its nature; so that such harshness is abhorred by men's instinct, even if their reason does not condemn it. Thus in the world of grace, as in that of nature, is affection the root of duty; and men's relation to the Church of their baptism is built on that fundamental law, which is the basis of social life. Our Catechism, therefore, rests religious as well as temporal authority on the Fifth Commandment, and deduces from it the obligation to obey spiritual as well as temporal masters. For "Jerusalem which is above is the mother of us all" [Gal. 4:26]. Hence the rule of Church obedience is limited only by that original duty of obedience to God, which cannot be superseded by any subsequent obligation. Such considerations suggest at once what are men's relations to Christ's body in that state or place where God's providence has fixed them, and also what they owe to the more extended system, in which it is their blessing to have an individual share. Towards their own mother Church they owe not only obedience in things lawful, but also reverence and thankfulness. So long as she continues to bless, they may not cease to obey. There are those who speak of themselves as the Church's friends, forgetting that such a term, which might be appropriate if employed by the holy angels, is the extreme of irreverence when employed by sinful men respecting the mystical body of Christ their Saviour. For it implies ignorance of their filial relation to the Church of Christ. Hence the common opinion that men are at liberty to join any religious community where statements are propounded, and where practices are pursued, which harmonize with their feelings. And hence men's attachment to their own part of the Church's body is measured less by their obedience to its rules than by their professed aversion to other systems.

All these errors result from a forgetfulness of the central truth, that the Church of Christ is his body; his presence, its life; its blessing, the gift of spiritual union with his man's nature. Where this is given, there is opened for men the gift of life and state of salvation. Our duty towards that portion of it in which our lot is cast arises from love to itself, not from hatred to others; the lines of our heritage are marked out by affection and not by antipathy. For in it lies our actual participation in the mediation of Christ. Through him only who is both God and man is there access to the Father. For such has been the appointment of his sovereign wisdom, "that so in the person of a Mediator the true ladder might be fixed, whereby God might descend to his creatures, and his creatures might ascend to God." [25]

CHAPTER XII:
OF COMMON WORSHIP AS A MEANS OF UNION WITH THE MYSTICAL BODY OF CHRIST

The actings of Christ our Lord since his ascension have been stated to be: first, his intercession on man's behalf with God the Father, and secondly, his spiritual presence through his man's nature with his brethren.[1] And this spiritual presence of the man Christ Jesus has been shown to be vouchsafed in his Church, whereby "we are members of his body; of his flesh, and of his bones" [Eph. 5:30]. For men are joined to his body natural which was slain, in his body mystical which is sanctified. The question which next arises respects the means of union with that mystical body in which men have title to the privileges of the gospel.

25. Bacon's Confession of Faith [*Works*, XIV, 48]

1. [ED.] Cf. R. I. Wilberforce, *The Doctrine of the Incarnation of Our Lord Jesus Christ* (London, 1848), 249.

Of these, the first and most comprehensive is common worship. This point must now be established. The considerations which lead to it are:

First — The nature of common worship.

Secondly — The grounds of its necessity.

Thirdly — The place which it occupied in the Jewish system.

Fourthly — Its connexion with the doctrine of mediation.

Fifthly — The necessity of an ordained ministry and public ritual.

I. The very nature of common worship shows its efficacy in maintaining our connexion with the mystical body of Christ. For what is it but the voice and action of the Christian community, which, if it has life, must by such symptoms show that it lives? Every organized body has some mode of giving expression to that pervading principle which renders it a whole. A tree puts forth leaves; animal life discovers itself by sound and motion. This is that simple method of rendering homage to God, which the psalmist ascribes to the whole visible creation. And if the Church be not a mere aggregation of men, who meet by accident within the same precincts, but the living exponent of a spiritual power, which renders it Christ's mystical body, then that quickening energy, with which it is instinct, must have some means of utterance. And since its office is not only towards men — whom it gathers for their own benefit into its fostering bosom — but likewise towards him, whose "praise is in the great congregation" [Ps. 22:25]; therefore its first object must be that the inhabitants of this lower world, "with Angels and Archangels, and with all the company of heaven" should "laud and magnify his glorious Name, saying: Holy, holy, holy, Lord God of hosts, heaven and earth are full of thy glory." [2] Now, if this be the Church's chosen function, to partake in it must be our first means of exercising our Christian privilege, and of claiming our portion in that mystical body of Christ wherein we are members.

II. How deeply this feeling was implanted from the first in the Christian community appears from the grounds on which the importance of public worship has always rested. Its indispensable necessity must have arisen from the nature of the case, inasmuch as it did not arise from positive enactment. No positive command to meet for united worship occurs in the New Testament, except that incidental one in the Epistle to the Hebrews [Heb. 10:25], which cannot have been relied upon in the Western Church, by which in early times the Epistle to the Hebrews was not received; and yet the first Christians not only encountered every

2. [ED.] From the Preface and *Sanctus*, Communion Service, B.C.P. (1662).

danger, but, what was a still stronger proof of their conviction, they violated those civil laws to which they usually paid such prompt obedience, rather than forego the privilege of that common worship whereby each man maintained his part in the fellowship of his Saviour. How could they be justified in disobeying Caesar, unless their duty to God had been peremptory and unquestioned? But it stood on no direct command of Scripture. It must have rested, therefore, on the very nature of the case — on the connexion of this service with those general duties and privileges which are set forth as the first principle of the Christian life — on the necessity of union with Christ as the new Head of the redeemed race — on the common obligation to honour God more than man — it must have been the very act by which men professed themselves Christ's servants, and claimed membership in the mystical body of the Crucified. The very publicity and danger of the deed makes the weight which was attached to it the more manifest. Instruction could be given by books or by single conference. The consecrated elements might be carried round singly to those who desired to partake them. But when the Roman law had expressly forbidden the meetings of religious bodies, the common worship of the Christians became, as Pliny expresses it, the very "sum of their crime." [3] It was forbidden therefore during the Diocletian persecution, even under the mild rule of Constantius; and its permission is the main point expressed in the tolerating edict issued by Galerius just before his death. Yet in the face of all this opposition, the Christian Church never intermitted its united worship; the duties which it could not perform in public and during the day were discharged secretly and during the hours of darkness; it retreated into the heart of the earth, and maintained itself in catacombs and the abodes of the dead, that it might issue forth when its season was come, and publish in the face of the sun those benedictions in which it calls on heaven and earth to partake.

III. The importance of common worship as our means of union with the body of Christ is further manifested if we consider wherein lay the peculiar privileges which were enjoyed by the Jews. Their peculiar blessing was plainly that covenanted access to God, which was allowed to them alone of ancient nations. "What nation is there," said Moses, "who hath God so nigh unto them as the Lord our God is in all things that we call upon him for?" [Deut. 4:7]. The wide distance which sepa-

3. [ED.] Pliny the Younger, *Letters*, Bk. X, 96 (Loeb ed. [New York, 1915], II, 402 f.).

rates man from his Maker was not bridged over indeed so effectually as since God has become man and man God, but a foundation was laid for this wonderful bond of union. For the first time in God's dealings with mankind was there a nation chosen to receive the privilege of accepted prayer. Private prayer there had been, doubtless, from the first: the instinct which leads men to pray in time of distress seems a sufficient sanction for it. And family prayer had probably commenced in the household of Seth, when "men began to call on the name of the Lord" [Gen. 4:26], and had since continued in the tents of the Patriarchs. But this usage had rested on natural instinct or individual communication; it was personal or family; it was not relevant to any peculiar promise, or any public institutions; it belonged to that patriarchal state in which the Most High was pleased to favour his dutiful followers by single and especial manifestations. Under this rule did Enoch, Job, and Abraham walk with God. But this rule waxed insufficient when, with the increasing extension of mankind, those lights which they possessed in early times were withdrawn. Hence the censure passed by our Lord upon the Samaritans, who thought their practice justified because their "fathers worshipped upon this mountain": "Ye worship ye know not what; we know what we worship, for salvation is of the Jews" [Jn. 4:20, 22]. It was not in the doctrines of a pure monotheism that the Samaritans of that age were wanting. Their habit was to address themselves to the Father of all, through the unaided service of their own devotion. But they worshipped they knew not what, because they had no certainty of acceptance. "Salvation is of the Jews." To them only belongs the assurance that the Father of all will hear them. This means of access no other nation possessed. They had the "lively oracles" [Acts 7:38] which afforded an intercourse with the Almighty.

Now, on what was this intercourse dependent? It could not rest only on a conviction of the existence of Jehovah; in this respect they were not superior to their fathers, the Patriarchs, even if they surpassed their contemporaries. That which marked them out as God's people was the national ritual, by which they were assured of access to him. The road indeed was narrow, painful, and circuitous; and yet it was a road of approach to God. All right of drawing near him was through their nation. Their family union conferred on each individual in their tribes a pre-eminence which was enjoyed by no other people. "All the earth is mine," declared Jehovah, but "ye shall be unto me a kingdom of priests, and an holy nation" [Ex. 19:5 f.]. Royalty lies in high descent, and priesthood in that peculiar consecration, which marks men out to draw near to the presence of God; and both these qualities centred in that whole society, all whose members were so much more favoured than the residue of mankind. The consciousness of this pre-eminence was felt when the high priest was observed to bear on him the symbols of the whole world, when he entered into the holy place because he was the representative of the whole creation.[4] If this were so, he was the type of him who stretched out his sacrificing arms upon the cross, that he might in truth embrace the universe. In this wise were the Jews favoured above the rest of men. And this privilege they enjoyed through their participation in those public acts which were the especial privilege and work of their nation. It was not that each individual Jew found his way to God through his individual excellency; but he had a claim to participate in that public service by which his nation was brought nigh to the Almighty. The national ritual was a bond of union which gave the individual a vantage ground in his approach to God. That general communing of his spirit with the Great Author of the universe, which was all that the heathen man enjoyed, was sanctioned and exalted by the mediatorial character of the public ritual, in which the Jewish nation had a common interest. The priesthood of Aaron did not derogate from the general privilege, which made Israel at large a royal priesthood; it was the very basis on which their blessing rested—it was the provisional appointment of that mediatorial office, by which God and man were bound together; the typical representation of that true High Priest, who is the perfect Mediator between earth and heaven. Therefore, to reject the Jewish ritual during that period, when it was the appointed means of foreshowing him who was to come, would have been in reality to reject Christ, and to slight the efficacy of his mediation. So that when Korah maintained that the separate priesthood of every individual Israelite dispensed with the necessity of that national ritual, which anticipated the mediation of Christ, it pleased God by immediate judgments to show who should "come near to offer incense before the Lord" [Num. 16:40]. Thus was it plainly seen what was that channel of mediation, through which individual prayers should ascend to heaven. And as such the holiest and most spiritual Israelites used it. Their ardent aspirations to God were grounded always on that peculiar privilege of

---

4. [ED.] Cf. Philo, *Moses*, II, 26 (Loeb ed. [New York, 1929–41] VI, 512–15). Wilberforce bases his statement on I. A. Dorner, *History of the Development of the Doctrine of the Person of Christ* (Edinburgh, 1878), Div. I, I, 33.

approach, which had its central and consecrating point in their national ritual. Such as voluntarily neglected those means of confederation whereby men maintained their portion in the public service were cut off from God's people. But those who by involuntary hindrances were precluded from actual association with their brethren were not left to that mere feeling after an unknown helper, which was all that the heathen possessed; their thoughts travelled to their native land, they associated themselves in spirit to that national worship which God had made the channel of heavenly gifts, and thus they claimed their part in the collective privilege of the nation. Thus did David in spirit go "with the multitude" from the "land of Jordan and the hill Mizar" [Ps. 42:4, 6]. Thus did Daniel pray, "his windows being open in his chamber towards Jerusalem" [Dan. 6:10]. This was the very principle of the Jewish service, which extended to those who were in distant lands as well as to those who, being gathered in the Temple's courts, "were praying without at the time of incense" [Lk. 1:10].

> They knew much better than the heathen, that God's throne of Majesty was in heaven, and yet were to tender their devotions unto him as extraordinarily present in his temple or sanctuary.[5]

For the principle of a public ritual does not depend on the actual presence of men, which may be interrupted by the accidents of our weakness, but on that actual presence of God, which he vouchsafes through his appointed means of intervention. The voluntary neglect of such opportunities on our part would be to despise the privilege of intercourse with God. It would be to prefer our own means of access to those which the appointed Mediator bestows. If we have a true belief that the privilege of union with God is bestowed through those especial channels of intercourse which he has himself ordained, we shall make such efforts as were made by the early Christians to use them. For the whole value of such a service depends on the reality of those blessings which God bestows, as he unquestionably bestowed them in former times on those who worshipped towards his mercy-seat, and as, since the Incarnation of Christ, they have been pledged in fuller measure to those who make up together the mystical body of the Lord.

IV. Now, this leads us to discern why such especial importance should be attached to common worship in the Church of God. For since Christ Incarnate is the real priest, through whom all Jewish service was effec-

5. Thomas Jackson, *Commentaries on the Creed*, Bk. XI, chap. 3, 11 [*The Works of Thomas Jackson, D.D.* (Oxford, 1844), X, 37].

tual — his body, the real victim; his members, the true temple — therefore to suppose that individual piety dispenses with the necessity of
participation in the Church's collective acts is the same thing as if a Jew
had maintained that it superseded the necessity of participation in the
ancient ritual. Communion with the Church in its united acts of worship
brings men into the same relation to Christ, the one true and abiding
Mediator, which was gained in their degree for the men of old time by
participation in that typical and imperfect service which was maintained
through the continual offering of the Levitical sacrifices. As a Jew could
not approach God save through the intervention of the expected Messiah,
so cannot a Christian save through the mediation of the Messiah who has
been manifested. The single prayers which were offered by the pious
Jew in the solitary temple of his heart ascended to God because, through
the privilege of the nation, heaven and earth were bound together. And
the solitary worship of the fervent Christian is not effectual through its
private merit, but by virtue only of that intercession which is offered for
the elect at large, and of that sacrifice, in which the whole Christian body
has common interest. To rest therefore on the mere separate intercourse
of man with his Maker, on the private aspirations of the individual soul,
would be to pass by the intervention of Christ as something unnecessary,
and to set up our own spirit as the mediator through whom the Father
of all could be approached. And this would be an idolatry which all
Christian men would abhor. Yet is this virtually the effect when personal
devotion, the importance of which cannot in itself be too much enforced,
is represented as a rival to that participation in the public ordinances of
his Church, whereby God is approached through Christ. True it is that
all Christian men are kings and priests, and thus have immediate access
to God. But then this access must be *in Christ* — it depends on their
character as members of his body — it is because that mediation is complete which in Jewish times was imperfect — because God and man
have been made one in Christ. The Jews likewise were all a royal priesthood, but this did not neutralize the necessity of that public ritual
whereby every individual had privilege of approach. Neither does the
privilege of single Christians interfere with the necessity of that mediation
of Christ, on which it is dependent.

> Albeit the temple of Jerusalem, wherein God's people only were
> to worship, were long since demolished; yet the sanctuary, wherein
> they were to worship God, is rather translated or advanced from
> earth to heaven than destroyed; for it was God's presence that made

the temple, and that is more extraordinary in Christ's body, than ever it had been in Solomon's temple.[6]

But then the question recurs, why is this reference to Christ our Lord especially connected with his public service? Why is it not satisfied by that mere regard which is paid to him singly, by those who do not choose to associate themselves with their fellow creatures? Cannot men's hearts travel forth towards him as their God in privacy and seclusion? There have been many who have professed to worship Christ singly, through the mere exercise of their private faith; and this is the real principle of all those Separatists, who, like the Quakers, have no sacramental union, and by whom common worship has been exchanged for simple teaching. Now, the reason why such a system is a disparagement of our Lord's mediation is because his mediation does not depend merely on our calling ourselves by his name, or on our entertaining certain feelings towards him; but results from that actual relation which he condescended to assume towards us when he took our nature into abiding union with his own. His mediation is a reality, external to ourselves, and not a mere matter of our own imagination. It is not enough to say that we gain certain blessings by resorting to that Divine Being who happened once to be upon earth — as though he accidentally undertook the office of speaking in our favour; but his mediation is the consequence of that permanent character which he was pleased to adopt by assuming manhood. He thus became the Head of the renewed family, who offered himself a sacrifice on behalf of the whole, and through whom all graces devolve upon the rest; and, therefore, by a certain singular fitness was he marked out to be the representative of his brethren. So that towards the completeness of his work, it was essential that those for whom he spoke should be as truly bound to his manhood, as by descent they were to their original parent. For this work was expressly declared to be undertaken on behalf of his mystical body. It is for those who believe on him through his apostles' words, and who are "one as we are one" [Jn. 17:22], that he intercedes with his Father. His advocacy results from his being "Head over all things to the Church, which is his body, the fulness of him that filleth all in all" [Eph. 1:22 f.]. Would we have part, then, in his intercession as Mediator, we must be members in that "family in heaven and earth" [Eph. 3:15] which is called after his name. This membership involves federal union with the collective Church: to be a member is to

6. [ED.] *Ibid.*, slightly abridged.

be part of a body, because the existence of parts implies the existence of a whole. And, therefore, the notion of a mere individual relation to our Lord, independently of that social tie which binds us to him as a part of his mystic body, would lead, when followed into its results, to the virtual denial of that office which he discharges as man: Christ would be viewed, according to the Sabellian theory, as a mere name or relation, under which in this present dispensation the Father of all has pleased to reveal himself; and his actual intervention as a person, other than the Father and the Holy Ghost, and as co-operating through that nature which he took of the Virgin, in the great work of bringing many sons unto salvation [Heb. 2:10], would be practically forgotten.

The permanency, therefore, of Christ's mediation, together with the importance of his present interference, is the true point which is asserted when the necessity of the Church's office is maintained. But if a present work is transacted on our behalf in the Gospel Kingdom, through the merits of Christ's ascended manhood, some means must be appointed through which his brethren may partake its benefits. A system of worship upon earth is the necessary correlative to a work of intercession in heaven. The one implies the other. And, therefore, in that early age of the Church, when our Lord's mediation was felt to be the life of the Christian community, there was an universal and unqualified assertion that as certainly as Christ's sacrifice was pleaded effectually above, it was likewise truly participated in gospel ordinances, and that those things which were done on earth in the Church's united acts made part of that grand sacrifice which has its consummation in heaven. So that while all other parts of the Christian ritual were spoken of as sacrificial in their character, that service by which men especially participated in the mediation of Christ, because they are most truly bound by it to his mystic body, *i.e.*, the Eucharist or Lord's Supper, was called emphatically the Christian sacrifice. And this is an act which, by its federal character, involves the necessity of that united worship whereby men partake in the collective privileges of the Church of God. "Irenaeus tells me," says our own Mede, "that there were offerings there, *i.e.* in the Old Testament; there are also offerings here, *i.e.* in the New Testament; there were sacrifices among the people, *i.e.* the Jews; there are sacrifices also in the Church." [7] And after mentioning that the Holy Communion was commonly called a sacrifice, "it would be infinite," he adds, "to note all the places and

7. [ED.] Joseph Mede, *Works*, Bk. II, chap. 4 (4th ed. [London, 1677], 361), quoting Irenaeus, *Against the Heresies*, IV, 18, 2 (*ANF*, I, 484 f.; *PG*, VII, 1025).

authors where and by whom it is thus called." He contents himself
therefore with citing those authors by whom it was so described in the
lifetime of the apostles. In justification of this mode of speaking, St.
Irenaeus adduces that prophetic description, which had been given by
Malachi of the services of the Christian Church: "From the rising of the
sun even unto the going down of the same, my name shall be great among
the Gentiles; and in every place incense shall be offered unto my name,
and a pure offering" [Mal. 1:11]. Now, the one of these things, incense,
is explained by St. John to typify the prayers of saints (Rev. 5:8); the
pure offering, therefore, must on its part have something to indicate.
Accordingly, it was understood to be the "new oblation of the New
Testament, which the Church receiving from the apostles offers throughout the whole world to God." [8] An oblation which is thus explained by
Mede:

> We are wont to conclude our prayers with, *Through Jesus Christ
> our Lord*. And this is the specification, whereby the worship of a
> Christian is distinguished from that of the Jew. Now, that which
> we in all our prayers and thinksgivings do *vocally*, when we say
> *through Jesus Christ our Lord*, the Ancient Church in her public
> and solemn service did *visibly*, by representing him, according as
> he commanded, in the symbols of his body and blood. What time,
> then, so fit and seasonable to commend our devotions unto God,
> as when the Lamb of God lies slain upon the holy table; and we re-
> ceive visibly, though mystically, those gracious pledges of his
> blessed body and blood? This was that sacrifice of the ancient
> Church the Fathers so much ring in our ears — the sacrifice of
> praise and prayer through Jesus Christ, mystically represented in
> the creatures of bread and wine.[9]

These assertions respecting the Holy Communion involve the two
following conditions: First, that this ordinance shall be allowed to be
as truly a sacrifice as any of those ancient rites to which that term was
commonly applied either in Scripture or by men; secondly, that its efficacy should be rested wholly upon that sacrifice of Christ upon the cross
once for all, which forms the basis of his mediation. The first of these
conditions is implied in the language of the early Church respecting the
Blessed Eucharist: it follows from the fact that "we have an altar" (Heb.
13:10), and that "this" is "our sacrifice." [10] The second results from the

8. Irenaeus, *Against the Heresies*, IV, 17, 5 [*ANF*, I, 484; *PG*, VII, 1023].
9. Mede, *Works*, Bk. II, chap. 2 (4th ed., 357).
10. [ED.] Prayer of Oblation, Communion Service, B.C.P. (1662).

reality of that system of mediation whereby man is reconciled to God. The principle of this mediation was, that he who undertook it partook truly of both natures, so that he was at once God's representative among men, and man's advocate with the Creator. And in this character, what valuable thing could he offer to God but the sacrifice of himself? His sanctified humanity was the only pure thing which could be gathered out the mass of corrupted mortality. And, therefore, no earthly accessions could increase its amount or enhance its value. If its value were not infinite, it would not suffice to atone for all sins; if its amount were not unbounded, it would not take in all offenders. To this sacrifice, therefore, no acts of ours can contribute anything; our hundred pence, if we could offer them, would add nothing to the value of his ten thousand talents. So that the only ground on which the Holy Communion can have that character of a sacrifice which has been assigned to it must be through its participation in the central work of mediation, the offering, *i.e.*, of the body of Jesus Christ once for all [Heb. 10:10].

But how can the Eucharist or Christian sacrifice be an "offering of the body of Jesus Christ"; since "Christ dieth no more" [Rom. 6:9], but "hath entered in once into the holy place, having obtained eternal redemption for us" [Heb. 9:12]? So that the body of Jesus Christ which he took of the Virgin, that through its sanctification (Jn. 17:19) he might sanctify the mass of humanity, has its material place in heaven, "until the restitution of all things" [Acts 3:21]. This body, therefore, cannot die again, nor can its material place be other than at God's right hand: yet must this be the very body which we present to the Father; for were it aught besides, our dependence would not be on that anointed first-fruit of man's nature which, that it might be the instrument of mediation, was made personally one with God. The offering must be made, then, in a manner not incompatible with the truth that the thing offered "ever liveth" [Hebrew 7:25]; and again, that according to its material place, it "is ever at the right hand of God" [Rom. 8:34]. Now, this is the exact manner in which the sacrifice of Christ is declared to be presented before God: as in reference to time past he was "the Lamb slain from the foundation of the world" [Rev. 13:8], so there "stood a Lamb as it had been slain" [Rev. 5:6] before the throne, in the vision of the utmost future. So that our offerings derive their value from the same source which gave their efficacy to the ancient sacrifices. For thus is Christ consecrated "a priest for ever" [Heb. 6:20], and his offering is "a perpetual sacrifice" (Heb. 10:12). "The substance or matter of the sacrifice" of Christ, says Dr. Jackson, "is of the same force at this day to remit sins, that it was of whilst it was offered; for his human nature was consecrated by death and by his bloody passion, to be a sacrifice of everlasting virtue, to be the continual propitiation for our sins." [11]

Now, it is because what is pleaded above as the ground of our acceptance is that true manhood which was taken for the purpose of mediation by the Son of God, that the Eucharist, rather than any other part of the Church's ritual, is declared to be the Christian sacrifice. For "as often as ye eat this bread and drink this cup, ye do show the Lord's death till he come" [1 Cor. 11:26]. Through its character of a sacrament, as shown in the next chapter, does the Holy Communion connect us with that slain humanity of the Incarnate Word, which is present by spiritual power in holy ordinances. Through this bread and this cup, that which is offered as a true sacrifice in heaven, is present as a real though immaterial agent in the Church ministrations. So that what is done by Christ's ministers below is a constituent part of that general work which the one great High Priest performs in heaven: through the intervention of his heavenly Head, the earthly sacrificer truly exhibits to the Father that body of Christ which is the one only sacrifice for sins; each visible act has its efficacy through those invisible acts of which it is the earthly expression; and things done on earth are one with those done in heaven.

But though the body of Jesus Christ, present materially in heaven, and present in holy ordinances through spiritual power, supplies the Christian sacrifice with its whole intrinsic value, yet those things which are contributed by his brethren obtain acceptance by union with him. To this circumstance the prayer and praise of Christains owe all their right to be admitted as a portion of the Christian sacrifice. For the virtue of the Mediator's service extends itself to that of all his brethren. And so is it likewise with those elements of bread and wine, which are presented to God as a sample and first-fruits of his creation, that they may afterwards be set apart by consecration to be the means whereby that Mediator who has sanctified this whole defiled universe may distribute himself to men. These elements, therefore, like the prayers of men, cannot be an acceptable offering except so far as they have received *his* hallowing presence, who corrects the evils of the Fall. But when Malachi described the sacrifice of the Christian Church, he looked plainly to some higher object than the mere material value of these preliminary offerings. For as incense typifies but is not prayer, so the "pure offering" could not

11. Jackson, *Commentaries on the Creed*, Bk. X, chap. 55, 6 [*Works*, IX, 592].

be the literal Mincha, or meat-offering, but that true sacrifice of which it was typical. And to what did all Jewish rites refer but the one real Mediator? So that the oblation which Malachi contemplated must have been that true Mincha, that hidden Manna, the body of Jesus Christ which was offered once for all. This it was which he declared should be presented in every place from the rising to the setting of the sun (Mal. 1:11), by those priests and Levites whom the Gentile Church should substitute for the ancient ministrants (Is. 66:21).

The account which has been given of the Eucharist will seem to some to make it too real a sacrifice, while to others it will seem wanting in reality. The latter will say that if the efficacious part of the eucharistic offering is performed by our great Mediator in heaven — if the thing of value which is presented before God has already been brought into the heavenly temple — then that which remains to be done upon earth can only be a symbolical, and not a real offering. And they fear, therefore, that no great importance will be attached to that portion of the work in which Christ's earthly servants are ministrants. But the statements which have been made are involved immediately by the central fact of the doctrine of mediation, that no perfect offering can be found among men except that manhood which was personally united to God. And that Christ's human body should have its material place in heaven does not interfere with that influence which it has by spiritual power; or diminish therefore the sacredness of those elements or means whereby men participate its presence. For if to rest its efficacy on Christ's work above is incompatible with the opinion that the Eucharist is a true sacrifice, then must this name be denied to the Passover also. What was the real virtue of the Passover, but that through its participation men had part in that acceptance which the Mediator effected? The lamb slain upon earth was not of intrinsic value, but that "Lamb slain from the foundation of the world" [Rev. 13:8], in whose effectual atonement it gave Israel participation. To the heavenly temple, therefore, do those ancient writers direct our thoughts, who speak most strongly of the reality of the Christian sacrifice. "There is an altar in heaven," says St. Irenaeus, "for to it our prayers and oblations are directed." [12] And therefore he speaks of "the Word" — Christ, according to his man's nature — as the oblation which is offered to God.[13] A similar statement is made by St. Ambrose:

12. Irenaeus, *Against the Heresies*, IV, 18, 6 [*ANF*, I, 486; *PG*, VII, 1029].
13. Irenaeus, *Against the Heresies*, IV, 18, 4 [*ANF*, I, 485 f.; *PG*, VII, 1027].
[ED.] The reading accepted by Wilberforce is open to question on textual grounds.

On one side is the shadow, on another the representation, on a third
the truth. The shadow is in the Law, the representation in the Gospel, the truth in heaven. In former times sacrifices consisted of
lambs and calves: now Christ is offered, but he is offered according
to his man's nature, according to that being in which he is receptive
of suffering; and as Priest he offers up himself as the ransom of our
offences; he does it here in representation, he does it in truth there,
where he mediates in the Father's presence as our Intercessor.[14]

The real point in dispute, therefore, supposing all verbal questions
excluded, is whether what is done in common worship, and especially
in its crowning act, the Holy Communion, is done merely within man
himself, in the region of his own feelings and intellect, or whether, besides this, it be something which belongs to the whole Church, which
extends not only to earth but to heaven, of which the agent is not only
the man who supplicates on earth, but the Church's Head who supplicates
in heaven. And this turns on the point whether man's salvation depends
on a real work, external to ourselves, which our great Advocate is still
carrying on by his intercession, and through the pleading of his slain
humanity. So that we fall back upon the original matter of controversy,
whether we are to accept the Church's doctrine that our Lord's Incarnation is a truth, or the Sabellian opinion that it is a fictitious representation.
Let Christ be believed to be truly God and man, pleading for us the
merits of that human nature which he has consecrated through his Godhead, and there must be reality in those means whereby we are continually associated to that sanctified humanity, in union with which is
all our hope. It is the certainty of this communion — the truth that on its
media is our life dependent, because the thing with which we are thus
connected is our life itself — which was so zealously contended for by
those contemporaries of the apostles, to whom Mede refers, when they
asserted the reality of a sacrifice and therefore of a priesthood in the
Church of Christ. For if there be such importance and reality in the
work which is done by Christ, then the means whereby we participate
it must be real and important. Through fear of a different error, many
persons in later times, who never doubted the reality of this work, have
used different language. Their anxiety has been merely to exclude the
notion that human acts have any value except through the sacrifice of
Christ. But this truth is so far from being incompatible with the assertion of a priesthood and a sacrifice by the primitive Fathers that it is the

14. Ambrose, *On the Duties of the Clergy*, I, 48, 238 [*NPNF*², X, 240; *PL*, XVI,
100 f.].

very ground upon which they based its importance. They maintained the reality of those means whereby we are joined to Christ, for the purpose of showing that we cannot be saved except through his "perpetual sacrifice." Now, since Christ's work is the work of the great Head of renewed humanity for all his brethren, therefore the means whereby we hold to him are an actual participation in his sacrifice. A sacrifice is not participated only by the sacrificing priest, but by all those who have a right in the action which is performed and a hope through the offering which is accepted. "Behold Israel after the flesh: are not they which eat of the sacrifices partakers of the altar?" [1 Cor. 10:18]. Both laity, therefore, and priesthood have a share in the Christian sacrifice — the one as participating in the virtue of the gift, the other as further contributing by their ministry to its common participation. Therefore, though it be a necessary result of our acceptance through the work of a Mediator, that the same party should be both Priest and Victim — though looking at that meritorious act on which man's acceptance is dependent, there is but one Priest and one sacrifice in heaven and earth — we yet may fitly apply the name both of priests and sacrifices to those media whereby that act which is continually pleaded in the heavenly sanctuary is participated by surrounding multitudes. Neither can we speak too highly of the value of what is effected by Christ's earthly ministers, provided we render them subservient to that perfect sacrifice of himself which can receive no augmentation.

Why then is it that the existence of a Christian priesthood, and a Christian sacrifice, have been questioned by those who never doubted the reality of Christ's intercession and atonement as an actual work external to ourselves? Two things have been principally alleged: first, that their assertion is inconsistent with the privilege of Christians; and secondly, that it is incompatible with the prerogative of Christ. These objections shall be considered in their order.

To be "kings and priests" has been declared in Scripture to be the privilege of individual Christians [Rev. 1:6; 5:10]. For to them more signally than to Israel of old has been given that right of access to God, which is at once a royal privilege and a priestly function. This is the meaning of that *sacerdotium laicorum* which was claimed in primitive times for all Christians. But on what does this title depend? It results solely from the fact that all members of the family of Christ are associated in their degree in those privileges of which the pattern Man was perfectly possessed. The abundance of supernatural grace which be-

longed to him by right was sufficient to ennoble all his brethren. Their
title, therefore, is no individual birthright — no natural superiority to
the residue of mankind — but that those privileges, which belong to the
Head of the Church by right, belong to his members by favour. On this
ground similar titles were bestowed even upon the Jewish people, because
their prospective participation in the promised Mediator gave them some
portion in his honours. Now, if this be the ground of that claim which
is made for individual Christians, how can it be interfered with by that
medium of intercourse with Christ, on which its very existence is dependent? For it is to Christ, as man, that the title belongs of right, in
which all Christians claim to participate. Now, it is for the very end of
providing a channel of intercourse with the man's nature of Christ that
all Church ordinances have been provided. Their professed purpose is
to add members to his body. So long, then, as the Christian sacrifice
and priesthood are merely made a means of union with the manhood of
Christ, they cannot interfere with the privilege of individual Christians.
As the same terms of royalty and priesthood, when applied in their degree
to the Jewish nation, were rendered available through the efficacy of
that national ritual whereby the whole people was united to God, so the
existence of such common worship as involves the reality of a Christian
priesthood is the very means of their maintenance in the Church of
Christ. The simple *name* of a Christian priesthood cannot be objected
to, as incompatible with the right of Christians, for otherwise, to monop-
olize the title of king would be equally inconsistent with their kingly
honour. So that such priesthood and such sacrifices in the Church of
Christ as are the means of maintaining the connexion between Christ and
his brethren are no disparagement to their birthright, but supply the very
basis on which it is dependent.

   We come then to the other objection. Is the continuence of a sacerdotal system incompatible with the prerogative of Christ? Those who deny
that a priesthood and sacrifice exist under the gospel suppose that they
interfere in some way with the propitiatory office, which is admitted
on all hands to belong exclusively to Christ. But why are they supposed
to interfere with it? If, indeed, Christ's work was entirely concluded
when he was upon earth — if when he had removed certain disabilities
which attached to man's position, he left men to find their way to heaven
as they could, with the help perhaps of that general influence of the
Great Spirit of the universe, in which all ages and nations have believed
— then indeed no place is left for the present action of a sacerdotal sys-

tem. But this would be to renounce belief in Christ's "continual sac-rifice" — to explain away the reality of his intercession and the truth of his nature — and to forget that he retains that manhood whereby he has become the new Head of our race. Now, if Christ is still maintaining a real intercession — if he still pleads that sacrifice, in the merit whereof we must partake if we would be truly joined to his man's nature — then is there ample place for that sacerdotal system, by which some actual *thing* is to be still effected, and in which some agents must be still employed. Now, this it is which is asserted by St. Ignatius and St. Irenaeus when they maintain that there exists an altar and a sacrifice in the Church of Christ. They maintain the reality of those acts of Christ, in which we participate through the intervention of his ministers. So that the real dispute is whether anything is still done by the God-Man in his Gospel Kingdom; or whether, as the Sabellians maintain, his work is over, and his office at an end. For if anything is still transacted, so that for its participation there need certain acts and the service of certain agents, we have an exact precedent in the Jewish system for bestowing the name of sacrifice and priesthood upon the media which are thus employed.

Now, to this it may be replied that the Jewish system was a temporary provision, which was superseded by the gospel. The high priest, it may be said, stood formerly in the place of Christ; and therefore now that the true Priest is come, a typical priest would not only be superfluous but intrusive. Such is the common argument; but such is not the argument employed by the writer to the Hebrews. His assertion is, not that the Levitical priesthood was so real and efficacious that had it continued, the priesthood of Christ would have been supererogatory; but, on the contrary, that had Christ's priesthood, like the Levitical, been only earthly and typical, there would have been no use in the transition from the one system to the other. "If he were upon earth, he should not be a priest, seeing that there *are* priests, that offer gifts according to the law" [Heb. 8:4]. Christ is asserted, therefore, to be a priest not after the order of Aaron, but after the order of Melchisedec [Heb. 7:11]. And the reason why the Jewish ritual has passed away is because now that the true sacrifice is offered, the media of commemoration have taken the place of the media of prediction. Had there been more than this in the Jewish ritual, how could the apostles have continued to observe it? Had it interfered with the work of Christ, it would not have been enough to leave it to die away under the light of the gospel. It would not have been sufficient for St. Paul to teach men not to trust; he must have forbidden any to practise it. But every privilege which has been bestowed in God's two great dispensations has flowed into them from that central fact of the mediation of Christ, which has been the quickening principle of both. For on it alone both the Old and New Testament were dependent, and in its blessings the old and new election, though in different degrees, have been partakers. Neither could inferior officers or means in either Covenant supersede that mediation of Christ, to which they were subordinate. Their sole purpose was to carry it out, to turn men to it, to unite them into such system and harmony, that they might profit by the blessings which it conveys. This is all which can be done by the ministers of Christ's Church; and all which could be done by the ministers of God's temple. And the very reason why we put the priestly office under the law in a line with the ministerial office under the gospel — why we assert that if the title of priest could be given fitly to the first, it belongs also to the second — is that otherwise we should place men on the same level with Christ, and derogate from his peculiar character. For to allow this distinction would be to assign too little to the mediation of Christ, and too much to the priesthood of men. It were to assign too little to Christ to say *merely* that when earthly priests had been long offering their insufficient sacrifices, he appeared in the fulness of time to offer that which was perfective and complete. Christ's office as Priest is the consequence of his nature: it differs in kind from the same work or title as discharged by others; it cannot be referred to the same rank, or compared with things which are incommensurable with it. Any persons who discharge an office which has reference to God, and who present to him what is offered by men, may be *called* priests (as was Melchisedec, because a type of Christ), but this no more places them in the same class with Christ than the title of Son as bestowed upon him assimilates him to the partakers in earthly sonship. That he is called Son and Priest in Scripture is no reason for degrading him to the class of earthly priests or earthly children. For his priestly office flows directly from that conjunction of two natures whereby he is Mediator between God and man. This rendered him by nature such a real representative of our race towards God as earthly priests can be only by office and appointment. Except for this true conjunction of Godhead and manhood, no acceptable offering could be rendered by man to God. As he is the only channel through whom graces flow from God to man, so he is the only medium through which worship ascends from man to his Maker. This is the very cause for that system of the Church whereby men are truly united to him and have a real share in his intercession. Now, to assert that if priests existed under the second as under the first Covenant, his sole and inalienable office would be impaired, is to allow that the Aaronic priests are to be put in the same class with him, and that they executed a function which he afterwards discharged. The perpetuation of a corresponding office could not interfere with the work of Christ, unless the priesthood of the sons of Aaron would have interfered with him. And thus is he degraded to a mere functionary who exercised a certain work by appointment, instead of being that great High Priest who is our Mediator by nature.

And as this is to assign too little to Christ, so it is to assign too much to men. For if the Aaronic priesthood is looked at in itself, and independently of him, how could it do anything towards man's salvation? It is a general declaration that it is "not possible that the blood of bulls and of goats should take away sins" [Heb. 10:4]. The importance then which was assigned to the Jewish law, and the benefits which were derived from it, show that it was only relevant to Christ — that its force depended on the constant application of Christ's merits — that its object was to bring men into union with him — and that except with this reference it was a splendid fiction. This assertion is as true respecting those media of communion which were used before the time of Christ, as respecting those which have been employed since his Advent; for it is only through "the Lamb slain from the foundation of the world" [Rev. 13:8] that the offerings of men, whether before or since, could be acceptable. If it be said therefore that a Christian priesthood is needless because the work of mediation is discharged by Christ alone; the answer is that such an argument proves a Jewish priesthood to have been useless also. If it be added that a Christian priesthood interferes with the sole merits of Christ by providing another way of approaching God, why then did not the Jewish priesthood the same? If men answer that the latter was specially appointed to show beforehand the Lord's death, is not a system of ministering equally required to fulfil the allotted office of showing "the Lord's death till he come" [1 Cor. 11:26]? But in truth, neither the one nor the other office has any tendency, when rightly viewed, to lead men away from Christ, their only object being to conduct men to him. The Manichees, indeed, who thought the ancient law a mischievous obstruction which shut men out from the Good Spirit of the universe, might entertain similar notions of the system whereby men are united to the body of Christ. But those who admit the divine authorship of that law under which the ancient priests ministered to Christ by type and sacrifice, need not doubt that the ministration of public officers in his Church may in like manner enable men to profit by his mediation. There is nothing in the privilege of Christians, nor in the work of Christ our Lord, inconsistent with such intervention. It is an intervention which unites, and does not separate. For it is obviously essential to that common and united worship which has been shown to be the appointed means of union with the mystical body of Christ. So that an ordained ministry and public ritual may be concluded to be required of necessity in the Church of God.

V. It has been shown that it is nowise inconsistent with the doctrine of our Lord's mediation that the Christian ministry should equally with the Jewish be called a priesthood, and that its service should equally be styled a sacrifice. And it has been stated what is that true and only sacrifice, on the pleading whereof depends the office of both systems; the one by typical representation — the other by sacramental union. As yet, however, nothing has been adduced but reasons for expecting a Christian ministry to exist; it is necessary to show further the fact of its existence. Now, it is essential to notice what it is which Scripture declares on this subject, and on what it is silent. The existence of a public ritual and ministry it declares either expressly or by implication: their nature, order, and mode of appointment are less clearly expressed. The existence of a public ministry follows (independently of various historical and incidental statements in Scripture) from that central portion of the Christian revelation with which we are particularly engaged. For the doctrine of our Lord's Incarnation, which is the beginning and end of the gospel, declares to us that the renewal of man's nature is effected through union with the manhood of Christ. All the supernatural gifts of grace were first concentrated in this representative of the human race and Head of the Christian family, that from his manhood they might afterwards flow forth for the replenishment of his brethren. Again, this union is declared to be vouchsafed to us in that mystical body of Christ our Lord, in which all Christians are engrafted. Again, our mean of partaking in the mystical body of Christ has been shown (in the present chapter) to be participation in its common actions. Those common actions, therefore, are essential to the effect of the Incarnation of Christ. And if there be public acts, there must be public agents: a ministry or system of some sort or other must be essential to the existence of that collective order whereby individuals become members of the body of

Christ. What is asserted then as a scriptural truth and necessary doctrine is that some public order and worship, with all which it implies, must forever exist in the Church of God. And by common worship is not to be understood that Christians have the right of meeting together, and those who please the right of uttering their minds (a thing which here is neither affirmed nor denied), but that the Church of Christ, regarded as a whole, has certain duties incumbent on it towards God — that those duties involve united worship, common action, a public service, and arise from that collective character which is stamped on the whole Christian community by its spiritual union with the body of its Incarnate God. To forego this relation is to leave the high ground of the Christian Revelation and to descend to the uncertainty of mere natural religion. It is to rest on that immediate relation to God through the intercourse of mind with mind, which belonged to unfallen man, but which since the Fall can only be restored through the intervention of a Mediator. So that to suppose the individual duties of religion to be anterior to common worship or independent of it is virtually to abandon the mediation of Christ. For all the private prayers, thoughts, actions of Christians, depend on that union with Christ our Lord which is attained through the communication of his man's nature. And he communicates it through those public acts whereby the Great Head of the Christian body joins all its members to himself.

Now, when it is further demanded by whom are these public acts done, in what circumstances, under whose presidence and authority, we can only refer to the practice of the Church, as she has been guided "into all truth" [Jn. 16:13] by the Holy Ghost, and to the example which was set by the apostles. It has been God's will that in this, as in many other cases, the New Testament should not comprise such an exact code of laws as was afforded by the Old. That the several books which compose the New Testament are inspired, and that they contain the rule of our faith, are facts of which we are assured because it was always so held by the apostles and their successors, although no such statement occur in Holy Writ. That worship should be solemnized especially on the first day of the week, so that we are authorized to depart from the letter of the Fourth Commandment, rests on the same authority. We have no other proof that children are fit partakers of the one, or women of the other sacrament. In all these cases we take as our guide the example of the apostles. In like manner must we act in regard to the nature and mode of that public agency whereby the united acts of the Christian community have their expression. That such united action exists, and that there must be a public system of worship, we believe on the authority of Scripture, and because they are indissolubly bound to the highest doctrines of religion. And the existence of such a system, even in the opinion of those who are least inclined to rest the Church's being on any doctrinal basis, involves the necessity of agents by whom it may be conducted.

> Any one who sanctions a society (says Archbishop Whately), gives in so doing his sanction to those essentials of a society, its government, its officers, its regulations. Accordingly if our Lord had not expressly said anything about "binding and loosing," still the very circumstance of his sanctioning a Christian community, would necessarily have implied his sanction of the institutions, ministers, and government of a Christian Church.[15]

Since the existence, then, of a system of common worship is a truth of Scripture, and since it implies the existence of a ministry, all that remains is to ask the nature and constitution of that ministry; and if on this subject Scripture has given us no express rule, yet as in the other cases mentioned, some guidance may be derived from the example of the apostles.

This accordingly has been the course adopted by the English Church. She prefaces her enforcement of the rule of Episcopacy by declaring that "it is evident unto all men diligently reading the holy Scripture and ancient Authors, that from the Apostles' time there have been these Orders of Ministers in Christ's Church: Bishops, Priests, and Deacons." [16] As we trace back from the present time, we find this rule to have universally prevailed among the spiritual predecessors of our present ministry. Each generation has professed to receive its commission from Christ through the intervention of the preceding one. Even Archbishop Whately allows that "the existence of such an order of men as Christian ministers, continuously from the time of the Apostles to this day, is perhaps as complete a moral certainty as any historical fact can be." [17] And when we draw near its fountain, we have the direct testimony of Tertullian, who lived shortly after St. John, that its first rank had its commission handed on to it by that apostle of Christ; [18] and St. Ignatius, St. John's contemporary, declares its intervention essential to the validity

15. Richard Whately, *The Kingdom of Christ* [New York, 1842], 123.
16. [ED.] Preface to the Ordinal, B.C.P. (1662).
17. Whately, *Kingdom of Christ*, 186 f.
18. *Cf.* Tertullian, *Against Marcion*, IV, 5 [*ANF*, III, 350; *PL*, II, 395].

of sacred ordinances. This is sufficient ground for justifying the English Church in her assertion of the apostolical descent of the three orders of ministers. It is a further question whether this apostolical succession is essential, and whether any break in it would impair the validity of sacred rites. Such a question, however, seems as needless as to ask whether the Church could safely reverse the appointment of the Lord's Day, or unsettle the observance of infant baptism. In all such cases, to follow the apostolic example is plainly the right, because it is the safest, course.[19] Since the purpose of a ministry is to keep up that public order whereby we hold perpetual communion with the Lord's body, any departure from its constituted usage is a needless risk. It is alleged, indeed, that to rest anything on the perpetuation of a chain which contains so many links is to subject our religious hopes to a painful uncertainty. This is to forget that the apostolical succession only supplies those who believe it with an additional security, over and above what others possess. Since each bishop has commission from three of his brethren, its effect, if traced back a few generations, is to identify his individual authority with that of the whole episcopate of the Church. Were it not that the same parties repeatedly consecrate, every bishop would have two hundred and sixteen spiritual predecessors in the fifth degree; and it can scarcely be doubted, therefore, that by going back a few years, his commission must have been transmitted by the whole body of his forerunners. The feeling thus engendered may be illustrated by that which prevailed among pious Israelites, from the hope that our Lord would descend from them according to the flesh. Considering the vast number of ancestors which each individual had in the twenty-seventh generation, there can scarcely have been a Jewish parent in the time of David, if we except those whose progeny became absolutely extinct, who was not, according to the flesh, a predecessor of our Lord. So truly was he the heir of the nation. And in like manner there can scarcely have been a bishop in the primitive Church — much less could there be one among the apostles — through whom every individual inheritor of the episcopal office may not trace his commission. Surely such a fact is not calculated to weaken the feeling of the Church's unity, or to relax that bond whereby all the members of the Lord's body are united to himself. And if it be said that there may in some case have been a secret failure, which may have impaired some one of the many parallel threads by which this bond is rendered con-

---

19. [ED.] Cf. *Tract Four: Adherence to the Apostolical Succession the Safest Course* (London, 1833). John Keble was the author.

tinuous, such a circumstance, instead of being fatal to the general law, seems the very exception for which some great divines have contended — that an *involuntary* breach of this apostolical rule is not fatal to the Church's existence.[20] If we saw persons whose descent we were unable to trace to Adam, but whose acts and character showed an exact congruity with those of his children, we should suppose that it had pleased God, in some way to us unknown, to amalgamate them with mankind. It would not be an unnatural exercise of faith to believe that God is pleased in like manner to supply the involuntary deficiencies of those who desire to be identified with his Church's existence.

But why, it may be asked, do we refer to this apostolical commission if it be not expressly affirmed to be essential? For the same reason that we assert Christian ministers to be as truly priests as those of the first Temple, and that their offering is as truly a sacrifice. It is possible that these particulars might not be essential to the existence of worship, and therefore to the reality of those acts whereby Christians claim their part in the body of Christ our Lord. But, independently of the fact that we have good authority for their assertion, they contribute to a reverent estimate of those public acts of the Christian body, from which the contrary tendency proportionably detracts. The thing of moment is that common worship is a real work, whereby the whole Christian community preserves its right as the collective body of the Lord. Its claim to a true life in him is thereby asserted, just as the privileges of Israel belong to all who had a part in its united ritual. By this means are we led to appreciate those external actions of the God-Man, on which his character of Mediator is dependent. Nothing hinders, indeed, but that the like results might have attended common worship, though it had been God's pleasure that the public officers, by whom it is directed, instead of being set apart for their work, had been chosen out of the mass for the occasion. But if common worship be really of the moment which has been described, such manner of selecting those who guide it could not be esteemed so suitable as that which has been handed down from the apostles. Accordingly, those who have adopted such an expedient have either begun or ended by depreciating the work itself. Instead of being an office which has reference to God, and may therefore be properly called sacred or divine, the task of ministering has before long been looked upon only in its reference to man, and as little else than that of an instructor. Thus

20. [ED.] For statements of the views of older Anglican theologians on this question, *cf.* E. R. Fairweather, *Episcopacy Re-Asserted* (London, 1955), 50–56.

the notion of common worship passes away. The collective sacrifice of the people's prayers is lost sight of. So that beginning by neglecting the example of the apostles, men have ended by disbelieving their doctrines. The life of the Christian community as the body of Christ has been destroyed. His mediation, whereby God and man are united, has been explained away into a mere natural religion. The necessity of being joined to his man's nature has been forgotten. Such has been the actual result in very many of those communities where the line of a living ministry has been broken. And to add to this tendency, where the ancient system of the ministry has been abandoned, the ancient ritual and liturgy have commonly been renounced. Here too the practice of early times, so far as it can be attained, affords an useful example; especially in points of such leading moment as the ministering of sacraments. But the material point is that such form of service should be maintained as may testify to the collective character of the Church's supplications. This is the very purpose of a public liturgy, which, by calling on the people to bear their part, finds place for the service of the whole community. Where this responsive system of worship is lost, the nature of a public service will soon be forgotten. Instead of regarding the minister as a public servant, whose office is to provide a centre of union for their collective prayers, men will look to him mainly as a teacher, whose office is not to address God but themselves. The very place of assemblage, instead of being known as God's "House of Prayer" [Is. 56:7], will be associated with the recollection of some favoured preacher. And the sure consequence will be a forgetfulness of the peculiar relation which men gain in common worship to Christ the Mediator, to whom at that moment they should address themselves as members of the one mystical body in heaven and earth, for which he is interceding at his Father's right hand.

Nothing has more contributed to the growth of that unbelief which has overspread many parts of the Continent than the evil which has been described. For with the collective character of worship, that real life of the Church has been lost, which depends on Christ's presence. The preservation of this among ourselves has not been owing merely to our attachment to great names or orthodox expressions, however important; for Christ only can maintain that quickening spirit, which he bestows through the ordinances of his grace. From himself must come the power which is sought through those federal acts which unite men in his mystical body. A neglect of those especial means by which this union is effected, issues in a practical undervaluing of the union itself. The In-

carnation of Christ ceases to be looked upon as the source of his continual presence among men, and a system of self-mediation grows up in
its place. The glowing words in which Scripture describes the privileges
of Christians are regarded as something bestowed on them as individuals,
as a reassertion of the claims of nature, and as though by themselves
they had access to God; whereas it is only through their great Head
that these blessings devolve on them. The royal and priestly nature has
been shown not to belong to them in themselves, but by union with him
who by his mediation has joined them to God. As fallen humanity was
first reconsecrated by union with the divine nature in Christ our Head,
so all consecrating virtue is bestowed upon his servants through that
union with him which belongs to them as members of his mystical
body. So that to abandon the connexion which is maintained by the
public ordinances of his grace is to renounce that highest birthright of
man's race, which is bestowed upon it through the mediation of Christ.
It is a bold statement of Dr. Bisse, in relation to the importance of daily
service, that the

> mother churches, the sure resting-place for the Ark of the Cov-
> enant, before which the daily offering never ceaseth to be offered
> morning and evening — these are our strength and salvation, and are
> of far greater use and security to our people and to our land, than
> all the watchfulness of our senators, or policy of our ambassadors,
> or valour of our mighty men.[21]

What was present to his mind was that by this collective service is
maintained our connexion with that mediation of the Son of God, from
which flow the highest privileges of humanity. This no doubt is the
Church's reason for requiring the public ministration of daily service,
except when "reasonably hindered," of all her clergy.[22] And well were
it if all who take part in public prayer, and especially all who worship
in those central churches, in which the whole diocese has a common
interest, would remember how high and responsible is the office which
they undertake. For not only those who officiate, but all who take part
in public prayer, are thereby uniting themselves to that great work, of
which the Head and Leader is the Son of God himself. This belongs to
the laymen who present prayers, as well as to the priest whose office is
to give them united voice and utterance. If the high priest in ancient

---

21. [ED.] Thomas Bisse, *A Rationale on Cathedral Worship or Choir-Service*, 2d ed.
(London, 1721), 54.
22. [ED.] Concerning the Service of the Church, B.C.P. (1662).

times bore with him into God's presence the symbols of the whole world, and claimed to be its common minister, much more so does the Christian, the heir of the world, for whose sake were the dispensations which are past, and on whom the "ends of the world have come" [1 Cor. 10:11]. On this account is man emphatically called "the creature" [Rom. 8:19–21] in Holy Writ, because he is the heir and representative of God's creation. A lofty title, but which one only individual bears in himself, and which, if others attempt to claim it for themselves, will but minister to their more signal overthrow. Those who seek to rule the world by themselves, or who claim for themselves its possession, do but demonstrate the imbecility of worldly talents and the instability of worldly success. The heir of the world, the ruler of the creation of God, is that Man only, whom a nature which was above humanity marked out to be the "first-born of every creature" [Col. 1:15]. In the elder son, all the prerogatives of birthright were exclusively inherent. To him only do those titles belong of right, which he bestows upon all his brethren by favour. He is the sole King, the only Priest; but they are all heirs, so far as they are one with him, in a kingly and priestly line. That sacerdotal system whereby we maintain communion with his man's nature, instead of derogating, as some have imagined, from the privilege of individual Christians, is the very circumstance on which their tenure rests. On the maintenance of their federal union with him depends their pre-eminence. To let go this connexion is to fall back into the imbecility of their natural state. Those public ordinances, therefore, through which as Mediator he unites them to his own manhood, are the very life of theirs. To be found in him their representative is to share his honour, because it is to share his nature. "For thou wast slain, and hast redeemed us to God by thy blood out of every kindred, and tongue, and people, and nation; and hast made us unto our God kings and priests: and we shall reign on the earth" [Rev. 5:9 f.].

CHAPTER XIII:

OF SACRAMENTS, AS MEANS OF UNION WITH THE
MANHOOD OF CHRIST

The actions of Christ towards men since his ascension have been said to be involved in the truth of his presence. His presence has been explained to be that spiritual presence of his manhood whereupon all the functions of his mediation depend. It is vouchsafed in his body mystical, the Church; and the offices of common worship, speaking comprehensively, are the means whereby men partake it. But there is one means of partaking it, so specific, peculiar, and signal, as to need separate notice — namely, sacramental grace.

Something has already been said respecting the Holy Communion as a sacrifice, a view, however, of this sacred ordinance, of which its character as a sacrament is the root. For it is by virtue of the connexion into which it brings men with Christ that it forms the leading feature of our public service, so that its relation to worship arises from that which is the characteristic and original distinction of both sacraments. There are other purposes which they serve, and other views which may be taken of them, but that circumstance on which all the rest depend, and which especially connects itself with the present inquiry, is that sacraments are "the extension of the Incarnation," [1] that through these means we are united to the man's nature of Christ. Other particulars which distinguish them are: First, that in sacraments there is the performance of a definite and peculiar act, which is likely to engender in us peculiar preparation. Hence, as our Article observes, they are "badges or tokens of Christian men's profession." [2] Christian burial consequently is not allowed except to those who have been partakers of the one, and who have not been formally excluded from the other sacrament. Now, this circumstance may not unfitly suggest the cautious preparation with which we should approach rites by which we are especially dedicated to God's service. But this is only a first, and as our Article is careful to observe, only a partial estimate of sacraments; it rests their use on our act only, not on that of God; it is merely subjective, human, tentative, and though useful as a direction to ourselves, falls far short of the sublime views which Scripture opens respecting these "holy mysteries." [3] It is such conception as a Socinian might entertain, but with which the Christian mind could never be satisfied.

We pass on then to the second purpose which our Article assigns to sacraments, *i.e.*, that they are "not only badges of profession," "but rather . . . certain sure witnesses and effectual signs of grace." Here, then, we have a divine, as before a mere human meaning in these sacred ordinances. They are not only subjective, as implying a feeling in our-

1. Jeremy Taylor, *The Worthy Communicant*, Bk. I, chap. 2 [*Works* (London, 1822), XV, 420].
2. [ED.] Thirty-nine Articles, XXV.
3. [ED.] Prayer of Thanksgiving, Communion Service, B.C.P. (1662).

selves, but objective likewise, as implying an act external to us on the part of the Almighty.

> Christ and his Holy Spirit with all their blessed effects, though entering into the soul of man we are not able to apprehend or express how, do notwithstanding give notice of the times when they use to make their access, because it pleaseth Almighty God to communicate by sensible means those blessings which are incomprehensible.[4]

This then is no doubt the peculiar end of sacraments, that they are channels to the faithful of those supernatural gifts whereby God renews the soul. And herein their tangible nature has this peculiar advantage, that it turns men's minds more completely to their Almighty Author, so that in times of doubt they are a stable comfort, and yet in times of steadfastness do not minister to pride. Their advantage in time of doubt is that their ground is God's promise and not man's confidence: so that they supply some fixed external standing-place in those hours of dejection when men's own feelings are in most need of succour. In such seasons comfort must come from without, for how are inward doubts to be solved by the mind, whose very complaint is doubtfulness? In such moments, then, how inestimable that gift whereby "thou dost assure us of thy favour and goodness towards us." [5] And yet such succour contains this antidote to pride, that whereas all inward movements of man's soul, even though we admit them to be God's works, may yet blend and confuse themselves with our own agency; on the contrary, "where God doth work and use these outward means, wherein he neither findeth nor planteth force and aptness towards his intended purpose, such means are but signs to bring men to the consideration of his own omnipotent power, which without the use of things sensible would not be marked." [6] This then being the main purpose of sacraments, and there being some peculiar advantages in the very simplicity of the vehicles which God has chosen for the communication of his gifts, we may yet go further, and inquire how far they connect themselves with his general dealings with mankind, and whether this connexion supplies any circumstances which explain what appears at first sight their anomalous nature. For what indisposes the minds of many to the doctrine of sacramental grace is that

---

4. Richard Hooker, *The Laws of Ecclesiastical Polity*, Bk. V, chap. 57, 3 [*Works* (Oxford, 1845), II, 257].

5. [ED.] Prayer of Thanksgiving, Communion Service, B.C.P. (1662).

6. Hooker, *Ecclesiastical Polity*, Bk. VI, chap. 6, 11. [*Works*, III, 94 f.].

it seems so completely a matter of *arbitrary appointment*. They require to discern greater congruity between the effect attained and the means of attaining it. We are used to see cause and effect linked together by a chain of interdependent circumstances; and the gap between a slight external act and a momentous internal alteration is intolerable to our fancy. Say what men will, the judgment revolts at it; man's faith is not strong enough for such a trial. This is why all the learned works which have been written on the sacraments fail to give confidence in their efficacy: the unbelief which is vanquished in the study reappears in the world, and men acquiesce in the formularies of the Church, but their reason remains unsatisfied. What they need, as Hooker expresses it after St. Augustine, is some "answer, such as not only may press them with the bare authority of custom, but also instruct them in the cause thereof." [7]

Now such a cause seems to be supplied by that particular subject with which we are at present occupied. The importance of sacraments rests on the Incarnation of Christ, and on their being the means through which his man's nature is communicated to his brethren. Let this be apprehended, and what offends men in their arbitrary appointment will pass away. For since this is a wholly supernatural work, we could not expect to see it effected, except through some means specifically provided by God's peculiar appointment; and the visible means employed are so far from appearing to be less suitable than any other with which the wisdom of God could have connected the secret working of his power, that in several respects we can discern them to be singularly appropriate. If man's connexion with the Supreme Being were the mere natural intercourse of mind with mind — if man were still, as Adam was before the Fall, the perfect image of his Maker, then indeed, to introduce such media of communication at all would be superfluous. And on this account the sacramental system is inconsistent with that rationalistic theory which supposes that the divine principle of holiness and truth is sufficiently possessed by nature. But allow the scheme of mediation to be essential to man's recovery, let it depend on union with that personal Being in whom holiness and truth became incarnate, and the sacramental system follows of course. In the mere intercourse of mind with mind, sacraments would be an unnatural interruption: but they are exactly suited to effect that union whereby the Divine Head of man's race is

7. [ED.] Hooker, *Ecclesiastical Polity*, Bk. V, chap. 64, 2 (*Works*, II, 308 f.), quoted from Augustine, *Epistle* 98, 7 (*NPNF*[1], I, 409; *CSEL*, XXXIV, 529).

bound to his fellows. Since this union is itself foreign to the course of nature, so must the media be by which it is effected; the work cannot depend on their natural influence, but on that influence with which they are supernaturally endowed. And that those outward means which we call sacraments are truly attended by an inward effect, that what is done on earth in holy mysteries effects a real change in the whole nature of those who are acted upon, is known to us by the distinct declarations of God's word. We are told in plain and indubitable terms that baptism and the Lord's Supper are the means by which men are joined to the body of Christ, and therefore by which Christ our Lord joins himself to that renewed race, of which he has become the Head. So that, as St. Leo expresses it, "He that is received by Christ, and that receives Christ, is not the same after the laver of baptism as he was before it, because *the body of the regenerate person becomes the flesh of the crucified one*." [8] Now, these facts we learn from the express statements of St. Paul. "For by one Spirit are we all baptized into one body" (1 Cor. 12:13). And again, "We being many are one bread and one body, for we are all partakers of that one bread" (1 Cor. 10:17). Herein it is expressly declared that the one and the other of these sacraments are the peculiar means by which union with the body of Christ is bestowed upon men. They are the "joints and bands" [Col. 2:19] whereby the whole body in its dependence on its Head has nourishment ministered. So that it is in the Church that union takes place with Christ, the new Adam or representative of our race, and it is by this actual union with the new Adam that the whole family of renewed men have that collective being whereby is derived to them their spiritual life.

And this, then, is the circumstance which puts the main difference between sacraments and those other means of grace wherein also we draw near to God. The profit of all other means of grace depends on that right of access to God which Christ the Mediator has dispensed. But the purpose of sacraments is to bind us to him on whom this right of access is dependent. Our prayers and praises avail not, unless we are part of that renewed race which our great High Priest has been pleased to identify with himself, covering the infirmity of their actions with the perfection of his own. But it is through that union of his man's nature with ours, which is compacted through the sacraments of his grace, that the Head of the body is identified with its members. Thus it is that the whole body is "fitly joined together, and compacted by that

8. [ED.] Leo the Great, *Sermon* 63, 12 (*NPNF*², XII, 177; *PL*, 54, 357).

which every joint supplieth" [Eph. 4:16]. So that sacraments differ from all other means of grace, in that whereas other things result from union with Christ, they on the contrary conduct to it. Their pre-eminence depends on a real diversity between their office and that of any other things appertaining to divine service, because through them Christ, the Head of mankind, joins himself to his brethren.

Sacraments, then, differ in purpose from other means of grace, in that through them the Head is united to its members. But why are they especially employed for such an office? What is that congruity which fits them for the work, and what the suitableness which may be found in such external portions of them as address themselves to our sense? It is not for us, of course, to lay down rules for the Omniscient, and yet we may contemplate with reverence what it has been his pleasure to appoint. Now, since the peculiarity of sacraments is that they are not merely inward actions, but that they touch likewise upon the external world — that they have, in fact, both "an outward visible sign" and an "inward spiritual grace" [9] — this compound nature marks them out as a singularly appropriate medium of intercourse between things, which are themselves compound, *i.e.,* man who is to be renewed, and the Mediator whose presence renews him. For thus it is that all graces are communicated to mankind, flowing into them from that manhood which has been made the fountain of grace through its personal oneness with Deity. Now, man consists of a material as well as an immaterial nature, and in body, soul, and spirit does he require to be renewed after the image of him that created him. It has not been an uncommon feeling, that in the material clay of man's composition lies all his vileness; let him be emancipated only from this, and the pure spirit would expatiate in the freedom of its native refinement. This was the inherent vice of the Gnostic system; [10] it resulted from that erroneous philosophy which represented simple immensity as the essence of Godhead, forgetful of those moral conditions whereby both through conscience and revelation the Father of all has been pleased to declare that his character is most adequately expressed. Thus are men blinded to the deformity of sin and to the hatefulness of that rebellion against an holy God, which is the real degeneracy of our state. An error, this, which is best corrected by remembering that Christ our Lord took our whole nature, and that our whole nature is to be

9. [ED.] Catechism, B.C.P. (1662).

10. [ED.] *Cf.* R. I. Wilberforce, *The Doctrine of the Incarnation of Our Lord Jesus Christ* (London, 1848), 138.

renovated in him. "For if our flesh had not admitted of redemption, the Word of God would not have become flesh." [11] And because the terms which are to be united are of this complex character, it is not unnatural that the sacraments, which are appointed to unite them, should show by their very constitution that even the material part of manhood is not to be forgotten. "Hadst thou been incorporeal," says St. Chrysostom, "God would have given these his gifts in a naked and incorporeal manner. But since thy soul is joined to thy body, the garb of sense is used in conveying a gift to thy mind." [12] Therefore does our Church remind us that by the baptism of Christ "in Jordan," water was consecrated "to the mystical washing away of sin." [13] The whole element, in all its multiform variety, was freed by this single use of it from the imputation of being naturally impure. So does Irenaeus maintain that all the simple ingredients of man's life were purified through their employment by that Head of our race, who could not be defiled.[14] To esteem man's spirit something so much purer than his animal nature that its acts may in themselves find an access to the Deity, which his material nature is unworthy to share, is not very unlike the fanciful heresy of the Gnostic Valentinus. The man Christ, he supposed, having been moulded by the Demiurgus, or maker of the world, with his utmost skill, had received, unknown to his creator, the seeds of a superior nature from the ultimate author of all, which discovered themselves as he grew up to the astonishment of the being who had produced him, and supplied the point of contact with that divine spirit which descended upon him at his baptism.[15] There is something almost analogous to this conception in the belief that a part of our nature has in itself a right of access to the holy God, independently of that means of approach which he has bestowed through Christ upon the whole of it. For Christ our Lord vouchsafed to come in the perfection of our nature, that all might be renewed. The representative of our race took our being in its completeness, that it might be wholly sanctified.

> For we could not taste of incorruption and immortality unless we had first been united to that which is immortal and incorruptible.

11. Irenaeus, *Against the Heresies*, V, 14, 1 [*ANF*, I, 541; *PG*, VII, 1161].

12. [ED.] John Chrysostom, *Homilies on the Gospel of St. Matthew*, 82, 4 (*NPNF*[1], X, 495; *PG*, LVIII, 743).

13. [ED.] Order of Holy Baptism, B.C.P. (1662).

14. *Cf.* Irenaeus, *Against the Heresies*, III, 11, 5 [*ANF*, I, 427; *PG*, VII, 883].

15. [ED.] Wilberforce cites Dorner as his authority for this account. *Cf.* I. A. Dorner, *History of the Development of the Doctrine of the Person of Christ* (Edinburgh, 1878), Div. I, I, 229–39.

But how should we be united to that which was incorruptible and immortal, unless he who was personally incorruption and immortality had first been made the same with ourselves, that so what was corruptible might be swallowed up by incorruption, and what was mortal by immortality, that we might receive the adoption of sons.[16]

The course then which God's infinite wisdom was pleased to adopt was, that since "the children were partakers of flesh and blood, he also himself" (in the person of the Eternal Son) "took part of the same" [Heb. 2:14].

He summed up the lengthened series of mankind in himself, affording us salvation in that epitome of our being; that what we had lost in Adam, *i.e.*, to be after God's image and likeness, we might recover in Christ.[17]

Thus then was there "one Mediator between God and men, the man Christ Jesus" [1 Tim. 2:5]. There was one common bond by which these two infinitely distant parties might be united. And this common term of union required to be truly and really joined to each of the extremes, which it was to couple to one another. It was truly joined to Godhead by that personal union whereby Christ our Lord was very God, of very God. The very nature of Godhead — whole God — was in the person of the Son of Mary united to our flesh. "God was manifest in the flesh" [1 Tim. 3:16]. All glory, purity, perfection, power, of which Godhead could not be emptied, were enshrined in a human frame. Thus was there sown a seed of life and immortality, which was to interpenetrate and pervade the whole nature of mankind. For this end, as the man Christ Jesus was joined to Deity by personal union, so is he allied to his brethren of mankind by sacramental grace. For "we are members of his body; of his flesh, and of his bones. . . . This is a great mystery, but I speak concerning Christ and the Church" [Eph. 5:30, 32]. Now, this union of the Mediator with men, whereby are transmitted to them those beams of glory which were centred in his flesh, needs to be as true and certain as that other union which he has with Godhead, whereby its self-originating excellencies were transferred into himself. As the fountain has its source in those unknown waters which issue from the throne of God, so from the fountain do the streams descend to water the earth. In the union, then, of God's nature with manhood in the person

16. Irenaeus, *Against the Heresies*, III, 19, 1. [*ANF*, I, 448 f.; *PG*, VII, 939 f.].
17. Irenaeus, *Against the Heresies*, III, 18, 1 [*ANF*, I, 446; *PG*, VII, 932].

of Christ, lies the cause of our union with the man Christ Jesus by sacramental grace. If the first be received as a true, real, abiding fact, such as can be founded on that diversity of persons in the Ever-Blessed Trinity, which forms the basis of the Christian system, the second also will be looked at not as a mere figurative expression, but as an actual operation. But let the first be denied, as by Socinians, or by Sabellians be resolved into a mere nominal transaction, and the reality of the second must evaporate. Therefore does St. Athanasius observe that a denial of the personality of God the Son of necessity involves a denial of the grace of baptism.[18] Or on the other hand, let our hold on that union which couples men with Christ be forgotten, and the functions of the Mediator will become an office discharged by some manifestation of the divine power rather than the result of God's actual oneness with our nature. So essential is each link in this golden chain to the integrity of the rest.

Now, as the mean of this union between Christians and Christ, the wisdom of God has employed the system of sacraments. Visible things have been taken, that with them might be associated that inward power and grace which is the living principle whereby the one of these is bound to the other. The union of the outward and visible sign and the inward and spiritual grace make up the sacrament. "Neither is it *ordinarily*" God's "will to bestow the grace of sacraments on any but by the sacraments." [19] And besides other advantages which have been stated to accrue from this appointment, there results from it this peculiar consequence, that the intervention of a means of grace which borrows its vehicle or organ from the external world is adopted in a case where that which consists both of body and soul is to be joined to that Head or representative who consists both of soul and body. Now, because the first effect of union with Christ is the removal of that defilement of our whole being which sin had engendered, this process commences with a rite which speaks to the outward eye of cleansing and purification. Again, because our subsequent life results from the continual influx of grace from him whose manhood has become its storehouse, therefore our further acts of union are through a means whereby our souls are strengthened and refreshed "by the Body and Blood of Christ, as our bodies are by [the] Bread and Wine." [20] Thus significant is the sensible

18. [ED.] Pseudo-Athanasius, *Fourth Discourse against the Arians* (*NPNF²*, IV, 443; *PG*, XXVI, 508).
19. Hooker, *Ecclesiastical Polity*, Bk. V, chap. 57, 4 [*Works*, II, 258].
20. [ED.] Catechism, B.C.P. (1662).

part of that process, which having its beginning in the truth, "The Word was made flesh" [Jn. 1:14], has for its conclusion, "that we might be made partakers of the divine nature" [2 Pet. 1:4]. Not that the connecting principle which binds together mankind and their Head is any material derivation. The things united, indeed, are on one side the whole constitution of man as it exists in each individual, and whole Christ on the other. But that whereby they are joined is the spiritual power by which it has been shown that Christ acts upon his brethren. This power has been shown to be immaterial, both by reference to what it is, and by reference to what it is not.[21] For it was to be the mysterious agent in this union that the third person in the Ever-Blessed Trinity vouchsafed his gracious concurrence on man's behalf. He came to join men to Christ, to supply the loss which would else have attended our Lord's ascension, that he who was withdrawn according to his carnal propinquity might be brought more near by spiritual presence. And the same thing follows from considering what it has been shown, that our Lord's mystical or sacramental presence is *not*. It is not that local presence of a material body which he maintains in heaven. "Christ as man according to the body is in a place and goes from a place, and when he comes to another place, is not in the place from whence he came." [22] That this local presence, therefore, of Christ's material frame is not upon earth is the very thing which is asserted when it is stated to be in heaven.

Here, then, it may be well to pause for a moment, in order to notice what is the exact point which *is,* and what that which *is not,* stated respecting the blessed sacraments.

I. It is not affirmed then that their external or sensible parts are so raised above their natural nothingness, as by their own efficacy to produce a spiritual result. In each sacrament the outward sign is produced by combining an appointed matter with certain chosen words. Unless the words and matter are properly combined (and hence arises the occasion for such caution and heedfulness in their ministration), there is no sacrament. But neither are these things aught by themselves but sounds or elements, nor when duly combined, though of course hallowed by being consecrated to a holy use, do they cease to be in themselves elements and sounds. For "sacraments are not physical but *moral instruments* of salvation." [23] This

21. [ED.] Cf. Wilberforce, *Doctrine of the Incarnation,* chap X.

22. [ED.] Augustine, *Homilies on the Gospel of John,* 31, 9 (NPNF¹, VII, 192; PL, XXXV, 1640), as quoted by Jeremy Taylor, *The Real Presence of Christ in the Holy Sacrament,* sec. XI, par. 15 (*Works,* X, 31).

23. Hooker, *Ecclesiastical Polity,* Bk. V, chap. 57, 4 [*Works,* II, 257].

is more readily admitted, perhaps, in the sacrament of baptism than in that of the Lord's Supper. Yet:

> The orthodoxal ancients use the same language for expressing Christ's presence in Baptism and in the Eucharist: they stick not to say that Christ is present or latent in the water, as well as in the elements of bread and wine. Their meaning is, that neither of these elements or sensible substances can directly cleanse us from our sins, by any virtue communicated to them or inherent in them, but only as they are pledges or assurances of Christ's peculiar presence in them, and of our true investiture in Christ by them.[24]

And as the element in one sacrament is on all hands allowed to continue water, so the element in the other is expressly called bread by St. Paul [1 Cor. 10:16], even when its sacramental use is referred to. And, indeed, why should aught else be expected? The only ground for questioning it must be, that Holy Scripture declares the body and blood of Christ to be our food in the Lord's Supper. Now, when we speak of our Lord's body and blood, the very words lead us of necessity to his manhood, to that same bodily substance which was born of the Virgin, and ascended into heaven after its sufferings on the cross. It being admitted, then, by all believers that this body is present after some real manner in the Holy Eucharist, those who deny that the consecrated elements continue to be materially bread and wine must do so under the idea that without derogating from the local presence of our Lord's body in heaven, the elements when consecrated become a part of his material body and blood. Their reason for maintaining it, if such an opinion is ever really maintained, must be first, the letter of Scripture, which however all believers accept; and secondly, an impression that unless such transmutation is admitted, there can be no true belief in the efficacy of sacraments. But it follows from what has been already stated respecting the nature of our Lord's presence: first, that the consecrated elements, even if they undergo a material change, have no more tendency than without such change to produce the real end which results from sacraments; and secondly, that to rest on such a change is incompatible with a reference to our Lord's ascended manhood as that Head of the renewed race, with whom it is the purpose of sacraments to unite us. For in the first place, suppose the consecrated elements to undergo some such change, that they should be found to be, we know not how, the material body

---

24. [ED.] Thomas Jackson, *Commentaries on the Creed*, Bk. X, chap. 55, 9 (*The Works of Thomas Jackson, D.D.* [Oxford, 1844], IX, 595).

of Christ. This would no doubt give them great sacredness; but how would it minister towards the purpose of a sacrament? Why should we be the better for the carnal devouring of our Lord's body? What spiritual efficacy would result from such a feast? A spiritual efficacy, indeed, our Lord's body has on all those with whom according to its proper laws of action it is brought into connexion; but would this action attend its material consumption? Is there any relevance between union with the flesh of the Son of Man and the carnal devouring him? We are united to Adam by one means, to Christ by another. The first is by the law of paternity, the second by that of regeneration. Why should we increase our relation to Christ by this carnal banquet, any more than we should to Adam by the eating of his flesh? "As is our eating," says Taylor, "so is the nourishing, because that is in order to this." [25] A spiritual effect of the manhood of our great Head must proceed through spiritual action from his purified humanity. Sacraments have been appointed as its medium of communication; but if baptism does not depend on the natural effect of the elements which it employs, why should the Lord's Supper? Such a supposition at all events is not essential to a belief in the sacramental system, and to a true acceptance of its divine results.

But further, it may be observed in the second place that to rest on a material transmutation in the consecrated elements is, so far forth, to detract from the influence of our Lord's ascended manhood as Head of the renewed race. For its consequence would be to turn our minds to the natural effect of those sacred elements which we partake, instead of building on the supernatural presence of that ascended manhood with which it should be our object to be united. The blessing in the one case would be to be fed with heavenly food — in the other to be united to a divine person. The first of these would, according to the supposition, be a blessing in itself, independently of the other. So that the main object of sacraments, their real life, that which separates them from all other means of grace — that in and through them we are joined to the true Head of man's race, and receive those blessings which through a spiritual medium he communicates in holy mysteries to all his members — would become a secondary consideration. Accordingly, those ancient writers who most insist on the real presence and action of Christ's manhood in holy mysteries declare plainly that the human body and blood which are ascended into heaven are not carnally consumed. And a single definite denial of this kind is more decisive in such a controversy than an hundred

25. Taylor, *The Real Presence of Christ*, sec. VII, par. 8. [*Works*, IX, 495].

passages in which our Lord's real presence in his Supper is asserted; because these last consist as well with the spiritual, while the first is incompatible with the carnal presence of Christ. Such are two quotations made by Bishop Poynet from St. Jerome and St. Augustine.[26] The celebrated letter of the latter to Dardanus has already been cited.[27]

This reference to the real manhood of Christ, as opposed to the conception that sacraments produce their effect through any efficacy inherent in their elements, is warmly supported by our own Hooker:

> For of sacraments the very same is true, which Solomon's wisdom observeth in the brazen serpent — "He that turned towards it was not healed by the thing he saw, but by thee, O Saviour of all" [Wisd. of Sol. 16:7].[28]

That which we commonly discern in the course of nature is a certain orderly series, wherein like results follow habitually from like premises. Hence arises the instinctive belief that in the construction of this material universe the Author of our being works in constant reference to the laws which he has himself ordained. Thus we say that food has a natural tendency to support life; not that we understand the secret mechanism by which it does so, but from observation of the facts, we discern that the Almighty Dispenser has been pleased to connect certain material agents with certain physical effects. This is what we mean by the course of nature. But we have no right to assume that material substances when once created are left to themselves, or that their action is the effect of their inherent principles. All that we can affirm is that for material agents to produce material effects is the natural order of things. And on the same principle, that material agents should be attended by spiritual effects belongs to an order of things which must be supernatural. But why should anyone assert that in this case the result is the effect of the agent itself, seeing that even in that class of subjects which are most strictly natural, no such assertion can be safely made? To affirm the truth of Christ's real presence, at all events, is not to attribute the efficacy of sacraments to the effect produced by the elements which are employed, in themselves, but to trace it to the immediate power of that Divine Being, with whom sacraments bring us into connexion.

26. [ED.] Cf. John Po[y]net, *Diallacticon* (London, 1688), 17–19. The more pertinent quotation is from Augustine, *Expositions on the Psalms*, 98, 9 (*NPNF*¹, VIII, 485 f.; *PL*, XXXVII, 1264 f.).

27. [ED.] Cf. Augustine, *Epistle* 187, 10 (*FC*, XXX, 228; *CSEL*, LVII, 89); Hooker, *Ecclesiastical Polity*, Bk. V, chap. 55, 6 (*Works*, II, 242).

28. Hooker, *Ecclesiastical Polity*, Bk. V, chap. 57, 4. [*Works*, II, 258].

II. The other of the two questions which have been raised requires to be no less guarded than that which has been considered. We must remember not only what is *not* asserted respecting sacraments, but what *is*. That there is in them some real influence and immediate power results from the actual presence of that Divine Being, who in these sacred ordinances binds men by holy instruments to himself. This is the very reason for asserting that the benefit of the Holy Communion does not result from the natural fruitfulness of the means employed, but from the actual presence of the Being with whom those means unite us. Much less can we rest in the belief that these ordinances are merely a lesson addressed to the senses, or that the expressions used respecting them are only metaphorical. For they rest on a basis external to ourselves — they depend on that which has a real, tangible, objective existence, *i.e.*, Christ our Lord, as he has been exalted into heaven, and by spiritual agency has become the Head of the redeemed race.

For when spiritual presence is spoken of, there are two notions which may suggest themselves. Such presence may either be supposed to result from the action of the mind, which receives an impression, or from the action of the being who produces it. The first would be a subjective and metaphorical, the second is an objective and real presence. We might think of a spectacle in Greece or Asia, and lay hold of it by internal impulse, as though it were present to our sight. But this would only be a figurative and visionary presence, because the movement would come altogether from within, and would be wholly irrespective of any action on the part of the object thought of. A real presence, on the contrary, is when there is some object external to ourselves, which produces upon us those effects which result from its propinquity.[29] And such presence may be said to be spiritual as well as real when the medium of communication, by which this external object affects, or is present with us, is not material contact, but spiritual power. Our reason, therefore, for asserting that spiritual presence in the sacraments is a presence of the second and not of the first kind; that it is actual not metaphorical — real not visionary — is because it is the presence of Christ, and results from what is revealed as the result of his Incarnation. For though the two natures which dwell in him remain within those limits by which they are severally bordered, yet they so far concur in his actings towards mankind that the inferior has received from the superior that property of having "life in itself" [Jn. 5:26], which renders it the source of life to

29. [ED.] *Cf.* Wilberforce, *Doctrine of the Incarnation,* 288.

others. And this life results from that spiritual presence of our Lord's manhood which has its medium of communication in the power of the Holy Ghost. When we speak, therefore, of spiritual presence in sacraments, what we refer to is not the vivacity of our spirits, which are able to fancy what is not truly near, but that spiritual power which was bestowed upon Christ's manhood when it was personally united to God. And therefore to disbelieve this spiritual presence, to resolve it into a figure of speech, to transfer it to the action of our own minds, would be equivalent to the denial of our Lord's real manhood; it would be to explain away his existence and substitute a Sabellian fancy instead of the Catholic truth. And what would be the result, but that the life-giving principle of holiness must have its seat, not in Christ, but in our own minds; and therefore in effect that we should be our own saviours? It may be asserted then respecting both sacraments, that their efficacy results from that spiritual power by which Christ's manhood is truly present; that in both of them some real external gift is bestowed upon mankind. That such is the teaching of Scripture shall be shown by what is said respecting each of them, as well as by reference to their common character.

Baptism, then, is

a sacrament which God hath instituted in his Church, to the end that they which receive the same might thereby be incorporated into Christ, and so through his most precious merit obtain as well that saving grace of imputation which taketh away all former guiltiness, as also that infused divine virtue of the Holy Ghost, which giveth to the powers of the soul their first disposition towards future newness of life.[30]

So that it is the especial purpose of baptism, that from that perfect fountain of grace and holiness which is vouchsafed in the manhood of Christ our Lord, the blessings of forgiveness and strength should be attained by every individual. Thus by conjunction with the purity of the second Adam may be regained what was lost by the transmitted defilement of the first. How should this be sought for but by union with him from whom was derived the guiding principle which shone originally in man's breast? The image of God, in which man was made, and which was impaired by sin, has been shown to have resulted from that illuminating power of God the Word, which in fulness of time took up its personal dwelling in our flesh. What means are there then of recover-

30. Hooker, *Ecclesiastical Polity*, Bk. V, chap. 60, 2. [*Works*, II, 265 f.].

ing that which was lost, save by union with him, in whom the light which was intended for each man in his degree has its perfect inhabitation? We come to the fountain-head of light, that our extinguished lamps may each one be replenished. The soul's regeneration, like the body's growth, is of course a protracted process, which the whole of life is not too long to complete. But what gives to baptism its especial character is that in that holy rite this process is begun. For then are men joined by heavenly agency to Christ, that the life of their souls may from that day forth have its development. Holy Scripture speaks everywhere of union with Christ as that new creation in man's being whereby the forfeited likeness of the Word is given back. For "if any man be in Christ, he is a new creature" [2 Cor. 5:17]. And "in Christ Jesus neither circumcision avails nor uncircumcision, but the new creation" [Gal. 6:15].

> In Christ, that is in his Communion or Church (says Olshausen), the ancient divisions are unimportant; everything there depends on the new creation, upon that true regeneration, whereby Christ the New Man is born within us.[31]

Therefore St. Paul tells the Ephesians, "that ye put off concerning the former conversation the old man, and that ye put on the new man, which, after God, is created in righteousness and true holiness" (Eph. 4:22, 24). To be created *after God* is further explained to be the recovery of the impaired image of Christ: "Ye have put off the old man with his deeds and have put on the new man, which is renewed in knowledge after the image of him that created him" (Col. 3:10). This perfect recovery of Christ's image is stated to be the very purpose of God's dealings with men in his Church: "For whom he did foreknow, he also did predestinate to be conformed to the image of his Son" (Rom. 8:29). And "we all are changed into the same image" (2 Cor. 3:18).

But how is this restoration to be effected? How can God's image be created anew in the soul? If man had never fallen, it had been sufficient to inherit it: fallen as he is, there must be the gift of a new life. And this new life had its commencement in the fact of the Incarnation. For by it was a beginning made in the person of him who was to be "the firstborn among many brethren" [Rom. 8:29]. Then did divine gifts take up their abode in humanity, that from the Head they might be distributed to all his brethren. For in the new as in the old creation is he "the firstborn of

31. [ED.] Hermann Olshausen, *Biblical Commentary on St. Paul's Epistles to the Galatians, Ephesians, Colossians, and Thessalonians* (Edinburgh, 1851), 105 f. (loosely quoted).

every creature" [Col. 1:15], "the beginning of the creation of God" [Rev. 3:14]. All its subsequent ramifications are but the result of the impulse which in his Incarnation was bestowed. For "he is the Head, even Christ, from whom the whole body fitly joined together, maketh increase to the edifying of itself in love" [Eph. 4:15 f.]. Whereof, that men "might be partakers of the divine nature" [2 Pet. 1:4] is the wonderful result. This work, therefore, follows from union with him in whom originated the new creation of God. It began with the Head, it extends itself to his members; it began with the new Adam, it reaches on to all his brethren. Thus is he in truth "made a quickening spirit" [1 Cor. 15:45]. Thus are we all "complete in him" (Col. 2:10). To suppose, then, that such a work could commence from a spontaneous, inherent action, would be the very heresy of Pelagius. The flame requires to be kindled from without, that it may burn within. There must be an external action to which the inward movement must respond. Renovation must have its root in regeneration. There must be a gift antecedent to our efforts. This gift is that first union with Christ, whereon all communication of graces from him to us depends. Out of this beginning arises the whole system of the Christian life. And this heavenly impulse is expressly declared in Scripture to be extended to us in baptism: "As many of you as have been baptized into Christ," says St. Paul, "have put on Christ" (Gal. 3:27). For "by one Spirit are we all baptized into one body" (1 Cor. 12:13). And in baptism, as the apostle asserts twice over, that death to the old nature takes place, whereby the new creation in Christ is commenced. "We are buried with him by baptism into death" (Rom. 6:4), "wherein also ye are risen with him" (Col. 2:12). So that St. Peter says, that "baptism doth also now save us" (1 Pet. 3:21). For our Lord himself had taught that in this ordinance lies the beginning of the spiritual life — "Except a man be born of water and of the Spirit, he cannot enter into the kingdom of God" [Jn. 3:5] — a passage whereof Hooker reminds us, "that of all the ancient, there is not one to be named that ever did otherwise either expound or allege the place than as implying external baptism." [32]

Since the statements of Scripture on this subject are so precise, how comes it then that any persons should have dissented from this universal opinion of our Lord's first disciples? The grounds of men's objection appear to be two: first, an attachment to the idea introduced, or at least systematized, by Calvin, that grace is not given to any except those who

32. Hooker, *Ecclesiastical Polity*, Bk. V, chap. 59, 3 [*Works*, II, 263].

will finally be saved; and secondly, the assertion that no visible results attend on baptism. The difficulties which these considerations involve induce men to refer to such passages of Scripture as express the full effect and ultimate consequence of regeneration, *i.e.*, victory over sin and final perseverance (1 Jn. 3:9; 5:18); and they infer that no gift has really been bestowed in baptism unless these ultimate consequences are discerned to be its effect. They deny in effect that any seed has been sown where fruit is not brought forth. They deny that there can be dead branches in the Christian vine. And the language in which Scripture and the Church speak of something as actually *done* in baptism, they consider to be merely a charitable hope that something will be done hereafter — a hope which, in the majority of instances, they say is not borne out by the result. Now, the passages of Scripture which they cite have in themselves no tendency to show that in baptism occurs no real work: for they only speak of this work as one, the completion whereof is the extinction of sin; and which must therefore spread itself through man's whole life. But all that is asserted of baptism is that since it is our first means of union with the manhood of Christ, the basis of our spiritual growth must be laid in it. "Baptism doth challenge to itself but the inchoation of those graces, the consummation whereof dependeth on mysteries ensuing." [33] The denial therefore that in baptism, as rightly and worthily participated, there is any real change made in the recipient of the ordinance — the assertion that the benefits ascribed to it are merely figurative, contingent, occasional — that they are spoken of prospectively as something to be hereafter attained, and not positively as something actually possessed — all this does not follow from any scriptural author-ity; the grounds for supposing it are men's antecedent difficulties. And as to the first of them, it is surely matter of surprise that any traditional attachment to the opinions of Calvin should interfere with the direct assurances of God's word. For it has been shown by Bishop Butler that the predestinarian theory is never carried out so rigidly as to preclude all the practical inferences to which it is intellectually opposed. This is far from being undesirable, considering how imperfect an instrument is man's understanding, and how much safer in many cases is the appeal to con-science than to argument. But those who can reconcile the doctrine of arbitrary decrees with the general invitations of Scripture to repentance and faith need not object surely to allow that the gifts of grace may be coextensive with the ordinances of the gospel. For do not faith and

33. Hooker, *Ecclesiastical Polity*, Bk. V, chap. 57, 6 [*Works*, II, 259].

repentance need grace as an unavoidable prerequisite? Why, then, should men deny the reality of baptism, even if on their theory it be "a seal perhaps to the grace of election before received," seeing it is declared to be "to our sanctification here a step that hath not any before it"? [34]

Neither is there reason why men should ground their disbelief in the reality of baptism on the small results which they see it effect. The very principle of faith is to admit that which sense does not discern: "Blessed are they that have not seen, and yet have believed" [Jn. 20:29]. And it is hard to say how much of the inefficacy of baptism is due to the popular unbelief, which prevents men from doing justice to it. When children are not instructed in the nature of the gift which they have received, we cannot wonder if it be allowed to be inoperative. Its result might be very different if they were accustomed to expect those effects which St. Cyprian assures us resulted from his own baptism. He speaks of his former difficulties; and how powerless he felt to escape those evil habits, which adhered to his nature.

> But (he says) after that the stain of former sins being washed away through the water of the new birth, a light from above infused itself into my acquitted and purified bosom; and after that, through a spirit drawn from above, a new birth had made me a new man — what was doubtful began immediately in a wonderful manner to receive confirmation; what was shut to be opened; what was dark to be enlightened; what was impossible to be attainable.[35]

But with this disbelief in the reality of baptism is joined an unreasonable estimate of the results, which, if real, it might be expected to effect. For the gifts of grace do not in any case supersede the responsibility of mankind. Those who think most highly of baptism regard it only as the appointed means for that union with Christ, whereby men may obtain strength to serve him. Baptism neither exempts devout men from the necessity of a watchful life, nor careless men from the necessity of conversion. It is a reason why the watchfulness of the one should be more unvaried, and the conversion of the other, more complete. To receive gifts of grace is in itself no security against losing them. In Adam himself, the image of God did not preclude the possibility of disobedience. Much less can this be expected in his descendants, on whom the concupiscence of the will has been entailed by his failure. It is sometimes forgotten that baptism does not determine what *shall be* men's future

---

34. Hooker, *Ecclesiastical Polity*, Bk. V, chap. 60, 3 [*Works*, II, 267].
35. [ED.] Cyprian, *Epistle to Donatus*, 4 (*ANF*, V, 276; *CSEL*, III/1, 6).

state, but what *is* their present position. And herein lies the defect of all
hypothetical interpretations of the language used respecting this holy
ordinance. For their purpose is to transform that which is essentially an
assertion respecting a present fact into a supposition about the future. It
is asserted, for example, respecting every child who is received into the
Church after private baptism, "that this child *is by Baptism regenerate.*" [36]
As in such cases no sponsors have been employed, the validity of the
ordinance cannot be attributable, as has sometimes been imagined, to
their faith. The Church, of course, supposes it to result from that reality
of union with Christ's manhood whereby those who were heirs of Adam's
sinfulness become heirs of grace. But what signification is assigned to the
words by those who deny that baptism is the appointed channel of grace?
Some children, say the parties in question, are no doubt regenerated at
baptism; it may be so in any individual instance, and it is charitable to
affirm that which it is impossible to deny. And this, they observe, is the
course adopted by the Church respecting the departed, concerning whose
future condition, because unable to predict it, we express a charitable
hope. But to confound conjecture with assertion is to destroy the
whole meaning of speech. Things future, being from their nature uncertain to us, do not admit of a positive affirmation. And in the case of
such present things as we feel to be dubious, we cannot do more than
express a hope, leaving it to the result to clear up what is uncertain.
Since hope, then, is in its nature conversant with things which are future
or contingent, its expression is compatible with the highest degree of
uncertainty. In the most unpromising morning we may hope that the
sun will shine at noon. And respecting the departed, supposing them to
die in the Church's communion, we can hardly do less than declare them
our brethren, and express hope that they sleep in Jesus. And this, with
thanks for their deliverance from this world's miseries, is all that is expressed by our service. What countenance is there here for the positive
assertion of a present fact, concerning which we have no knowledge?
It is obvious what would be said respecting a man who asserted unequivocally that the sun was shining at present, and who afterwards
justified himself on the ground that he hoped it was, but possessed no
means of informing himself. And what else can be thought of those who
assert respecting every baptized child that "this child *is* regenerate,"
when they believe in their consciences that in all probability it is not?

But to leave the Church's language and come to the positive effect of

36. [ED.] Reception of Children after Private Baptism, B.C.P. (1662).

this system. It rests plainly on the notion that the benefits of baptism do not depend upon the present act, but on the future results which attend a devotion to God's service. These no doubt are many and great. They associate the party with Christians — they suggest such feelings as should attend an early dedication to God, and thus lead to those efforts on the part of man, which God's grace will doubtless meet with a proportionable blessing. But in all this there is one radical defect — the need of some predisposing grace on the part of God, whereby the first movement may be made towards holiness. For this the Church refers us to baptism. It considers this first gift of life to be derived from that union with Christ which he originally bestows. What was said to the disciples, not excluding the one on whom the gift was conferred ineffectually, is in baptism uttered to all Christians: "Ye have not chosen me, but I have chosen you" [Jn. 15:16]. The enslaved will of man was first restored to its perfect freedom in that great representative of our race, in whom the concupiscence which Adam entailed upon his descendants was counteracted by the full influx of God's Spirit. The first of Adam's progeny who possessed that perfect liberty in which our original parent was created was the second Adam, Jesus Christ. Now, it is only through union with our disenthralled representative that we also can escape bondage. "If the Son shall make you free, ye shall be free indeed" [Jn. 8:36]. Unless the beginnings of the spiritual life are laid in this antecedent gift of union with Christ, we pass over of necessity to the rationalistic principle which would attribute them to that natural relation of the soul to God, which it had by creation. A new birth, then, is needed as preliminary to the first actings of the will, because upon it depends our admission into "the glorious liberty of the children of God" [Rom. 8:21]. And, therefore, *regeneration* does not merely imply the second birth of every individual, as opposed to his primary birth by nature (though this doubtless is referred to); but it also points to that state of freedom in which man was originally created, but into which every heir of Adam's sin requires to be *readmitted*. This birth *back again* into the condition in which man was made when he was fashioned after God's likeness is not complete till his will has laid full hold on that freedom, into which he was admitted by God's grace. Therefore, the complete and general development of the Christian Covenant is described by our Lord as "the regeneration, when the Son of Man shall sit upon the throne of his glory" [Mt. 19:28]. For then shall the ancient state be again perfectly possessed by those who, "being made free from sin," have become "servants of righteousness" [Rom. 6:18]. But the beginning of this work in every individual must be through God's act, and not through the act of man, because its very object is to give man the power of acting, by the enfranchisement of the will from its hereditary bondage. And the act whereby God bestows this blessing is especially connected by St. Paul with that sacrament of baptism which our Lord himself appointed: "According to his mercy he saved us by the washing of regeneration and renewing of the Holy Ghost" [Tit. 3:5]. But such a preliminary act on the part of God is negatived when the real, objective influence of baptism is denied, and it is asserted not to be the appointed channel of grace. Hereby everything is thrown on man's part; and thus the Pelagian doctrine is in reality introduced, and man's salvation is made to depend originally upon his own exertions. This is not the meaning of many who deny that a new birth is conferred in baptism; their intention is to refer regeneration to the immediate act of God, and they exhort the young to ask and desire it. But on what are prayers and good desires to be built? To say that it is on natural goodness were Pelagianism. Yet if we are referred to God's grace, by what event except baptism are those who are born in sin entitled to it previously to the first actings of their understanding? What we are speaking of is the case of those who have not yet been able, by any act of their own, to take part in that which is necessary to their will's freedom. Yet what Christian parent but would associate prayers to God with the very first lispings of infant speech? Either men must be prepared, then, to adopt the Pelagian hypothesis, or their conduct to the young *assumes* the presence of that very gift which baptism has been appointed to convey. And the only alternative is such rigid adherence to the Calvinistic theory as, by declaring Christian education needless and impossible, would go counter to the instincts of nature and the word of God.

But it may be objected, are not the heathen exhorted to prayer, as a preliminary to baptism? They doubtless are; and in their case the appeal rests upon that universal presence of the Word, by which every man is in a measure enlightened. Unless there were some remnant of that original influence which the Word exercised over his creatures, no basis would exist for their first conversion.[37] But their prayers and efforts are not built upon that union with Christ which is the principle assumed in Christian education. To deal with Christians as heathen men should be dealt with is to shut our eyes to the freedom and fulness of the gospel;

37. [ED.] Cf. Wilberforce, *Doctrine of the Incarnation*, 134 f.

it is to treat the "joint-heirs with Christ" [Rom. 8:17] as though they were bondmen. The principle of Christian education is avowed in the Church Catechism, wherein every child is taught to declare at the outset that in baptism it was made "a member of Christ." And after praying for them that they "may ever *remain* in the number of" God's "elect children," [38] we teach every child to affirm that the Holy Ghost "sanctifieth me, and all the elect people of God." This principle is consistently carried out by the Church, for she limits the use of Christian burial to those children whose bodies have been consecrated in baptism by union with the body of Christ. And even those who have not had the advantage of her guidance proceed usually upon an analogous system. For their plan of education is professedly built on the plan of the gospel and on the expected succour of the Comforter. And yet how are men entitled to his help, save by virtue of the mediation of Christ? And what right have we to Christ's mediation unless we have been brought into the same relation to the new man, into which our birth brings us to the old one? It were contrary to the whole theory of the gospel, to assume the existence in man of Christian graces antecedently to their participating in the mediation of Christ. And yet that Christian principles are to be acted upon is the very foundation of the gospel scheme, seeing that it begins by assuming a belief, the practical effect whereof is afterwards to be developed. The existence, therefore, of an external and objective mean, whereby we may in the first instance be united to Christ, is the very basis of subsequent obedience. And this is why its denial is more plainly inconsistent with our ritual and Catechism than with the Articles, in which doctrines are abstractedly exhibited. For the evil to which it leads is a practical denial of the gospel — an undervaluing of that union with Christ our Lord which is consequent upon his Incarnation — an overestimate of human efforts — and such a tendency will conflict more plainly with those parts of our established formularies, in which our dependence upon Christ our Lord and our constant adherence to him are actually exhibited.

In respect to the Lord's Supper, it may be doubted whether the same amount of belief is entertained on all hands as in Hooker's days was universally prevalent.

> It is on all sides (he says) plainly confessed, first, that this sacrament is a true and a real participation of Christ, who thereby imparteth himself, even his whole entire person, *as a mystical head* unto every

38. [ED.] Order of Holy Baptism, B.C.P. (1662).

soul that receiveth him, and that every such receiver doth thereby incorporate or unite himself unto Christ as a *mystical member* of him; and secondly, that to whom the *person of Christ* is thus communicated, to them he giveth by the same sacrament his Holy Spirit to sanctify them, as it sanctifieth him, which is their Head.[39]

In these words the union with Christ's manhood by mystical participation is put forth as the leading characteristic of this holy ordinance. But since the time of Hoadly [40] a different system has become prevalent. The mere human side of this sacrament has been mainly thought of: it has been considered to be a sermon preached to the senses — an act whereby we commemorate the death of Christ, and testify our reverence for his memory. This account of its uses, to the exclusion of that deeper view, which is founded on the application of our Lord's Incarnation to the wants of men, and on the necessity of external grace, having been introduced by Socinian writers, has since found advocates in the Church. As baptism is explained away into the mere expression of a charitable expectation, so the Lord's Supper into a simple commemoration. How are we to decide whether this holy service is to be considered a divine rite or a human ordinance; whether it is the supernatural means, by which whole Christ gives himself to his people, or a mere accommodation to the taste for acted services? The letter of Scripture surely represents the eating and drinking of Christ's body and blood to be a mystical means of obtaining heavenly benefits. But those who question the apparent meaning of such passages of Scripture deny that the sixth chapter of St. John can refer to an ordinance which was instituted after the narrative which it records. It is not here affirmed that the spiritual communion of his members with our Lord's manhood is confined to that holy feast which is the signal and peculiar means of maintaining it; but if the participation of Christ in his Holy Supper be not at all referred to in the sixth chapter of St. John, then it is hard to see how Holy Scripture could be intended for the instruction of ordinary readers. For surely no simple persons, whose minds were not preoccupied by some theory, could ever read that chapter without the most palpable misconception. And how could St. John have delivered it to the Church, when the Holy Communion had been habitually celebrated for half a century, without taking care to guard it from such obvious misapprehension? But, in fact,

39. Hooker, *Ecclesiastical Polity*, Bk. V, chap. 67, 7 [*Works*, II, 354 f. (abbrev.)].

40. [ED.] Benjamin Hoadly's *Plain Account of the Nature and End of the Sacrament of the Lord's Supper* (1735) was perhaps the most notorious Anglican instance of a bare "memorialism" in eucharistic theology.

that this dialogue should have been prophetic of what was to come is so far from an objection that it is in exact consistency with other parts of our Lord's instruction. How much did it contain, which even "his disciples understood not at the first" [Jn. 12:16]? He spoke of being "lifted up from the earth" [Jn. 12:32] — he promised "living water" [Jn. 7:38] — he declared the necessity of taking up the cross and following him [Mt. 16:24]: in all these cases his prophetic words received their interpretation from the event. And the sixth chapter of St. John contains a direct assurance that its meaning would not be apparent till our Lord's ascension. "What and if ye shall see the Son of Man ascend up where he was before" [Jn. 6:62]? So that we have express authority for interpreting it by events which were to come. Hooker accordingly points out to us how exactly what the apostles had "learned before — that Christ's flesh and blood are the true cause of eternal life" [41] — was explained by our Lord's institution of the Holy Communion. And as this is the natural conclusion which would be adopted by untaught readers of Scripture, so is it supported by the unanimous testimony of early writers. "Both the Greek and Latin Fathers," says Bishop Poynet, "refer the words of our Lord in the sixth chapter of St. John with great unanimity to the sacrament of the Eucharist." [42] Our Church sanctions the same interpretation in her ritual — "then we eat the flesh of the Son of Man and drink his blood, then we dwell in Christ and Christ in us." [43] As Dr. Jackson expresses it:

> This present efficacy of Christ's body and blood upon our souls, or real communication of both, I find as a truth unquestionable amongst the ancient Fathers, and as a Catholic confession. They all agree that we are immediately cleansed and purified from our sins by the blood of Christ; that his human nature, by the inhabitation of the Deity, is made to us the inexhaustible fountain of life.[44]

One further argument for the reality of that union with the body of Christ which is bestowed in the Holy Eucharist is supplied by the circumstances under which its observance was commenced. On our Lord's ascension, his disciples returned to Jerusalem to wait for that gift of the Holy Ghost which was shortly to be dispensed. It had been declared to be the work of the Blessed Comforter to provide some new and closer

41. Hooker, *Ecclesiastical Polity*, Bk. V, chap. 67, 4 [*Works*, II, 351].
42. Po[y]net, *Diallacticon*, 15 [paraphrased].
43. Long Exhortation at Holy Communion, B.C.P. (1662) (slightly adapted).
44. Jackson, *Commentaries on the Creed*, Bk. X, chap. 55, 12 [*Works*, IX, 598, abbrev.].

means of union with that manhood of the Son which was to be withdrawn from mortal sense. By this means he who in appearance departed was in reality to be brought more near. The new Head of the renewed race, the second Adam of reformed humanity, was about to provide that principle of supernatural union whereby all his members were to be engrafted into himself. Now, it is through the Holy Communion that this connexion is especially maintained. Its great purpose is to bring the members of Christ into mystic union with their Head. Thereby does the manhood of Christ act upon his brethren. In this circumstance surely we have the reason why, during that first assemblage at Jerusalem, no mention is made of an observance, which so soon as the Holy Ghost had bestowed the fulness of his gifts, became the main act of Christian worship. "These all continued in one accord with prayer and supplication" [Acts 1:14]. But no sooner had the lifegiving medium been bestowed, than "they continued in *breaking of bread*, and in prayer" [Acts 2:42]. The Holy Communion, it seems, could not have effect till the pouring out of that quickening Spirit by which the members of Christ mystical are attached to their Head.

> The one Holy Catholic Church and Communion of Saints, did not begin to be *in esse* or bear true fruit, until the effusion of the Holy Ghost, which is the soul of the one Holy Catholic Church, or of the mystical body of Christ.[45]

But how different had it been if the Communion of Saints were only a figurative expression, and the Holy Communion a mere commemoration. When were the disciples more united by natural bonds than in this hour of their desertion? When were they more likely to commemorate their Lord than while his departure was so fresh? The Holy Eucharist cannot, therefore, have been a merely human rite; its force was not that it addressed their senses, and set forth what they had lost; it depended for its efficacy on that new gift of the Holy Ghost whereby Christ their Head came back to them with power; it was their perpetual means of union with his glorified humanity, their soul's food, the medium of the body's immortality.

It remains only to recall that which has been already stated as applicable to both the sacred ordinances which have been considered. The reality of both of them has been maintained: it has been affirmed that baptism is not merely the expression of a charitable hope; that the Lord's

45. Jackson, *Commentaries on the Creed*, Bk. IX, chap. 41, 4 [*Works*, VIII, 486, abbrev.].

Supper is not a bare act of pious recollection. The essential principle of each of them has been shown to be union with the perfect manhood of Christ our Lord. Let it be remembered only in conclusion, that to deny their reality is to assail the great principle of the mediation of Christ. For the doctrine of our Lord's mediation does not rest only on the divine power of Christ as a partaker in the nature of self-existent Godhead; it implies also that, by associating man's nature to his own, he has made created being the channel of his gifts. Now, as the media through which these gifts are dispensed to his brethren; as the ramifications, whereby his divine nature distributes itself on the right hand and the left, these two sacraments go together — their importance is equal — their effect alike — and to disparage them is to derogate from that principle of action which the wisdom of God has seen fitting to adopt. Every attempt to explain them away, every contrivance for extenuating the real import of what they effect, is a virtual detracting from the reality of that objective and actual influence which Christ the Mediator is pleased to exert. Its tendency is to resolve his actions into a metaphor, and his existence into a figure of speech. His specific and personal agency as the Eternal Son, who in the fulness of time conjoined himself to man's nature for the recovery of a fallen race, is merged in the general action of that ultimate Spirit, whom none but atheists professedly reject. For the real objection against the sacramental system does not arise from any deficiency in its scriptural authority, which has been shown to be ample, but from the abstract improbability that external ordinances can be the means of obtaining internal gifts. Now, this improbability rests on the circumstance that the *natural* mean of connexion with God is the intercourse of mind with mind, and consequently that the intercourse through sacraments is *supernatural*. The connexion with God, *i.e.*, which man received by creation, and which rationalism affirms to be sufficient for his wants, is more compatible with men's natural position than that new system of mediation which has been revealed in the gospel. But let the doctrine of mediation be admitted, and it ceases to be an argument against the sacramental system that it does not accord with that scheme of nature which the gospel professes to supersede. And the rationalistic argument against these means of grace is of equal avail against that whole scheme of mediation upon which they are dependent. If the natural intercourse of mind with the unembodied mind of the Creator supersedes the necessity of sacramental ordinances, does it not supersede equally the humanity of Christ? If man has still that immediate communion with God, of which Scripture affirms that the Fall deprived him, what need is there of a Mediator between them? Thus does the objection mount up from earth to heaven — from Christ feeding men below through sacraments to Christ mediating above by his atonement and intercession. For "if we have told you earthly things, and ye believe not, how shall ye believe if we tell you of heavenly things" [Jn. 3:12]? If the sacraments be thus emptied of their meaning, it is because the present actings of Christ as the Son of Man are not appreciated; and the purposes of his Incarnation are forgotten. And this forgetfulness again may be traced to unbelief in that real diversity of persons in the Blessed Trinity, in which all creaturely existence has its ultimate root. Thus does a practical Sabellianism respecting Christ's person coincide with that rationalistic theory by which the reality of his sacraments is disputed. And their surrender is fatal to the true doctrine concerning himself, even as the true doctrine of his nature sets the importance of these instruments in a proper light.

APPENDIX TO CHAPTER XIII:
WILBERFORCE'S *Doctrine of the Holy Eucharist*

Editor's introduction. Wilberforce followed up his *Doctrine of the Incarnation* with two sequels: *The Doctrine of Holy Baptism* (1849) and *The Doctrine of the Holy Eucharist* (1853). The last-named work both illustrates the evolution of his thought concerning the distinctive gift of the Eucharist and suggests the implications of his ideas for sacramental practice. Illustrative excerpts follow.

❖   ❖   ❖   ❖

Whether Christ is truly present or not in the Holy Eucharist; whether we are to behave as though he were really with us, and are truly responsible for a divine gift; and again, whether in that holy ordinance there is a real sacrifice — these are in great measure practical questions, on which it is possible to produce distinct evidence from Scripture and the primitive Church. But the manner in which Christ's presence is bestowed, whether it be by transubstantiation or according to any other law, is a point which did not come under consideration during the first eight centuries. On this subject therefore it will not be necessary to enter. But that Christ's presence in the Holy Eucharist is a real presence;

that the blessings of the new life are truly bestowed in it through communion with the New Adam; that consecration is a real act, whereby the inward part or thing signified is joined to the outward and visible sign; and that the Eucharistic oblation is a real sacrifice, these points it will be attempted to prove by the testimony of Scripture and of the ancient Fathers.[1]

It is obvious, . . . both from the practices of the first Christians, and from their doctrines, that they supposed consecration to be the essential characteristic of the Holy Eucharist. They considered the validity of the ordinance to turn upon the setting apart of the sacred elements; they supposed our Lord to speak not of bread and wine at large, but of *This,* which he held in his hands, and which his ministers after his example are to break and bless. They would not otherwise have supposed that it was necessary that a peculiar class of men should be set apart for the performance of this action, that it could not be effected without a special commission, and that on its validity depended the perpetuation of gospel blessings.

It will throw further light upon this subject if we compare the Holy Eucharist with that which in many respects possesses a corresponding character — the sacrament of baptism. Both of these ordinances were instituted by Christ himself; and both have an immediate connexion with those blessings which he bestows upon his mystical body. In both there is an inward grace and an outward sign. In both the union of form and matter is necessary to the completeness of that which is outward and visible. But in baptism the inward part consists only of the benefit bestowed, whereas in the Holy Eucharist, as our Catechism reminds us, the thing signified is distinct from the benefit by which it is attended. Baptism, that is, implies two parts only, the outward symbol and the inward gift; but the Holy Eucharist implies three — the outward sign, the inward part or thing signified, and the accompanying blessing. In baptism therefore the outward sign has no permanent relation to the inward grace, since the rite has no existence save in the act of administration; but in the Holy Eucharist the outward sign has something more than a momentary connexion with the thing signified. As respects baptism, therefore, our Lord used no words which imply that any particular portion of the element employed is invested with a specific character: it was not *this*

1. [ED.] R. I. Wilberforce, *The Doctrine of the Holy Eucharist* (London, 1885), 4 f.

water, but the element at large which was sanctified to be a pledge of the "mystical washing away of sin." And the Church has always acted upon this principle. It is orderly and decent that the water should be set apart with prayer, and that the ceremony should be performed by Christ's minister; but the absence of these conditions does not invalidate the act, either according to the belief of the ancient Church or according to the existing law of the Church of England. For the setting apart of the element confers only a relative holiness; it is not necessary to the validity of the sacrament; the inward grace is associated with the act, and not with the element; and does not require that the outward part should be brought into an abiding relation with any inward part or thing signified. And for the same reason, the intervention of the minister, however desirable, is not essential. A deacon, in the priest's absence, is as much authorized to baptize as a priest. No doubt it might have pleased God to assign the same limitations in the case of baptism which obtained in regard to the Holy Eucharist; but such limitations are not expressed in Scripture, nor has the thing been so understood by the Church. The priestly office, indeed, is essential to the validity of baptism, because without it there can exist no living branch of Christ's Church, into which new members may be engrafted; but its relation to this sacrament is general and not specific, because baptism depends upon an act which all Christians may perform, and not upon any consecration which requires a special commission.

Now the reverse of all these things is true of the Holy Eucharist. Here it is not the element at large which is spoken of, but *this bread,* and *this cup.* The intervention of the minister is not matter of decent ceremonial; it is essential to the validity of the ordinance. For valid baptism is that which is ministered to a competent receiver, but a valid Eucharist is that which is received, after consecration by an authorized priest. It is obvious, then, that consecration is the essential characteristic of this sacrament, since, but for it, the inward part and the outward part cannot be brought together. And this fact is testified by that law of our Church which renders the services of the priest indispensable in the celebration of the Holy Eucharist, as it was testified by the practice and assertions of antiquity.[2]

. . . When we speak of sacraments as moral instruments, we are merely discriminating between the order of grace and the order of nature; we

2. [ED.] *Ibid.,* 11–13.

affirm that sacraments pertain to the first, whereas those things which are called physical instruments belong to the second. For it has pleased God that the whole material creation should obey a certain set of laws, which are called the laws of nature. Every individual object, therefore, has its peculiar dimensions, bulk, and qualities; and by virtue of these does each act upon the others, in a certain uniform and appreciable course. The only exception would seem to be those responsible beings to whom their great Author has given that power of spontaneous action which renders them in this respect an image of himself. Hence it is that we are able to speak of the permanence of the laws of nature, and can calculate upon the regularity of their effects. And this we do without implying that they are independent of the will of God or can produce their effects without his co-operation.

But in sacraments the order followed is not that of nature, but a higher one, which is referable to the immediate interference of Almighty God. As a king might govern his dominions by unalterable laws, without laying down such general rules in his own family, so the gifts which the Most High bestows through sacraments in the household of faith are regulated by a different law from those which are bestowed in the king-dom of nature. In the last there is nothing which to our observation betrays his interference; he allows things to move on according to the invariable law of physical causation; but the means which are employed in the first derive their whole efficacy from his continual intervention. It is not meant, then, that sacraments are less certain in their effects than physical agents; nor yet that their *reality* depends upon those circum-stances in their receivers which are essential to their *utility*. But they are called moral instruments because they derive their validity from the immediate appointment of him, who acts in common according to that law which he has imposed upon the material creation; because they belong to the order of grace, and not to the order of nature.[3]

How is it possible that those who admit the reality of consecration should deny the efficacy of the elements? For is it not for this very purpose that they are set apart? With what intention can they be conse-crated, except that they should be effectual? Why is *this* especial portion separated from the element at large, except to be the medium of a bless-ing? What other conclusion can reason dictate; for why should they be subjected to this ordinance unless they are the recipients of its effect?

3. [ED.] *Ibid.*, 15 f.

And as this conclusion has the sanction of reason, so does the authority of all ages witness in its behalf. In this particular do the Fathers of the first centuries agree with the innovators of the last. The former ascribed efficacy to the elements because they believed the validity of consecration: the latter deny it, because the validity of consecration is the very conclusion from which they wish to escape. Both allow, then, that consecration and the efficacy of the elements must stand together. Neither is it possible to suppose that those who reject one can seriously intend to uphold the other. Those who deny that a gift is communicated through the elements cannot really believe the validity of consecration. They may be willing to retain the rite as a harmless tribute to ancient usage, but it is impossible that they should believe in the reality of consecration unless they believe in its results. If they are content to retain the pregnant expressions of the early Church, it is with the understanding that they mean nothing. Yet what a mockery is a priestly commission which confers no powers, and a form of consecration whereby nothing is made holy! If these things are real, their consequences should be admitted: if unreal, they had better be discarded. *Legem credendi lex statuat supplicandi.* But if a certain ritual was ordained by Christ, and handed down by his apostles, can it be indifferent whether or not it is observed? As it would be presumptuous to invent, so to abandon it would be impious. And yet either, perhaps, were less heinous guilt than to retain holy and sublime usages, pregnant with great truths and associated with the love and devotion of all saints, yet to regard them with the cold contempt with which men treat the unmeaning and obsolete fashions of a barbarous age.[4]

. . . It was the exclusion of the mass of men from the Christian sacrifice which made it necessary to substitute other offices, by which the daily Eucharist has been practically superseded. Now no circumstance has had more influence than this upon the belief of the people. We may trace to it the popular conviction, which no argument can efface, that congregations meet together merely for the quickening of their feelings, or for the imparting of instruction, and not that they may obtain their petitions. And thus the notion of the Church's *work,* as an actual operative transaction, is well-nigh lost.

The effect of such errors in diminishing men's practical sense of the mediation of Christ, it is impossible to overestimate. The *mediation* of Christ means that work which he effects through his human nature,

4. [ED.] *Ibid.,* 62 f.

because it is not the interference of any casual intercessor, but results from that position which he has vouchsafed to take between God and mankind. He is the sole Mediator between God and man because he only can stand midway between both. Let the efficacy, then, of his man's nature be forgotten, and his mediation is lost. Yet how does the efficacy of his man's nature display itself, save through those sacraments wherein he bestows himself as the sustenance of his people, and presents himself as their perpetual Intercessor with God? So that when the Holy Eucharist ceases to be regarded as a real action, wherein Christ's very presence is exhibited on earth, and whereby prayer is truly rendered available, men fall back upon some other system of approaching to God, and with a change in belief comes a change in the principle of worship. Thus do individual prayer, and private faith, and single piety take the place of that collective action whereby the whole Church was supposed in ancient days to offer itself to God; and are supposed not only to be necessary, which they are, to the Christian life, but to have right in themselves to acceptance. Whereas nothing has a claim to acceptance but the sacrifice of Christ; and the Church's claim is that she is his mystical body; and it is the oblation of the perfect Head which gives efficacy to that of the imperfect members.[5]

5. [ED.] *Ibid.*, 340 f.

EDWARD BOUVERIE PUSEY

The Presence of Christ in the Holy Eucharist
(SELECTION)

Editor's introduction. On October 16, 1852, Dr. Pusey — who, unlike certain less serious-minded Anglo-Catholics, held a high view of the preacher's responsibility in the sight of God and in the face of the congregation — was already wondering what to say on January 16, 1853, when his turn would come to appear in the university pulpit.

My last two sermons [he told Keble] have been on the Roman subject, "The Rule of Faith" and "The Unity of the Church." I had thought of preaching on the Unity of the Faith (which I touched upon in the sermon on the Rule of Faith) as a sort of Irenicon, following Le Blanc, Cassander, and the like, as showing approximations of doctrine where there seemed to be difference, real agreement in differing words. I have since thought whether there may not be reasons rather for taking one doctrine, the Holy Eucharist, with a practical application to young men, not to profane It when it is part of the College system to receive It. I preached before "The Holy Eucharist, a comfort to the penitent." This would be on danger to the impenitent. This would give it a practical character. The reasons are (1) the Bishop of Oxford has asked me to explain myself (my Letter which I began has stuck): (2) I am still under a slur, for my former condemnation, among a large party; while the University is committed to condemnation of these doctrines in the eyes of others: (3) I suspect that Roman doctrine is increasing on the one side, while there is a vague fear of any definite doctrine among others. . . . My line would be, as in my Letter and my sermon, to inculcate the doctrine of the Real Presence and to speak of the elements as remaining; as the obvious teaching of Holy Scripture and of the Fathers. . . . Will you, after a little time, tell me

368

what you think? There is no hurry. But I must write the sermon next term in Oxford, where I have books.[1]

Keble seems to have doubted the wisdom of Pusey's plan, but the latter set to work almost immediately, submitting "little fragments," as he wrote them, for Keble's criticism. The result was the sermon on "The Presence of Christ in the Holy Eucharist," in which the main lines of Pusey's eucharistic teaching were painstakingly sketched.

It differed from the earlier sermon on the Eucharist, as a careful statement of doctrine might differ from a devotional appeal. The doctrine enunciated was the same in both sermons; but the first was the language of unguarded fervour, the second that of precise definition on this side and on that. Thus the second sermon differs from the first in the distinctness with which it insists not only on the Reality of the Sacramental Presence resulting from consecration, but also it deals with the continued existence of the substance in those consecrated elements, which are the veils of our Lord's presence. This latter side of truth was as much present to Pusey's mind when he preached his first sermon as the fact of the Objective Presence itself: but he had then supposed that unfriendly critics would take this for granted, and he now put it forward as an explanation of his earlier language which, had opportunity been allowed, he should have given ten years before. The sermon abounds in passages of great beauty; it is penetrated through and through with Pusey's intense reality, and it closes with an appeal to the junior portion of his audience, based on the obligations of the sacramental life in Christ, which few who heard it can ever forget.[2]

We may find ourselves in disagreement with one aspect, at any rate, of Liddon's assessment, because it is hard to see that "precise definition" is a notable quality of this sermon. No doubt it is clear enough what Pusey is against — on the one hand, a reduction of the Eucharist to a piece of pictorial symbolism; on the other hand, any notion of the effects of consecration that would cast doubt on the continuing reality of the outward and visible signs. But even the reader who pursues the problem through the massive "concluding unscientific postscript" with which Pusey followed up his sermon [3] may well be at a loss to say what his positive teaching is, beyond the assertion that the glorious body and

1. H. P. Liddon, *Life of Edward Bouverie Pusey*, D.D., 4th ed. (London, 1894-98), III, 423 f.

2. *Ibid.*, 425

3. E. B. Pusey, *The Doctrine of the Real Presence, as Contained in the Fathers from the Death of S. John the Evangelist to the Fourth General Council, Vindicated, in Notes on a Sermon, "The Presence of Christ in the Holy Eucharist"* (London, 1855).

blood of Christ are somehow present beneath the substantial, tangible veils of bread and wine. In reality, however, this is just where Pusey intended to leave his hearers and readers. For more reasons than one, perhaps, but most obviously because he was determined to distinguish his own doctrine from "transubstantiation" — above all other Roman dogmas the *bête noire* of traditional Anglicanism — he carried his opposition to theological speculation to a climax in his treatment of the Eucharist. From his various statements it is not at all evident that he really understood either the dogma of the Fourth Lateran Council or what Thomas Aquinas had to say on the subject, but he insisted on construing both dogma and theology as an illegitimate attempt to account for the supernatural mystery of Christ's sacramental presence. Over against all such essays in "precise definition" he sought at once to affirm the truth of faith and to vindicate its mysterious character.

Granted, however, the terms on which he was prepared to discuss the mystery of the Eucharist, the austere Pusey, for all his habitual distrust of rhetorical effects, could rise to remarkable heights of eloquence on this beloved theme. Here Liddon's estimate is altogether accurate. No feature of the Christian dispensation moved Pusey more deeply than the sacrament of the altar. In it he saw God's tabernacle among men, the supreme event of Christian worship, the closest bond of union among believers in Christ. To it, moreover, he believed that the Catholic voice of Christendom bore glowing witness.

> Yes! along the whole course of time, throughout the whole circuit of the Christian world, from East and West, from North and South, there floated up to Christ our Lord one harmony of praise. Unbroken as yet, lived on the miracle of the Day of Pentecost, when the Holy Spirit from on high swept over the discordant strings of human tongues and thoughts, of hearts and creeds, and blended all their varying notes into one holy unison of truth. From Syria and Palestine and Armenia; from Asia Minor and Greece; from Thrace and Italy; from Gaul and Spain; from Africa Proper, and Egypt, and Arabia, and the Isles of the Sea; wherever any Apostle had taught, wherever any Martyr had sealed with his blood the testimony of Jesus; from the polished cities, or the Anchorites of the desert, one Eucharistic voice ascended: "Righteous art Thou, O Lord, and all Thy words are truth." Thou hast said, "This is My Body" "This is My Blood." Hast Thou said, and shalt not Thou do it? As Thou hast said, so we believe.[4]

❖   ❖   ❖   ❖

4. *Ibid.,* 721 f.

1 Cor. 10:16. The cup of blessing which we bless, is it not the communion of the blood of Christ? The bread which we break, is it not the communion of the body of Christ?

The Holy Eucharist is plainly the closest union of man with God. Through the Incarnation God took our nature, took the manhood into God. But although we had that unspeakable nearness to himself, in that the Coeternal Son, God *of* God and God *with* God, took not the nature of angels, but took the manhood into God, this was a gift to our whole race. It was a gift which, by its very nature, must overflow to us individually; yet still it required a further act of God's condescension fully to apply it to each one of us. God the Word became flesh. Yet hereby he was in his human nature one *with* us; we were not, as yet, made "one with him."

We belonged to him as his creatures. Unutterable was the love whereby, when man was fallen, he took part of all our miseries, except our sins and the sinfulness of our nature; and these which he could not take *to* himself, he took *on* himself: what *we* could not bear, he bare *for* us. But although we were thereby reconciled to God, as his creatures, we were not yet united to him individually. We could not be united to him, save by his communicating himself to us. This he willed to do by indwelling in us through his Spirit; by making us, through the sacrament of baptism, members of his Son; by giving us, through the Holy Eucharist, not in any carnal way, but really and spiritually, the flesh and blood of the Incarnate Son, whereby "he dwelleth in us, and we in him; he is one with us, and we with him." [1] Through these, he imparteth to us the life which he himself is. He, the Life of the world, maketh those alive in whom he is. This is the comfort of the pentitent, the joy of the faithful, the paradise of the holy, the heaven of those whose conversation is in heaven, the purity of those who long to be partakers of his holiness, the strengthening of man's heart, the renewal of the inward man, the fervour of divine love, spiritual peace, kindled hope, assured faith, burning thankfulness — that our Lord Jesus Christ, not in figure, but in reality, although a spiritual reality, does give himself to us, does come to be in us.

But nearness to God has also an awful aspect. "Our God is a consuming fire" [Heb. 12:29]. Your consciences, my younger brethren, can best tell you whether your souls are arrayed in the wedding garment which Christ gives, and which Christ requires in those who would approach to his heavenly feast, the wedding garment of faith and love unfeigned,

1. [ED.] Long Exhortation at Holy Communion, B.C.P. (1662) (adapted).

an upright and holy conversation, cleansed and made pure by the blood of Christ; or whether, "grieving the Spirit of God, whereby ye were sealed" [Eph. 4:30], and "not led by the Spirit of God" [Rom. 8:14], ye are now (God forbid that ye should remain so) "none of his" [Rom. 8:9]. I speak not now of the present, but of the past. Ye yourselves best know how far ye differ from that past. But no one at any time can have known in any great degree what were the habits of a large portion of the young in this place, or even the very outward fact, how, when man required it, almost all received the Holy Communion; how few, when God only called, and the young were left to their own consciences — none can have observed this without greatly fearing that if too few are present in the one case, too many are present in the other.

The Church requires as conditions: repentance, faith, charity, a loving memory of the passion of our Lord, and a steadfast purpose to lead a new life. This you are to ascertain for yourselves, by examining yourselves. God bids you by St. Paul [1 Cor. 11:28]; he exhorts you by the Church: "Search and examine your own consciences, and that not lightly and after the manner of dissemblers with God, but so that ye may come holy and clean to such a heavenly Feast." [2] Would that one were not compelled to think that many sought rather to forget themselves than to examine themselves; to hide themselves from themselves; to put away their sins for a day or two, in order to resume them as before; as though the wedding garment which God requires might be laid aside as soon as the feast was over; or as if this unwilling abstinence of a few days from some besetting sin were the clothing of "the new man, which after God is created in righteousness and true holiness" [Eph. 4:24].

I would then, once more, my younger brethren, set before you the doctrine of the Holy Eucharist on both sides. And this, both because some, looking for too much clearness in their intellectual conception of divine mysteries, are tempted to undue speculation in defining the mode of the sacred presence of our Lord; and others, practically, can hardly be thought to believe any real presence at all; else they would not approach, as they do, so unrepenting and so careless.

[Pusey here supplies several examples of excessive precision in theological explanation.]

And so, as to the Holy Eucharist, men *can* conceive that the elements after consecration are only what they seem and what they were before,

2. [ED.] First Long Exhortation, appointed for giving notice of Holy Communion, B.C.P. (1662).

not the vehicle of an Unseen Presence; or, again, they *can* imagine that they are nothing but an outward show, and that the body of Christ alone is present; they can forget either the Unseen Presence or the visible form, but they have difficulty in receiving the thought which the Church of England suggests in her words: "Of the due receiving of the blessed body and blood of our Saviour Christ *under* the form of bread and wine"; [3] that the sacramental bread and wine "remain still in their very natural substances"; [4] and yet that under these poor outward forms, "his creatures of bread and wine," [5] "the faithful verily and indeed take and receive the Body and Blood of Christ." [6]

And yet Holy Scripture, taken in its plainest meaning, affirms both that the outward elements remain, and still that there is the real presence of the Body of Christ. And I may, in the outset, say, that when the Articles reject transubstantiation, they themselves explain what they mean to reject — a doctrine which "is repugnant to the plain words of Holy Scripture," [7] *i.e.*, those words in which our Lord and St. Paul speak of the natural substances as remaining. The Articles call it also "a doctrine which overthroweth the nature of a Sacrament," in that the outward and visible part is supposed to have no real subsistence. They except against no statement which does not imply that the natural substances cease to be.

[Pusey explains further that he does not mean to substitute "consubstantiation" — an idea, he notes, incorrectly ascribed to Lutherans — for "transubstantiation."]

To receive literally, then, those words of our Lord, "This is my body" [1 Cor. 11:24], does not necessarily imply any absence, or cessation, or annihilation of the substance of the outward elements. In taking them literally, we are bound to take equally in their plain sense his other words, in which he calls what he had just consecrated to be sacramentally his blood, "this fruit of the vine" [Mt. 26:29]; or, again, those other words of Holy Scripture: "the bread which we break" [1 Cor. 10:16]; "as often as ye eat this bread" [1 Cor. 11:26]; "whosoever shall eat this bread"

3. [ED.] From a note at the end of the *First Book of Homilies* (*Certain Sermons or Homilies Appointed to Be Read in Churches* [London, 1864], 155). *Cf.* E. B. Pusey, *The Real Presence of the Body and Blood of Our Lord Jesus Christ the Doctrine of the English Church* (Oxford, 1857), 4–159.

4. [ED.] Declaration on Kneeling ("Black Rubric"), Communion Service, B.C.P. (1662).

5. [ED.] Prayer of Consecration, Communion Service, B.C.P. (1662).

6. [ED.] Catechism, B.C.P. (1662).   7. [ED.] Article XXVIII.

[1 Cor. 11:27]; "so let him eat that bread" [1 Cor. 11:28]; "we are all partakers of that one bread" [1 Cor. 10:17]. Our Blessed Lord, through those words, "This is my body," teaches us that which it concerns us to know, his own precious gift, the means of union and incorporation with himself, whereby he hallows us, nourishes our souls to life everlasting, re-forms our nature and conforms it to his own; re-creates us to newness of life; binds and cements us to himself as man; washes, beautifies, kindles our minds, strengthens our hearts; is a source of life within us, joining us to himself our Life, and giving us the victory over sin and death. Yet he did not deny what himself and Holy Scripture elsewhere seem in equally plain language to affirm.

[Pusey observes that Scripture very frequently speaks to the point immediately at issue, with no concern for systematic completeness. Almost every heresy has arisen from a failure to understand this. The words, "This is my body," do not contain all of Christ's teaching on the Eucharist.]

The presence of which our Lord speaks has been termed sacramental, supernatural, mystical, ineffable, as opposed *not* to what is real, but to what is natural. The word has been chosen to express, not our knowledge, but our ignorance; or that unknowing knowledge of faith, which we have of things divine, surpassing knowledge. We know not the manner of his presence, save that it is not according to the natural presence of our Lord's human flesh, which is at the right hand of God; and therefore it is called sacramental. But it is a presence without us, not within us only; a presence by virtue of our Lord's words, although to us it becomes a saving presence, received to our salvation, through our faith. It is not a presence simply in the soul of the receiver, as "Christ dwells in our hearts by faith" [Eph. 3:17]; or as, in acts of spiritual, apart from sacramental, communion, we, by our longings, invite him into our souls. But while the consecrated elements, as we believe (because our Lord and God the Holy Ghost in Holy Scripture call them still after consecration by the names of their natural substances, and do not say that they cease to be such) — while the consecrated elements remain in their natural substances, still, since our Lord says, "This is my body," "This is my blood," the Church of England believes that "under the form of bread and wine," so consecrated, we "receive the body and blood of our Saviour Christ." [8] And since we receive them, they must be there, in order that we may receive them. We need not then (as the school of

8. [ED.] *Cf.* p. 373, n. 3, above.

Calvin bids men) "ascend into heaven, to bring down Christ from above" [Rom. 10:6]. For he is truly present, for us truly to receive him to the salvation of our souls, if they be prepared by repentance, faith, love, through the cleansing of his Spirit, for his coming.

[Pusey compares the Eucharist with other unfathomable mysteries — the Virgin Birth and Resurrection of Christ.]

This acknowledgment of our ignorance is a refuge from our perplexity about the things of God. We acknowledge, since Scripture saith it, that the natural substance remains. "What was bread remains bread; and what was wine remains wine." [9] But faith regards not things visible, only or chiefly; as it regarded not the outward dress of our Lord, save when it touched the hem of his garment, and virtue went out of him, and healed those who touched in faith (Mt. 9:20–22; 14:36). Yea rather, faith forgets things outward in his unseen presence. What is precious to the soul is its Redeemer's presence, and its union with him. It acknowledges, yet is not anxious about, the presence of the visible symbols. It pierces beyond the veil. It sees him who is invisible, and receives him in the ruined mansion of the soul; and by him is strengthened; in him has peace; in his presence has the pledge of forgiveness and of everlasting union with its Lord and its God. It owns as a truth of fact, and as taught in God's word, the presence of the outward symbols. Its joy, the contentment of its longings, its hope, its strength, its stay, its peace, its life, is the presence of its Lord.

[Pusey continues his argument with frequent appeals to Scripture and the Fathers. He concludes with an address to the undergraduate members of his congregation, beginning and ending as follows.]

Christ redeems us not, my younger brethren, to part with us. He cometh not to us, to part from us; he cometh to abide with us, if we will have him. He will come to us in holiness, righteousness, sanctification, redemption, if we will long for him — if in faith and charity we will receive him. He will cleanse your dross, slake your feverishness, chase away foul thoughts, re-create your decay, drive off Satan, gather you up into himself. He will strengthen you against temptation, lift you up above those miserable, maddening, seducing pleasures of sense, and give you a foretaste of heavenly sweetness, of blissful calm, of spiritual joy, of transporting love, of unearthly delight, in his own ever-blessed, ever-blessing presence. . . .

Wait but a little, pray your Redeemer for endurance, and all ye long

9. [ED.] J. H. Newman, *Parochial and Plain Sermons*, IV (London, 1908–18), 147.

for ye shall have, not against the will of God, but from his love and the fulness of his good pleasure. Then for these feverish pleasures, ye shall be filled and overflowed with the torrent of his pleasure; then, for maddening joys, ye shall enter into, be immersed in, the joy of your own Lord. Then shall your soul be irradiated with the light of divine wisdom, your mind be enlightened with divine knowledge, your body be clothed with the glory of God, wherewith ye shall be encompassed. Then shall ye gaze unceasingly on beauty which eye hath not seen — the face of God. The brightness of his glory, and the infinity of his love, and the unchangeableness of his joy, and the hidden treasures of his knowledge, and his incomprehensible essence, shall be in your measure apprehended by you. Then shall all truth be open to you, all love shall fill you; soul and body shall be satisfied with his likeness; they shall rest in his love; they shall have all they long for, and long for all they have. All you long for shall be forever yours; for the All-Holy Trinity shall be forever yours; the glorified humanity of your Lord shall be forever yours; and meanwhile, if you pray him to cleanse his dwelling place, your soul, he will cleanse it. He will empty it of what is not his; he will fill it with what is his; he will fill it with his grace, fill you with himself, the Author of grace, as he saith: "If a man love me, he will keep my saying, and my Father will love him, and we will come unto him, and make our abode in him" [Jn. 14:23]. Amen.

III

JOHN KEBLE

On Eucharistical Adoration
(SELECTION)

Editor's introduction.

> O God of Mercy, God of Might,
> How should pale sinners bear the sight,
> If, as Thy power is surely here,
> Thine open glory should appear?
>
> For now Thy people are allow'd
> To scale the mount and pierce the cloud,
> And Faith may feed her eager view
> With wonders Sinai never knew.
>
> Fresh from th' atoning sacrifice
> The world's Creator bleeding lies,
> That man, His foe, by whom He bled,
> May take Him for his daily bread.
>
> O agony of wavering thought
> When sinners first so near are brought!
> "It is my Maker — dare I stay?
> My Saviour — dare I turn away?"

* * *

> Sweet awful hour! the only sound
> One gentle footstep gliding round,
> Offering by turns on Jesus' part
> The Cross to every hand and heart.

Refresh us, Lord, to hold it fast;
And when Thy veil is drawn at last,
Let us depart where shadows cease,
With words of blessing and of peace.[1]

It seems a far cry from this word-picture of Christian souls in communion with their crucified Saviour to the often rather shabby sacramental controversies of the mid-nineteenth century, and in fact its author was no eager combatant in the warfare that raged over the holy ground of the eucharistic mystery. Nonetheless, when the doctrine of Christ's real presence in the sacramental gifts was challenged by men in high places in the Church, he felt it his duty to speak out — and, just as he had spoken once before with notable effect, he spoke out now. As it happened, two challenges came close together, and Keble had a word to say in response to each of them. When Archdeacon Denison was condemned, he wrote *On Eucharistical Adoration;* when Bishop Forbes was attacked, he addressed *Considerations suggested by a Late Pastoral Letter on the Doctrine of the Most Holy Eucharist* to the Scottish Episcopal clergy.[2]

The Denison case, which directly concerns us here, began in 1853, when George Anthony Denison, Archdeacon of Taunton, preached the first of three sermons on the Eucharist in Wells Cathedral. As examining chaplain to the Bishop of Bath and Wells, he had earlier rejected several candidates for ordination because of their views on baptismal regeneration, and a number of Evangelicals, not content with their judicial victory in the Gorham controversy, promptly seized what looked like a golden opportunity for revenge on another opponent. Denison, it was alleged, had taught:

> That the Body and Blood of Christ being really present after an immaterial and spiritual manner in the consecrated bread and wine, are therein and thereby given to all, and are received by all who come to the Lord's Table — that to all who come to the Lord's Table, to those who eat and drink worthily, and to those who eat and drink unworthily, the Body and Blood of Christ are given, and that by all who come to the Lord's Table, by those who eat and drink worthily, and by those who eat and drink unworthily, the

1. John Keble, "Holy Communion," in *The Christian Year* (*The Christian Year, Lyra Innocentium, and Other Poems* [London, 1914], 186–88).

2. Both works are contained in J. Keble, *On Eucharistical Adoration, with Considerations suggested by a Late Pastoral Letter (1858) on the Doctrine of the Most Holy Eucharist,* 3d ed. (Oxford, 1867). On the Denison case, *cf.* H. P. Liddon, *Life of Edward Bouverie Pusey, D.D.,* 4th ed. (London, 1894–98), III, 427–48; and on the Forbes case, *cf. ibid.,* 448–59.

Body and Blood of Christ are received — that the universal reception of the inward part or thing signified of the Sacrament in and by the outward sign, is a part of the doctrine of the Real Presence itself — that worship is due to the real, though invisible and supernatural, presence of the Body and Blood of Christ in the Holy Eucharist under the form of bread and wine — that the act of Consecration makes the Bread and Wine, through the operation of the Holy Ghost, to be Christ's Body and Blood — that in the Lord's Supper the outward parts or signs and the inward parts or things signified are so joined together by the act of Consecration, that to receive the one is to receive the other — that all who receive the Sacrament of the Lord's Supper receive the Body and Blood of Christ.[3]

Given the climate of opinion in the Church at large, these were likely to prove damaging charges, if only they could be verified.

In the end Denison escaped, but only by a legal technicality, and not before he had been condemned by a court presided over by the Archbishop of Canterbury, John Bird Sumner — the first Evangelical to become Primate of All England. Under the circumstances, the Tractarian party could hardly refrain from bearing witness to their cherished convictions. Keble's characteristic contribution to the joint effort was, of course, his *On Eucharistical Adoration, or, The Worship of Our Lord and Saviour in the Sacrament of Holy Communion*, first published in 1857.

❖ ❖ ❖ ❖

CHAPTER I:
PROMPTINGS OF NATURAL PIETY

1. The object of this essay is to allay, and, if possible, to quiet, the troublesome thoughts which may at times, and now especially, occur to men's minds on this awful subject, so as even to disturb them in the highest act of devotion. For this purpose it may be well to consider calmly, not without deep reverence of heart: First, what natural piety would suggest; secondly, what Holy Scripture may appear to sanction; thirdly, what the Fathers and liturgies indicate to have been the practice of the primitive Church; fourthly, what the Church of England enjoins or recommends.

2. For the first: is it not self-evident that, had there been no abuse,

3. *Ibid.*, 430.

or error, or extravagance connected with the practice, all persons believing and considering the real presence of our Lord in Holy Communion, in whatever manner or degree, would in the same manner or
degree find it impossible not to use special worship? — the inward worship, I mean, and adoration of the heart: for that, of course, is the main
point in question; the posture and more are secondary and variable, and
may and must admit of dispensation.

The simple circumstance of our Lord Christ declaring himself especially present would, one would think, be enough for this. Why do we
bow our knees and pray, on first entering the Lord's house? Why do we
feel that during all our continuance there we should be, as it were,
prostrating our hearts before him? Why is it well to breathe a short
prayer when we begin reading our Bibles, and still as we read to recollect
ourselves, and try to go on in the spirit of prayer? And so of other holy
exercises: in proportion as they bring with them the sense of his peculiar
presence, what can the believer do but adore? I firmly believe that all
good Christians do so, in the Holy Sacrament most especially, whatever
embarrassment many of them may unhappily have been taught to feel
touching the precise mode of their adoration.

And this may well be one of the greatest consolations in the sad controversies and misunderstandings among which our lot is cast. It is as
impossible for devout faith, contemplating Christ in this sacrament, not
to adore him, as it is for a loving mother, looking earnestly at her child,
not to love it. The mother's consciousness of her love, and her outward
manifestation of it, may vary; scruples, interruptions, bewilderments may
occur; but there it is in her heart, you cannot suppress it. So must there
be special adoration and worship in the heart of everyone seriously
believing a special, mysterious presence of Christ, God and man, expressed by the words, *This is my body*.

3. I say a *special* adoration and worship, over and above what a religious man feels upon every occasion which helps him to realize, what
he always believes, that God is "about his path, and about his bed, and
spieth out all his ways" [Ps. 139:2, B.C.P.]; that in him he "lives, and
moves, and has his being" [Acts 17:28]. And this for very many mysterious and overpowering reasons. I will specify three, the most undeniable and irresistible. First, the *greatness* of the benefit offered; next,
its being offered and brought home to each one *personally* and *individually;* thirdly, the deep *condescension* and *humiliation* on the part of him
who offers the benefit.

[Keble gives a number of Old Testament illustrations of response to the greatness of a gift.]

5. So, and much more, in the Christian Church. If we kneel, and bow the knees of our hearts, to receive a blessing in the Name of the Most High from his earthly representatives, father, priest, or bishop, how should we do other than adore and fall prostrate, inwardly at least, when the Son of Man gives his own appointed token that he is descending to bless us in his own mysterious way? And with what a blessing! — "the remission of our sins, and all other benefits of his passion"! [1] His flesh, which is meat indeed, and his blood, which is drink indeed [Jn. 6:55]! mutual indwelling between him and us; we living by him, as he by the Father [Jn. 6:57]! Surely these are gifts, at the very hearing of which, were an angel to come and tell us of them for the first time, we could not choose but fall down and worship. And now it is no angel, but the Lord of the angels, incarnate, coming not only to promise, but actually to exhibit and confer them.

6. Further, the Eucharist is our Saviour coming with these unutterable mysteries of blessing, coming with his glorified humanity, coming by a peculiar presence of his own divine person, *to impart himself to each one of us separately*, to impart himself as truly and as entirely as if there were not in the world any but that one to receive him. And this also, namely, the bringing home of God's gifts to the particular individual person, has ever been felt by that person, in proportion to his faith, as a thrilling call for the most unreserved surrender that he could make of himself, his whole spirit, soul, and body: *i.e.*, of the most unreserved worship.

[Keble again illustrates his point with Biblical examples.]

9. Thus it would appear that God's holy word from beginning to end abounds in examples to sanction those natural instincts of the devout and loving heart, which prompt to deeper and more intense adoration, in proportion to the greatness of the gift, and the directness with which it comes straight to the receiver from Almighty God.

Now the gift in the Holy Eucharist is Christ himself — all good gifts in one; and that in an immense, inconceivable degree. And how can we conceive even Power Almighty to bring it more closely and more directly home to each one of us, than when his Word commands and his Spirit enables us to receive him as it were spiritual meat and drink? entering into and penetrating thoroughly the whole being of the renewed man, somewhat in the same way as the virtue of wholesome meat and drink

1. [ED.] Prayer of Oblation, Communion Service, B.C.P. (1662).

diffuses itself through a healthful body: only, as we all know, with this
great difference (among others) — that earthly meat and drink is taken
up and changed into parts of our earthly frame, whereas the work of
this heavenly nourishment is to transform our being into itself; to change
us after his image, "from glory to glory" [2 Cor. 3:18], from the fainter
to the more perfect brightness; until "our sinful bodies be made clean
by his body, and our souls washed through his most precious blood; and
we dwell evermore in him, and he in us": [2] "we in him," as members
of "his mystical body, which is the blessed company of all faithful
people"; [3] "he in us," by a real and unspeakable union with his divine
person, vouchsafed to us through a real and entirely spiritual participation of that flesh and blood which he took of our father Adam through
the Blessed Virgin Mary; wherewith he suffered on the cross, wherewith
he now also appears day and night before his Father in heaven for us.
So that a holy man of our own Church was not afraid thus to write of
this sacrament:

> By the way of nourishment and strength
>   Thou creep'st into my breast,
>   Making thy way my rest,
> And thy small quantities my length,
> Which spread their forces into every part,
>   Meeting sin's force and art.

* * *

> Thy grace, which with these elements comes,
>   Knoweth the ready way,
>   And hath the privy key,
> Opening the soul's most subtle rooms.[4]

10. The sum is this. Renewed nature prompts the Christian, and Holy
Scripture from beginning to end encourages him, to use special adoration to Almighty God at the receiving of any special gift — adoration
the more earnest and intense as the gift is greater, and the appropriation
of it to the worshipper himself more entire and direct. So it is with all
lesser, all partial gifts; how then should it not be so when we come to
the very crown and fountain of all, that which comprehends all the rest
in their highest possible excellency, and which is bestowed on each re-

---

2. [ED.] Prayer of Humble Access, Communion Service, B.C.P. (1662).
3. [ED.] Prayer of Thanksgiving, Communion Service, B.C.P. (1662).
4. [ED.] George Herbert, "The H: Communion" (F. E. Hutchinson, ed., *The Works of George Herbert* [Oxford, 1941], 52).

ceiver by way of most unspeakable participation and union — that gift
which is God himself, as well as having God for its Giver? "Christ in us,"
not only Christ offered for us; a "divine nature" set before us, of which
we are to be made "partakers" [2 Pet. 1:4]. Must we cease adoring, when
he comes not only as the Giver, but as the Gift; not only as the Priest,
but as the Victim; not only as "the Master of the Feast," but as "the Feast
itself"? [5] Nay, but rather this very circumstance is a reason beyond all
reasons for more direct and intense devotion.

5. Jeremy Taylor, *Holy Living*, sec. IV, x [add. sec. 10: *the petition; Works*
(London, 1822), IV, 310].

A Select Bibliography

PRIMARY SOURCES

COLLECTIONS AND ANTHOLOGIES

Tracts for the Times, by Members of the University of Oxford (London, 1834–41). 6 vols.

CHADWICK, O., ed., *The Mind of the Oxford Movement* (London, 1960). A broad selection of short passages, with an excellent introduction.

HUTCHINSON, W. G., ed., *The Oxford Movement: being a Selection from Tracts for the Times* (London, 1906).

BRICKNELL, W. S., ed., *The Judgment of the Bishops upon Tractarian Theology* (Oxford, 1845). A classified collection of critical comments from episcopal charges.

INDIVIDUAL WORKS

ARNOLD, THOMAS, *Principles of Church Reform* (London, 1962) An historic statement of the ecclesiastical "liberalism" which the Oxford Movement opposed.

CHURCH, R. W., *The Oxford Movement: Twelve Years, 1833–1845*, 3d ed. (London, 1892). A fine piece of historical writing and the great firsthand account of the Oxford Movement.

FORBES, A. P., *A Primary Charge delivered to the Clergy of his Diocese at the Annual Synod* (London, 1857). An important statement on the Eucharist, by the greatest of Scottish Tractarians.

———, *An Explanation of the Thirty-Nine Articles* (Oxford, 1867).

R. H. FROUDE

Remains of the late Reverend Richard Hurrell Froude, 4 vols. (London-Derby, 1838–39).

HAMPDEN, R. D., *The Scholastic Philosophy considered in its Relation to Christian Theology*, 3d ed. (Hereford, 1848). The fullest statement of the theological "liberalism" attacked by the Tractarians.

J. H. HOBART

HOBART, J. H., *An Apology for Apostolic Order and its Advocates* (New York, 1807). A characteristic work by the most important living link between the older American High Churchmanship and the Oxford Movement.

The Posthumous Works of J. H. Hobart; with his Life by W. Berrian (New York, 1833). 3 vols.

JOHN KEBLE

KEBLE, JOHN, *The Christian Year, Lyra Innocentium, and Other Poems* London, 1914).

———, *Sermons, Academical and Occasional*, 2d ed. (Oxford, 1848).

———, *On Eucharistical Adoration* (Oxford, 1857).

MAURICE, F. D., *The Kingdom of Christ* (London, 1958). 2 vols. The major work (first published in 1838) of one of the Tractarians' greatest contemporaries.

———, *Reasons for Not Joining a Party in the Church* (London, 1841).

J. B. MOZLEY

Letters of the Rev. J. B. Mozley, D.D. (London, 1885). Contains interesting observations on the Oxford Movement by a distinguished and sympathetic contemporary.

MOZLEY, J. B., *The Baptismal Controversy*, 2d ed. (London, 1883).

J. H. NEWMAN

NEWMAN, J. H., *Works* (London, 1874–1921). 40 vols. The comprehensive collection of Newman's published writings. Earlier editions of the major Anglican works are listed below.

———, *Parochial and Plain Sermons* (London, 1868). 8 vols.

———, *Lectures on the Prophetical Office of the Church* (London, 1837).

———, *Lectures on Justification* (London, 1838).

———, *Apologia pro vita sua* (Garden City, N.Y., 1956). An important source for the general history of the Movement.

BARMANN, L. F., ed., *Newman at St. Mary's: A Selection of the Parochial and Plain Sermons* (Westminster, Md., 1962).

DESSAIN, C. S., ed., *The Letters and Diaries of John Henry Newman* (Edinburgh, 1961–   ). Vols. XI–XII the first to be published.

MOZLEY, ANNE, ed., *Letters and Correspondence of John Henry Newman during His Life in the English Church* (New York, 1911). 2 vols.

TRISTRAM, H., ed., *John Henry Newman: Autobiographical Writings* (New York, 1957).

PALMER, W., *A Narrative of Events connected with the Publication of the Tracts for the Times*, 2d ed. (London, 1883). An important account by a High Churchman closely associated with (though often critical of) the early Tractarians.

E. B. PUSEY

PUSEY, E. B., *Nine Sermons, preached before the University of Oxford, and printed chiefly between A.D. 1843–1855, now collected into One Volume* (Oxford, 1879).

———, *Sermons preached before the University of Oxford between A.D. 1859 and 1872* (London, 1872).

JOHNSTON, J. O., and NEWBOLT, W. C. E., eds., *Spiritual Letters of Edward Bouverie Pusey* (London, 1898).

LIDDON, H. P., *Life of Edward Bouverie Pusey, D.D.*, 4th ed. (London, 1894–98). 4 vols. An important primary source for the general history of the Movement. Contains full list of Pusey's published works (Vol. IV, 396–446).

WARD, W. G., *The Ideal of a Christian Church* (London, 1844).

WILBERFORCE, R. I., *The Doctrine of the Incarnation of our Lord Jesus Christ* (London, 1848).

———, *The Doctrine of Holy Baptism* (London, 1849).

———, *The Doctrine of the Holy Eucharist* (London, 1853).

———, *An Inquiry into the Principles of Church Authority, or Reasons for Recalling my Subscription to the Royal Supremacy* (London, 1854).

ISAAC WILLIAMS

PREVOST, G., ed., *The Autobiography of Isaac Williams* (London, 1892).

SECONDARY AUTHORITIES

REFERENCE WORKS

The Cambridge Bibliography of English Literature (Cambridge, 1940), III, 854–60.

Dictionary of National Biography (London, 1885–1900), 63 vols.; Supplement (London, 1901), 3 vols.

CROSS, F. L., ed., *The Oxford Dictionary of the Christian Church* (London, 1957).

OLLARD, S. L., CROSSE, G., and BOND, M. F., eds., *Dictionary of English Church History*, 3d ed. (London, 1948).

GENERAL SURVEYS AND INTERPRETATIONS

BRILIOTH, Y., *The Anglican Revival: Studies in the Oxford Movement* (London, 1925). Easily the best comprehensive study of Tractarian theology.

————, *Three Lectures on Evangelicalism and the Oxford Movement* (London, 1934).

BROSE, O. J., *Church and Parliament: The Reshaping of the Church of England 1828–1860* (Stanford, Calif., 1959).

CLARKE, C. P. S., *The Oxford Movement and After* (London, 1932).

CROSS, F. L., *The Oxford Movement and the Seventeenth Century* (London, 1933).

DAWSON, C., *The Spirit of the Oxford Movement* (London, 1933). A discerning study by a Roman Catholic historian.

DE MILLE, G. E., *The Catholic Movement in the American Episcopal Church*, 2d ed. (Philadelphia, 1950).

FABER, G., *Oxford Apostles: A Character Study of the Oxford Movement*, 2d ed. (London, 1936). Sprightly and tendentious.

FAIRBAIRN, A. M., *Catholicism, Anglican and Roman*, 5th ed. (London, 1903). Provocative reflections of a liberal Congregationalist.

FROUDE, J. A., "The Oxford Counter-Reformation," in *Short Studies on Great Subjects* (London, 1890), IV, 231–360.

HARDY, E. R., JR., "The Catholic Revival in the American Church, 1722–1933," in Williams, N. P., and Harris, C., eds., *Northern Catholicism* (London, 1933), 75–116. Clear, concise, and well documented.

KNOX, E. A., *The Tractarian Movement, 1833–1845*, 2d ed. (London, 1934).

MACKEAN, W. H., *The Eucharistic Doctrine of the Oxford Movement: A Critical Survey* (London, 1933).

OLLARD, S. L., *The Anglo-Catholic Revival: Some Persons and Principles* (London, 1925).

————, *A Short History of the Oxford Movement*, 3d ed. (London, 1963). An accurate, compact account of the Oxford Movement and later Anglo-Catholicism.

OVERTON, J. H., *The Anglican Revival* (London, 1897).

PERRY, W., *The Oxford Movement in Scotland* (London, 1933).

STEWART, H. L., *A Century of Anglo-Catholicism* (London, 1929). An instructive study by a Canadian philosopher.

STORR, V. F., *The Development of English Theology in the Nineteenth Century, 1800–1860* (London, 1913).

VOLL, D., *Catholic Evangelicalism: The Acceptance of Evangelical Traditions by the Oxford Movement during the Second Half of the Nineteenth Century* (London, 1963).

WALSH, W., *The Secret History of the Oxford Movement*, 5th ed. (London, 1899). The classic interpretation of the Oxford Movement as a "popish plot."

WARRE CORNISH, F., *The English Church in the Nineteenth Century* (London, 1910). 2 vols.

WEBB, C. C. J., *Religious Thought in the Oxford Movement* (London, 1928).

WILLEY, B., "Newman and the Oxford Movement," in *Nineteenth Century Studies: Coleridge to Matthew Arnold* (London, 1949), 73–101.

WILLIAMS, N. P., and HARRIS, C., eds., *Northern Catholicism: Centenary Studies in the Oxford and Parallel Movements* (London, 1933). A valuable symposium, despite the dubious theory expressed in its title.

WOODWARD, E. L., *The Age of Reform, 1815–1870* (Oxford, 1938).

SPECIAL TOPICS

WORSHIP

DAVIES, H., *Worship and Theology in England*. Vol. III: *From Watts and Wesley to Maurice, 1690–1850* (Princeton, 1961); Vol. IV: *From Newman to Martineau, 1850–1900* (Princeton, 1962). A mine of information, with perceptive accounts of Anglo-Catholic developments.

GASELEE, S., "The Aesthetic Side of the Oxford Movement," in Williams, N. P., and Harris, C., eds., *Northern Catholicism* (London, 1933), 423–45.

WHITE, J. F., *The Cambridge Movement: The Ecclesiologists and the Gothic Revival* (Cambridge, 1962). A lively study of the theory and practice of early "ritualism."

RELIGIOUS ORDERS

ALLCHIN, A. M., *The Silent Rebellion: Anglican Religious Communities, 1845–1900* (London, 1958).

ANSON, P. F., *The Call of the Cloister: Religious Communities and Kindred Bodies in the Anglican Communion* (London, 1955). An encyclopedic work by a Roman Catholic writer.

SOCIAL THOUGHT

LASKI, H. J., "The Political Theory of the Oxford Movement," in *Studies in the Problem of Sovereignty* (New Haven, 1917), 69–119.

PECK, W. G., *The Social Implications of the Oxford Movement* (New York, 1933).

ECUMENICAL RELATIONS

BRANDRETH, H. R. T., *The Oecumenical Ideals of the Oxford Movement* (London, 1947).

SHAW, P. E., *The Early Tractarians and the Eastern Church* (Milwaukee, 1930).

Biographical Studies

Battiscombe, G., *John Keble: A Study in Limitations* (London, 1963).

Beek, W. J. A. M., *John Keble's Literary and Religious Contribution to the Oxford Movement* (Nijmegen, 1959).

Bennett, F., *The Story of W. J. E. Bennett* (London, 1909). The adventures of a pioneer "ritualist."

Boekraad, A. J., *The Personal Conquest of Truth according to J. H. Newman* (Louvain, 1955).

Bouyer, L., *Newman: His Life and Spirituality* (London, 1958). An outstanding study.

Brooke, A., *Robert Gray, First Bishop of Cape Town* (London, 1947). The life of a zealous contender for the independence and spiritual authority of the Church.

Chadwick, O., "The Limitations of Keble," in *Theology*, LXVII (1964), 46–52.

Church, M. C., *Life and Letters of Dean Church* (London, 1894).

Coleridge, J. T., *A Memoir of the Rev. John Keble* (Oxford, 1896).

Cross, F. L., *John Henry Newman* (London, 1933).

Davidson, R. T., and Benham, W., *Life of Archibald Campbell Tait, Archbishop of Canterbury* (London, 1891). 2 vols.

Dolling, R. R., *Ten Years in a Portsmouth Slum*, 6th ed. (London, 1903). Memoirs of an unconventional "ritualist."

Fairweather, E. R., "A Tractarian Patriarch: John Medley of Fredericton," in *Canadian Journal of Theology*, VI (1960), 15–24. A sketch of Tractarianism at work in a Canadian diocese.

Guiney, L. I., *Hurrell Froude: Memoranda and Comments* (London, 1904).

Harrold, C. H., *John Henry Newman: An Expository and Critical Study of His Mind, Thought and Art* (New York, 1945). Contains good "Select Bibliography" (440–52).

Kelway, A. C., *George Rundle Prynne: A Chapter in the Early History of the Catholic Revival* (London, 1905).

Ketchum, W. Q., *The Life and Work of the Most Reverend John Medley, D.D., First Bishop of Fredericton* (Saint John, N.B., 1893).

Lathbury, D. C., ed., *Correspondence on Church and Religion of William Ewart Gladstone* (London, 1910). 2 vols.

Lock, W., *John Keble: A Biography* (London, 1891).

Lough, A. G., *The Influence of John Mason Neale* (London, 1962). A study of a distinguished liturgiologist and founder of a great religious order.

Lowder, C. F., *Twenty-One Years in St. George's Mission* (London, 1877). Memoirs of a famous Anglo-Catholic slum priest.

Charles Lowder: A Biography (London, 1882).

MAURICE, J. F., *The Life of Frederick Denison Maurice* (London, 1885). 2 vols.

McGREEVY, M. A., "John Keble on the Anglican and the Church Catholic," in *The Heythrop Journal*, V (1964), 27–35.

MIDDLETON, R. D., *Newman at Oxford: His Religious Development* (London, 1950).

OSBORNE, C. E., *The Life of Father Dolling* (London, 1903).

PATTISON, M., *Memoirs* (London, 1885).

PERRY, W., *Alexander Penrose Forbes, Bishop of Brechin, the Scottish Pusey* (London, 1939).

PRESTIGE, G. L., *Pusey* (London, 1933).

PURCELL, E. S., *Life of Cardinal Manning, Archbishop of Westminster* (London, 1895). 2 vols. A somewhat tendentious account of an early (and temporary) supporter of the Oxford Movement.

RUSSELL, G. W. E., *Arthur Stanton: A Memoir* (London, 1917). The story of a famous Anglo-Catholic preacher.

SMITH, B. A., *Dean Church: The Anglican Response to Newman* (London, 1958).

STANLEY, A. P., *The Life and Correspondence of Thomas Arnold* (London, 1844). 2 vols.

T[OWLE], E. A., *Alexander Heriot Mackonochie: A Memoir* (London, 1891). The life of the great hero of "ritualism."

———, *John Mason Neale, D.D.: A Memoir* (London, 1906).

TREVOR, M., *Newman.* Vol. I: *The Pillar of the Cloud;* Vol. II: *Light in Winter* (London, 1962). The latest full-scale biography.

TUCKER, H. W., *Memoir of the Life and Episcopate of George Augustus Selwyn, Bishop of New Zealand, 1841–1867; Bishop of Lichfield, 1867–1878* (London, 1879). 2 vols. An account of a missionary pioneer who was strongly influenced by the Oxford Movement.

WARD, W., *The Life of John Henry Cardinal Newman* (London, 1912). 2 vols.

———, *William George Ward and the Oxford Movement* (London, 1889).

———, *William George Ward and the Catholic Revival* (London, 1893).

WEBSTER, A. B., *Joshua Watson: The Story of a Layman, 1771–1855* (London, 1954). A glimpse of High Churchmanship outside the Tractarian circle.

WHATELY, E. J., *Life and Correspondence of Richard Whately, D.D., late Archbishop of Dublin* (London, 1866). 2 vols.

WILLIAMS, T. J., *Priscilla Lydia Sellon: The Restorer after Three Centuries of the Religious Life in the English Church* (London, 1950).

WOODGATE, M. V., *Father Benson: Founder of the Cowley Fathers* (London, 1953).

YONGE, C. M., *Life of John Coleridge Patteson, Missionary Bishop of the Melanesian Islands* (London, 1874). 2 vols. The story of a great missionary and martyr.

Index

Aaron, 313, 325, 327
Abbott, Jacob, 63 n.
Abraham, 89, 188, 214, 253 f., 287, 290, 312,
absolution, 12, 179 n., 233, 271–79, 286
Adam, 206 f., 219, 221, 235–37, 254, 256, 287, 289, 292, 294, 298, 302, 304, 332, 338, 346, 349, 353–55
Adam, second (Jesus Christ), 237, 255, 286, 288, 292, 294, 298, 300, 311, 316, 323, 328, 339, 345, 348 f., 355, 357, 360, 363
Aerius, 140
Alphonsus Liguori, St., 181 n.
Amalekites, 43, 46
Ambrose, St., 136, 141, 275 n., 278, 321 f.
Ammonites, 40
Andrewes, Lancelot, 108, 150
Anglican Communion, Anglicanism, 8–10, 13, 34, 54, 78, 94–114, 144–48, 154–56, 195, 203. See also England, Church of; via media.
Anglo-Catholicism, 8–10, 12 f., 20, 108–12, 124, 148, 159, 203. See also papalists, Anglo-Catholic.
Antichrist, 85, 125 f.
antiquity, Christian, reverence for, 127–43
apostles, 8, 47, 80–82, 98, 107, 117 f., 120, 130 f., 136, 154, 243, 247 f., 268, 275, 277, 315, 325, 329, 333, 366
apostolic succession, 7, 9, 43 f., 54–59, 63, 77, 82 f., 87 f., 126, 155, 201, 215, 330–33
apostolic tradition, 7, 9, 63–89, 116–19, 129–31, 155
"Apostolicals," 63, 109
Arches, Court of, 173 n.
Arianism, 27 n., 79 n., 135, 152, 217
Aristotle, 265 n.
Arnold, Thomas, 61, 159, 191 n., 201 f.
asceticism, 12, 160, 178 f., 182, 193, 195 f.
Ashtaroth, 295 f.
Athanasius, St., 79 n., 146, 343
Atonement, 48, 126, 204, 218, 227, 230, 233, 245–47, 264 n., 265–70, 286, 288, 318–20, 323–28, 362

Augustine of Hippo, St., 79 n., 80, 125, 140, 142, 146, 206, 212, 214 n., 215, 217 f., 248 f., 252, 273, 278, 293, 338, 344, 347

B

Baal, 295
Bacon, Francis, Baron Verulam, 293 n., 309
baptism, 69, 141, 151 f., 202, 226, 230–33, 250–52, 271–75, 277, 285, 297, 339, 349–57, 363 f.
  baptismal regeneration, 203–15, 353–57
  of infants, 77, 130, 207, 329, 331, 354–57
  sprinkling in, 131
Baptists, 116, 122
Barberi, Dominic, 145
Bellarmine, St. Robert, 134, 137 f., 139 n., 140 n.
Ben Sira, 245
Bentham, Jeremy, 191
Bible. See Scripture.
Bickersteth, Edward, 126 n.
bishops, 7 f., 44, 55–59, 140, 158 n., 175 f. See also episcopacy; ministry, threefold.
Bisse, Thomas, 334
Bonald, Louis-Gabriel-Ambroise, Vicomte de, 3
Boniface VIII, Pope, 307
Book of Common Prayer (1662), 112, 150, 172, 178, 208, 216, 261, 334
  Baptismal Office, 224, 341, 354, 357, 364
  Catechism, 205–07, 232, 308, 340, 343, 357, 373
  Communion Service, 31, 310, 318, 336 f., 359, 371–73, 381 f.
  Commination, 31
  Ordinal, 57, 83, 330
  Service for King Charles the Martyr, 150 n.
Bossuet, Jacques-Bénigne, 134, 136, 143
Bourke, Richard, 36 n.
Breeks v. Woolfrey, case of, 173 n.

393

Breviary, 172
Brilioth, Yngve, 6, 10, 15, 215
British Critic, The, 160–63, 165 f., 168–79, 184, 186 f., 194, 197
Bucer, Martin, 148 n.
Bull, George, 134–36, 236
Burnet, Gilbert, 249 n.
Burton, Edward, 36 f.
Butler, Joseph, 86 n., 95, 108, 133, 265 n., 352

C

Cajetan (Thomas de Vio Caietanus), 139 n.
Calvin, John, 213, 351 f.
Calvinism, 109, 123, 160, 241, 356
Canada, Anglican Church in, 7
Canons of 1604, English, 124 n., 154
Cashel, diocese of, 36 n.
Cassander, Georg, 368
Catherine of Genoa, St., 140 n.
Catholic emancipation. *See* Roman Catholic Relief Act.
Catholicism, Catholicity, 5, 9–11, 13, 61, 70, 109 f., 124, 132–34, 147, 153 f., 161, 185–89, 193 f.
celibacy, 178 f., 195 f., 202
Chadwick, W. O., 135 n.
Chalcedon, Council of, 82 n.
Chalcedonian Definition, 146
Charles I, King of England, 103, 126, 150 n.
Charles II, King of England, 109, 249
Chillingworth, William, 81 n.
Christ Church, Oxford, 93
Church, 5, 8, 11, 14 f., 23, 32, 97–101, 160, 288–309
    authority of, 5, 7 f., 20, 30, 55–59, 64, 95–143, 201 f., 284 f., 305 f.
    as Body of Christ, 67, 256, 288–362
    order of, 9, 80, 82
    primitive, 87, 111, 118–20
    and state, 5–7, 37–49, 63 f., 87 f., 156, 284 f.
Church, R. W., 34 f., 60, 95 f., 160 f., 164, 260, 262 f.
Church Temporalities Act, 35 f., 48, 63
Churton, Edward, 5 n.
Churton, T. T., 157
Clarendon, Edward Hyde, first Earl of, 81 n., 104
Clark, F., 148 n.
Clement of Alexandria, 135
Clement of Rome, St., 76
Collier, Jeremy, 109

Communion, Holy. *See* Eucharist.
confession. *See* absolution.
confirmation, 233, 299 n.
Connecticut, High Church tradition in, 9
consecration of churches, 24
conservatism, political, 3–5
Constance, Council of, 141 f.
Constantinople
    First Council of, 82 n.
    Second Council of, 82 n.
    Third Council of, 82 n.
Constantius, Flavius Valerius (Chlorus), 311
Convocations
    English, 36, 62 n., 102
    Irish, 36
Corporation Act, 3, 35
Councils, ecclesiastical, 81 f., 118, 129 f., 152–54, 201
Counter-Reformation, 9
Cranmer, Thomas, 148 n.
creeds, 78 f., 83, 97, 201
    Apostles' Creed, 69, 73, 100
    Nicene Creed, 77–79, 146, 205, 207, 230, 255, 291
    see also Quicumque vult
Cross, F. L., 142 n.
Cuvier, Léopold-Chrétien-Frédéric-Dagobert (Georges), Baron, 98
Cyprian, St., 66 n., 79 n., 110, 275 n., 353
Cyril of Alexandria, St., 131, 275 n., 276

D

Daniel, 32, 314
Dante Alighieri, 191
David, 32, 43, 224, 279, 314, 331
Denison, Edward, 162
Denison, George Anthony, 378 f.
Diocletian, 311
disciplina arcani, 142 f., 186
Dissent, Dissenters, 35 f., 56, 60 f., 102, 110, 126, 177, 197, 261
doctors of the Church, 134
doctrine, development of, 135
dogma, 7, 20, 61–63, 130
Donatism, 146
donum superadditum naturae, 236
Dorner, I. A., 284, 304, 313 n., 341 n.
Dublin Review, The, 146

E

Eastern Orthodoxy, 9, 13
ecumenism, 13, 283 f.
Elisha, 240

Elizabeth I, Queen of England, 9
England, Church of, 5–9, 13, 20, 34 f.,
    44–49, 53–59, 63 f., 83, 88 f., 101–04,
    108–12, 127, 146–48, 159–98, 249, 273,
    305, 364, 379
Enoch, 312
Ephesus, Council of, 82 n.
Ephraim Syrus, St., 131
Epicureanism, 172
episcopacy, 6, 9, 102, 155, 307. *See also*
    bishops; ministry, threefold.
Erastianism, 48, 87 f.
Erskine, Thomas, 63 n.
Essays and Reviews, 62 n.
Eucharist, 12 f., 79, 82, 160, 232 f., 250 f.,
    259, 273, 298, 302, 329, 339, 362–83
  communion in one kind, 131, 141 f.
  consecration, 80, 82, 363–66
  eucharistic presence, 12, 85, 344–47, 357–
    60, 368–76
  eucharistic sacrifice, 9, 12, 77, 82, 286,
    317–23, 332, 363, 366 f., 377
  fast before Communion, 12
  see also Mass; transubstantiation
Eutyches, 131
Evangelical party, 5, 10 f., 19 f., 161, 172,
    251, 260–62, 379
evidences of Christianity, 28, 30
Ezekiel, 39

F
Fairbairn, A. M., 4
Fairweather, E. R., 37 n., 58 n., 206 n.,
    332 n.
faith, 4, 8, 41, 62, 65, 160, 210, 253, 261,
    279, 298 f., 352–54, 371 f., 377, 380 f.
  deposit of, 68–71, 87–89
  justification by, 11, 151 f., 204 f., 215–
    17, 222 f., 227, 232, 246, 248, 250, 254
  and reason, 14, 20, 23–33, 111, 374 f.
  rule of, 72–75, 104, 112, 329, 368
Fall, the, 178, 286, 320, 329, 338, 362
fasting, 12, 182, 202
Fathers, 14 f., 70, 75, 81 f., 94 f., 113, 118,
    120 f., 128 f., 130 f., 133 f., 211, 214,
    217 f., 236, 247, 275, 298, 322 f., 363,
    375, 379
  Ante-Nicene, 134 f.
  consent of, 82, 95, 128 f., 133
  Greek, 140, 205 f., 359
  Latin, 140, 359
  Roman Catholic attitude towards, 127–
    43
Firmilian, St., 275 n.

Fisher, St. John, 139 f.
Florence, Council of, 136
Forbes, Alexander Penrose, 378
"Four Tutors," 157
Fox, George, 298 n., 301–03
Franciscans, 141
François de Sales, St., 181 n.
Friday abstinence, 12
Friends, Society of. *See* Quakers.
Froude, Richard Hurrell, 19 f., 35, 53 f.,
    148 n., 159 f., 167, 260, 283
Froude, Robert Hurrell, 54
Fulgentius, St., 278 n.

G
Galerius, 311
Genesis, Book of, 117, 235
Geneva, 110
Gentiles, 42, 47
George II, King of England, 109
Gerizim, 130
Gerlach circle, 3
Germany, 110, 284
Gibbon, Edward, 135
Gibeonites, 43
Gladstone, William Ewart, 284, 285 n.
Gnosticism, 86, 340
good works, 151 f., 216–18, 248–70
Gorham, George Cornelius, 285
Gorham Judgment, 6 f., 284 f., 378
gospel, 5, 11, 65 f., 68, 70, 74, 79, 160, 179,
    188, 204, 209–11, 216, 224 f., 229 f.,
    233–35, 237, 240 f., 251–54, 257, 261 f.,
    267 f., 285, 291, 295 f., 298, 301, 308 f.,
    317, 324–26, 328, 352, 356 f., 361
Grabe, Johannes Ernst, 110
Grabmann, Martin, 203
grace, 5, 9, 11, 20, 152, 172, 201, 208, 218,
    222, 227, 229, 257–61, 286–88, 305–08,
    323 f., 343, 352–57, 364 f.
Gratian, 139 n.
Gray, Robert, 7
Great Rebellion (English Civil War),
    301
Gregorian Reform, 6
Gregory the Great, St., Pope, 131, 142,
    275 n.
Gregory VII, St., Pope, 307
Gregory XI, Pope, 136
Gregory of Nyssa, St., 131
Grey, Earl, 35
Griffiths, J., 157
Günther, Anton, 284
Guillemard, H. P., 164

H

Habakkuk, 223
Hammond, Henry, 108, 150
Hampden, Renn Dickson, 60–63, 86 n.
Hebrews, Epistle to the, 272, 310, 325
Henry VIII, King of England, 102, 139
Herbert, George, 160, 382
Herod Antipas, 47
High Church party, 5 f., 9, 11, 20, 34, 54,
    61, 109, 148, 158 f., 161, 175, 194–97
Hildebrand. See Gregory VII.
Hippolytus, St., 70
history, appeal to, 5 f., 14 f., 127–43
Hoadly, Benjamin, 109, 249 n., 358
Homilies, 151, 153, 216, 224, 373 f.
Hook, Walter Farquhar, 95, 148, 158 f.
Hooker, Richard, 14, 58 n., 80, 84 n., 150,
    208, 209 n., 213, 275 f., 291 n., 300 f.,
    337 f., 343 f., 347, 349, 351–53, 357–59
Hume, David, 24
Hutcheson, Francis, 24 n.

I

idealism, 4
Ignatius of Antioch, St., 76, 100, 110, 253,
    325, 330 f.
Ignatius Loyola, St., 181 n., 182
images, 187
Incarnation, 5, 11, 74 f., 82, 106, 126, 202,
    veneration of, 82
    239, 285–362, 371
Independents, 116, 122
indulgences, 139 f., 187
infallibility, doctrine of, 95 f., 127–43, 175
Ireland, Church of, 4, 6, 35–37, 48, 60, 63
Irenaeus, St., 72–74, 76, 135, 248, 317 f.,
    321, 325, 341 f.
Israel, 40, 43, 47, 152, 232, 287. See also
    Jews.

J

Jackson, Thomas, 301, 314–16, 319 f., 345,
    359 f.
James, St., 152, 236 n., 249
James II, King of England, 109 n.
Jansenism, 136
Jelf, R. W., 159
Jeremiah, 103
Jerome, St., 70, 79 n., 140, 142, 275 n., 347
Jerusalem, 130
Jesuits, 134–36, 260

Jesus Christ. See Adam, second; Atone-
    ment; Incarnation; Resurrection;
    Virgin Birth.
Jews, 22, 37–43, 98, 103, 154, 178 f., 256,
    259, 311–14
Job, 312
John the Baptist, St., 21, 213 f., 268
John the Deacon, 70 n.
John the Divine, St., Revelation of, 235 f.,
    318
John the Evangelist, St., 330
    Epistles of, 72, 74–76, 229
    Gospel of, 22, 71, 76, 130, 358 f.
John Chrysostom, St., 66 n., 79 n., 125,
    205 f., 273, 341
Joshua, high priest, 234
Jowett, Benjamin, 62 n.
Judah, 43
Jude, St., 45
judgment, divine, 3, 20, 29, 39, 43, 85, 98,
    220, 261, 268, 272, 275, 355
July Revolution, 53
justification, 9, 11, 151 f., 160, 204 f., 215–
    59
    effects of, 233–47
    nature of, 219–33
Justin Martyr, St., 135

K

Keble, John, 3 f., 34–37, 63, 93, 148, 158,
    262 f., 283, 331 n., 368 f., 377–79
    on apostolic succession, 82 f.
    on apostolic tradition, 63–89
    on Christians in an apostate nation, 43–
        47
    on the clergy and the Church-state
        crisis, 63–68
    on the deposit of faith, 68–71
    against Erastianism, 48 f., 87 f.
    on the Eucharist, 379–83
    against nominalism, 86 f.
    on Scripture and tradition, 71–82
    on the state and religon, 27–49
Ken, Thomas, 109, 160
Knox, Alexander, 204
Korah, 313

L

Lacey, T. A., 146 n.
Lamennais, Félicité-Robert de, 3
Lateran Council, Fourth, 370
Latitudinarians, 108 f., 135, 249, 252
Laud, William, 105, 108
Laurence, Richard, 213 n., 214 n.

Lazarus, 239
Le Blanc, Guillaume, 368
Lent, 12
Leo the Great, St., Pope, 146, 339
Leslie, Charles, 298 n., 303
liberalism, 3, 7 f., 19 f., 31 f., 41 f., 53
Liddon, Henry Parry, 93 n., 211 n., 272, 369 f., 378 n.
Lightfoot, John, 213 n.
liturgies, ancient, 81, 211 f., 214, 379
Lord's Day, 24, 80, 130, 287, 329, 331
Low Church party, 109 n., 158
Lowder, Charles Fuge, 12 f.
Luke, St., 22, 55
Luther, Martin, 139, 217 f., 220 f., 247
Lutheranism, 9, 110, 160, 216, 222, 254
Lyttelton, A. T., 283

M

Machiavelli, Niccolò, 191
Maistre, Joseph de, 3
Malachi, 318, 320 f.
Maldonatus, 139 n.
Manichaeism, 327
Martha, 239
martyrdom, martyrs, 55, 105
Mary, Blessed Virgin, 131, 183 f., 187, 239, 287, 293 n., 317, 319, 342, 345, 382
Rosary of, 184
Mary II, Queen of England, 102 n., 109 n.
Mason, A. J., 58 n.
Mass, Canon of, 79 n.
Matthew, St., Gospel of, 72
Maurice, Frederick Denison, 181 n., 285
Maurists, 136
Mede, Joseph, 317 f., 322
mediation, principle of. See Incarnation.
Medina, Miguel de, 140
meditation, mental prayer, 12, 182
Medley, John, 7, 54 n., 110 n.
Melanchthon, Philip, 216
Melbourne, William Lamb, second Viscount, 61
Melchizedek, 79, 325 f.
Mercersburg Review, The, 284
Mill, John Stuart, 159
Milner, John, 134
ministry, threefold, 77, 154 f., 330 f.
miracles, 23, 74, 240
Möhler, Johann Adam, 284
Monophysitism, 146 f.
Montanism, 131
moral sense
Hutcheson and Shaftesbury on, 24 n.
Newman on, 23–28

Morley, John (Viscount Morley of Blackburn), 4
Moses, 152, 238, 296, 311
Mosheim, J. L. von, 137 n.
Mozley, James Bowling, 271 f.
Mozley, Jemima, 144 n., 145
Mussus, Cornelius, 142

N

"National Apostasy," 4, 6, 37–48
Naylor, James, 303
Nebuchadnezzar, 103
Nevin, John Williamson, 284
New Jersey, High Church tradition in, 9
New Testament, 22, 38, 76, 118–21, 329
canon of, 72–76, 82, 119 f.
New York, High Church tradition in, 9
New Zealand, Anglican Church in, 7
Newman, Jemima. See Mozley, Jemima.
Newman, John Henry, 4, 7–10, 14, 19–21, 34, 37, 53 f., 60 f., 63 n., 93–96, 144–48, 157–59, 161–64, 178, 181 n., 192, 201, 203, 215–18, 283, 285, 375
on the Anglican position, 96–114
on apostolic succession, 55–59
on authority in the Christian religion, 96–143
on the controversial strategy of the Anglican church, 114–27
on general councils, 152–54
on justification, 151 f., 215–59
on the papal supremacy, 154–56
on reason and religion, 21–33
on the Reformation as cause of rationalism, 29 f.
on the Roman doctrine of infallibility, 127–43
on the Thirty-nine Articles, 148–56
Newman, Mary, 19
Newton, Sir Isaac, 98
Nicaea
First Council of, 79, 82 n.
Nicene Anathema, 136
Second Council of, 82 n.
See also creeds
Nicholas of Cusa, 142
Nichols, J. H., 3 f., 284 n.
Nicodemus, 207, 213
"noetics," 19
nominalism, 86 f.
Nonconformists, 9
Nonjurors, 6, 9, 36, 102 f., 108 n., 109, 110 n.
Novatianism, 211, 279

O

Oakeley, Frederick, 173
office, divine, 12
Old Testament, 22, 37 f., 75 n., 76, 80, 228 n., 329
Ollard, S. L., 260
Olshausen, Hermann, 284, 350
ordination, 56–59, 69, 83, 233
Oriel College, Oxford, 19, 34, 283
Origen, 131
Oxford Movement
  as assertion of ecclesiastical authority, 7 f.
  beginnings of, 19–21, 34–37
  as completion of Anglican "Counter-Reformation," 8–11
  continuation in "ritualism," 12 f.
  ecumenical consequences of, 13
  first Tracts for the Times, 53 f.
  incarnational theology of Church and sacraments, 11
  "Hampden persecution," 60–63
  renewal of spiritual discipline, 12
  revival of religious life, 12
  as revival of supernatural religion, 3–5
  secessions of 1845, 145, 164, 203
  as struggle for ecclesiastical liberty, 6 f.
  theological achievement of, 13–15
  Tract Ninety crisis, 147 f., 157–59
Oxford, University of, 60–63, 93, 157–59, 164, 273, 368

P

Pacian, St., 275 n., 277 f.
Paley, William, 28 n., 56 n.
Palmer, William ("of Worcester"), 94 n., 136 n., 147 n., 148, 158, 159 n., 163, 165, 173–77, 187
pantheism, 298
papacy, 102, 123, 132, 154–56, 175
papalists, Anglo-Catholic, 9, 159–64
Parliament, British, 3, 7, 35 f., 48, 158
Passover, 321
patriarchalism, Christian, 3
Patriarchs, 312
Pattison, Mark, 62 n.
Paul, St., 47, 55, 61, 65–72, 74, 82 f., 85 f., 178, 188, 218, 223–25, 229, 231, 234–40, 246, 253 f., 290 f., 325, 339, 350 f., 356, 372 f.
Pelagianism, 206 n., 218, 244, 286, 351, 356
Petavius, Dionysius, 135 f., 243 n.

Peter, St., 72, 223, 225 f., 240, 243, 275, 351
Pharaoh, 23
Pharisees, 270
Philippians, 66
Phillips, W. A., 48 n.
Philo Judaeus, 313 n.
Pilate, Pontius, 47, 69, 105
Pilgrim Fathers, 307
Pius IV, Creed of, 128
Plato, Platonism, 291, 299
Pliny the Younger, 291, 299
Polycarp, St., 100
Po[y]net, John, 347, 359
predestination, 131, 252
presbyterian order, 102, 307
Presbyterians, 116, 122
priesthood
  of Christ, 256–59, 323–28, 335, 339, 383
  Christian, 258, 323–33
  Jewish, 257, 313, 325–28
  of laity, 323 f.
Protestantism, 9–11, 13, 81 n., 99 f., 102, 107–11, 114–27, 144, 167, 181, 201, 216 f., 233 f., 254
punishment, eternal, 126, 131
purgatory, 125, 131, 137, 139 f.
Puritans, 38, 107, 109, 301
Pusey, Edward Bouverie, 5, 10, 93 f., 99 n., 148, 158, 202 f., 271–73, 283 f., 368–70
  on baptismal regeneration, 203–14
  on the eucharistic presence, 371–76
  on the power of absolution, 274–79
Pythagoreanism, 107

Q

Quakers, 296–98, 301–03, 306, 316
Quicumque vult, 31, 62

R

rationalism, 20 f., 61–63, 85, 110, 294, 298, 361 f.
reason, place in religion of, 21–33, 168–70
Record, The, 205
Reformation, Reformers, 9 f., 29 f., 102, 124, 148, 155, 159 f., 162, 166, 176 f., 182, 190, 195, 197
Reformed Churches, 9
religious life, 12, 195 f.
Restoration Settlement, 9, 144
Resurrection of Christ, 208, 210, 224, 238 f., 246 f., 275, 287, 289, 375
retreats, 12, 182
revelation, divine, 11, 20, 97

Revolution of 1688, 102–04, 109
Ridley, Nicholas, 148 n.
righteousness
  Christ as our righteousness, 234–42, 248–59
  imparted, 204, 219 f., 224–33, 248
  imputed, 204, 219–21, 234, 248
ritualism, 7, 12 f.
Rogers, Frederic (Baron Blachford), 146
Roman Catholic Relief Act, 3, 35, 48
Roman Catholicism, 9 f., 13, 35 f., 64, 71, 81, 84, 94–96, 99–102, 107–11, 114–48, 154–58, 160–65, 171, 173, 175, 179–85, 187 f., 215–17, 220–23, 232–34, 247–49, 252, 254
Roman Empire, 154, 291
romanticism, 4

S

Sabbath, 130
Sabellianism, 293, 302–04, 317, 322, 325, 343, 349, 362
sacraments, 5 f., 11, 87 f., 126, 155, 160, 193, 201–04, 208, 232 f., 249, 256, 265, 284, 286 f., 289, 294, 296–303, 333, 364 f. See also baptism; Eucharist.
St. Mary the Virgin, Oxford, Church of, 19, 94 n., 203
St. Peter's, London Docks, 12 f.
saints, 187, 189
  invocation of, 131, 187
Salazar, Francisco de, 181 n.
Samaritans, 240, 312
  Samaritan woman, 226
Samuel, 38–41, 43 f., 45 f.
sanctification, 9, 218 f., 242–47
Satan, 85, 221, 230, 232, 255, 307, 375
Saul, 43, 46
Schaff, Philip, 284
Schleiermacher, Friedrich Daniel Ernst, 63 n., 284, 304 f.
Scotland, Nonjurors in, 9
Scott, Thomas, 241
Scripture, 13 f., 81 n., 83 f., 102, 242, 261, 265–68, 279, 289, 291, 305 f., 326, 334 f., 345, 349, 351 f., 361–63, 374 f., 379–82
  authority of, 30
  interpretation of, 8, 32, 61 f., 79 f., 82, 114–16
  and tradition, 71–80
Selwyn, George Augustus, 7
Sennacherib, 23
serpent, brazen, 152, 246
Seth, 312

Sewel, W., 301–03
Shaftesbury, Anthony Ashley Cooper, third Earl of, 24 n.
Shakespeare, William, 191
Sikes, Thomas, 99 n.
Simon Magus, 240
sin
  actual, 206–08, 372
  forgiveness of, 205–08, 218, 221, 224–26, 230, 271–79, 285, 341, 343, 355, 371, 375
  original, 126, 178, 206–08, 285, 355
"Six Doctors," 273
Smith, Goldwin, 62 n.
Socinianism, 109 f., 135, 241, 303, 336, 343, 358
Socrates, 291
Sodor and Man, diocese of, 108
Solomon, 347
  temple of, 291, 315 f., 332
Song of Solomon, allegorical interpretation of, 79
South Africa, Anglican Church in, 7
Spiritual Combat, The, 181 n.
Stillingfleet, Edward, 139 n., 142 n.
Stoicism, 172
succession, apostolic. See apostles.
Sumner, John Bird, 379
Sunday. See Lord's Day.
Supremacy, Oath of, 154, 156

T

Tacitus, 191
Tait, A. C., 157
Taylor, Jeremy, 139 n., 140 n., 141 n., 142 n., 298, 336, 344 n., 346, 383
Temple, Frederick, 62 n.
Temple, William, 14
Tertullian, 66 n., 72, 76, 105 n., 131, 330
Test Act, 3, 35
Thessalonians, 72, 85
Thirlwall, Connop, 162 f., 261 f.
Thirty-nine Articles, 60, 62, 75 f., 109, 112, 144–58, 161–64, 172 f., 216, 224, 244 n., 336, 357, 373
Thomas Aquinas, St., 181 n., 370
Tillotson, John, 249 n.
Times, The, 158
Timothy, St., 55, 65–72, 82 f., 86
Titus, St., 68
Tories, 5
Tracts for the Times, 4, 19, 54, 93 f., 157, 162, 201
tradition. See apostles.
traditionalism, 3

transubstantiation, 85, 131, 362, 370
Trent, Council of, 125, 137, 142
   decree on justification of, 247, 249
   decree on purgatory of, 125, 137
Trinity, 229, 292 f., 303, 305, 343 f., 362, 376
   dogma of, 62, 77, 82, 86 n., 126, 135, 304

U

Unitarians, 116, 228, 241
Utilitarians, 5, 20, 159

V

Valentinus, Valentinians, 300, 341
Vasquez, Gabriel, 216
Vermigli, Peter Martyr, 148 n.
via media, 9, 95 f., 100 f., 107 f., 110 f., 144–48, 159, 215
Victoria, Queen of England, 184
Vincent of Lérins, St., 70, 77, 86 n., 129 f., 132 f.
Virgin Birth of Christ, 375

W

Ward, William George, 159–64, 215
   on the Church's corruption, 165–68
   defence of his critical writings, 170–74
   on duty to the English Church, 174–79
   on the first steps towards reformation, 192–97
   on his loyalty to the English Church, 197 f.
   on reforming the English Church, 164–98

   on the responsibility of Christian intellectuals, 168–70
   on Rome as the model for an Anglican reformation, 179–92
Wesleyans, 116
Whately, Richard, 19 f., 61, 63 n., 305 f., 330
Whigs, 35
White, Joseph Blanco, 63 n., 86 n.
Wilberforce, Robert Isaac, 10, 35, 283–88, 362
   on apostolic succession, 330–33
   on baptism, 349–57
   on the Christian priesthood, 323–33
   on Christian worship, 309–35
   on the Church as Christ's Body, 288–309
   on the Eucharist, 317–23, 344–47, 357–60, 362–67
   on "mediation" as the basic principle of Christianity, 285–362
Wilberforce, Samuel, 62 n., 283, 285, 368
Wilberforce, William, 283
William III, King of England, 102, 109 n.
Williams, Isaac, 4, 35, 260–63, 283
   on the place of good works in Christianity, 263–70
Wilson, H. B., 157
Wilson, Thomas, 108, 160
Wiseman, Nicholas, 146
Woodgate, Henry Arthur, 61 n., 261
Woodward, E. L., 36
works. *See* good works.
worship, Christian, 309–35

Z

Zacchaeus, 267
Zwingli, Ulrich, 212 f.

M